Praise for *Blood and Treasure*

"Drury and Clavin together have given us a half dozen elegantly written narratives of exhilarating episodes in American history. . . . Their latest collaboration . . . is among the most redolent of time and place."
—*The Wall Street Journal*

"For anyone who loves the adventurous side of American history, *Blood and Treasure* is a gem. It's full of action, thorough, and wide. Seek out this treasure and you won't be disappointed."
—Terri Schlichenmeyer, *Wyoming Tribune Eagle*

"Bob Drury and Tom Clavin challenge conventional wisdom about an American origin story and, in the process, weave a tale fit for the big screen."
—*The Washington Free Beacon*

"*Blood and Treasure* is a splendid book, well researched and beautifully written, by two very fine authors. I heartily recommend it."
—Dave Tabler, Appalachian History

"Bob Drury and Tom Clavin have done a good job and a great service in presenting the story of our nation's westward expansion during the years before most people had ever dreamed about the Trans-Mississippi West."
—James A. Crutchfield, *Roundup Magazine*

"Throughout *Blood and Treasure,* Drury and Clavin intersperse the events of Boone's life with big-picture perspectives. The book opens a gap of sorts in a complex chain of colonial treaties, tribes, wars, and land grabs, leading the reader to an appreciation of the many combatants in the conflict over Kentucky's 'dark and bloody ground.'"
—James Dittes, *Chapter 16*

Praise for the Work of Drury and Clavin

"A ripping yarn."

—Laura Miller, *Salon*

"Vivid . . . Lively . . . A tale of lies, trickery, and brutal slaughter."

—Christopher Corbett, *The Wall Street Journal*

"A page-turner . . . The narrative has a remarkable immediacy."

—Kate Tuttle, *The Boston Globe*

"Exquisitely told . . . remarkably detailed."

—*USA Today*

"Filled with an overabundance of details."

—*The Dallas Morning News*

"Drury and Clavin have now given us the fullest and most readable account . . . against which all subsequent efforts must be measured."

—Joseph J. Ellis, Pulitzer Prize–winning author of *Founding Brothers*

"The word 'epic' is overused these days. Not here. This is big, blazing history writ large."

—S. C. Gwynne, author of *Empire of the Summer Moon*

BLOOD
AND
TREASURE

Daniel Boone and the Fight for
America's First Frontier

BOB DRURY AND TOM CLAVIN

ST. MARTIN'S GRIFFIN
NEW YORK

Published in the United States by St. Martin's Griffin,
an imprint of St. Martin's Publishing Group

www.stmartins.com

Map illustrations by David Lindroth

Frontispiece image: National Portrait Gallery of Eminent Americans portraits
by Alonzo Chappel (steel engraving), New York: Johnson, Fry & Co., 1862

Designed by Michelle McMillian

The Library of Congress has cataloged the hardcover edition as follows:

Names: Drury, Bob, author. | Clavin, Thomas, author.
Title: Blood and treasure : Daniel Boone and the fight for America's first frontier /
  Bob Drury and Tom Clavin.
Other titles: Daniel Boone and the fight for America's first frontier
Description: First edition. | New York : St. Martin's Press, [2021] | Includes
  bibliographical references and index.
Identifiers: LCCN 2020048552 | ISBN 9781250247131 (hardcover) |
  ISBN 9781250277626 (signed) | ISBN 9781250247148 (ebook)
Subjects: LCSH: Boone, Daniel, 1734–1820. | Pioneers—Kentucky—Biography. |
  Explorers—Kentucky—Biography. | Indians of North America—Wars—
  1750–1815. | United States—History—Revolution, 1775–1783—Biography. |
  Frontier and pioneer life—Kentucky. | Frontier and pioneer life—United States. |
  United States—Territorial expansion.
Classification: LCC F454.B66 D78 2021 | DDC 976.9/02092 [B]—dc23
LC record available at https://lccn.loc.gov/2020048552

ISBN 978-1-250-24715-5 (trade paperback)

First St. Martin's Griffin Edition: 2022

10 9 8 7 6 5 4 3 2 1

To David Joseph Drury, a tougher man than I . . .

To Bob Schaeffer, for whom there were no boundaries to friendship

CONTENTS

PART II: THE EXPLORERS

PART III: THE SETTLERS

PART IV: THE CONQUEST

A NOTE TO READERS

The spelling and pronunciation of eighteenth-century Native American names and places was, in the era, notoriously diffuse. To take just one example of many, the Indian nation referred to herein as the Shawnee was variously described by European Americans as the Shawnoe, the Shone, the Chaouenon, the Shawun, and dozens of other appellations. Within the tribe itself, members usually refer to themselves as Shawano, sometimes given as Shawanoe or Shawanese. For narrative's sake, throughout the following text we have endeavored to present readers with the most standardized tribal designations recognized and accepted today.

Further, regarding the term Indian: as two white authors chronicling a historical epoch so crucial to the fate of America's indigenous peoples, we relied on historical context. Indian was not only in common usage during the era we write about, but it is nearly as common today. For a previous book, *The Heart of Everything That Is,* we went to pains to check with our indigenous sources regarding the word. No less a personage than the late Maka Luta Win—who also went by the Anglicized name Mary Ann Red Cloud and was the great-great-granddaughter of the legendary Lakota warrior-chief known to whites as Red Cloud—personally suggested to us that Native American, American Indian, and Indian were all accepted descriptive terms.

Finally, throughout the following text we have presented the quixotic spellings, capitalizations, and punctuation in letters, journals, and military reports from the era precisely as the writers themselves put their words to paper.

Stand at the Cumberland Gap and watch the procession of civilization, marching single file—the buffalo following the trail to the salt springs, the Indian, the fur-trader and hunter, the cattle-raiser, the pioneer farmer—and the frontier has passed by.

—FREDERICK JACKSON TURNER,
The Frontier in American History

BLOOD
AND
TREASURE

PROLOGUE

Daniel Boone was too far away to hear his oldest boy's screams as the tall Indian tore out the sixteen-year-old's fingernails one by one.

James Boone was already bleeding out from a gunshot wound. Now, prostrate on the frozen scree beneath the Cumberland Mountain's shadow line, he begged the Shawnee with the high cheekbones and misshapen chin to just kill him. His persecutor was not moved. Young Boone knew the sullen warrior understood English. His family had often welcomed the Indian, known as Big Jim, into their hearth.

The raiders had sprung the ambush just before daybreak. While James Boone and his seven companions slept beneath rough woolen blankets and buffalo robes, a mixed band of painted Delaware, Cherokee, and Shawnee crept into their camp. It was not much of a fight. The two Mendinall brothers were killed instantly, their scalps lifted with trilling shrieks. Only the evening before, the others had laughed when the young farm boys had been frightened by the howls of a wolf pack.

At the first rifle report the woodsman Crabtree, a veteran Indian fighter, sprang from his bedding and plunged into the thick spinneys of chestnut, oak, and ash on either side of the mountain trail. His rapid reaction saved his life. And one of the two slaves escaped by burrowing unnoticed into a nearby pile of fallen timber. The other, an older black man, was not as spry; his life would end with a tomahawk cleaving his skull.

The youngster named Drake, whom James Boone had only just met, took a ball to his chest yet still found the strength to lurch into the woods; his remains would be discovered months later wedged between two ledges of rock face less than a mile from the scene.

Both James Boone and the seventeen-year-old Henry Russell had been gutshot, the lead balls lodging in their hips. Incapacitated, fair game.

Several of Russell's fingers were sliced away fending off the scalping knife. His throat was finally slit and his head stove in with a war club. James Boone cried out for the same. He was eventually accommodated, but not before his toenails were also ripped away.

It was October 10, 1773, and several miles up the road Daniel Boone was growing impatient. His son James's party should have returned by now. The stolid frontiersman was preparing to pilot the first company of settlers through the Cumberland Gap and into the trackless territory of Kentucky. He was eager to be off.

Boone's company of a half dozen families had made camp the previous morning a mere one hundred miles east of the renowned notch in the Cumberland range. There they had been joined by a troop of several dozen mounted men from Boone's North Carolina community, who had traversed the Blue Ridge by a different route. The plan was for the lone riders to travel with Boone's packhorse caravan into Kentucky, establish farmsteads and plant spring crops, and return to retrieve their wives and children the following summer. A number of Virginia men who had attached themselves to the rough trekkers expected to do the same.

All that remained to set the expedition in motion was his son's return with the additional stores supplied by the enterprise's nominal boss, the Virginia military leader, Captain William Russell. It was to Capt. Russell whom Boone had dispatched James and the teenage John and Richard

Mendinall the previous day. James was to inform Russell that he should bring along extra horses and livestock.

It was late afternoon when James Boone had found Russell not far from his homestead on the Clinch River. The captain informed him that he would see what he could do about rounding up more cattle and horses before he and his small troop set out at sunrise the next day. In the meanwhile, Capt. Russell and his son Henry laded an array of packhorses with scythes and hoes, sacks of flour and seed corn, and bags of salt. At the last moment the elder Russell wrapped a parcel of books in oilskin and jammed them into a crook of his son's saddlebag. Among the tomes was his family Bible. He then instructed Henry, the youth named Drake, and the two black slaves to accompany the Mendinalls and James Boone back to his father's campsite. The local long hunter Isaac Crabtree volunteered to help them manage the small drove of cattle trailing behind.

From nearly the first moment European emigrants set foot on the New World's fatal shores, white men and red men had engaged in constant, bloody, and usually one-sided combat. This was not by accident. In 1607 the London directors of the Virginia Company that established the Jamestown Company had for good reason named the soldier of fortune John Smith as one of the expedition's leaders. Similarly, when English pilgrims dropped anchor near Plymouth Rock thirteen years later, they looked to an experienced military officer named Miles Standish for direction.

The wars of conquest that followed had combined with starvation, disease, and societal collapse to result in the extinction of almost 90 percent of North America's pre-Columbian population—an estimated nine million indigenous peoples perished. By the time Daniel Boone and his migrating pioneers were preparing for their journey into Kentucky, Native American tribes from the Canadian border to the Piney Woods of Georgia were being swept from their ancestral lands by the onrushing tide of intruders from across the sea.

In effect, it was a slow-motion genocide for the Hurons and Iroquois in the North; for the Delaware, Shawnee, Wyandot, and Mingoes of the mid-Atlantic; for the Cherokee, Chickasaw, Creek, and Choctaw in the South. In the Floridas the Seminoles were being hunted to extermination by the Spanish, whose conquistadors had taken to unleashing bloodhounds to track them, and vicious Irish wolfhounds to tear them apart. And even the more northwesterly peoples, such as the Ottawas, Chippewa, Miami, Kickapoo, and Sauk and Fox were experiencing the ripple effects of the white infestation in the forms of germ-ridden European goods traveling ancient trade routes. The violent treatment of North America's Eastern Woodlands tribes forecast the blood trails that would crisscross the prairies of the American West a century later.

For the first European Americans spilling over the Appalachians, the very notion of the ever-shifting and expansive frontier was a "galvanizing vision," as one borderlands observer noted, "a space for reinvention unburdened by society, history, and one's own past." The "tawny serpents" who stood in their way were viewed, as the noted American historian Frederick Jackson Turner had it, as no more than a brutish people temporarily impeding "the procession of civilization."

Conversely, to the continent's indigenous tribes, Turner's "meeting point between savagery and civilization" represented less an intersection of cultures than a deliberate and violent collision. A succession of Cherokee wars had failed to stem the tide, and Pontiac's subsequent rebellion had similarly ended in Native American ignominy.

Yet for a portion of tribal warriors now facing an overwhelming second wave of agents of empire traversing the eastern mountains in the guise of traders, mapmakers, and surveyors with their ubiquitous "rod and chain," it was again time to make a stand. Particularly aggressive nations, such as the Shawnee, stoked the resentful embers among the disparate indigenous peoples up and down North America's eastern timberland.

On that brisk autumn morning of October 1773, the slaying of Daniel

Boone's teenage son James and his company so close to the Cumberland Gap was merely the latest casualty in that existential clash.

It was on toward noon when Capt. Russell came upon the mutilated bodies splayed across the trail. The horses, cattle, flour, and salt were gone. The Russell family Bible was still packed tight in his son Henry's saddlebags. Henry's corpse, nearly unrecognizable beneath great splotches of brown dried blood, had been pocked by a cluster of birchwood arrows, as had James Boone's mangled remains. Their fletchings riffled in the morning breeze.

Russell and his men unpacked shovels and handpicks. They were still breaking the near-frozen ground when Daniel Boone's younger brother Squire Boone arrived with a party of riflemen. Up the road a camp straggler had already sounded the alarm about Indians prowling the trail, and Daniel had instructed Squire to carry with him several woolen burial sheaths sewn by James's mother, Rebecca. Shrouds for a journey farther than Kentucky. The bodies were wrapped in the coverings before being lowered into the ground.

The assailants had positioned painted hatchets and death mauls in a circle around the slain. It was a well-known show of bravado—and a declaration of war. Squire Boone told Capt. Russell that his brother Daniel was already hewing saplings and shrubs to throw up a defensive barricade. No one could tell precisely how many Indians had taken part in the massacre, nor if they would now set their sights on the larger company of whites up the trail. Their sign indicated they were headed north. But it was not unusual for war parties to feign retreat and circle back. There was nothing to do but prime flintlocks and wait.

PART I

THE FRONTIER

Europeans . . . did not conquer wilderness; they conquered Indians. They did not discover America; they invaded it.

—Francis Jennings, *The Founders of America*

1

A PATIENT PATHFINDER

It was the miniature war club that foretold the boy's future. Young Daniel Boone had crafted it himself Indian-style, grubbing up a maple sapling by the roots and shaving and sanding the rough nubbins while leaving the rounded burl at the killing end. He was almost ten years old when he began carrying the weapon into the deep wilderness to snag birds and small game. Crawling through the clover and peavine that carpeted Pennsylvania's forest floor, he could take down a wild turkey from thirty feet and stun a darting squirrel from more than half that distance. His prey would grow in size and ferocity after his father presented him with a short-barreled fowling piece three years later. Still, it was his hunts with his war club that presaged his role as North America's premier pathfinder.

It was sometime in the mid-1740s when Daniel, not yet a teenager, began to accompany his mother, Sarah; his infant sister, Hannah; and his one-year-old brother, Squire, Jr., to a cleared glade some five miles north of the Boone homestead in the Upper Schuylkill River Valley. There he would work the grazing season from spring to late fall, tending the family's small drove of milk cows fattening on the tall timothy grasses that thrived in the twenty-five-acre meadow.* His mother, meanwhile, spent the days churning butter or at work on her looms in the ramshackle cabin on the edge of the pasturage. The surrounding woods—thick stands of sycamore, oak, and box elder that blanketed what was then America's western borderlands—constituted the poet's "forest dark," filled with untamed beasts moving silently through a permanent twilight beneath the treetops' proscenium canopy.

Yet in a place where most men's fears were set loose, young Boone was at home. It was within this checkerboard chiaroscuro that he became expert at imitating all manner of birdsong while toting his club along Indian trails and game tracks trod for millennia by deer, bear, elk, and panther.

It was apparent early on that Daniel had inherited his mother's dark coloring. A sketch from his youth depicts a lad with thick, wavy tufts of coal-black hair pushed back off his broad forehead and parted in the middle. His thin Roman nose lent him the corvine appearance of a raven or a crow, and his hollow cheeks, yet to fill in, emphasized a long and tawny neck that seemed to support an outsize head whose blue eyes were the shade of the North Atlantic in winter.

At the summer pasturage Daniel was charged with tending the wandering livestock and bringing them in at dusk for milking in the cow pens. Yet so great was his curiosity about the backcountry's contours and creatures that he would disappear into its depths for prolonged stretches. When his mother chided him for leaving the cattle lying out at night with their udders near to bursting, the boy would apologize and promise that it would never happen again. But his propensity for woodland wanderlust only increased when he was presented with his fowling piece.

The key to the boy's skill as a hunter was his patience, a virtue he would display for the rest of his life. He would spend hours on end studying the habits peculiar to the thousands of white-tailed deer roaming the

*Timothy grass, also known in Northern Europe as meadow cat's-tail or common cat's-tail, was probably named after Timothy Hanson, a New England agriculturist who introduced the perennial into America in the early eighteenth century.

forest, noting how they were drawn to creeks and rivers at dawn and twilight not only to drink, but to gorge on the tender fountain moss that grew streamside. Trial and error taught him that in the fall months it was easier to steal upon a herd near daybreak, when the dew-moistened fallen leaves would muffle his footsteps. And when he spotted a black bear in late summer or early autumn, instead of shooting it on sight for its meat, oil, and hide, he would instead track it to its masting grounds. There, a sleuth of the creatures would be gathered among flocks of wild turkeys to fatten on acorns, walnuts, blueberries, blackberries, serviceberries, cherries, and crabapples before denning up for the winter. In this way his targets would not only be many, but he marked well the spot to return to the next season.

Thanks to the young Boone, the rafters of the little grazing shack on the edge of the woods—and later, during lean winter seasons, the Boone homestead on the Schuylkill—never wanted for fresh game, jerked meat, and pelts to trade for powder, lead, and flints. It was obvious to all who knew him that Daniel Boone was not cut out for a farmer's life. You could not plow a furrow with a war club.

A half century earlier, bent over his loom in the Devonshire town of Bradninch in southwest England, it is unlikely that George Boone or his wife, the former Mary Maugridge, imagined that their grandson would one day grow into a mythical figure across the Atlantic. Nor is it probable that George and Mary Boone—who had renounced the Church of England, pledged themselves to the Society of Friends, and hatched a plan to flee across the sea to William Penn's religiously tolerant colony—would have alighted on the New World's shores knowing that it virtually teemed with Boones.

As early as 1670 a small band of adventurers that included several Boones set sail from England to plant the first seed of a colony in South Carolina, while in 1704 a Massachusetts census recorded a pamphleteer named Nicholas Boone as the proprietor of a Boston bookshop. There

were also the Catholic Boones of French stock—probably originally calling themselves De Bones—who had sailed from the Isle of Wight early in
the seventeenth century to settle the American colony dedicated to Saint
Mary. Their progeny had since spread from Maryland into New Jersey and
Pennsylvania. They were soon joined by a Swedish community of Bondes,
who Anglicized their names to Boone upon reaching America and founded
a farming settlement along the Delaware River near Philadelphia.

In 1712, Daniel Boone's grandfather George dispatched his three oldest children—his namesake George III; younger brother, Squire; and their
seventeen-year-old sister, Sarah—to explore the possibility of emigrating
to Penn's colony. Upon George's return to Devonshire a year later—Squire
and Sarah remained in America—such were his tales of the opportunities
and freedoms of Pennsylvania that his parents soon sold their property and
weaving business and sailed from the port of Bristol with their remaining
seven children, arriving in Philadelphia in October of 1717.

From Philadelphia the Boone clan migrated into what was then Pennsylvania's interior and eventually settled in the predominantly Welsh community of Gwynedd, some twenty-four miles north by northwest of the
capital city. It was there, on the sixth day of May in 1720, that the twenty-
five-year-old tenant farmer Squire Boone married Sarah Morgan in the
Gwynedd Quaker Meeting House. According to interviews conducted by
the near-contemporaneous Boone biographer Lyman Draper, Daniel
Boone's father, Squire, was a composite of Anglo-Saxon stock, "a man
of rather small stature, fair complexion, red hair and grey eyes." On the
other hand, his nineteen-year-old bride's appearance—"a woman something over the common size, strong and active, with black hair and eyes"—
spoke to her Welsh forebears.

Some years after Squire and Sarah's wedding, the family patriarch
George Boone purchased a 400-acre tract about forty miles northwest
of Gwynedd in what was then known as Oley Township. There he constructed a stone manse among the rolling fields of the Upper Schuylkill
in the shadow of the growing Pennsylvania town of Reading. Though

George's son Squire and his daughter-in-law Sarah remained behind in Gwynedd, Squire Boone proved a dogged farmworker who, in addition to tilling his landlord's fields and tending his cattle, worked late into the evening as a gunsmith repairing weapons for the community. By 1731 Squire had managed to save enough money to buy out his tenancy and obtain 250 acres of prime red-shale land several miles south of his father's property. Three years later, on November 2, 1734, Sarah Boone gave birth to Daniel, the family's sixth child and fourth son.

As a free landowner, Squire Boone's work ethic never flagged, and his children rarely lacked for sustenance. The Boone clan enjoyed hearty

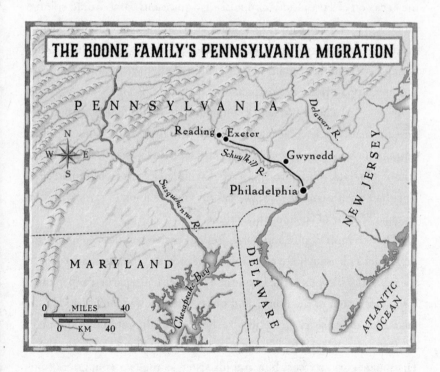

Upon landing in the New World from southwest England in 1717, the Boone family—led by patriarch George Boone, Daniel's grandfather—steadily migrated deeper into the Pennsylvania interior, from Philadelphia to the Welsh enclave of Gwynedd and finally to large tracts of farmsteads in the shadow of today's city of Reading. This area was eventually named Exeter in honor of George Boone's British ancestry.

breakfasts of bread and milk, dinners of venison, turkey, or good pork or bacon with dumplings, and simple evening repasts of hominy with milk, butter, and honey. Moreover, early in Daniel's life his father and several neighbors pooled their funds to purchase a seine net, and thereafter the Schuylkill's annual shad run provided the family with enough salted fish to last through the harsh Pennsylvania winters.

Sarah's industriousness on her several spinning wheels matched her husband's work ethic, and the toddling Daniel grew up watching his mother weave every stitch of her growing brood's linen and woolen apparel. At times Sarah found time to take in outside sewing work, and on the occasion of a propitious commission Squire and Sarah would splurge on chocolate mixed with maple sugar as a family treat. Though Daniel never had the luxury of a formal education, the wife of his older brother Samuel—yet another Sarah—taught him to read, to write, and to perform rudimentary arithmetic. An apt and avid student, Boone's writings later in life may have been rife with grammatical and spelling errors, but they bore the mark of a sensible man who knew how to get to the point. Further, despite the Kentucky historian Ted Franklin Belue's assertion that Boone "though literate, was far from lettered," in his later years Boone often cited Jonathan Swift's *Gulliver's Travels* as his favorite book to carry with him across a lifetime of far-flung adventures.

Though both Squire and Sarah Boone received endless compliments on Daniel's pleasant if not charming demeanor, the youngster also proved the most mischievous of the Boone children. He had a particular penchant for sneaking out of the house, and once, when he was four years old, he talked his older sister Betsy into stealing off in the middle of the night to peek in on a neighbor family rumored to be afflicted with smallpox. His innate curiosity cost him and his sister, as the two youngsters came away with the disease. And though their subsequent illnesses were mild by comparison, the stunt enraged their parents.*

---

* Like the three American presidents, George Washington, Andrew Jackson, and Abraham Lincoln,

Squire Boone, like most fathers of the era, was not a man to spare the rod when one of his sons stepped out of line. Unlike most colonial patriarchs, however, he was also known to genuinely rue the beatings he administered. It was thus probably best for all that Daniel's father went to his grave wondering why one morning he discovered his favorite horse splayed across the lane near his front door, dead of a broken neck.

As Daniel later related the story, the tale begins after Squire and Sarah retired for the evening. Daniel had heard of a "frolic," or coed barn dance, being held not far from the Boone homestead. And though his parents were not the most religious of Quakers—it is hinted in contemporaneous minutes kept by the Society of Friends that Squire was known to enjoy a jar of the forbidden corn whiskey—the teenage Daniel knew better than to ask their permission to mix with unchaperoned girls. After making sure his father and mother were asleep, he surreptitiously saddled Squire's horse and rode off to attend the party. Later, returning home in the early-morning hours in a daring mood, he attempted to leap a sleeping dairy cow. The recumbent animal, startled awake by the hoofbeats, rose to its feet mid-jump and sent both horse and rider tumbling. Daniel, unhurt except perhaps for his pride, removed the dead horse's saddle and bridle, returned them to their place in the barn, and snuck into bed, never to speak of the incident until his old age.

The youthful Daniel's interests were particularly drawn to the Indians who frequented the Oley Township farmsteads to trade. He found the Native Americans—predominantly small bands of Delaware and Shawnee hunters but sometimes minor chiefs with their entire families in tow—a source of wonder. Even then the phrase "standing straight as an Indian" was in vogue, and when the erect and sinewy braves strode into view, he studied with a boy's inquisitiveness for form and function the cut of their buckskin breechclouts, their leggings worn ankle to thigh to

who survived youthful bouts with the millennia-old virus, Boone's natural inoculation would serve him well as an adult.

absorb copperhead and timber rattlesnake strikes, and their moccasins—which they called *mockeetha*—whose meticulous stitching was equal to that of any Philadelphia cordwainer. During the cold months most men also sported cloaks, or matchcoats, made of a coarse woolen fiber called stroud and worn clasped about the shoulders.

Young Boone also marveled at the jewelry—ear and nose rings, arm-bands and wristbands—sported by both sexes. Some pieces were molded from the white man's bartered silver, but most had been fashioned out of the raw copper mined by Great Lakes tribes and passed along ancient Indian trade routes. And while it was not unusual for women to have hundreds of beads, ribbons, and brooches sewn into their one-piece shifts, he noted that the men were particularly partial to crescent-shaped gorgets and to swan's plumes woven into their hair.

Of particular fascination were the distended earlobes favored by many Eastern Woodlands warriors of the era. The ornamentation was achieved with considerable pain. First a brave's ears were slit from their apex to the lobe, and the wound was kept open by stuffing it with beaver fur. It was then slathered with bear oil or slippery elm bark pounded into gel. Lead weights were attached to the bottom of the lobes, elongating them nearly to the shoulders, and the hanging flesh was bound with brass wire to support the copper or silver rings or bells or turkey spurs affixed to the hoop. To a young Anglo-American like Boone, the indigenous peoples must have seemed as alien as the fantastical creatures from the realm of Prester John.*

Adding to the young Boone's admiration of the Indians' unearthly aura was the manner with which their medicine seemed to mystically commune with nature, particularly their ability to use various plants to concoct healing

---

* Every European American man, woman, and child was familiar with the legend of Prester John, the Christian king-priest whose territory was variously located either in the heart of Africa or in "the Far East beyond Persia and Armenia." Conjured by devout medieval European chroniclers as the Muslim faith spread throughout the Mideast and the Sahel, this potential Christian ally was said to rule over all manner of strange creatures, including men and women with horns, cyclopes, and humanoids with no heads but eyes, ears, noses, and mouths in their chests.

potions and salves. He learned that a poultice of Indian cornmeal or tur-
nips was quick to soothe burns, that the leaves of the white plantain weed
boiled in milk was a fair antidote to poisonous snakebites, and that apply-
ing a dressing of well-chewed slippery elm bark mixed with flaxseed to a
gunshot wound would lessen the chances of infection.

It was also from the indigenous visitors that Boone was taught to tan
hides into leather using the rib bones of an elk, bear oil, and the brain
matter of the animal itself, which contains a chemical agent that breaks
up the mucous membranes that cause a hide to harden. He also learned
how to construct a rudimentary "round boat" of a single deerskin or elk
skin stretched taut and perforated at the edges. After a loop of pliant hazel
or cherrywood was woven through the holes and fastened with leather
strings, the craft was left to bake in the sun with the hair side in. Thus was
created a waterproof shell in which to deposit kit, clothing, and weapons
that could be pushed ahead of a swimmer across streams or small rivers.

Perhaps most unusual was the family dynamic Boone witnessed among
the Native Americans. The adults doted over what to most whites appeared to be a scrum of ill-disciplined children. Those who had graduated
from the portable cradleboards were near naked and were allowed to run
free and engage in rough play in a manner that was anathema to Oley
Township's staid Quaker community. Not once did Boone see an Indian
boy physically disciplined. Moreover, he watched in awe as male clan leaders consulted their female elders regarding major decisions about the
time for hunts, the placement of temporary villages, and the arrangements
of religious feasts. Not even the most enlightened Anglo-American men
treated their women with such egalitarianism.

But, of course, Boone being Boone, he was most intrigued by the visitors' weaponry, particularly the ancestral totems Native Americans had
carried for millennia.

By the mid-eighteenth century most Indian warriors owned muskets
obtained by bartering furs and pelts. These "trade guns," as they were
called, were predominantly French-manufactured fusils, generally lighter

and shorter than the "widder-makin'" long rifles carried by American frontiersmen. Although the smoothbore fusils were only accurate to some 70 yards—as opposed to the 250 yards of the rifled-barrel arms—the tribes considered them a leap forward in weaponry.*

Moreover, with the Spanish introduction of the horse to North America over two hundred years earlier, Eastern Woodlands warriors and huntsmen had supplemented their supple hickory longbows with shorter versions more conducive to mounted pursuit. Boone particularly admired the craftsmanship of their powerful arrows—feathered missiles devised around the time the ancient Greeks were besieging Troy. A strong maple-wood shaft could take down a rampaging elk or stun a charging bear. Most of the men also wore scalping knives on leather loops about their necks—the traditional bone, jade, or obsidian blades now replaced by European steel—and the tomahawks tucked into their buckskin belts were interspersed with powder horns, pouches made from the hide of a polecat, and the topknots of vanquished tribal enemies. Finally there were the fearsome war clubs they carried, often called death mauls, that likely planted in Daniel the germ of the idea for his own small cudgel.

Many of Boone's frontier contemporaries surmised that it was the boy's early interactions with the itinerant indigenous peoples that laid the foundation for his affinity and understanding of them later in life. While most Europeans arriving on America's shores viewed Indian behavioral habits as atavistically chaotic and heathen, Boone saw through the veneer. He respected, if not completely understood, the spirituality and philosophy that underpinned their culture. Whether parleying with Indians or fighting against them, Boone never underestimated their intelligence.

For their part, the Delaware, Shawnee, and other Native Americans who came into contact with the borderlands settlers of Pennsylvania were nearly as new to the territory as the whites.

---

* Although traditionally associated with Kentucky—thanks in large part to Daniel Boone—the long rifles were originally crafted by German American gunsmiths in and around Lancaster, Pennsylvania, in the mid-1700s. They thus should by rights be known as "Pennsylvania long rifles."

2

"THE SINGLE NATION TO FEAR"

It was a quirk of New World geopolitics that allowed the Boone clan and its neighbors to become so conversant with American Indian culture. William Penn alone among the founders of the thirteen colonies had never stipulated that Pennsylvania's charter include the establishment of a formal militia to defend against the red peoples whom the Massachusetts clergyman Cotton Mather called the "Children of Satan."

Instead, Penn and his coterie of Quakers made it a point—in theory, at least—to treat the indigenous peoples as they would any other residents. This meant, among other anomalies of the era, negotiating over landholdings instead of taking them outright. This led to semi-amicable relations not only with the Delaware and members of the Iroquois Confederacy to the north—the most powerful bloc of Native Americans inhabiting the continent's Eastern Woodlands—but also attracted to the area a host of lesser-known displaced tribes whose names—Nanticoke and Conoy, Tutelo and Susquehannock—have been virtually lost to the mists of time.*

The three factions that made up the Algonquian-speaking Delaware

---

* The original Iroquois Confederacy consisted of five tribes—the Mohawk, Cayuga, Oneida, Seneca, and Onondaga Nations. In the early 1720s the Tuscarora joined the league.

tribe—the Leni Lenape, or "True People," in their native tongue—had originally occupied territories farther east along the river that gave them their Anglicized name. At first the Delaware had welcomed the few Europeans looking to make new homes in what today constitutes the coastal portions of America's Middle Atlantic states. But as influenza, measles, diphtheria, smallpox, and alcoholism weakened their numbers and fissured their culture, they were forced westward piecemeal. Roughly speaking, it took America's first colonial settlers about a century of forest-felling to push some hundred miles west from the Atlantic littoral. The result was that by the 1720s an entire faction of the Delaware had already been forced over the Appalachians into the Ohio River Valley. Despite Quaker good intentions, the rest would soon follow, as white and red concepts of land negotiation left a psychological bruise that the tribe never forgot.

In 1737, for example, the remaining Pennsylvania Delaware were approached by settlers with a proposition that came to be known as the "Walking Purchase." On its face the offer appeared simple and fair. The newcomers to North America, already encroaching into Indian territory, promised to pay dearly in European manufactured goods in exchange for inland tribal holdings. A treaty was consummated and the merchandise presented. All that was left was to measure the land, which according to the negotiated terms would be calculated by the distance a team of men could walk in thirty-six hours. Thus the "Walking Purchase."

The Indians took the timetable to mean a walk commenced at a "common" pace, with stops for meals and perhaps even a rest. But the Pennsylvania authorities had assembled a detachment of the territory's most able runners, who at the arranged signal sprinted sixty miles to four corners of a huge tract within the allotted thirty-six hours. Thus were vast portions of the Lehigh and Upper Delaware Valleys, rich in coal, timber, and iron ore, lost to the tribe.

Years later, ensconced in their new homes on the far, or western, side of the mountains, Delaware bards would illustrate the repeated thefts of their territories with allegorical metaphors. One tale involved the whites asking for a piece of land that could be covered by a bull's hide. When the Indians agreed, the whites sliced the hide into thin strips that encompassed miles. Another told of the Pennsylvanians requesting a land grant only as large as the seat of a cane chair. Again the Delaware acquiesced, and this time the whites unraveled the woven cane cords into thin strings that, when tied together, stretched over the horizon. These were parables—legal chicanery, false promises—that would be told in one form or another and in one Indian language or another for over a century to come.

Meanwhile, as the Delaware inexorably retreated over the mountains and established themselves along the Muskingum River in southeastern Ohio, they were greeted by their Shawnee cousins, already renowned as "the most bloody and terrible" of all the Algonquian-speaking peoples. The Shawnee were the southernmost of a linguistically related bloc of societies that constituted more than thirty independent tribes inhabiting a swath of North America arcing from the Carolinas to Quebec. Their name was in fact derived from the Algonquian word *shawunogi,* meaning "southerner," relative to their more northwestern "elder and younger brothers," among them the Ottawa, Wyandot, and the Twightwee, or Miami tribe. The Miami to the northwest were the Shawnee's closest neighbors and welcomed them into the Ohio Country as a buffer against the troublesome whites.

The Shawnee that Europeans encountered had descended from a prehistoric mound-building culture whose original territorial boundaries, viewed clockwise, followed a rough parabola from southern Ohio to western Virginia to northern Kentucky. Although their towns and villages were concentrated along the watercourses of the Ohio Valley, they were truly America's wanderers—Dutch maps from the 1600s place large bands of Shawnee east of the Delaware River, and Indians from Florida to Illinois described to early Spanish and French chroniclers their multiple encounters with the tribe's emissaries, whose language had become the lingua franca at indigenous trade fairs.

This penchant for wandering prevented the Shawnee from ever really coalescing into a single society. Yet as the sublime Shawnee historian Colin G. Calloway notes, by the eighteenth century, "No Indian people had moved so often, traveled so widely, or knew better how the [white] invaders had eroded Indian country." In a twist of fate, it was their fellow Native Americans who had induced the first great Shawnee diaspora.

Around the mid-1660s, Iroquois from the north swarmed into the Ohio Valley in search of new hunting grounds with which to maintain their beaver fur trade with the Dutch and British. Unlike most of their Indian neighbors who either fled or sought to make accommodations with the invaders, the Shawnee stood and fought a series of battles in what came to be known as the Beaver Wars. These were one-sided affairs. Already outnumbered four to one, the Shawnee tree-bark body armor and animal-hide shin greaves were no match for the trade guns carried by the Iroquois. Despite the defeat, it was here that the Shawnee solidified their reputation among their fellow indigenous peoples as the staunchest defenders of their land and culture. Twenty-five hundred years earlier the Greek historian Thucydides had observed that wars were fought for either honor, interest, or fear. No one who battled with or against the Shawnee ever accused them of timidity.

Nonetheless, in the wake of the Iroquois victory, Shawnee survivors were scattered and the Ohio Valley was virtually depopulated.* French

---

* Earth scientists point out that the decimation if not annihilation of the indigenous populations of America's northern woodlands tribes in the wake of the Europeans' arrival—the "Great Dying"—also prompted a worldwide climate effect. The resulting terrestrial carbon dioxide intake from trees and plants reforesting once-cleared Native American farm fields—a combined area about the size of France—had a detectable impact. The resulting "Little Ice Age" phenomenon that lasted approximately from the mid-1500s to the early 1700s saw London's Thames River freeze over regularly, blizzards bury Portugal, flooding in Timbuktu, and the decimation of centuries-old citrus groves in eastern China. In two somewhat piquant consequences of this weather phenomenon that reverberate to this day, it also allowed Antonio Stradivari to construct what are still considered the world's most famous violins from slow-growing European spruce, willow, and maple trees, and inspired the writer Mary Mapes Dodge to introduce to the world a fictional character named Hans Brinker, whose silver skates carried him across frozen Dutch canals that would never again ice over.

missionaries recorded Shawnee clans and factions arriving in Saint Louis, while others wandered south to Georgia's Savannah River Country. By the 1680s Shawnee villages had sprouted in western Virginia, South Carolina, and along Alabama's Tallapoosa River, where they forged an alliance with the Creek Indians. The seventeenth-century French explorer Pierre Le Moyne d'Iberville noted the Chaouenons' preternatural mobility and extraordinary adaptability, and described the tribe as "the single nation to fear" in America. In the meanwhile, farther north, bands of Shawnee also began crossing the Allegheny Mountains and moving into eastern Pennsylvania.

Like the Delaware—whom the Shawnee referred to as "grandfathers"— the tribe was initially welcomed by William Penn. The hamlets of Pottstown and Reading—the latter but ten miles from Daniel Boone's grandfather George Boone's farmstead in Oley Township—grew into large, multiethnic Native American hubs. But as more colonists poured into the territory, the Indians were once again pressed hard. Upon Penn's death in 1717, relations with the settlers bottomed out. In the first recorded instance of organized, large-scale violence between Pennsylvanians and Native Americans, a band of starving Shawnee attacked a white settlement near Reading that had refused to give them food.

George Boone, serving as the jurisdiction's justice of the peace, sent an urgent message to colonial authorities in Philadelphia requesting reinforcements; old George knew the Shawnee well and suspected the episode would escalate into general warfare. But aside from a small skirmish that left two settlers wounded, the incident proved a one-time aberration. Most whites soon forgot it. Not the Shawnee, who took the Indian tenets of honor and vengeance to a further extreme than most tribes. The price of insult was blood. In the decades to come many a pioneer mother put her children to bed with the warning that if they did not go to sleep, the Shawnee would come for them.

Meanwhile, with the Shawnee again looking beyond the Appalachians to their former homelands, tribal leaders recognized the strategic geographic importance of the Ohio Valley as a bulwark between New France to the north and west and the British colonies in the east. As such, they shrewdly dispatched emissaries to Montreal to gauge French interest in an alliance to counter the British-Iroquois coalition. This so alarmed the English that, in 1739, Crown representatives proffered a treaty that promised peace between the Shawnee and the British-Iroquois alliance in return for a pledge of Shawnee fealty. When the Shawnee initially refused to sign, the word "fealty" was replaced with "amity." Though Shawnee diplomats agreed to the pact, they continued to communicate in secret with French Canada. They did not trust the British, the Iroquois, or the Americans. They had good reason.

Only five years later, in 1744, the British were on the verge of their third war of the eighteenth century with the French. Known as King George's War in America, it was fought primarily across western New York, New England, and Nova Scotia. Although the four-year conflict in the New World was but a peripheral skirmish in the larger War of the Austrian Succession, which encompassed most of Europe, Pennsylvania authorities nonetheless found the moment expedient to sign the Treaty of Lancaster with the Iroquois.* In retrospect, observes the historian Fred Anderson, the treaty "marked the high point of Iroquois influence in dealing with the English colonies."

The agreement stipulated that much of the land in western Pennsylvania, western Maryland, and western Virginia that the Iroquois had conquered almost a century earlier would now be ceded to the colonists. In exchange, the Confederacy received currency and gold worth nearly $2.5 million today, as well as a guarantee of safe passage through those colonies when the tribe's warriors traveled south to raid ancient enemies such as the Cherokee. As Anderson also notes, this was "a concession that evidently included an agreement to provision war parties while in transit."

---

* In the end, the 1748 Treaty of Aix-la-Chapelle, which ended King George's War, failed to resolve any of the outstanding American territorial disputes.

That the Shawnee had since reoccupied the territories traded away made no more difference to the Iroquois than it did to the whites. Acting on the theory of *a fortiori*—"from the stronger"—the Iroquois had granted tacit permission for the Anglo-Americans to do what they wished with the territory.

By the 1750s, white traders had penetrated deep enough into the heartland to report a thriving Shawnee town and tribal ceremonial center with a population of close to two thousand. Named Chillicothe after a faction of the tribe, it was located on the Scioto River, a north–south running watercourse that bisects the current state of Ohio before emptying into the Ohio River across from Kentucky. The Chillicothe were one of the five principal divisions of the Shawnee Nation, and the bloc from which tribal chiefs were generally selected. Wherever the band lived was known as Chillicothe Town, and a rough translation of Chillicothe as "Fire That Won't Die" is a reference to the Shawnee's sacred council flame kept alive by the eponymous division.*

Chillicothe had risen on a great plain, or "barrens," created by controlled burns at the confluence of the two rivers. Like most Shawnee towns, it was dominated by a large council house, in Chillicothe's case an immense, four-doored building over 150 feet in length and nearly 40 feet wide. Spreading from the council house in all directions were domed, oval wigwams constructed of large sheets of bark and, beyond, vast communal farm fields sown with the holy trinity of squash, beans, and corn of multicolored kernels—the "three sisters" of the earth. Women tended the farm fields, collected crustaceans and shellfish from the watercourses,

---

* The multiplicity of relocations for Shawnee "Chillicothe Towns" throughout Ohio in the eighteenth century—on the Scioto River, on the Little Miami River, and on the Big Miami River—is a continuing source of bewilderment to modern-day chroniclers. The current Ross County, Ohio, seat of Chillicothe, for example, was never an Indian town nor village. Moreover, contemporaneous whites affixed adjectives to the hamlets—"new," "big," "little"—that only add to the confusion. Daniel Boone, for instance, always referred to the second Chillicothe Town on the Little Miami as "Old Chillicothe." For clarity's sake we will refer to the three locations as Chillicothe on the Scioto, New Chillicothe on the Little Miami, and the Third Chillicothe on the Big Miami.

and scoured the forest for fruits and medicinal plants. Men, meanwhile, hunted from late summer to December, often crossing the Ohio River to stalk the game herds and flocks of wild fowl that darkened the skies over what are now West Virginia and Kentucky. Chillicothe on the Scioto was as fine a place as any for the Shawnee to buy time, for the French were not the only potential confederates to whom the tribe dispatched diplomats.

The Shawnee, like most Indians, sensed that King George's War was but a preliminary clash between the two great European powers vying for hegemony in the New World. Having reassembled in the heart of the multicultural Ohio Country, the Shawnee were perfectly positioned to take a leadership role among the manifold Indians with whom they had formed intimate connections over the decades. Those tribes were like spokes on a wheel, with the Shawnee at the hub, and whoever directed or even influenced their actions stood astride the gateway to the North American interior.

As it happened, the outsize Shawnee leverage in the subsequent French and Indian War—known as the Seven Years' War when it erupted in Europe in 1756—was merely a precursor to marshaling their red brethren for the true and ultimate test of defending their lands and cultures against any and all white interlopers.

3

THE LONG HUNTERS

As the eighteenth century crept toward its midpoint, Oley Township's population and Squire Boone's agitation accelerated in tandem. The sparse Pennsylvania borderlands territory to which the Boone clan had migrated over a decade earlier had become so overrun with homesteaders that it had to be municipally divided, with the Boones successfully lobbying the Quaker town fathers to rename their section as Exeter in honor of their English origins. Yet despite the civic influence of the burgeoning family—Squire's wife, Sarah, would give birth to a total of eleven children—all was not well in the Boone household.

The Boones' ascendency in Pennsylvania coincided with the rise of an evangelic movement known as the First Great Awakening. With mesmeric preachers stoking religious fires on both sides of the Atlantic, the new creed's theology had riled Britons and North Americans of all denominations to ever more strident interpretations of God's "true calling." The ostensible spirituality of the movement reckoned less with heretics than with apostates, and it was amid this pious revolution that, in 1742, Squire Boone's eldest daughter, named after his wife, Sarah, was excommunicated, or "disowned," by the Friends of Exeter Meeting. Her crime was marrying a German immigrant outside the faith, and Squire himself was formally rebuked by the town's religious establishment for blessing the union.

Five years later he was again reprimanded when his eldest son Israel also wed a non-Quaker. Both marriages were considered rebelliously disloyal to the Society of Friends, particularly as the dissenters hailed from such a prominent family. In 1748, when Squire Boone failed to properly disassociate himself from his married children and their spouses, he was excommunicated. By then it may not have mattered. Four years earlier the family patriarch and devout Quaker George Boone had died at the age of seventy-eight, further fraying Squire's connection not only to the religion but to the lands of the Upper Schuylkill.

In the meanwhile, Squire and Sarah Boone had remained assiduous and frugal laborers, and if not for their defiance of the Quakers would have been considered notable luminaries in Exeter's political and social circles. The Boone cattle herd had multiplied exponentially, and savings from the couple's farming, gunsmithing, and weaving endeavors had allowed Squire to purchase an additional 250 acres of prime bottomland adjacent to his late father's estate. In addition, the family's smokehouse was rarely empty due to Daniel's increasing proclivity with his rifle, which his father had presented to him on his thirteenth birthday. Yet Squire Boone remained restless. Rumors of a fertile valley nearly five hundred miles to the southwest had begun to reach Exeter around this time, and the fifty-two-year-old Squire still considered himself hale enough for one more adventure.

Reports from Pennsylvania pioneers who had settled along North Carolina's Yadkin River—which splashes out of the Blue Ridge Mountains before joining the Pee Dee River in South Carolina as it winds to the sea—emphasized the area's secluded beauty, abundant game, and loamy soil. The more descriptions Squire Boone heard of this backcountry, the more intrigued he became. He reckoned the territory to be the kind of place where a diligent and energetic man could make a fine life for his family without an overly righteous board of Quakers dictating his choices—a new territory, as the Boone biographer Lyman Draper noted with a nod toward the Society of Friends, "where conscience was free."

Squire and his wife spent the winter of 1749–1750 consulting with their older children about the benefits and drawbacks of relocating to the Yadkin Valley. It was no secret that the conclusion of King George's War had left the southern borderlands in a state of flux. The French were not keen on the idea of Anglo-Americans edging ever closer to their inland territory, not least for fear that their Ohio Country Indian allies might forsake them for English trading partners. But for Squire, any fears of French provocations against settlers in the Yadkin were fairly moot. After all, they weren't planning to cross the Appalachians, merely looking to settle on the lee side of the range.

Squire Boone made his decision that spring. His brood would sell their Exeter properties, auction off their surplus animal stock and any household items too bulky to be transported overland, and move to the Yadkin. Israel and his wife and Sarah and her husband, whose family now included a baby, would join the exodus, as would several of Squire's grown nephews. Young Daniel was ecstatic when he learned that his father had agreed to take along Daniel's best friend, the thirteen-year-old Henry Miller, who years earlier had been informally "adopted" into the Boone clan and worked as Squire's gunsmith apprentice.

Relocating an entire household was a languorous affair in the mid-eighteenth century, and it took the Boone wagon train nearly two years of pushing through Pennsylvania, Maryland, and across the Potomac into Virginia before reaching North Carolina. Conestoga wagons of the era were not generally constructed to carry passengers, although Squire Boone had kept his horse-drawn vehicle's pullout lazy board free of supplies and equipment to accommodate his daughter Sarah and her infant. With the rest of the women and girls walking beside the wagons, and most of the men and boys following on foot driving a small cattle herd, much of that traveling time was spent traversing the "Great Valley" of the Shenandoah in northwestern Virginia. There the party spent at least two growing seasons not far from the homestead belonging to the husband of Squire's sister Sarah, the girl with whom he had emigrated to North America four decades earlier. Each night after pitching camp, the now-fifteen-year-old Daniel would shoulder his rifle and disappear into the forests to hunt, inevitably returning before dawn with an ample supply of venison or wild-fowl.

It was these nightly patrols through the deep forests of Virginia that sparked in the teenage Boone his thirst for the "long hunt."

Just as the contours of a river dictate the pilot's course, America's Eastern Woodlands shaped the route of Daniel Boone's journey into manhood. In the late summer of 1750, while his family remained camped in the Shenandoah, the teenage Boone and his friend Henry Miller took leave to depart on their first long hunt.

Though they have since been lost to the fog of history, long hunters— also known as pelt-getters and market hunters—once occupied a pan-theon of American mythology alongside such fictional folk heroes as Paul Bunyan, John Henry, and Johnny Appleseed. Their heyday was brief— perhaps the fifteen-year period between the early 1760s and the mid-1770s—and unlike the farmers and bog-iron miners who followed them in order to subdue nature, they made little permanent physical impression on the wilderness. But their early packhorse journeys into North Amer-ica's interior served as prologue to the country's narrative of westward expansion.

Long hunting in North America's interior was a dangerous, stinking, and brutish undertaking. The weather itself presented all the challenges of any two-legged or four-legged adversary, ranging from debilitating heat to bone-numbing cold. It was through this climate that men who believed themselves up to the task were burdened with dragging and dismember-ing the bloody carcasses of white-tailed deer and elk—the former often weighing up to 150 pounds; the latter between 500 and 700—over long distances through trackless and unyielding terrain. Stalked by wolves, panthers, and sometimes even bears eager to pounce on their kills, long hunters were also swarmed by blinding black clouds of mosquitoes and blowflies drawn to their blood-caked buckskins. In the inevitable emergencies that arose in the wild, these frontiersmen needed to possess the rudimentary skills of doctors, blacksmiths, boatbuilders, gunsmiths, and coopers—all, incidentally, professions that budding pioneers would soon rely on.

The irony lay in the fact that this was not their purpose at all. For the most part these were men—and they were all men—who preferred woodland solitude to the company of other people. That they could earn a living at their craft was a side benefit.

Generally hailing from Pennsylvania, Virginia, and North Carolina, long hunters traveled in small groups or occasionally even alone, sometimes setting off for only a season of deer hunting or beaver trapping and other times planning on being away for a year or more. Trailed by their dogs, they ignored boundaries set by the British and respected no Indian claims to the lands on the far side of the Appalachians. Although their racist disdain for America's indigenous peoples was manifest—here Boone was the outlier—they adopted Indian dress and hunting techniques as their own.

Few long hunters wore breeches or trousers into the woods, and Boone was no exception. He rapidly and easily acquired the frontiersman's habit of dressing more expediently in an Indian breechclout—a length of cloth or buckskin perhaps a yard long that passed between the legs under a deerskin belt. Thick and tough animal-hide moccasins and leggings held up by garter straps protected the hunter against snakebites. A billowing linsey-woolsey hunting shirt completed the uniform. The thigh-length garments were made by spinning wool fibers on a loom for the warp, and linen for the weft. They were sashed at the waist with the same belt that kept a breechclout in place, with enough room in their folds to stash small amounts of tobacco, ball and powder, or even a memento from home.

These coarse woven tunics were the distinctive mark of an eighteenth-century backwoods hunter, as surely, Boone's biographer Lyman Draper notes, "as a snuff box was the mark of a gentleman dandy." If a hunter had a particularly prolific season, he might order a new linsey-woolsey embroidered with colored silk thread. As was the woodsman's custom, Boone had also let his dark hair grow long enough to be plaited and tied at the nape with a ribbon or rawhide string.

When not stalking prey, long hunters spent their days and nights toiling on a plethora of mundane tasks. Boiling salt from brackish springs to be used in smoking and curing jerky was a necessity, as was rendering bear oil and tallow for candles, with a good-sized bear yielding close to twenty-five pounds of lard. The dried bladders of the largest animals were filled with a pounded mixture of marrow, fat, jerked meat, and berries and coated with suet to make a portable and nourishing pemmican. But, of course, the hunt itself was the raison d'être for the entire enterprise.

On an average day an experienced long hunter could take down between ten and thirty white-tailed deer. But as venison was considered inferior eating, bear meat and, to a lesser extent, opossum and raccoon were the preferred meals. What the deer *were* prized for were their summer and early-autumn hides, when their coats were known to be "in the red." When not bringing down game, the long hunter's most important, if time-consuming, task by far was dressing their deerskins. It began with a process called graining, wherein the hair and outer grain of the animal's flesh was scraped clean with a sharp hunting knife or, in a pinch, an elk's rib bone. The remaining pelt was then scuffed back and forth across a rough board or log until it was soft and pliant. A pack of one hundred or so deer hides was stacked and covered with elk or bearskins to protect them from the weather. As rope was a luxury in the wilderness, the entire parcel was then secured by what the frontiersmen called *tugs*—long strips of hide twisted into a sturdy leather twine. Lastly, the packs were hoisted onto platforms erected atop cane scaffolding high enough to be out of reach from scavenging wolves.

When it came time to pack out, the skins were baled and bundled on either side of a horse's withers. A robust horse could carry up to 250 pounds of hides, and a man with a marksman's eye and the skill and luck to emerge from the woods in one piece might earn more than $1,000 from his haul—the equivalent of nearly $40,000 today. By comparison, in the mid-eighteenth century a butcher made about 44 cents a day, a blacksmith 67 cents, and a farm laborer 33 cents. The latter would need more than eight years to earn $1,000.

Serendipitously, it was also long hunters who introduced the term "buck" into the American vernacular as a synonym for "dollar." The hide of a full-grown male white-tailed deer was worth about one of the Spanish pesos in wide circulation along the American frontier. As a peso was often referred to by its German name of *thaler, thaler* became "dollar," and "dollar" became "buck."

Despite the vastness of America's eastern forests, they were not as empty of humanity as one might suspect. As hunters from white cultures combed the frontier's intersecting paths and trails, they often encountered one another. On such occasions it was not unusual for the strangers to spread their blankets and animal skins beneath the stars, strike a campfire from the flint of their gunlocks, and share a pipe of tobacco or kinnikinnick, a pungent admixture of herbal bark and bearberry and sumac leaves. Over an uncorked leather flask they would trade snippets of news in a pidgin patois that included English, French, German, Dutch, and even Algonquian words and phrases spoken in a variety of brogues, dialects, and accents. It was during these encounters that young Boone was schooled in a way of life that bridged European and Native American cultures.

Boone and Henry Miller at first planned to limit their long-hunting sojourn into the Shenandoah Mountains. But finding game there scarce, they worked their way south to the Roanoke River in southwestern

Virginia, where they lingered for weeks accumulating skins. They next followed the river through the Roanoke Gap in the Blue Ridge, which led them to the high piedmont country along the Virginia–North Carolina border that teemed with deer, bear, and elk. Although it was as yet too early in the season to strike out for the higher elevations to the west, which were flush with beaver and otter, by late fall their haul of hides was substantial enough for them to turn back north with their packhorses piled high.

They paused briefly in the Shenandoah to relate their adventures to Squire and Sarah Boone before continuing on to Philadelphia to sell their treasure. There, as Miller later told the story, the payment for their several months' worth of backcountry labors allowed the two teenagers to embark on a three-week "jamboree" of taverns and gaming houses, which left their pockets empty by the time they returned to Virginia to join the Boone train setting off for North Carolina.

Though Miller came to look back on their profligacy with a sense of "disgust," Boone's carefree abandonment of any fiscal responsibility foreshadowed a trait he would exhibit for the rest of his life. Decades later, long after Henry Miller had established himself as an emblem of probity as the owner of a Virginia ironworks factory and a string of sawmills and paper mills, his old friend Daniel Boone was still combing the woods and still falling and climbing in and out of debt.

4

INTO THE YADKIN

There is speculation, never verified, that Daniel Boone's father, Squire, acting as a sort of advance scout, may have accompanied his son and Henry Miller as far as the Yadkin River Valley on the boys' long hunt. In any case, that the clan definitively reached the forks of the Yadkin some time in 1752 is attested to by court records revealing that in the fall of that year the nineteen-year-old Elizabeth "Betsy" Boone—Daniel's old smallpox-peeking partner—married a farmer named William Grant, a transplanted Marylander who had put down stakes in the valley two years earlier. Squire, Sarah, and their extended family in the meanwhile settled on a 640-acre swath of level land in the eastern shadow of the Blue Ridge. Squire, assuming his late father's, George's, old role as the Boone family's paterfamilias, purchased the tract from agents of the British speculator John Carteret, 2nd Earl of Granville, whose family had been deeded much of western North Carolina by a royal land grant. The price was three shillings, or a little over twelve dollars today.

Folklore has it that the itinerant Boones and their various in-laws lived for a time in a large cave while their neighbors helped them raise cabins near the confluence of two creeks that emptied into the north fork of the Yadkin. One can glean from colonial census records that the building processes were likely accomplished fairly rapidly by many hands. Those figures show that the number of fighting-age men inhabiting the three counties that made up western North Carolina spiked from one hundred in 1746 to some three thousand by 1753.

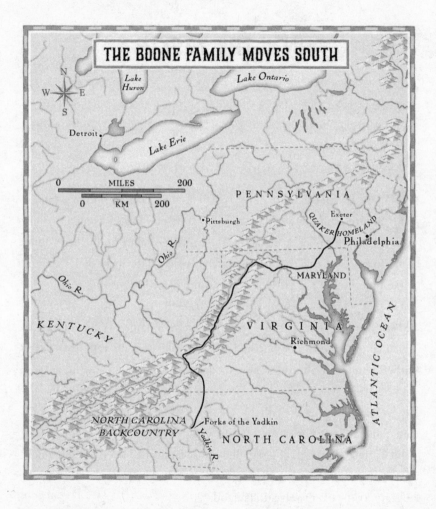

Feeling squeezed by newly arrived European immigrants settling in Pennsylvania, in 1750 the sixteen-year-old Daniel Boone's parents, Squire and Sarah Boone, sold their Exeter property and, with Daniel's ten brothers and sisters in tow, embarked on an arduous two-year, 525-mile journey from "Quaker Country" to the forks of the Yadkin River in the shadow of North Carolina's Blue Ridge Mountains.

The expanse surrounding the Boone compound was composed of a series of "rich and undulating" meadows of luxuriant tall grass cross-hatched by dozens of small creeks. In many places these streambeds were overspread by thickets, or canebrakes, of *Arundinaria gigantea*, a thinner species of indigenous bamboo. Wherever canebrakes grew, colonial settlers took that to indicate fertile land. These canebrakes could rise to twenty feet and served as cover and nesting grounds for all manner of wild-fowl and small game. The edges of the grasslands gave way to clusters of berry bushes, grapevines, and walnut trees that thrived in the moist, brick-red clay soil. Wild fruit trees also abounded, and the the Boone women never lacked for resources to stock their root cellars with preserves made from peaches and pawpaws, a yellowish-green fruit about the size of a mango whose custardy pulp tastes like a combination of mango, banana, and pineapple.

Meanwhile, the forks of the Yadkin were a constant source of shad, flathead catfish, and largemouth and smallmouth bass, while the towering spinneys of hemlock, oak, and hickory that surrounded the Boone pastur-ages lent the valley its Indian name—Yattken or Yattkin, meaning "Place of Big Trees" in the Siouan tongue. As a bonus, the piedmont country was also a meteorological delight whose elevated location hundreds of miles inland from the pine-forested North Carolina coast tempered high summer's oppressive heat.

With the Boone family expanding—Daniel's older brother Samuel had taken a bride not long after Betsy's wedding—and certain to grow larger, in 1753 Squire Boone purchased a second, 640-acre grant from Lord Carteret's estate some two miles to the west of his cabin on a stream that would come to be known as Bear Creek. In a mere two generations the descendants of the religiously persecuted Boones of England's Devonshire peninsula had discovered halfway around the world a life, as Quaker scrip-ture has it, "guided by that light [which] will achieve a full relationship with God." Squire Boone in fact envisioned the fat and happy days of a gentleman farmer's existence ahead for himself and his progeny, most of them at any rate. For despite the lush agricultural bounty offered by the Yadkin River basin, the fire inside his son Daniel to roam the western forests had only been stoked by his long hunt with Henry Miller.

Boone, at nineteen, was now the oldest male still living under his parents' roof. As such he was duty bound to partake in what he considered the drudgery of family farming during the spring, summer, and early-fall cropping seasons. Once finished in the fields, however, he wasted no time lighting out for the frontier to spend his days and nights slipping through the hardwoods tracking prey in his breechclout and linsey-woolsey shirt. What he discovered in the deep North Carolina forests were deer, bear, and elk so plentiful—over thirty thousand deerskins were exported from the colony in 1753—that a stealthy hunter's biggest challenge was fending off wolves and panthers as he dressed the carcasses. In the fall, when black bears rampaged more openly for food in search of hibernation weight, a rifleman with Boone's skill could fell enough of the *Ursus americanus* to cache a season's worth of fatback bear meat, salted to make bear bacon. Legend had it that the Bear Creek that ran through the Boone property acquired its name from the ninety-nine bears that Boone killed along its banks over the course of a single autumn.

Daniel Boone was no longer taking down game for recreation, practice, or even sustenance. He was now a full-time market hunter, jouncing his peltry-laden wagon along the rough road to the "trading town" of Salisbury some twenty miles to the southeast, a municipality that was rapidly becoming a literal and metaphorical crossroads of Anglo-American and Native American societies.

The Indian villages nearest to the Boone's Yadkin Valley homestead were occupied by the Catawba tribe, a rump faction of the Siouan people who had remained behind in North America's southeast when the great Sioux Nation decamped for Minnesota sometime in the 1500s. The Catawba villages were congregated about the western North Carolina river named for them near what is present-day Charlotte.

Like the Delaware and Shawnee who had visited Oley Township to feast and barter, the Catawba—whose six thousand men, women, and children included an estimated fifteen hundred warriors—often pitched temporary camps near Salisbury for great trading fairs. It was an arrangement amenable to both sides, with the Indians arriving with loads of furs and hides to exchange for iron pots, hand mirrors, the strands of pounded silver with which they ornamented their bodies and, most essential, guns and ammunition to keep their ancestral enemies, the Cherokee, at bay.

Much Indian lore was exchanged during these jubilees, and Daniel Boone was delighted to learn that Catawba warriors amputated buffalo hooves and bear paws to attach to the soles of their moccasins to lure the Cherokee into ambush. It was also likely from the Catawba that he was taught the natural healing powers of the twiny mistletoe vine so common to the southern frontier that, as Boone grew older, he would use it to treat his arthritic joints.*

By this time Boone had established a reputation among both white and red men as one of the most skilled marksmen, if not *the* most skilled, along the Blue Ridge. He was a regular at shooting competitions held in Salisbury town, and such was his haughtiness that he was known to hit the middle of his target with trick shots before advising his competitors to save their money and their pride. This arrogance did not sit well with a prominent Catawba warrior and tracker named Saucy Jack, whose star Boone had eclipsed.

One night not long after Boone again bested Saucy Jack in a shooting contest before departing for a short hunting excursion, the Indian repaired to a Salisbury tavern, where he loudly boasted of his plans to ambush the upstart Boone upon his return. It is not unlikely that the

---

* Peoples as far back as the Druids had distilled the parasitic plant, which attaches itself to a host tree, into a tea used to ease seizures, headaches, and, in the case of Boone's later years, arthritis.

Catawba's threats were fueled by the ferociously potent corn liquor ubiquitous to the ramshackle pot-and-plank alehouses, known as "ordinaries," that dotted America's upland crossroads. Nonetheless, when word of the Indian's provocations reached Squire Boone the next morning, he jammed a hatchet into his belt and set off to strike first.

No blood was spilled. Saucy Jack, now presumably sober, sensibly took leave of the territory after hearing that the elder Boone was coming for him. However, the story—admittedly but a minor episode in Boone's life—is nonetheless illustrative. For not only did it limn the young Boone's burgeoning public prominence, but it also impressed upon him a lesson in humility that he would carry with him always. Not least, the tale also says a bit about the hearty, fifty-seven-year-old Squire Boone's tenuous relationship with his Quaker faith. To the Society of Friends, the killing of another human being—the most heinous crime that can be perpetrated—is never justified. Squire Boone's conscience was indeed free along the Yadkin.

Discounting Saucy Jack's whiskey bravado and the annoyance of the occasional stolen pig or hen, the white settlers across the North Carolina Piedmont for the most part maintained friendly relations with the Catawba. The same cannot be said for what the homesteaders called the "Northern Indians," particularly the fierce Shawnee. By now all the Shawnee factions had been forced west of the Appalachians by Anglo-American settlers. And their once tentative relations with the French had evolved into an informal alliance.

For well over a century, Britain and France had been engaged in a lethal contest for control over what was then called the Northwest Territory— the immense tract of land roughly bounded by the Great Lakes to the north, the Mississippi River to the west, the Cumberland River to the south, and the Appalachians to the east; the chain runs some fifteen hundred miles from Newfoundland to the foothills of Alabama and Georgia, with its width ranging from ninety to three hundred miles. The mountains had risen between 540 million and 295 million years ago, the result of sedimentary sandstone, shale, siltstone, limestone, and dolomite being lifted, compressed, weathered, and eroded by the repetitive rise and fall of ancient shallow seas. The prehistoric swamps left behind by the outflowing water eventually formed the coal beds for which the region may be best known today, but at the time it was considered as formidable a barrier as the walls of Jericho.

On the far side of the peaks lay the Ohio River. Fed by myriad tributaries, the Ohio was the nucleus of the country as it flowed along a rough southwesterly course through the center of this bountiful expanse and into the Mississippi. Kings and ministers in London and Paris recognized that whoever laid claim to the river would hold sway over an untapped and unmapped domain the likes of which the western Europeans could barely envision. Thus the race for dominance of the American frontier had three times led England and France to formal declarations of war—in 1688, in 1702, and in 1744.

But declared wars were expensive. More often than not the European powers found it more expedient to employ Native American proxies to help achieve their territorial goals. When reports of Shawnee restiveness in the heart of the Ohio Country reached Paris, Louis XV and his advisors—not least his influential mistress Madame de Pompadour—envisioned a set of tumblers clicking into place and locking the English into a commitment against a prolonged guerrilla struggle that would not only drain the British treasury but sap the morale of the British Army. To that end the Shawnee, fueled by French-supplied brandy and rum, would periodically pour south to raid Catawba and Cherokee villages known to be partial to the British-aligned settlers.

White pioneers along the southern borderlands were often swept up in these conflicts and sometimes even specifically targeted. The year after the Boones relocated from Pennsylvania, a small war party of Shawnee descended on the Yadkin country and burned a number of isolated cabins.

The raids only subsided when an overwhelming force of Catawba rallied to the homesteaders' defense, killing and scalping a good many Shawnee and putting the rest to flight. Among the spoils the Catawba collected from their fallen foes were silver crucifixes, glass beads, and hand mirrors quite obviously of French manufacture.

Over the next three years, these backwoods skirmishes escalated. What the French had not foreseen, however, was the British employing proxy troops of their own in the form of the American colonists. So it occurred that in the spring of 1755, the twenty-year-old Sergeant Daniel Boone of the North Carolina militia packed his rucksack, picked up his long rifle, and volunteered his services to the Crown. Naturally, he had no way of knowing that before the conflagration that came to be known as the French and Indian War was even officially declared, he was destined to take part in one of the most embarrassing defeats in the history of the British Empire.

5

THE OHIO COUNTRY

I f the Ohio River was the beating heart of the Old Northwest Territory, the Mississippi was the key to the continent. For France, the river meant unfettered trade and communication routes connecting Canada and the Great Lakes to French holdings in the West Indies. To England, control of the immense North American watercourse would form a defensive barrier protecting her seaboard colonies from foreign intrigue. Perhaps most significant for each country, control of the Mississippi River promised the containment of the other's colonial aspirations in the New World. The irony lay in the fact that the Spanish had gotten there first.

Although Christopher Columbus was erroneously rumored to have sailed past the mouth of the Mississippi during his third exploratory voyage in 1498, the first white man to record the existence of the river bisecting North America was the Spanish navigator Alonso Álvarez de Pineda. Álvarez de Pineda entered his "discovery" into his ship's log on June 12, 1519, christening the flow the Rio del Espiritu Santo in honor of the feast of the Pentecost. There is no record of Álvarez de Pineda's ships sailing up the Mississippi, and a succession of subsequent Spanish explorers who dropped anchor off Florida could only marvel at the tales the Indians related of the mighty "Father of Waters" beyond the western horizon.

It was not until 1541 that the gold-seeking conquistador Hernando de Soto, at the head of a party of six hundred soldiers and a handful of priests, hacked his way from the Florida panhandle to the banks of the Mississippi near what is today the city of Memphis, Tennessee. There he constructed flatboats, crossed over to present-day Arkansas, and became the first European to explore the Mississippi Valley. Boots of Spanish leather trod soil as far south as Louisiana and as far north as Missouri in de Soto's fruitless search for treasure and heathen souls to convert or enslave. A year after de Soto's initial crossing of the Mississippi, he was still recording his findings for the court of Charles I when he succumbed to fever on the river's western bank. As Spanish friars chanted the first requiems ever heard along the watercourse, de Soto's weighted corpse was slipped into the current.

Nearly a century passed before a group of Indians described in detail for the royal governor of Virginia, Sir William Berkeley, the fruitful world of plenty that stretched from the far slope of the Appalachians to the great river to the west. Berkeley found himself at sixes and sevens. The territory beyond the mountains may as well have been marked on maps as "Here Be Dragons." As far as most Anglo-Americans were concerned, the land was populated by a menagerie of wild beasts and even wilder "savages." The English word, derived from the French *sauvage,* has its roots in the Latin *silva,* meaning "wood." It was used by allegedly civilized Europeans to describe black Africans, brown Indians populating the Asian subcontinent, and even the forest-dwelling clans of northwest Ireland. Along America's eastern seaboard it was taken for granted that the country's interior teemed with entities lusting to maim or kill: black bears and wolves, rattlesnakes and panthers, and feral humans whose mode of dress, clannish culture, and chopped, guttural languages struck European ears as barely a step up from the grunts of apes.

Yet as Governor Berkeley and his Virginians processed the descriptive stories of the rolling green hills and river valleys to the west abounding with game and beaver pelts, of rich bottomland waiting to be converted into pasturage, of pristine streams meandering through thousands upon thousands of acres of thick deciduous forest, the tiniest shoots of "westering fever" took root.

Sensing an opportunity to expand Great Britain's colonial holdings, in the summer of 1650 Gov. Berkeley commissioned a six-man expedition to chart the alleged arcadia that lay beyond Appalachia's skyscraping heights. With an Appamattuck Indian as their guide, the group departed Fort Henry near present-day Petersburg, Virginia, and pursued a course through the Roanoke Gap, the same route Daniel Boone and Henry Miller were to explore a century hence. The expedition returned a mere nine days later, having laid a rather grandiose claim in the name of England to all the territory west of Petersburg. Thus began an era of British exploration, which culminated in 1699 when the English king, William III, the infamous William of Orange, affirmed his country's proprietorship of the American heartland. Theoretically, the royal land grab extended to the Mississippi and beyond. This, however, created an international dilemma, for the French were already plying the big river's waters.

During the same half century that disparate parties of British agents and Anglo-American colonists traversed the continent's wooded interior on behalf of the British Crown, French explorers approached the same territory from points north. Nearly one hundred years before William of Orange laid his claim, French missionaries had trekked out of eastern Canada to proselytize as far west as Lake Superior. And in the summer of 1673, while British-backed expeditions were still wandering the "near west" on the far side of the Blue Ridge, the black-robed Jesuit priest Jacques Marquette and the French Canadian geographer and fur trader Louis Jolliet became the first white men since de Soto to skim the surface of the Mississippi River in their birchbark canoes.

Nine years later the French explorer Robert de La Salle entered the river by way of the Great Lakes, and on this and subsequent missions

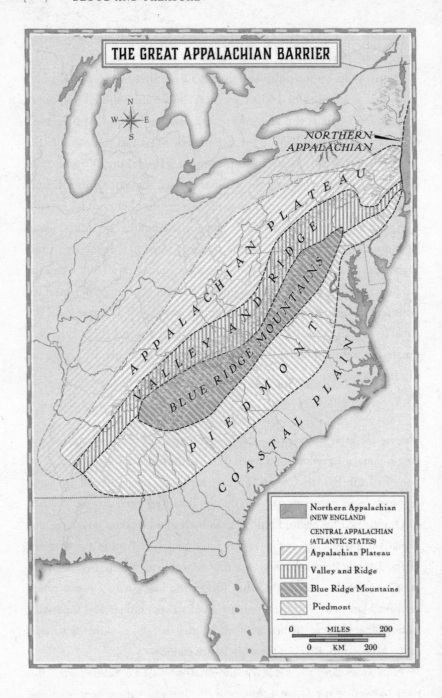

THE GREAT APPALACHIAN BARRIER

NORTHERN APPALACHIAN

APPALACHIAN PLATEAU

VALLEY AND RIDGE

BLUE RIDGE MOUNTAINS

PIEDMONT

COASTAL PLAIN

Northern Appalachian
(NEW ENGLAND)

CENTRAL APPALACHIAN
(ATLANTIC STATES)

Appalachian Plateau

Valley and Ridge

Blue Ridge Mountains

Piedmont

0   MILES   200

0   KM   200

he and his crew journeyed as far south as present-day New Orleans. La Salle erected makeshift forts while mapping the contours of both the river and its watershed, and formally took possession of the entire territory of what he called La Louisiane as sovereign French soil. For the next seventy years, England and France vied for preeminence across the verdant North American interior.

The antagonism came to a final head in May 1756 when England formally declared war on France. The three previous wars between the two countries had done little to affect the territorial contours of North America. This time, both nations vowed, would be different. The conflict that raged across Europe for the next seven years sucked in nearly every great Western power, with the Prussians, Portugal, and a confederation of smaller German states and duchies allying with Great Britain against a coalition of French, Russian, Swedish, Spanish, and Austro-Hungarian armies. Incongruously, the entire European conflagration was touched off by an incident that occurred nearly four thousand miles away in the deep forests of western Pennsylvania. It was instigated by the man destined to become the first president of the United States.

In May of 1754, two years before European hostilities officially commenced, a twenty-two-year-old lieutenant colonel in Virginia's colonial corps named George Washington entered the Ohio Country leading a company of a little over one hundred militiamen at the behest of the colony's governor, Robert Dinwiddie. His orders were to assist a detachment of British regulars erecting an outpost called Trent's Fort on the triangular peninsula formed by the confluence of the Allegheny and Monongahela Rivers that formed the mighty Ohio—the site of the future city of Pittsburgh.

MAP ON LEFT: *During the nascent settlement of North America, the Appalachian Mountain system, rising from Georgia to Canada, effectively boxed in colonists eager to appropriate Native American lands west of the range into a sliver of the Atlantic Coastal Plain.*

Washington, who still retained his natural teeth, was the logical choice to carry out the mission. A year earlier he had been tasked with delivering a letter from Governor Dinwiddie to the commander of the French garrison at Fort LeBoeuf in northwest Pennsylvania. The stockade was one of a string of outposts that the French had either built or planned to erect to secure their hold on territory stretching from the Saint Lawrence River to the Mississippi. To King Louis XV, the necklace of forts, when pulled tight, would strangle King George's ambitions in North America's interior. To the British, it was land piracy.

In the communiqué Washington had carried on his first trip into the interior, the colonial governor informed the French commander at Fort LeBoeuf that he and his troops were trespassing on ground claimed by His Britannic Majesty. They were, the message warned, to immediately withdraw.

The French politely laughed off the pretensions of the governor's young representative, and sent Washington on his way. Upon his return to Virginia, however, Washington's expeditionary journal was published by a local broadsheet. His stirring tales of traversing Allegheny Mountain passes through waist-deep snow and fording icy rivers that froze the legs off his packhorses during his thousand-mile-round-trip journey caused an immediate sensation in the colonies—as did his reports of English and American traders taken captive and even murdered by Indians allied with the French. This was particularly galling considering that Canadian-based trappers and traders known as *coureurs de bois* were crosshatching the Ohio Country with impunity. Washington's travel narrative was soon reprinted in British newspapers and magazines from London to Edinburgh, and the adventures of the fourth-generation colonial planter became the talk of Great Britain's salons and coffeehouses.

Now, twelve months later, in May 1754, Washington was back in the Ohio Country at the head of his Virginia irregulars as well as a small contingent of Mingo warriors who, in return for British muskets, had turned on their French allies. In late May, Washington was informed that the French had captured Trent's Fort on the Ohio and renamed it Fort Duquesne. Further, his Indian scouts warned him that the tracks of a thirty-three-man enemy reconnaissance patrol had been discovered not five miles from his position. Washington, leading a party of close to forty troops and a dozen or so Indians through the early-morning hours of May 27, stalked the French to their camp and fell on them at dawn. The firefight lasted but moments; ten fusiliers were killed with another twenty-two captured. One Frenchman managed to slip away through the woods and bring word of the ambush to Fort Duquesne.

Among the dead bodies mutilated by the Indians was their commander, the French nobleman Joseph Coulon de Villiers de Jumonville. A Virginia militiaman later claimed that as Jumonville lay wounded, the Mingo war chief Tanacharison—known as the "Half King"—personally split his skull, decapitated and scalped him, and affixed the head to a pole after ritualistically washing his hands with the Frenchman's brains as a symbol of fealty to the Anglo-Americans. When news of the incident reached Fort Duquesne, the French commander—Jumonville's older brother—claimed that he had been in the process of carrying a diplomatic message to the British and was thus traveling under a flag of truce.

In the wake of Jumonville's death, Washington's column was pursued by a French and Indian force of some seven hundred fighters to a spot about seventy miles southeast of Fort Duquesne. There, in an open meadow on the edge of a dank swamp, they hastily threw up a wooden barricade named Fort Necessity. Though Washington's ill-equipped corps of frontiersmen had never seen action against trained soldiers, he was confident that their woodland wiles and Indian-fighting skills would stand them well, particularly as he had now been reinforced by some one hundred British regulars. In the battle that ensued, however, his unseasoned recruits withered under concerted and coordinated enemy fire.

As Washington attempted to cohere a defensive front with the contingent of Redcoats, the despairing Virginians ignored him and instead broke into their rum supply. Though Washington kept his composure throughout the one-sided battle, he was inevitably forced to raise a white flag. He was then informed by the French commander that he and his surviving troops would be allowed to return to Virginia upon signing surrender terms. The details, written in French, were poorly translated by Washington's Dutch interpreter. As a blistering downpour obscured the ink on the document, Washington affixed his name to papers attesting that he had "assassinated" Jumonville. It was an admission that haunted him for the rest of his life. For the moment, the young colonial officer so lately the toast of London was now considered a war criminal in Paris. Washington had also, in effect, fired the first unofficial shots of the French and Indian War. As the French philosopher Voltaire was to observe, "So complicated are the political interests of the present times that a shot fired in America shall be the signal for setting all Europe by the ears."

Voltaire's prediction was soon validated as European nations and kingdoms raised armies in preparation for the inevitable, including a vicious proxy war that was to blaze across North America. Although British and French regular troops fought in the conflict, the French and Indian War is best recalled for the extreme barbarity carried out by militiamen from both factions as well as the confusing mélange of Indian tribes allied to either side who hewed to no "civilized" rules of war.

Writing about the French and Indian War, the prize-winning historian Joseph Glatthaar notes the dichotomy of expectations versus the reality on the ground. "Linear warfare may have been effective in Europe where there were vast open fields and both sides played according to the same rules," Glatthaar writes. "But in the colonies Indians did not fight that way. Amid extensive forests, Indians attacked in raiding parties, using speed and surprise. They would strike and press their advantage and retreat when they lost it, utilizing the terrain and cover to their benefit. Colonists responded by adopting tactics that were similar to the Indians, attacking by surprise, taking advantage of the topography, and burning down villages, seizing hostages, and taking scalps. When the British attempted to use linear tactics against the Indians, the colonists considered them fools."

It was in the spring of 1755 that Daniel Boone entered the maelstrom Glatthaar described as a teamster assigned to accompany the British general Edward Braddock's expedition into the French-held American frontier. Braddock, dispatched from London with two regiments of regular troops to finish the job that Washington had failed at, planned his campaign with several lofty if elusive goals. Initially, he would capture Fort Duquesne, and from there march north to raze the New France strongholds at Niagara and Quebec. Along the way he would also construct the first great road into America's trackless wilderness. To his American allies who knew the country and its defenders, this was hubris unchecked.

6

KANTA-KE

Portraitists of the era did the sixty-year-old Gen. Braddock no favors. In a string of renderings, his obligatory British gentleman's frizzed white wig appears several sizes too small, emphasizing a pair of coal-dark eyebrows that resemble nothing so much as a brace of fruit bats arrayed over a long, spiky nose mottled with gin blossoms. Perhaps his reputation for an imperious arrogance played into the artists' subconscious as they wielded their brushes.

Comeliness, of course, had never been a prerequisite for a keen military mind. But Braddock's strategy for driving the French from America's interior left many colonials baffled. Particularly puzzling was his derision for the Native Americans' fighting skills. When one Shawnee chief approached him with an offer to attach his warriors to the Redcoats in exchange for the promise of sovereign territory, the general responded with a sneer. "No Savage Should Inherit the Land," he wrote. When he further announced that the British would simply take the Indian homelands as spoils of war, Versailles's most gifted propagandists could not have devised a sharper recruiting message.

In late May 1755, Gen. Braddock departed Fort Cumberland in western

Maryland at the head of some fourteen hundred British regulars and between three hundred and four hundred militia auxiliaries from Virginia, Maryland, and North Carolina. The nominal leaders among the colonials were the Virginians, whose governor had initially raised the call to arms to the neighboring colonies. But, in truth, Braddock and his inner circle regarded the provincials as little more than camp labor. Even militia officers such as Washington, whom Braddock had specifically requested to join the expedition despite the debacle at Fort Necessity, were treated as second-class soldiers. As such, sharpshooters like Boone were assigned to the rear of the column as wagoneers hauling the regimental baggage. Braddock's target, Fort Duquesne, rose 110 miles to the west.

It was during the march that Boone first met his cousin Daniel Morgan, at nineteen almost two years Boone's junior. That Morgan was descended from the same Welsh stock as Sarah Morgan Boone was evident. Well over six feet tall and broad of shoulder with a frontiersman's ruddy complexion, the leonine Morgan towered over his cousin. Morgan had migrated from New Jersey to Virginia two years earlier and had since worked clearing land, operating a sawmill, and hiring out as a teamster. Though technically unschooled, he possessed an uncanny business acumen, and by the time of Braddock's expedition he had put aside enough money to purchase his own wagon and draft team, which the British had conscripted for the campaign. Perhaps more pertinent, Morgan's reputation as a roustabout across Virginia's Shenandoah Valley equaled Boone's renown as a tracker and hunter along North Carolina's Blue Ridge. If Morgan were weather, he'd have been a hailstorm.

Morgan was known to walk into one of the motley public houses that dotted the Shenandoah and challenge any and all comers to a wrestling match. He rarely lost. The rough company Morgan kept along America's borderlands can be ascertained from a letter to *The Virginia Gazette* from an itinerant preacher published in 1751. The clergyman, whose sensibilities had been refined in the East, was aghast at the rampant immorality inherent to the liquor-purveying "ordinaries." Like so many of his fellow citizens, he viewed the unruly westerners as barely a step above wild savages in manners, clothing, and taste. Their backwoods barrooms, he wrote, "are the common Receptacle and Rendezvous of the very Dreggs [sic] of the people, even of the most lazy and dissolute where Time and Money are vainly and unprofitably squandered away, where prohibited and unlawful Games, Sports, and Pastimes are used, followed, and practiced almost without any intermission; namely Cards, Dice, Horse-racing, and Cock-fighting, together with Vices and Enormities of every other Kind."

The parson ended his screed with a flourish, charging that within the walls of the taverns, "Drunkenness, Swearing, Cursing, Perjury, Blasphemy, Cheating, Lying, and Fighting are not only tolerated, but permitted with Impunity; nay, abound to the greatest Excess." To the irate cleric this may have been literal hell on earth. To Dan Morgan, it was a night out.

Morgan also proved a fair marksman, and as Braddock's column inched west he and Boone traded hunting techniques and family lore while often communicating with each other via coded turkey gobbles that flummoxed the Redcoats. Somewhere along the route the two fell in with a thirty-three-year-old Irish-born teamster named John Findlay, an Indian trader whose adventures had taken him well west of the Appalachians. Findlay's experience was sketched in the deep lines of his face, and in the flickering shadows of nightly campfires he would regale Boone and Morgan with exuberant and exhaustive paeans to the rich country over the mountains. He was most keen on a huge tract to the southwest that the Shawnee called Kanta-ke and the Iroquois Ken-tah-ten—both translated variously as "Place of Lush Meadows" or "Land of Tomorrow."

As Findlay described it, the Indians who had named it had not missed the mark; Kanta-ke was a tramontane paradise replete with fertile soil, a mild climate, a vast inland navigation system of rivers and—Boone's ears pricked at this—enough game to feed every colonist from Boston to Savannah.

One night, Findlay related an adventure story, which Boone and Morgan later decided was mostly true. Three years earlier, Findlay began, he and four *voyageurs* for hire had set off down the Ohio from western Pennsylvania in a small fleet of canoes piled high with trade goods. The birchbarks, riding low in the current, were weighted with the usual powder and ball as well as the obligatory kettles, beads, blankets, silver gewgaws, and a surfeit of hand mirrors and mother-of-pearl combs. The most fragile cargo was packed in "good English hay" acquired in Lancaster, Pennsylvania, to minimize damage.

The small flotilla had descended the river as far as present-day Louisville, a mere 274 miles from its mouth on the Mississippi. There they were blocked by the Falls of the Ohio—a series of cataracts where the river dropped 26 feet in less than 3 miles.* So dangerous was the white water and so laden was the party with merchandise that even the *voyageurs*— short, stout professional canoemen admired for their combination of strength and diminutive size, so as to leave room for more cargo—agreed that they had no choice but to turn back. Before they did, Findlay said, with only a hint of his birth country's blarney, they dined like kings on the hundreds of plump geese and ducks sucked over the falls by the strong current and bashed to death on the rocks below.

After paddling some eighty miles back upriver, Findlay and his associates found themselves at the confluence of the Ohio and a wide and swift tributary they had somehow missed in the fog on their trip downstream. It was here that they happened upon a Shawnee hunting party about to follow what the Indians called the "Cantucky" River into the territory to the south. The Shawnee showed the white men the natural wonder of what the traders took to be the bleached skeletons of at least seven elephants

---

* A series of canals, dams, and modern river maintenance has virtually eliminated the chute today.

along a freshet appropriately named Big Bone Creek.* Then they invited Findlay's party to accompany them through a lush tract so thick with game, the Indians promised, that they would soon have mounds of peltry to exchange for the white men's manufactured goods.

After paddling some seventy miles up the Cantucky, the Indians and Findlay's party reached the site of a small village enclosed by a log palisade. Eskippakithiki, they called it, which roughly translates "Place of Blue Licks" or "Blue Licks Town," after the cerulean hue of the nearby salt deposits on Lulbegrud Creek. The Shawnee told Findlay that a band of their "grandfathers" had arrived there years earlier after being driven from Ohio by the Iroquois. Findlay and his troop were surprised to find a few other white traders awaiting the hunting party's arrival. The competition did not matter.

As the Indians had promised, within days the camp was so awash in furs and hides of such fine quality that the traders were forced to fell several of the towering tulip trees that lined the river in order to hollow out planked, flat-bottomed bateaux to transport their haul. It proved an empty effort. As they were about to depart in midwinter, a force of French soldiers and their Ottawa and Ojibwa allies fell on the "Englishmen." The raiders killed three of the white men and captured another six. They also made off with hundreds of pounds of peltry. Only Findlay and another man managed to slip away.

What Findlay likely did not tell Boone and Morgan, as he quite probably did not know himself, was that the Shawnee had abandoned Eskippakithiki two years after his narrow escape. Since then the Native Americans to the north and south of Kentucky—primarily the Shawnee and Cherokee but also the Delaware, Miami, Mingoes, Creek, and Chickasaw—had abided by an unofficial pact never to settle the land. Kanta-ke was, in essence, a forty-thousand-square-mile game park where all might hunt and

---

* In 1738 a party of French Canadians descending the Ohio River—perhaps the first white men to set foot in Kentucky—discovered what they also concluded were elephant bones near a marshy salt lick some five miles inland from the riverbank. The remains of the long-extinct mastodons and mammoths drawn to the site at some point during the Pleistocene epoch gave, and still gives, the area its name—Big Bone Lick.

KANTA-KE { 57 }

trap but none might erect a permanent town or village at the risk of brutal war. This included white men.

Boone was not completely unaware of the expanse beyond the far horizon that Findlay described. In a widely publicized speech to the Colonial Congress one year earlier, Benjamin Franklin was one of the first to recognize that the conquest of the Ohio Valley was the key to America's future.* Extolling "the great country back of the Appalachian Mountains," Franklin suggested that two new colonies be settled immediately in the territory— one based on Lake Erie and the other on the Scioto. That the Scioto River basin was home to scores of Shawnee villages that revolved around their main municipality of Chillicothe Town was apparently beside the point to Franklin, much as it had been to the Iroquois and, for that matter, to Boone.

Moreover, it was not lost on the Americans marching toward Fort Duquesne under Gen. Braddock's Union Jack that the war with France was a mere precursor to a larger conflict as to whether the red race or the white race would control the verdant lands to the north and south of the Ohio River. For now, however, it was Findlay's poetic homages to the seemingly magical kingdom of Kanta-ke that set spark to Boone's imagination.

Most intriguing was Findlay's description, gleaned from the Shawnee, of a V-shaped notch in the hundred-mile long Cumberland Mountain that afforded easy access through the highlands. This cleft in the Appalachians, part of an ancient buffalo trace, sat astride a major Native American road taken by the southern and northern tribes when they raided each other's holdings. Athiamiowee, the Northern Indians called the trail in the Algonquian tongue, the "Path of the Armed Ones" or, more succinctly, the "Warrior's Path." And though Findlay had never seen it, he was told that this corridor into Kentucky—well known to the tribes but still hidden to most whites—lay somewhat to the west of Boone's Yadkin Valley home. It was the first Boone had heard of the Cumberland Gap.

---

* It was Franklin's Philadelphia printing house that would publish the first rough maps of the Ohio Country, including Kentucky, in the same year as Braddock's expedition.

7

BRADDOCK'S FOLLY

As much as the idea of a secret breach in the mighty Appalachians intrigued Daniel Boone, he had business at hand. Braddock's progress into the interior was proving tedious; the 110-mile journey to Fort Duquesne that Boone, Daniel Morgan, or any other competent backwoodsman would have completed in less than a week became a monthslong slog.

The British column, four miles long, moved west at the rate of three or four miles per day, pausing often while its military engineers leveled hills and bridged fast-moving creeks to accommodate the cannons, howitzers, and mortars being dragged behind the wagons. If this was Braddock's great turnpike into America's interior, he was unaware that he was constructing his own via dolorosa. Moreover, the march itself was not without incident, as constant Indian sniping from the deep woods took a psychological toll on soldiers unaccustomed to close forest fighting. As he neared his target, Braddock committed what many military tacticians consider his fatal mistake—dividing his army into a flying column of eight hundred soldiers and eight artillery pieces while leaving the rest to catch up. Finally, on July 8, 1755, the vanguard of the British force was less than ten miles southeast of Fort Duquesne.

That evening a small delegation of Indians suddenly appeared in the English camp requesting an audience. A bemused Braddock refused to treat with the "savages," and instead sent Washington and an American scout named John Fraser to discern their intent. The Indians told the two white men that if the British general would only hold off his attack for a few days, they were certain they could convince the French to negotiate a withdrawal. When Washington and Fraser eagerly brought the offer to Braddock, the general scoffed at the proposal. Braddock was a protégé of William Augustus, Duke of Cumberland—the notorious "Butcher of Culloden" who nine years earlier had led an army that mercilessly destroyed the Jacobite host of the young pretender to the throne, Prince Charles Edward Stewart. Given his overwhelming firepower advantage, Braddock was certain he could duplicate his mentor's victory. His reasoning was not without some logic.

Braddock's intelligence officers had informed him that the log fort the French had thrown up was defended by a mere 250 fusiliers and Canadian militiamen with but a single cannon. Those troops were fortified by some 700 Ottawa, Shawnee, Delaware, Chippewa, Potawatomi, Seneca, and Wyandot warriors. The latter tribe was a rump faction of the once-powerful Huron Confederacy that had drifted south from the north shore of Lake Erie after having been shattered by the Iroquois a century earlier. All were aware of Braddock's stiff-necked attitudes toward Indians. Whether anyone in the offensive thrust knew that the Ottawa contingent was led by a feared chieftain named Pontiac is not recorded. It would not have mattered.

On the morning of July 9, Braddock's troops forded the Monongahela River. Following the rigid military formations more suited to the open battlefields of Europe—and pointedly ignoring the American militia officers who pleaded with him to fan scouts out to either flank—Braddock arrayed his soldiers "with colors flying, drums beating, and fifes playing the Grenadier's March." Soon they were approaching a twisting forest path that descended into the thick and dank timberland leading to the fort. Boone and his fellow American irregulars, a half mile to the rear, were certain that they were walking into a trap.

Fort Duquesne's commander was aware that his barely completed stockade could not withstand an artillery bombardment. To that end he had left a small rearguard at the fort while he and his combined troops slipped away under cover of darkness and positioned themselves among the bushes, fallen logs, wild tall grass, and massive oak trees, some of them fifteen feet in circumference, on either side of the British pathway. The resultant ambush turned the trail into an escape-proof enclosure, the holding pen of an abattoir. Braddock's forward companies were cut down within moments, and as the main body of his army huddled in utter bewilderment, they, too, were picked apart by the musket balls and arrows of an unseen enemy.

Despite this suicidal error in judgment, it should be noted that all first-person accounts of the massacre—including a thorough after-action report penned by George Washington—described the gallantry with which the British officers, most notably Braddock himself, attempted to re-form their troops into both offensive and defensive postures during the four-hour fight. Most of these officers, in the words of one eyewitness, "were sacrificed by the soldiers who declined to follow them, and even fired upon them from the rear." Inevitably, the leaderless and panicked Redcoats "broke and ran like sheep before the hounds." Braddock was one of the last to fall when a ball of unknown provenance passed through his right arm and lodged in his lung. He fell from his horse like a man in slow perish and was carried from the field by, among others, the young Washington. He would die from the wound four days later.

In the meanwhile, as war cries echoed through the trees and Indians darted from the woods to lift the scalps of fallen enemies, the ripping-silk sounds of musket balls cleaving the air began to encompass Boone, Morgan, and the rest of the teamsters. Boone fired off several rounds at the approaching mass of French and Indians before cutting his team's lead horse loose from its harness, jumping on its back, and plunging into the surrounding forest. Morgan was not as fortunate. As he leapt from his lazy board and attempted to slice his horses' reins, a ball punctured the back of his neck and exited his left cheek, taking with it his upper and lower molars. The wound did not immobilize Morgan, however, and while the Indians paused to plunder the baggage train, he and Boone managed to

It is difficult to list the miscalculations made by the hubristic British general Edward Braddock in his army's march from Maryland's Fort Cumberland into western Pennsylvania to drive the French and their Native American allies from their foothold in North America's interior at Fort Duquesne, the site of present-day Pittsburgh. That list would have to begin with Braddock's loudly proclaimed denigration of the Indians' fighting abilities. As it happened, with more than an assist from a confederation of indigenous warriors, the outnumbered and outgunned French succeeded in decimating Braddock's force of 1,400 British regulars and some 400 American militiamen—among them a young George Washington and an even younger Daniel Boone—at the Battle of Monongahela in July 1755.

join the jangled survivors falling back across the Monongahela. Among them was the garrulous Irishman John Findlay.

The final tally of what came to be known as "Braddock's Folly" told a macabre tale. During three hours of fighting, 26 British and colonial militia officers were killed, and another 37 were wounded, while 714 British privates and noncommissioned officers were slain. These included 12 British captives, whom the Indians marched back to Fort Duquesne, staked to poles on the banks of the Allegheny, and burned alive one by one. The fort's French commander later testified that he was helpless to stop the gruesome executions.

In the wake of the encounter, the highest-ranking British officer left standing was Washington, who managed to rally a small company of Virginia militiamen to cover the retreat. Two horses were shot from beneath Washington during the withdrawal, and another four balls pierced his greatcoat and hat. Several days later, when Washington judged what was left of the army to be out of harm's way, he paused to bury Gen. Braddock on the road and had the surviving troops march over the grave to conceal it from the Indians—although not before retrieving the general's sash to display at Mount Vernon as a memento of that fateful day.

It is likely that Boone crossed paths with Washington during the trek back east, and Boone's youngest son would later mention that his father had met the future president on that mission. There is, however, no record of the Virginia planter interacting with the North Carolina market hunter.

When word of the catastrophe reached London, Washington's grace under fire prompted Lord Halifax, the president of England's Board of Trade, to inquire, "Who is Mr. Washington? I know nothing of him but that they say he behaved in Braddock's action as bravely as if he really loved the whistling of bullets."

In response, a staggered Washington confided to friends that he felt as if "Providence was saving him for something larger."

The destruction of Braddock's army prompted Great Britain to officially declare war on France. With operational theaters encompassing

Europe, North America, the Caribbean, West Africa, and India, Winston Churchill would years later be prompted to describe the conflict as the first true world war. It also left French and Indian hegemony along the American frontier unchecked. The Shawnee in particular took advantage of the British military absence by spreading terror among the isolated homesteads and small farming communities in backcountry Pennsylvania, Maryland, and Virginia. Directing these war parties was a chief named Hokoleskwa, a man in his mid-thirties whose name the whites translated as "The Cornstalk" or merely "Cornstalk."

Although most Shawnee had sided with the French against Braddock, there was an expedient nature to the commitment. They certainly felt a kinship with the Algonquian-speaking Great Lakes tribes who had formed alliances with France stretching back decades. But Shawnee tribal leaders, concerned with preserving their own future independence from both European powers, bore no illusions. They understood perfectly that a pact with either France or Britain brought with it the countless bacilli of an alleged civilized refinement. To that end Cornstalk's raids had one goal—to ensure that no matter who emerged victorious in the white man's war, their lands remained in Shawnee hands.

The dozen or so clans that made up the Shawnee were divided into five distinct patrilineal divisions, with each band assuming hereditary responsibilities that fulfilled the obligations of tribal culture as a whole. The Mekoche faction, for instance, provided both diplomats and medicine men, while the Pekowi were charged with keeping ancient religious rituals alive. Men from the Chillicothe and Thawekila bands generally shared the burdens of political leadership in times of peace—thus the keepers of "The Fire That Won't Go Out"—while war chiefs were usually, but not always, chosen from the more martial Kispoko.

Like almost all Eastern Woodlands tribes, the Shawnees historically alternated between quasi-hereditary village chiefs in times of peace and war chiefs to lead them into conflicts. The former, sometimes called sachems, were relied upon to navigate the internal and external needs of the community in relation to allies as well as to negotiate with those outsiders, be they tributaries or supposed equals. The latter, usually younger men, were temporarily appointed by the sachems. In the past, when a conflict concluded, war chiefs relinquished their authority and, like Cincinnatus, returned to their old roles. On this occasion, however, the tribe had found an anomaly in Cornstalk.

Cornstalk, from the Mekoche division, was a dignitary equally adept at diplomacy and military strategy and tactics. He was, in fact, a natural selection. For by the time of Braddock's invasion, the drums of war were beating so incessantly throughout the Ohio Country that the Shawnee as well as neighboring tribes looked to Cornstalk to guide them through the maze of negotiation versus battle.

It is not known if Daniel Boone was present when his cousin Daniel Morgan survived the punishment of 499 lashes for striking a superior officer in the wake of Braddock's defeat. Boone would certainly have been sympathetic. To his dying day he cursed the incompetence of the British general and his officers, yet also admitted to learning much from his first true experience fighting Indians. Equally enlightening was the glimpse he had gotten of at least a small portion of the lonely and beautiful Upper Ohio Valley beyond the mountain ranges.

Before returning to the Yadkin, he packed his kit and, as he had lost his horse, began walking toward his old Pennsylvania homestead in Exeter. His stated purpose was to renew ties with kinfolk who still lived in the area. It is not beyond the realm of possibility, however, that having undergone the trauma of military rout, a trip to his boyhood home would allow him to reflect on happier memories from his arcadian youth, when freedom of the forest did not include storms of musket balls and scything tomahawks.

Though he was heading east, his mind was on the West. For he was now more than ever determined to find the mysterious Cumberland Gap that led to the Irishman Findlay's fabled land of Kanta-ke.

8

REBECCA BRYAN

By the summer of 1755 Daniel Boone had returned to the Yadkin Valley. Twelve months later he was a married man. He had met Rebecca Bryan, a third-generation North Carolinian, three years earlier at the wedding of his sister Mary. Rebecca's grandfather, Morgan Bryan, had arrived in America from Northern Ireland at the end of the previous century and begun his new life as a rough-and-tumble market hunter. By the time Boone proposed to Morgan's granddaughter, the Bryan clan had accrued some five thousand acres on the Yadkin and expanded into milling and blacksmithing. They also owned a substantial cattle herd.

Rebecca was the eldest daughter of Morgan Bryan's oldest son, Joseph, and despite his family's appreciating wealth and prestige, Grandfather Bryan's evident discomfort with the trappings of "civilization" had been passed down to his seven sons and one daughter. The Bryans preferred homesteading on the fringes of society, a lifestyle choice that naturally fell in line with Boone's own prerogatives.

Described by a contemporary as a "flaxen-haired beauty," Rebecca was sketched in her youth in a black-and-white line drawing depicting a handsome woman of dusky complexion with pert lips and a cascade of beribboned ringlets falling about her face. Her most arresting features were her large, dark eyes, which seemed to be staring off toward some space in the middle distance. This alone would have entranced a restless suitor like Boone, although, contrary to sylvan legend, he did not first "shine" eyes on Rebecca during a fire hunt on the night before his sister's wedding ceremony.

Rifles at the ready, fire hunters ventured into the forest on moonless nights following a mounted scout who held aloft a blazing pitch-pine torch. When the firebrand reflected in the eyes of white-tailed deer, their eyes would "shine" the flame, making them easy targets. Though Boone was known to fire-hunt mostly in cases of food shortages, no one in either the Boone nor the Bryan family ever vouchsafed the yarn of Boone nearly mistakenly shooting his future wife during a fire hunt.*

One anecdote pertaining to Boone's courtship, however, does shine a light on the calculations of his own character. It occurred when Boone invited Rebecca to join a group of young men and women on a cherry-picking outing, a fairly standard courtship ritual for the time and place. For the rest of his life Boone delighted in relating the story of how, as they sat upon a log eating the cherries, he began playing with his knife. In the course of his mumblety-peg-like game, he twice pretended to absentmindedly nick and cut the edges of Rebecca's cambric apron. The bleached, lightweight-cotton cloth was a luxury along the frontier, and, as Boone recalled, he was testing the girl's temper. Instead of offering remonstrations, however, Rebecca simply removed the apron out of harm's way. This was the moment, Boone attested, when he decided to marry the woman whom for the rest of his life he would refer to as "my little girl."

By now, nearing his twenty-first birthday, Boone's stout chest and strong, narrow shoulders had grown into his elongated neck, and his plaited dark hair, when not amply bear-greased, still fell in waves across a

---

* This did not deter early Boone biographers from including the "shining" moment as fact in their profiles.

broad forehead down to his sun-bleached eyebrows. In the few portraits from the era, usually drawn from memory, his lips appear stretched tight across a curiously wide mouth, forming a line of demarcation between his strong jawline and a straight, thin nose. Like so many of his peers on the frontier, Boone's wide, horseman's hips flared out to a brace of muscled thighs, and his leathery hands were strong enough to break a wolf's jawbone. Though he had retained his mother's coloring as he matured, his father's genes dictated that a five-foot-eight-inch frame was all that would carry his 175 pounds, a perceived deficiency that led Boone to stiffen his spine and walk tall for the rest of his life. Though he was often likened to a pony who could outwork and outrun the largest horse, it was also speculated that his self-consciousness regarding his physical stature was the reason—contrary to centuries of misinformation—that he eschewed a flat coonskin cap in favor of a high-crowned and wide-brimmed felt hat, which made him look taller.

Rebecca Bryan was seventeen when she took Boone's hand in marriage on August 14, 1756, in a ceremony that galvanized the territory. By this time the tracts along the Yadkin had been formally incorporated into North Carolina as Rowan County, and Boone's father, Squire, was now an established power in the district, having been appointed to the municipal court that oversaw both judicial and administrative tasks. It was Squire Boone who officiated over the wedding.

Given that the daughter of the area's largest landowner was marrying the celebrated son of a respected local civic leader, the observance and its reception was as much a political as a social affair. Rebecca's father, Joseph Bryan, though at first put off by what he considered Boone's coarse manners—once during their courtship Boone had gifted the Bryan family with a deer, dressed it on a stump outside their home, and arrived at the dinner table without having washed the blood and guts off himself—soon came around to his new son-in-law. And in another sign that old Squire Boone's Quaker roots had withered, he had only recently opened a public house astride what was known as Squire Boone's Old Mill Road. On the day of his son's nuptials, the cider, rum, and corn whiskey for which he normally charged six shillings a gallon flowed for free.

While the newlyweds Daniel and Rebecca moved into a small cabin on Squire's property, the Boones joined the Bryans in constructing an extensive single-story log farmhouse for them. The structure, located on Morgan Bryan's property several miles north of the Boone compound, was an extravagance for the borderlands, with glass windows, a separate summer kitchen, and a manual-pump well. The extra space was needed, for Daniel was not the only Boone to whom the teenage bride was now charged with tending. Several months earlier Boone's older brother Israel, Israel's wife, and their two young daughters had died of what was at the time called "consumption," what we now know as tuberculosis. In the interim, Israel's two surviving boys, Jesse and Jonathan, had grown increasingly close to their Uncle Daniel, and Rebecca had agreed to take them in. This was far from an unusual arrangement on the frontier, where sprawling broods were often left orphaned by any number of natural or man-made caprices.

In the meanwhile, Rebecca, like the majority of pioneer wives, was responsible for chopping wood, fetching water, cooking, cleaning, weaving, and washing. To take in extra money on market days, she also planted several varieties of crops, including corn, soybeans, cabbage, cucumbers, and potatoes, on a small "truck patch" of their property. For his part, Boone remained a hunter at heart and by trade. As he would for the rest of his life with a few dramatic interruptions, he spent most of the autumn and winter of his first year as a husband stalking the surrounding woods and acquiring meat to salt for the winter months and furs and pelts for trade. The following May, nearly nine months to the date of their marriage, Daniel and Rebecca's first son, James, was born.

Although the French and Indian War continued to rage, Boone declined to take part in any more military campaigns. He did occasionally contract out to the British as a freight hauler or offer his blacksmithing services to a passing company of mounted colonial militiamen known as Rangers. But news from the north was too worrisome for him to venture far from the Yadkin. By this point in the conflict the French and their Indian allies were largely confining their frontier raids to the western peripheries of New England, New York, and Pennsylvania. But rumors nonetheless circulated throughout the southern borderlands of enemy emissaries, both white and red, infiltrating the Cherokee towns and villages of the South in attempts to nobble the tribe's allegiance. All understood that any Cherokee pact with the French would inflame the frontier.

When Hernando de Soto first encountered factions of the vast Cherokee Nation in the mid-1500s, their power and numbers, estimated at close to thirty thousand, had dwarfed those of the Native American tribes and coalitions to the north, including the Iroquois Confederacy. In the three centuries since, however, disease and displacement had reduced the Cherokee—the Aniyunwiya, meaning "Real People" or "Principle People"—to some ten thousand souls divided into three blocs, the Upper, Middle, and Lower factions. Cherokee villages were predominantly grouped on the flanks and hollows of the north-south-running Great Smoky Mountains, a southern spur of the Blue Ridge, straddling what is today's Tennessee–North Carolina border, although outlying affiliated communities trailed down into South Carolina and northern Georgia.

The tribe had originally been composed of seven matrilineal clans, and much like the Delaware, the Cherokee had initially accepted the European newcomers to the point of sending a delegation to London in 1730 to sign the Treaty of Whitehall, which recognized King George II as their protector. Though fierce enemies of the Shawnee and the Creek, who had befriended the wayward former tribe a century earlier, to this point the Cherokee had continued to maintain cordial if wary relations with the whites. Their leaders, in the spirit of their forefathers, had even signed a peace treaty with a delegation of North Carolina authorities at the outset of the French and Indian War.

But by 1757, blood was in the air, and as a precaution the far-flung

white communities along the southern frontier began erecting fortifica-
tions to which the settlers could retreat in case of Indian attack. Not long
after Boone's wedding, Fort Dobbs sprung up in the center of the Yadkin
Valley for just such a purpose. Named in honor of North Carolina's royal
governor, the twenty-two-hundred-square-foot structure was fairly typical
of a mid-eighteenth-century frontier stockade, with its corner bastions and
its log-and-plank walls dotted with some one hundred musket loopholes.

Although few British regulars could be spared to garrison these backwoods redoubts, provincial fighters were in long supply, particularly with
more and more families migrating into the Carolinas to escape the butch-
ery in the northern colonies. The refugees brought with them a recognition that violent mortality was the rule of existence, telling tales of settlers
burned alive in their cabins, of captives staked to the ground or tied to
trees for use as target practice (though only with arrows, as powder and
shot were too dear), and, of course, of the ubiquitous scalping of men,
women, and children. A few of the newcomers to the Yadkin had even
survived this latter ordeal, with the gruesome scars to show for it.

Contrary to myth, rarely was an entire head of hair severed from a
scalping victim's skull. For the most part, scalpers—who have existed
since time immemorial—would grab and pull on a hank of hair from the
crown of the head and cut to the bone with an incision about the circumference of a silver dollar. Some who survived a scalping underwent a primitive surgery called "pegging the head," wherein scores of tiny holes would
be bored into the now-exposed skull with a sharpened awl to allow the
pinkish cranial fluid to ooze out. If the fluid formed a scab, the area would
be swabbed with a poultice of medicinal herbs, and the wound would be
wrapped against infection. As might be imagined, the healing process was
slow, painful, and a vivid reminder to the Yadkin inhabitants that quarter
was rarely given in Indian fighting.

Yet, as is often the case during wartime, the defensive posturing of
the Carolina settlers triggered the immutable laws of unintended consequences. Though the Catawba remained loyal allies, so many skittish

white men with guns pouring into forts on the fringes of Cherokee territory only managed to arouse the tribe's suspicions. Moreover, following Braddock's failed expedition, the Redcoats suffered a string of defeats in rapid succession that shook the Cherokee faith in British hegemony.

The harbinger of what many foresaw as Britain's demise in the New World was the surrender in 1757 of Fort William Henry on New York's Lake George to an overwhelming French force of some seventy-five hundred fusiliers and sixteen hundred Huron, Ottawa, and Abenaki warriors under the command of the Marquis Louis-Joseph de Montcalm.

With Montcalm's artillery raining down on the half-starved and undermanned Redcoat garrison, and French sappers extending trenches ever nearer to the fort's walls, it took less than a week before the post's British commander understandably capitulated. After terms were struck, however, Montcalm's Indian allies, "incited by French propaganda and rum," in the words of the historian Ted Franklin Belue, attacked and slaughtered the surrendering survivors after they'd limped through the gates. Hundreds of soldiers and civilians were killed, and hundreds more were taken hostage.

A famous French painting of Montcalm, sword raised as he attempted to hold back the Indians, did little to mollify Anglo-American outrage. Such was the sustained reaction to the atrocity up and down the frontier that sixty-nine years later its memory was still fresh enough to be memorialized in James Fenimore Cooper's *The Last of the Mohicans*.

Such French triumphs, their barbarity notwithstanding, were not lost on the Cherokee Nation. Despite the goodwill they had shared and the treaties of amity they had signed with the British, the southern Indians sensed a shift in the winds. And then, as remorseful as the tides, the war's fortunes turned.

One year before the fall of Fort William Henry, the theatrical and ostentatiously colloquial William Pitt was named Great Britain's secretary of state. From his previous position as the British Army's paymaster general, the forty-eight-year-old Pitt had studied well his country's catastrophic Pennsylvania and New York campaigns. What he saw was a military system that was intact, as opposed to one that was working. Upon assuming his new position, Pitt rapidly went to work reinventing his country's North American strategy. In particular, he calculated that Great Britain was wasting its greatest martial asset—the Royal Navy—by continuing a course of land warfare across the frontier. Pitt proved prescient. Under his muscular guidance, the British had within two years regained the upper hand in the Western Hemisphere.

The first domino to fall, in 1758, was the French fortress of Louisbourg, the so-called "Gibraltar of the New World." Constructed three decades earlier on Nova Scotia's Cape Breton Island, Louisbourg's thirty-five-foot stone walls and 250 cannons stood athwart the mouth of the Saint Lawrence River, in theory protecting all of New France from a northern invasion. During the last week of May, a British fleet of 40 warships and 150 troop transports carrying fourteen thousand Redcoats dropped anchor in Gabarus Bay some three miles south of the citadel. Soon thereafter the besiegers, who outnumbered French defenders two to one, commenced a six-week naval bombardment that saw large sections of the fortress crumble. When Louisbourg finally fell on July 26, the British were left in control of the Saint Lawrence.

With its northern flank unprotected, Lake Ontario's Fort Frontenac—key to the French supply lines to its interior outposts—surrendered to an English force a month later, effectively bisecting France's holdings in North America. Farther south, the commander of Fort Duquesne, Colonel François-Marie Le Marchand de Lignery, recognized that he and his garrison had been left to wither without adequate supplies or the hope of reinforcements. Further, news that an overwhelming British expedition led by General John Forbes was bearing down on Fort Duquesne from the east led to the desertion of his Shawnee, Delaware, and Mingo allies. The

French officer faced little choice. In November he ordered his powder magazine blown and his troops withdrawn without a fight.

In the span of six months the French had suffered three calamitous defeats. Adding insult to injury, when Forbes's army reached what was left of the outpost on the confluence of the Monongahela and Allegheny Rivers, he renamed it Fort Pitt and immediately began rebuilding. A year later, the Royal Navy destroyed France's Atlantic fleet off the French coast in what would be looked back upon as the decisive battle of Churchill's "first true world war."

9

THE CHEROKEE WARS

The conflict between Britain and France was to drag on across the globe for another four years, but from a strategic point of view it was essentially all but concluded in the Western Hemisphere. England had won. Counterintuitively, however, the bloodshed along America's frontier only increased as France's fading fortunes in the New World brought the first sustained fighting to the southern colonies. Before the British column led by Gen. Forbes had even reached the abandoned Fort Duquesne, for instance, a host of deserting Shawnee ransacked its supply stores and made off with copious caches of rum. They then headed south, where they generously shared their plunder as well as their war belts with their former enemies, the Cherokee.

Though some Cherokee factions expelled the Shawnee from their villages, and the staunch Catawba remained on peaceful terms with the white settlers along the borderlands of both Carolinas and Virginia, skirmishes between roving bands of hostiles and settlers increased exponentially through the end of 1758. These collective, multifront engagements came to be known as the Cherokee wars. It was a murderous conflict, with white outposts besieged, Indian towns razed, no quarter given, and no age or gender barriers respected. Women and children from both sides were butchered as eagerly as fighting men were, and the contemporaneous accounts from the warpath veritably drip crimson off the page.

The fates of 150 settlers in the process of abandoning their homesteads along the western fringes of South Carolina is indicative of the carnage. On their march east they were attacked in an open glade by a hundred mounted Cherokees. Within thirty minutes some fifty white bodies of all ages and genders lay splayed across the ground while the survivors fled into the surrounding forest. A militia company riding to the rescue stumbled upon another two dozen mutilated corpses in a separate clearing in the woods and eventually rounded up some twenty half-naked and starving children, several of whom had been scalped and left for dead.

On another occasion a British officer captured by the Cherokee was forced by a group of braves to dance while their elders decided whether to kill him or trade him for imprisoned Indians. Overstepping their authority, the warriors lopped off both of the man's hands while whipping him to keep dancing. When their overseers discovered the damaged goods, the obvious decision was made: the officer's legs were severed, he was scalped, and he took his last breaths as his torso was tossed onto a bonfire.

Perfidy was not limited to the mounting Indian attacks. A company of North Carolina Rangers who happened upon a small party of Cherokees skinning an elk fired on them despite their offer to share the meat. The militiamen then chased the Indians into an abandoned cabin, made fast the door and chimney, and set the structure ablaze. They waited with guns cocked for their roasting victims to break down the door. None did. And volunteer frontiersmen manning backwoods trading posts gleefully hung from the ramparts the trophy scalps they had taken from Cherokee men, women, and children. "We fatten our dogs with their carcasses," wrote one of the white combatants, "and display their scalps, neatly ornamented, on the tops of our bastions."

By April of 1760, with these sickening reports of violence from the southern theater of war finally trickling into London, British authorities dispatched a contingent of some six hundred Scottish Highlanders into the area. Abetted by about three hundred mounted militia Rangers from both Carolinas as well as a smattering of Catawba scouts, the force penetrated deep into the backcountry, indiscriminately burning any and all Cherokee towns and farm fields regardless of whether the Indians had taken up arms.

Either inadvertently or with purpose—some historians maintain the latter—they also touched off a smallpox epidemic that spread far beyond their march. As humans infected by the virus can communicate the disease for upward of a month through their clothing, their bedding, and other personal items, it proved a tenacious and patient killer as it spread along Native American trade routes. It is estimated that 80 percent of the six thousand or so Cherokees infected by the Highlanders succumbed to the pox. An unintended byproduct of the spreading disease was the effect it had on the Catawba fighting alongside the Scotsmen. When the Indian scouts returned to their villages they set off an epidemic that felled over half the tribe's men, women, and children. Lacking immunity, the once-fierce Siouan people were so devastated by the pox that by late 1760 the Catawba population had dwindled to just 4 percent of what it had been a century earlier, able to field a mere sixty healthy warriors.

Around the same time, in a particularly deceitful incident, South Carolina's royal governor, William Henry Lyttelton, sent runners to the Cherokee camps inviting the tribe's headmen to parley under a flag of truce. When an Indian delegation arrived at the designated wood-and-clay outpost where the peace talks were to be held, Lyttelton had them seized and thrown into a dilapidated hut on the premises. He then sent word to their tribesmen that his hostages would be hanged unless the two dozen perpetrators of a recent raid on a frontier settlement were handed over. When instead a large war party unsuccessfully assailed the fort, Lyttelton ordered the hostages killed.

The Indians were swift to retaliate. Not long afterward a contingent of Upper Cherokee from the west side of the Great Smoky range led by the war chief called Standing Turkey encircled the isolated trading post of Fort Loudoun in what is now southeastern Tennessee. For months the besiegers stood watch over the stockade, capturing or killing every messenger dispatched to summon help. On August 6, with his garrison having eaten the last of their dogs and horses, Fort Loudoun's commander agreed to surrender the fort as well as all its armaments in return for safe passage to the east. Standing Turkey accepted the terms, unaware that the whites had already broken the accord by destroying their rifles, spiking their cannons, and throwing the lot into a tributary of the Little Tennessee River that coursed beneath the ramparts.

Three days later a bedraggled procession of some 150 troops and a few wives, children, and camp followers abandoned Fort Loudoun. They marched for ten miles before stopping for the night to camp on a small pasture surrounded by woodland. Back at the fort, the incensed Cherokee discovered the destroyed guns and called a war council. The unarmed whites awoke the next morning to the battle cries of some seven hundred Indians emanating from the forest, immediately followed by a rain of falling arrows that darkened the dawn sky. Between 25 and 40 whites died that day, with another 120 or so survivors taken captive. As the prisoners were marched away they were beaten with sticks and slapped in the face with the scalps of their fallen comrades. Most were eventually tortured and killed.

Though the majority of the fighting during the Cherokee wars took place along the South Carolina and northern Georgia frontiers—with some, such as the siege of Fort Loudoun, seeping into what is today eastern Tennessee—North Carolina was not immune to the carnage. The Yadkin Valley and Fort Dobbs were the scenes of vicious encounters between white and red men, with one weekly municipal posting from Rowan County listing a dozen of the valley's homesteaders killed in ambushes and several families burned out of their cabins. With his community aflame and many of the Boone clan having fled to the safety of Fort Dobbs, in the spring of 1759 old Squire Boone led a faction of his family east rather than endure the cramped, increasingly disease-ridden quarters of the stockade. His journey took him over a rough, two-hundred-mile trail to the tobacco country of Culpeper County in northeastern Virginia, and thence to the Georgetown section of Maryland near the Potomac, where a cousin lived.*

Among the evacuees accompanying Squire and Sarah Boone and their three youngest children were Daniel, Rebecca, and their expanding brood—their second son, named Israel in honor of Daniel's late brother, had been born in January 1759. While Squire and the rest moved on to Maryland, Daniel and his family remained in Virginia. There, despite the settled farm community's scarcity of game, they rented a small cabin in which to await the birth of their third child. There is no little irony to the fact that Boone, who carried a hatred of the smell of tobacco smoke with him for his entire life, could find no work in Culpeper County other than hiring out his two-horse rig to haul "flats" of the harvested crop to the nearest market town of Fredericksburg.

Susannah Boone, the couple's first daughter, was born on November 2, 1760. As soon as mother and child were well enough to travel, the family set back off for North Carolina. Rowan County municipal records indicate that sometime before Daniel Boone's return, his father sold him a 640-acre tract of Yadkin land for £50, about $10,000 today. Boone did not immediately occupy the homestead upon reaching the valley, and instead joined his remaining family within the walls of Fort Dobbs. Later in life Boone was often happy to discourse on his familiarity with the nooks, crannies, and musket loopholes of the first stockade in which he had ever "forted up."

In the wake of the Cherokee movement into the area, Fort Dobbs had become the headquarters to some four hundred North Carolina irregulars charged with patrolling the Indian frontier. Boone immediately joined their ranks. In the fall of 1760, likely on one of these scouting patrols, he

---

* Georgetown, incorporated by the Maryland assembly in 1851, later, of course, became part of the District of Columbia.

ventured west over the Great Smoky Mountains and dropped down into eastern Tennessee.

Whatever his military purpose or objective for the trip, he tarried long enough to note what fine hunting grounds the area would make. It would not be long before he returned. For as 1761 dawned, the royal governors of Virginia, North Carolina, and South Carolina decided at conference that their piecemeal expeditions against the rampaging Cherokee were the wrong military approach. Instead, they petitioned the commander in chief of all British forces in the Americas, General Jeffery Amherst, to undertake a concerted offensive into the western fringes of the three colonies. Amherst subsequently supplied enough regular troops to carry out the southern half of a pincer thrust from South Carolina. Farther north, Boone was a member of the all-militia force that comprised the claw that was to set out from North Carolina. His participation proved anticlimactic.

For while the southern portion of the campaign under the British lieutenant colonel James Grant included about twenty-six hundred men, perhaps half of them regulars, seven hundred packhorses, and over four hundred head of cattle, the northern army floundered. This was due in no small part to Gen. Amherst's refusal to supply its commander, Colonel William Byrd, with any regulars. Byrd had succeeded George Washington as leader of the Virginia militia, Washington having retired from military service after marrying the widow Martha Custis and being elected to a seat in the colony's House of Burgesses. Byrd's tenure was brief. A lack of ammunition as well as a dearth of horses and carts to carry supplies so angered the vainglorious colonel that he resigned his post midway through the expedition. While Byrd's second-in-command attempted to rally the few militiamen who remained, including Boone, Grant's southern force struck out beyond Fort Loudoun in June 1761.

Within a month Grant had thoroughly routed the combined resistance of the Lower and Middle Cherokee factions, killing hundreds who stood against him while burning their towns and villages and destroying their crops. By the time the much smaller party of some five hundred to eight hundred irregulars under Byrd's successor were prepared to take the field against the Upper Cherokee, Grant had so completely humbled his adversaries that the entire Cherokee Nation sent representatives to sue for peace. That November a formal treaty was signed between the royal governors of Virginia, North Carolina, South Carolina, and Georgia on the one side, and the Cherokee, Creek, Chickasaw, and Choctaw on the other.

Despite the peace pact, however, the violent nature of the western hinterlands ground on, weary and wild.

10

"BOONE'S SURPRISE"

With the southern tribes momentarily cowed, the withdrawal of British troops from the frontier left a law-enforcement void that was rapidly filled by roving gangs of outlaws. Their depredations had actually begun during the Cherokee wars, when the abandoned cabins and plantations of settlers seeking the safety of stockades proved easy marks for looters, who helped themselves to everything from livestock to farm equipment to kitchen utensils before vanishing into the backcountry. Even in the few communities where there were peace officers to spare, those who were not bribed proved feckless at locating the bandit camps hidden deep in the swamps or high in the mountains.

This early iteration of American organized crime was especially acute in South Carolina's rough borderlands of impenetrable cane and trackless marsh. Despairing of legal redress and already prone to an informal and self-enforced style of retributive justice, coalitions of settlers calling themselves Regulators formed posses to chase down the perpetrators. The most common punishments were on-the-spot lashings followed by banishment from the territory. But serial lawbreakers, if not lynched, often had their faces branded as a warning. It did not take long for the British to view the growing strength of these Regulators as a threat not only to law and order, but to colonial authority. In response, the Crown rushed to establish a court system enforced by sheriffs that extended deep into the American interior.

Though North Carolina was by comparison spared the more pervasive lawlessness afflicting its southern neighbor, there was one particular ring of brigands led by a husband and wife named Owens who preyed on the Yadkin Valley. Rumor had it that the Owens gang had established a rude fort somewhere high in the crags of the Blue Ridge, but several attempts to locate the hideout failed. Sometime not long after the signing of the treaty with the Cherokees, word spread through the Yadkin that a young girl tending her family's small cattle drove had been kidnapped by two of the gang members. Boone, who had only just arrived home from his militia service in the southwest, was approached by a group of settlers to lead a posse to recover the girl. Few had any idea that he was confronting a family drama of his own.

Between his scouting missions and Col. Byrd's aborted backcountry campaign, Boone had been absent from the Yadkin for just over a year. What greeted him upon his return came to be passed down in family lore as "Boone's Surprise": on October 4, 1762, his wife Rebecca had given birth to a second daughter, whom she named Jemima. Given the timing, Boone could not possibly have fathered the child.

When Boone asked Rebecca about the girl's father, his wife tearfully explained that she had thought Boone dead, and in her grief had relied upon his younger brother Edward, called Neddie, for comfort and solace. Neddie was unmarried, and though a studious sort more at home carrying a Bible or a farmer's hoe than a rifle, he bore a striking physical and facial resemblance to Daniel. Frontier widows with small children, as Rebecca had fashioned herself, were left with few good choices to carry on. She told her husband that in time she had not been able to help herself from becoming romantically attached to Neddie.

As his grandchildren were to later tell the story, the imperturbable Boone listened to his wife's tale and came to a swift decision: he had married a woman, not a painting of a saint. He confessed to Rebecca his own dalliances over the years with several Indian maidens and pronounced Jemima's paternity, "So much the better, it's all in the family." It was a typical Boone moment—slow to anger, quick to understand, and anxious to see life's ironies from another's point of view. Moreover, it never affected his relationship with either his new "daughter" nor his younger brother.

It was this same outsize sense of humanity that also led Boone to see that, given his knowledge of the backcountry, he was the logical choice to lead the posse to find his kidnapped young neighbor. He and a band of Yadkin Regulators did rescue the child when she managed to escape while her abductors fought over who would be the first to rape her. But the trail to the Owens gang's mountain lair remained cold.

Some months later the circle was squared when a cache of stolen goods was discovered hidden under a pile of fodder on the property of a heretofore-respected homesteader named Cornelius Howard. Howard found the guns leveled at his head by an angry citizenry a persuasive line of reasoning, and agreed to lead a posse to the Owens gang's mountain refuge. With Boone at the head of some forty riders, the troop was bushwhacking through a thick spinney of mountain laurel when Howard paused and pointed up toward an enormous cave. It was an ingenious hideout, with its mouth guarded by makeshift pickets and an overhanging rock face protecting it from attack from above. While a segment of Boone's contingent set off to round up stolen horses and cattle spotted grazing in a nearby meadow, Boone and the rest shot their way into the loot-filled grotto, killing Owens in the process.

In a small side chamber not far inside the cavern's mouth they found Owens's wife splayed across a bed of hay. She claimed to be dying of some unnamed disease; Boone suspected she was feigning her illness. His hunch proved correct when, at the appearance of Cornelius Howard, the Owens woman rose and lifted a pistol hidden in the folds of her dress. Boone disarmed her before she could get off a shot.

Aside from the female gang leader, another half dozen outlaws were captured (and ultimately hanged) by the Yadkin Regulators. They also recovered bolts of silk, log chains, plows, and wagonloads of sundry dry goods, some of it stashed in the hollows of nearby gum trees. Before they bound and gagged her, the Owens woman loudly branded Howard a "second Judas," and called down a mortal curse on his head. She may have been a more effective witch than actress playing sick. Not long afterward, Cornelius Howard was shot from his horse and killed while crossing a stream not far from his cabin. The murderer was never caught.

Although old Squire Boone served for many years as Rowan County's justice of the peace, his son Daniel never held an official municipal post in the Yadkin. He was, however, respected up and down the valley as a soft-spoken if forceful community leader and a generous neighbor who was known to drop by the homesteads of roving long hunters to ensure their families were provided for. It was his inherent sense of justice that had led him to form the posse that corralled the Owens gang. Still, the incident and others like it only reinforced his notion that civil society, with all its contents and discontents, would inexorably cycle on with or without his participation. Further, with the threat of Indian warfare subsided, more and more homesteaders were pouring into the Lower Yadkin. The valley's population had quadrupled since the Boones had arrived twelve years earlier.

As the newcomers slashed and burned extensive farm clearings, the territory's already-disappearing game became even more scarce. In its stead arrived a human wave of clergymen and shop owners, sheriffs and judges, clerks and lawyers, and the dreaded taxmen. With his lonely hunts now taking him farther afield, Boone found plenty of time to contemplate not only the vagaries of his life, but the paths of his future. As he approached his thirties, one idea abided.

During his return home from the aborted Byrd campaign two years earlier, he and a small coterie of Yadkin men had sought and received permission to split off from the main body of militia to wayfare across and through the secluded hills and vales of southwestern Virginia and what is now eastern Tennessee. The area not only teemed with game, but its untrammeled location also led Boone to believe that it might hold the key to the gateway of Kanta-ke.

With a wife, four children, and two stepsons to provide for and his property-tax debt accumulating, over the next few years Boone was forced to roam deeper and deeper into the frontier on his market hunts. Leading packhorses laden with powder, ball, and traps as well as sundry pots, pans, and rudimentary smithing tools into the unknown, Boone marveled at the majestic views from the Appalachian highlands as he traversed western North Carolina, southwestern Virginia, and eastern Tennessee. At one point he crossed the eastern Continental Divide, the fall line where the wellspring of the Yadkin River coursed east into the Atlantic, while a rose petal dropped into the headwaters of the Watauga, but a few miles away, would course into the Holston, then the Ohio, and down the Mississippi before curdling in the salt water of the Gulf of Mexico.

Along these journeys he was particularly intrigued by the three forks of the Holston River that carved a remote valley to the west of the Blue Ridge and, beyond that, the fertile Clinch River Valley. Years later, as the first settlers edged into the Clinch River territory, they discovered an inscription carved into the bark of a beech tree overhanging a spring that fed the river. It read, "Daniel Boone . . . Come on boys . . . heres [sic] good water."

Boone was sometimes accompanied on these long hunts by his Yadkin Valley neighbor Nicholas Gist, a superb marksman whose father, Christopher, had been one of the first Englishmen to record his explorations of the Ohio Country. The elder Gist, an experienced scout and surveyor, had journeyed into the interior by way of the Ohio River in 1750 at the behest of a consortium of Virginia land speculators to whom the Crown had granted a half million acres on the condition that they settle the territory within seven years. The colonials invested in the consortium included George Washington and his half brother Lawrence.* Among Gist's orders were to "take an exact Account of the Soil, Quality, & Product of the land, and the Wideness and Deepness of the Rivers [and] observe what Nations of Indians inhabit there, their Strengths & Numbers."

Along his travels Christopher Gist deceived the various tribes who generously housed and fed him, including the Shawnee, Mingo, Wyandot, and Miami peoples. He told the Indians that the whites beyond the mountains wanted nothing more from them than friendly trade, and he was acting as an advance scout to gauge their willingness to do so. Settlements and farming, he said, were out of the question. Yet all the while he kept a compass and measuring cord hidden deep in his saddlebag to survey tracts as far west as the Falls of the Ohio. His final report concluded that the territory "in short, wants Nothing but Cultivation to make it a most delightful Country."

After nearly three months of exploring and mapping, Gist began to fear that the French and their Indian allies suspected his true aims, and he returned to his home in the Yadkin. But he saw enough of Kanta-ke south of the Ohio River to excite his financial backers. He reported watercourses teeming with shad, sturgeon, catfish, and mussels sluicing through meadows of wild rye and clover tromped by countless elk, buffalo, deer, and bear, all encompassed by "Walnut, Ash, Sugar Trees, Cherry Trees, &c."

Now, over a decade later, Boone and Christopher Gist's son Nicholas habituated themselves to hunting expeditions just east of that territory. Their routine rarely varied. Over a predawn breakfast of hickory nuts, dried fruit, or a handful of the ubiquitous parched corn carried by every woodsman, they would divide the day's range between them. They then set off separately on ten-hour treks to check traplines and haunt the salt

---

* At one time Washington personally controlled over seventy thousand acres of land for speculation in what is now West Virginia.

springs and creeks where unwary animals gathered. Sometimes upon their return to camp, Boone, ever the cautious man when it came to Indians, would sense it too dangerous to light a night fire. On those occasions the two shared quiet meals of jerked meat and johnnycakes, a sort of cornmeal flatbread. But for the most part they feasted on their catch. Like many a frontiersman, Nicholas Gist was said to consider beaver tail seared crispy over a bed of red-hot charcoal as the ambrosia of the forest. Boone found the delicacy too greasy for his taste, and much preferred elk liver sizzled in bear fat or a slow-roasted wild turkey suspended over a flame and basted in its own juices.

Light fades fast in the mountains, and when all the tales of the day's hunt were shared, the two would take a last gulp from their flasks and retire to their respective "half-face camps"—three-sided lean-tos fashioned from saplings and bark and chinked with brush. Sometimes, when wolf sign was strong, they would stoke three or four fires and bed down in the middle with their pelts. They slept on mattresses of collected leaves or, on a lucky night, a soft chaise of Queen Anne's lace. Though but a young man, Boone's joints and bones already suffered from the arthritis so common to his profession and lifestyle, and after lacing his moccasins to his long rifle in case he was forced to hastily flee barefoot from intruders, he would toss a few last lengths of timber onto the flames and position his lower back, hips, and knees as close to its warmth as possible.

Boone appreciated the company of skilled long hunters like Nicholas Gist. But as he waited for his son James to grow old enough to join him on his sallies, he much preferred journeying into the wilderness with his horses and dogs as his only companions. He was said to enjoy the sublime "habit of contemplation" that he had cultivated in the Pennsylvania forests of his youth. And though not a conspicuously religious man—he admitted to holding the red man's Great Spirit in the same esteem as the white man's Christian God—he would sometimes tote a Bible in his saddlebag next to his *Gulliver's Travels* to keep him company by the firelight.

In the meanwhile, despite the cessation of hostilities between England

and France, Boone surely understood that though the blue-coated fusiliers might be sailing home, the Indians were not about to give up their
homelands without a fight. He may have even heard the vague rumors of a
British plan to placate the Native Americans by forbidding white pioneers
and hunters from venturing west of the Appalachians. Being aware of such
a decree, however, and abiding by it were two separate matters.

PART II

---+---

THE EXPLORERS

The Americans . . . acquire no attachment to Place;
But wandering about Seems engrafted in their Nature; and . . .
they Should for ever imagine the Lands further off, are Still better
than those upon which they are already settled.

—John Murray, Lord Dunmore, colonial governor of Virginia

11

"AN EXECRABLE RACE"

Alexander McKee arrived at the sprawling trading post on the Scioto known as Lower Shawnee Town in the last week of January 1763. He did not bear glad tidings for the various Shawnee, Delaware, Mingo, Wyandot, and Miami peoples gathered there. This was likely the reason Gen. Jeffery Amherst had selected the stout and plump-cheeked McKee as his messenger. The twenty-eight-year-old, the son of a Scots-Irish immigrant father and a captive white woman raised in the Shawnee culture, had spent his life on the frontier straddling both worlds.

Given McKee's fair standing with the Ohio tribes, Gen. Amherst may have concluded that there was less chance of McKee's scalp being lifted when he informed the assembled Indians that, as part of the terms dictated by England to the surrendering French, King Louis XV had ceded to the British all North American lands east of the Mississippi, including Canada.*

Gen. Amherst was an odd fellow. Handsome to the point of rakishness

---

* As part of the 1763 Treaty of Paris ending the Seven Years' War, all French holdings west of the Mississippi were transferred to Spain. In 1795, with Spain weakened by war, the Spanish King Charles III gave the Americans perpetual rights to navigation on the Mississippi. Napoleon won back the territory in 1801, and President Thomas Jefferson negotiated the Louisiana Purchase two years later.

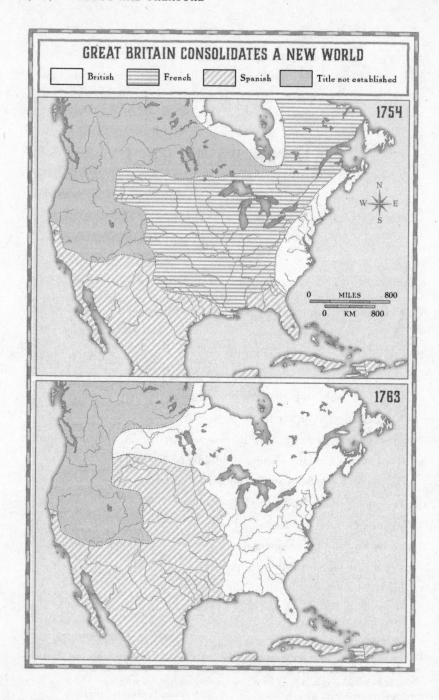

GREAT BRITAIN CONSOLIDATES A NEW WORLD

British   French   Spanish   Title not established

1754

N
W · E
S

0   MILES   800
0   KM   800

1763

and famously soigné in his signature scarlet greatcoat with blue facing adorned by gold-braided epaulets, his successful campaigns through French Canada during the French and Indian War allowed his superiors in England to look past his personal peculiarities. These included a genocidal desire to wipe clean from the face of the earth the "Execrable Race" of Native Americans, as well as a penchant for posing for portraits in medieval suits of armor.

Like Braddock before him, Amherst also belittled the notion of Native American fighting ability unless their opponents were helpless and exposed. "Indians," read one of his general orders during the Canadian campaign, "are the only Brutes & Cowards in the Creation who were ever known to exercise their Cruelties upon the Sex, and to scalp and mangle the poor sick Soldiers and defenceless Women." Of the eight thousand British troops stationed in the New World, Amherst felt he needed no more than five hundred or so west of the Appalachians. Most would be dead within the year.

Alexander McKee's pronouncement struck the majority of the tribes like a suddenly loosed rick of cordwood. The Shawnee, however—whose cabins and wickiups dominated Lower Shawnee Town's loose string of villages— were quick to sense the repercussions of the news. Unlike their Algonquian cousins, particularly those in the North who occupied the *pays d'en haut,* or "upper country," of what had been New France, they had never harbored any great love for the *habitants Français.* They merely hated the British more. They could also read a bottom line. The Redcoats had garrisoned each of the captured French forts throughout the Ohio Country. This had not been done on a whim. Fort Pitt itself was, to Indian eyes, a

MAP TO LEFT: *Britain's 1763 defeat of France in the French and Indian War—known as the Seven Years' War on the European continent—drastically rearranged land holdings in eighteenth-century North America, virtually eliminating the French as major players in the New World.*

monstrous six-sided bastion built to project a single vision: British power in North America's interior. Deftly interpreting Amherst's intentions, the mixed-blood Shawnee war leader called Corn Cob by the British told his fellow chiefs, "The English want to dispossess you of your lands, cheat you, and, at last, extirpate you."

Corn Cob's indignation was not uncommon among the indigenous peoples north of the Ohio River. The reasons, often complicated by intertribal dynamics, were myriad—real or potential loss of land and autonomy, creeping alcoholism, the disappearance of game, the spreading of heretofore unknown diseases. However, two new British policies instigated by Gen. Amherst stood out in particular.

The first was the cessation of gifts. The French, like vanquishers from the Romans to the Mongols, had established their authority through multiple forms of allegiance and repression based on competing Native American social mores. Firearms had certainly played a role. Over 150 years earlier, on a still July morning in 1609, Samuel de Champlain had decided a battle for the Hurons against their archenemy Mohawk by killing three Mohawk war chiefs with a single volley from his matchlock, or fuse-lit, harquebus. In the intervening decades, however, French authorities had more often than not drawn on the loyalties of clans, bands, and tribes via the distribution of presents. This custom carried important symbolic meaning to sachems, war chiefs, and medicine men, whose redistribution of the manufactured European goods secured their leadership roles.

Moreover, the French in North America tended to live among the Native American populations they subsumed, whereas the English were intent on displacing them. This French familiarity made their gift-giving all the more congenial. But now, with the British ascension, the flow of brandy and refined sugar, of metal-worked knives and cook pots, of silver jewelry and hand mirrors, of needles and thread came to a halt. Amherst abhorred the notion of bribing what he considered a subhuman species who had, after all, been conquered on the battlefield with their French allies. The Indians took the insult as it was intended.

Perhaps more pertinent was Amherst's proscription of trading lead and gunpowder for peltry. As it was impossible to confiscate the Indians' arms, denying them ammunition was the next best strategy for poisoning at the root any potential uprising. The British general knew well that a major cause for the collapse of the opposition during the Cherokee wars was a shortage of powder and shot. That the new trade ban would have the opposite effect of what Amherst intended was recognized by more than a few of his associates, including Sir William Johnson, the Crown's super-intendent for the Department of Indian Affairs.

The Irish-born Johnson was one of those outsize characters who flit through history without their import being appreciated at the time or much remembered for posterity. Early in the war with France, Prime Minister William Pitt had commissioned the civilian Johnson a major general in the New York militia, and he was subsequently charged with establishing a fortress at the southern tip of New York's Lake George as a buttress between Albany and enemy-held Montreal. After leading his irregulars to victory over a French expeditionary army, Johnson oversaw the construction of the ill-fated Fort William Henry.

But even that citadel's fall to Gen. Montcalm two years later did not dim Johnson's star in Whitehall.* Prior to Johnson's appointment, Great Britain's relationship to the New World's indigenous people had been vexed, marked by a piecemeal approach at best and, at worst, haphazardly rudderless. On the strength of Johnson's personal rapport with the Iro-quois Confederacy, this had been rectified, and in return King George III appointed him England's sole superintendent of the Indian Affairs De-partment for North America. The king also awarded Johnson the title of baronet, making him Amherst's peer. The assignation meant that Johnson now reported directly to London and could ignore or even overrule the authority of colonial governors and other Anglo-American officials. This

---

*In a supreme irony given the slaughter of Fort William Henry's surrendering garrison by Montcalm's Huron allies, two years earlier it was Johnson who personally saved the French commander Jean Erdman Dieskau from death at the hands of the Mohawk.

effectively gave Johnson a civil power roughly equal to Amherst's military command when it came to dealing with Native American affairs.

Though Johnson was to resign his military commission before the conclusion of the French and Indian War, his expertise at recruiting Indian allies—not least because of his facility with their languages— kept him entwined with the British military. This was most evident during the Battle of Fort Niagara in 1759. Johnson, arriving on the scene with one thousand Iroquois reinforcements, discovered that the officer leading the British forces had been killed. Johnson, much given to spirited speech- making, not only roused the Redcoat and Indian force to capture the fort, but also to rout a French relief force.

Johnson, as a civilian, was also with Amherst during the latter's capture of Montreal a year later, the final great campaign in North America. He then traveled to Detroit to prepare the Great Lakes tribes for the transfer of power on the continent. When he returned to New York, the Iroquois Confederacy awarded him a tract of 170,000 acres upstate, making him the third-largest landowner in North America behind the scions of Wil- liam Penn and the Dutch patroon Kiliaen Van Rensselaer.

Over the succeeding years, Johnson used his grant to found the city of Johnstown, about twenty-five miles west of present-day Schenectady, New York, naming the new settlement in honor of his son, John. There, at Crown expense, he established a free school for both white and Mohawk children. Outside the town he constructed his huge two-story home, Johnson Hall, which still stands to this day. Johnson recruited numerous Irish immigrant tenant farmers for his extensive lands and lived essen- tially as a feudal landlord. He also purchased some sixty African-American slaves as laborers—an amount comparable to those working the major plantations of the South.

Tall, dark, and roguishly handsome, Johnson, had he remained in Ireland, undoubtedly would have fallen into that category of cavalier who regularly emanated a scent of strong tobacco, single malt, and other men's wives. As it was, when not hunting, horse racing, drinking, or all

three, Johnson did his utmost to help populate his Upstate New York
fiefdom. Aside from the six acknowledged children he fathered with his
two common-law wives—the former German-born indentured servant
Catherine Weisenberg and the Native American Elizabeth "Molly" Brant,
older sister to the feared and famed Mohawk war chief Joseph Brant—he
is alleged to have sired another seven hundred or so Indian children with
various Native American concubines. An acquaintance, half-heartedly
defending Johnson's reputation, wrote to London that though he considered that number an exaggeration, "Johnson certainly took much pleasure
in the warm-tinted forest beauties."

That Johnson's carnal exertions never distracted him from being an
able colonial administrator as well as a loud advocate for Indian rights
was not lost on the tribes. Nor were his words regarding the Native Americans taken lightly in London. He reported that the Indians in general
and the Shawnee in particular would never accept subjugation, "whilst
they have any men, or an open country to retire to." He also recognized
that the tribes viewed Gen. Amherst's arms trade ban as a prelude to a
British invasion. Alexander McKee's journey to Lower Shawnee Town
was merely the first step in that process, the overture to an orchestrated
conflict to fulfill Amherst's desire to rid the country of the red race.

In the wake of McKee's message, war belts rapidly circulated from the
Mississippi to the Alleghenies. The only surprise was that the first blow
was struck not by the bellicose Shawnee, but by a relatively obscure
Ottawa war chief in his late thirties named Obwandiyag. He was known
to the whites as Pontiac.

Like most of the Algonquian-speaking peoples, Pontiac had allied his
warriors with New France during the French and Indian War. Since the
conflict's end he had fallen under the sway of a Delaware prophet named
Neolin. Neolin himself never traveled to Ottawa territory, but his teachings
that the Native American race had brought perdition upon themselves

by embracing the white man's guns, goods, and particularly his alcohol spread far and wide among the tribes. Purge themselves of these base desires, Neolin preached, and the Indians would also rid themselves of the European infestation. Pontiac agreed, to a point. He and his followers were not about to give up their rifles. He also had another motive.

Although it was long suspected that Pontiac and the other belligerent Native Americans had been prodded into an uprising by French agitators, more recent scholarship holds the opposite view: the Indians and Pontiac in particular believed that a major conflict with the English would draw the French back into North America. In either case, Pontiac's reaction to Amherst's policies was swift. In early May, three months after Alexander McKee's announcement to the tribes at Lower Shawnee Town, he led a contingent of three hundred Ottawas, Ojibwa, and Potawatomi—the Council of Three Fires—in a surprise raid on Fort Detroit.

Pontiac's fighters failed to dislodge the fort's defenders, but they did devastate a British column of reinforcements, killing or capturing sixty-one of the ninety-six-man regiment. Those taken prisoner were tortured to death in view of their comrades in the fort before the corpses were heaved into the Detroit River to float past the citadel's parapets. When the Red-coats attempted a counterattack on the Indian encampment, Pontiac easily beat them back, killing and wounding a fifth of the assailants. Pointedly, no British soldier allowed himself to be captured. It was rumored that the Redcoats had taken to carrying rawhide tugs bowed at both ends into battle. Were they about to fall into Indian hands, a soldier would loop one end of the cord around his boot, the other end around his trigger, and turn the gun to blow off his own head.

Pontiac's audacity had two immediate consequences: an additional nine hundred warriors from the north and west, momentarily overcome with a pan-Indian synchronicity that supplanted clan loyalty, flocked to his siege site. And Gen. Amherst placed a bounty on Pontiac's head equal to about $40,000 in today's dollars.

Over the next several months of what came to be known as Pontiac's

War, more than half the Redcoats stationed in the Ohio Country and hundreds of settlers and traders were killed or captured by a mélange of Ottawas and Ojibwa, of Shawnee and Delaware, of Kickapoo and Hurons, of Mingoes and Miami, of Piankashaw, Mascouten, and Wea.* One by one the lesser British forts in the interior fell, eight in all, until only three remained—Fort Detroit, Fort Niagara, and Fort Pitt, the latter under siege by a host of Shawnee, Delaware, and Mingoes. In desperation, Amherst and his top field commander, the Swiss mercenary Colonel Henry Bouquet, resorted to the first germ warfare ever to be authorized in the Americas. The victims were a negotiating party of Ottawas who had ventured into Fort Pitt under a flag of truce.

As Amherst planned and Pontiac suspected, nothing substantive came of the talks. But as the Indians departed they were surprised to be gifted with beads and blankets—blankets purposely infected with the smallpox virus from the fort's infirmary. Portraits of Bouquet depict a rotund man with predatory eyes and a plump lower lip that, in the right light, looks as if it could cast a shadow on his expansive jaw. Unsurprisingly, his feelings toward the Indians mirrored Amherst's—"vermin for vermin," he said of the smallpox ploy. Not satisfied with biological attacks, Bouquet also asked to be allowed to follow the example of the Spanish conquistadors and import packs of hunting dogs to sic on the tribes.† Although his canine scheme came to naught—Amherst regretfully pointed out that most of the dogs would perish during the transatlantic passage—the smallpox strategy worked to devastating effect. Within months the pestilence had jumped from the Ottawas and spread through most of the Eastern Woodlands tribes.

---

* Historians are quick to point out that the Ottawa whom Anglo-Americans called Pontiac was but one of many tribal war chiefs resisting British authority. However, so embedded in America's cultural sensibility is Francis Parkman's best-selling 1851 book *The Conspiracy of Pontiac* that, despite Parkman's retrograde worldview, even the most meticulous scholars have acquiesced to the common usage describing the conflict as "Pontiac's War."

† Henry Bouquet had also been present when the Highlanders ravaged the Cherokee villages three years earlier, which leads conspiracists to this day to suspect that the smallpox outbreak among the southern nations was not accidental.

Nevertheless, to the inexpert eye, the Indians seemed to be winning Pontiac's War. Within months they had managed to spring ambushes of British relief columns and outposts that resulted in the death of nearly two thousand Redcoats and colonial civilians. But as the fighting ground on through the summer of 1763, neither Pontiac's forces to the west nor the Shawnee coalition to the east could dislodge the British from Fort Detroit or Fort Pitt. An atrocity-pocked stalemate settled over the Ohio Country as hideous torture, rapes, and in some cases even ritualistic cannibalism marked the conflict. In the meanwhile, as Pontiac's name and fame spread and the British—still not understanding the Indian mentality—elevated him to the king of all the Algonquians, warriors of all stripes gradually realized just how much they had depended upon French supplies, particularly guns and ammunition, in their previous conflicts with the English.

With cracks in the Native American consortium opening and then widening, the tribes began to pursue their own agendas. The Illinois Territory Indians, whose lands had never really been threatened, slowly peeled away. Farther east, though the Shawnee, Delaware, and Mingoes under Cornstalk continued to raid and burn through the Pennsylvania and Virginia borderlands, their elders surreptitiously put out feelers to the British at Fort Niagara regarding a truce. In October, with Pontiac finally convinced that a French fleet would never hove into view on Lake Huron's horizon, he abandoned the siege of Detroit.

Meanwhile, across the Atlantic, Great Britain's finance ministers were growing alarmed. They informed George III and the new prime minister, George Grenville, that the royal treasury, severely depleted from nearly a century of conflict with France, could not long continue to bear the costs of a prolonged Indian uprising in North America. At the onset of the Seven Years' War, the country's national debt had stood at £74.6 million. By the time of its conclusion, the royal exchequer put that number at £122,603,336, carrying an annual interest rate of nearly 4.5 percent.

One wonders how Pontiac, Cornstalk, and the others—their towns and villages racked with disease, their people facing winter food shortages—would have reacted to the knowledge that they were on the verge of bankrupting Great Britain. They were never to know. For in mid-autumn the British king, convinced by his counselors that the white and red races could never cohere, finally announced a segregation strategy that had been in the works for years.

In his Royal Proclamation of 1763, George III promised the Native Americans that in return for peace, the crest of the Appalachian Mountains would delineate a hard and fast boundary between colonial settlements and indigenous lands. Markers were chopped, or "blazed," into trees and pounded into the ground signifying the border—including one within a day's ride of Daniel Boone's homestead in the Yadkin Valley. Only traders licensed by the British government, read the king's proclamation, would be allowed to cross this "Eastern Divide."

On the surface it appeared that a loose coalition of indigenous peoples had forced an empire's hand. This was of course far from the case. It had been long accepted in Europe that England had no friends, only interests. Now, across an ocean, the Royal Proclamation proved that the Crown's transactional notion of diplomacy had spread to the New World. The calculus was twofold. With the French withdrawn, allowing the Indians to return to a simulacrum of their previous tribal rhythms guaranteed a British monopoly on North America's lucrative peltry trade, including the precious beaver. On a more immediate note, Great Britain was falling further into debt fighting wars with the Native Americans, and the pledge of peace in exchange for a vast Indian reservation between the mountains and the Mississippi would stanch the financial bleeding. If, in the future, circumstances were to change, then so would the law, rendering the king's proclamation a mere palimpsest.

What London had not factored into the cynical equation was the uproar it would cause among its colonists.

12

PONTIAC'S DEMISE

The original royal charters issued to England's American colonies had theoretically extended from the Atlantic coastline to the Mississippi River or, some argued, even to the South Seas. This engendered what the historian Frederick Jackson Turner called an overriding "search for soil" that set off a dizzying array of maneuvering between colonial governments.

Seven of those colonies claimed portions on the far side of the Appalachians on the basis of their charters. As such, Massachusetts men bled into the western reaches of Maine, New York, and Pennsylvania and formed a land company that planned a community in Marietta, Ohio. Connecticut settlers peopled what is today Pennsylvania's Wyoming Valley and continued west to the shores of Lake Erie, claiming Cleveland across the water. Authorities in lowland Pennsylvania and Virginia contested for control of territory west of the Alleghenies, including the site of the future city of Pittsburgh. And a New Jersey outpost was planted in what is today Cincinnati. On British maps of the era, Saint Louis anchored the western rim of Virginia, while the two Carolinas would one day have to squabble over proprietorship of Memphis.

But with the stroke of a quill, the Royal Proclamation of 1763 had handed over to the Indians those vast sources of future wealth that land speculators—including George Washington, Thomas Jefferson, Patrick Henry, and a host of southern statesmen—considered fairly won from France. Given the era's racial attitudes, few Indians nor colonists disagreed with the concept of fixing a firm line between the red and white peoples, not least for safety's sake. There was, however, a mighty argument about where exactly that line should be drawn. The colonies were growing dramatically, close to doubling in population every twenty-five years, and nearly a century before President Andrew Jackson's Indian removal policies were put into effect there were already influential Americans who eyed the Mississippi River as that boundary.

Given the toll that European diseases continued to take on the Indians, there is no doubt that both English and American authorities recognized that contact with the red race could be fatal without a single musket being fired. Yet even if George III's royal proclamation included a shred of humanitarian motive for the plight of the Indians, a move that favored only the indigenous peoples and did not benefit the Americans struck the latter as a bridge too far.

Equally irritating to the colonists were the onerous taxes London had begun levying on them. It seemed reasonable to the Crown that the Americans should bear some brunt of the financial burden it had taken to evict the French from the New World. Yet it made little sense to the colonists that they were being asked to pay for a war whose victory they had had no little hand in ensuring while being denied the opportunity to reap the spoils. This territorial disagreement would fester beneath the surface of all British-American relations for the next decade until bursting into rebellion. For now, however, there was yet another war of mutual assistance to be pursued against Pontiac and his followers.

In late 1763, Gen. Amherst was recalled to London. Few if any in Parliament or Whitehall voiced moral qualms about Amherst's use of germ warfare. Nor were there questions over his policy of paying for the scalps of any Indian, male or female, over the age of ten—although how the age

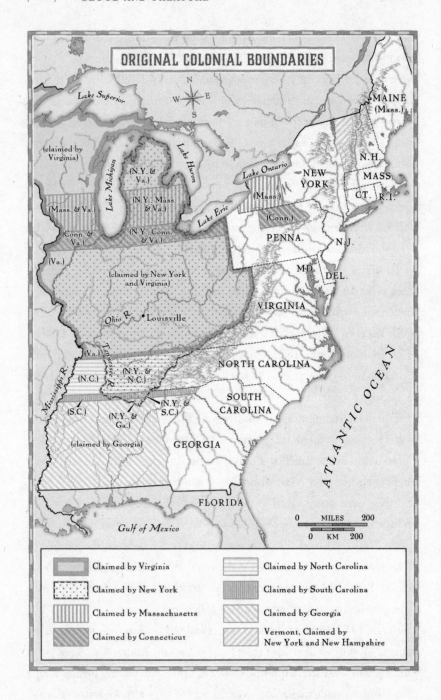

ORIGINAL COLONIAL BOUNDARIES

of a hank of hair was to be determined was left in the abstract. It was Amherst's literal, take-no-prisoners protocol that hastened his political demise. Officials overseeing England's drained exchequer lobbied ceaselessly to terminate the North American conflict, and as the Indian Affairs superintendent Johnson complained, Amherst's rigid orders to kill all Native Americans on sight was not only insane, but would leave Johnson no room in which to propose truce terms.

Amherst's replacement, General Thomas Gage, was also a veteran of the French and Indian War; he and George Washington had retreated side by side after Gen. Braddock's disaster at Fort Duquesne. Although Gage was now in command of more than fifty New World garrisons, stretching from Newfoundland to Florida, his signal contribution to the military was the creation of the British Army's first light-infantry regiment specifically designed for woodland combat in the North American interior. Gage was a savvy campaigner, and not long after his arrival he recognized that Native American enthusiasm for Pontiac's War was waning. After studying the geography of the conflict, he deployed his forest-fighting force to implement a divide-and-conquer strategy. If the royal proclamation was his carrot, the wedge he would drive between the Ohio Country hostiles and Pontiac's warriors to the northwest would be his stick. The Shawnee were his first target.

In the summer of 1764, Gage ordered two British armies, one marching south from Fort Niagara and the other west from Fort Pitt, to converge on Shawnee encampments on the Tuscarawas River in northeast Ohio. The latter column was headed by the infamous Col. Bouquet. Gage was aware that emissaries representing the Ohio tribes had already begun outlining tentative peace terms with British representatives at Fort Niagara. Bouquet

MAP ON LEFT: *Eight of the original thirteen British colonies claimed portions of territory on the far side of the Appalachians on the basis of their original charters, which theoretically stretched to the Mississippi River. Most of these lands would not be ceded to other states until the 1780s, 1790s, and in Georgia's case, the early nineteenth century.*

carried orders overriding any arrangements previously struck. The Shawnee were to be given an unambiguous choice: total surrender or death.

Upon Bouquet's arrival on the banks of the Tuscarawas he was invited by Shawnee, Delaware, and Mingo leaders to present his terms. Speaking through an interpreter, likely Alexander McKee, Bouquet first addressed what the tribes had long viewed as their ultimate chimera. He told the Indians that their longed-for French patrons were gone and were not coming back. As such, the Royal Navy controlled the Ohio and Mississippi Rivers as well as the Great Lakes. "And we now surround you," he continued. "It is therefore in our power to extirpate you from being a people."

Bouquet paused for effect, allowing the threat to sink in. He then attempted to soften the blow by relaying the highlights of the previous year's royal proclamation and its boundary line, explaining that this restraint on the part of the English king was far more generous than any arrangement that the French had ever offered. The Indians were of course skeptical but saw no recourse when McKee concluded the "negotiations" by giving them two weeks to collect and turn over the hundreds of white prisoners they held, soldiers and civilians alike. This would be a sign, he said, that they had accepted British demands. It was not lost on the Shawnee that among the captives were men, women, and children who had years and even decades before been adopted and acclimated into Indian culture.

But the Ohio tribes, pinioned beneath disease, imminent starvation, and the British Empire's might, saw little recourse. Within the allotted timeframe two hundred prisoners were delivered to Bouquet, with the Shawnees promising to retrieve another hundred from outlying villages. And so was lost the Ohio Country Indians' last bargaining chips.

The following spring, in May 1765, a delegation of Shawnee chiefs and warriors arrived at the gates of Fort Pitt singing peace songs and rattling pebble-filled gourds to the slow beat of tribal tom-toms.* Once inside

---

* By this time in their interactions with whites, most Indians made their drums—for millennia constructed from gourds—by stretching a deerskin tight over the open end of an old brandy or rum keg.

the stockade they acknowledged and accepted the British presence at all eleven former French forts as necessary to maintain the boundary line of the royal proclamation. They also volunteered their most able scouts and diplomats to accompany British emissaries to the Illinois Territory to help negotiate with Pontiac and the northern and western tribes still holding out.

More momentous, while presenting Gen. Gage and Superintendent Johnson with a wampum belt representing the "Chain of Friendship" between the two nations, the chiefs for the first time formally referred to the English as "fathers." This designation was not given lightly, and both sides knew it. The word represented not only a declaration of kinship between the two peoples but the formal recognition of British authority over the Ohio Country. What may have been lost on the white men, however, was the fact that in the Shawnee culture the term "father" indicated a teacher and benevolent protector, as opposed to a superior who demanded subservience. It was a semantic misunderstanding that would have grave results.

In the meanwhile, true to their word, the Shawnee provided escorts to accompany a British diplomatic mission west. Pontiac surely had mixed emotions when, in the summer of 1765, he received a wampum belt of peace from Johnson's deputy George Croghan. The Ottawa war chief held no illusions about the British ability to hold back the hordes of land-hungry Americans. He had likely never heard of King Canute and his futile fight against the ocean tides, but long experience with the whites had taught Pontiac the folly of relying on the British Crown to staunch the coming waves. Yet with the Ohio tribes no longer protecting his southern flank, he saw no choice but to negotiate. Ignoring the advice of the influential Shawnee clan leader Corn Cob to answer Johnson's overture by burning Croghan at the stake, he agreed to travel to western New York to meet with Johnson. A year later, in late July 1766, the two signed a formal pact of peace on the banks of Lake Ontario.

Corn Cob and a few scattered renegades from the Great Lakes area and the Illinois Territory accused Pontiac of betraying his people and his principles. Pontiac's response was terse: he had ceded no Indian territory to the whites, nor, unlike the Shawnee capitulation to their English "fathers," had he agreed to return any prisoners. He further argued that he, and by extension all his tribesmen, had emerged victorious in that they had forced the foreign enemy to not only abandon Gen. Amherst's racist policies, but to recognize Indian rights to all the land between the eastern mountains and the great river to the west. To the militants like Corn Cob his justifications rang hollow. Vowing never to accept British sovereignty, Corn Cob and several other Indian leaders led their bands across the Mississippi to settle in Spanish territory. Those who remained may have agreed to live under the terms Pontiac had negotiated. But they also began to view the great warrior in a new light.

The events surrounding Pontiac's postwar years remain shrouded. White historians and Native American lore keepers agree that following the conclusion of his eponymous "war," he began to believe the legendary deeds attributed to him by the British. After a failed attempt to proclaim himself the leader of all the western Indians, he was expelled by the Ottawas and spent his last days wandering the Illinois Territory. There, in 1769, Pontiac was stabbed to death by a Peoria warrior who, as best can be discerned, was taking revenge for the killing of his uncle.

Though the British had promised to enforce the royal proclamation with writs and guns, the agitated colonists need not have worried. The law was destined to failure before the ink on the king's signature was dry. The lands beyond the Appalachians were rich in soil, game, and minerals, and Americans continued to explore, chart, and tentatively settle the Ohio River Basin against feeble British Army attempts to check them. After all, as Jeffrey Amherst had contended, the French had been driven off, their Indian allies defeated. It would be another half century before the New York senator William Marcy coined the phrase, but the concept was already well understood—"to the victor belong the spoils of the enemy."

Hearty pioneers and gentlemen land speculators alike regarded the English king's decree as either a suggestion, a nuisance diktat soon to be forgotten or, in the extreme, a constraint worth fighting over. It would come to that soon enough.

13

BY ROYAL PROCLAMATION

In the late summer of 1765, not long after the Shawnee made their tentative peace with the British at Fort Pitt, five of Boone's old militia companions from the Braddock expedition rode into the Yadkin. They were passing through North Carolina on their way from Virginia to the new British colonies of East Florida and West Florida. At the conclusion of the French and Indian War the land had been ceded by French-allied Spain as reparations, and the royal governors of the new entities were offering inexpensive tracts to any settlers willing to live on and work the spreads. Emigrants from Scandinavia to the Greek Islands were flocking to the territory. Boone was intrigued.

After thirteen years in one place Boone was restless. There was also a psychological impetus for new horizons. His father, Squire, had died eight months earlier at the age of sixty-eight, further loosening whatever bonds existed between Boone and the Yadkin Valley. With his mother, Sarah, now living with his sister Mary—Mary, too, had married into the Bryan clan—he felt that Florida might provide strong enough shears to sever the North Carolina connection altogether. He later admitted to his children that his father's smiling face had appeared to him in dreams whenever his wanderlust gripped him strongest, as it did now. He took this as a good omen.

Boone had lately begun taking along his oldest son, the eight-year-old James, on some of his shorter backcountry jaunts to indoctrinate him into the intricacies and mysteries of the huntsman's life. James had proved a resourceful companion in the wild, and the boy was anxious to accompany his father to Florida. But Boone felt him still too young for the rugged six-hundred-mile journey. Not so Boone's twenty-year-old brother Squire, who had not only inherited his father's given name but the family patriarch's sense of restiveness. Also joining the company was a young Yadkin Valley settler, John Stewart, married to Boone's younger sister Hannah. In early fall, eight men set out for the southernmost fringes of North America. Boone promised Rebecca and his family that he would return in time for Christmas dinner.

The expedition did not go well. The promised journey through the land of sunflowers, magnolias, and orange groves proved instead a rough slog across mosquito-infested swamps and barren sand hills that exhausted man and beast. The few pine, cypress, and palmetto hammocks on which the party camped were so devoid of game that for long periods the party subsisted on snakes, bullfrogs, and alligators. At one point they became lost in a dark, boggy mire and nearly starved to death before a band of Seminoles happened upon them. The Indians, hounded from their ancestral lands by the Spanish and reduced to subsistence living under the harshest conditions, could have easily slaughtered the intruders. Instead they took pity on them and nourished the northerners back to health with venison and honey.*

Once recovered, Boone, as was his wont, kept a keen eye out for the main chance. If the territory was not a hunter's paradise, perhaps farming was the answer. Upon departing the venerable Spanish town of Saint

---

* Honeybees did not exist in the New World until European settlers transported hives across the Atlantic. Although Native Americans, like the Seminoles who rescued Boone's party, developed a taste for honey, the importation of the bees proved a double-edged sword. Indians called them English flies and took their appearance near their towns and villages as a sign to decamp, as the intruding white man could not be far behind.

Augustine on the Atlantic coast—the oldest continuously inhabited settlement in continental North America—he stopped often to examine the soil near rivers and creeks. He found it favorably arable, particularly on either side of the Saint Johns, Florida's longest river. But mere yards from the banks the earth turned into a sandy mix that he felt would never support crop cultivation.

Thinking they might have better luck in West Florida, the troop made their way to the panhandle port of Pensacola, a village not much larger than the original presidio constructed by the Spanish six decades earlier. There, Boone was so entranced by the beauty of the enclosed bay that he impulsively purchased a lot overlooking the crystalline water. His enthusiasm proved momentary. As promised, he arrived home in the softening predawn dark on Christmas Day, 1765, in time for the holiday dinner. Rebecca had a gift waiting: she was four months pregnant with their fifth child. In the weeks that followed she protested as strongly as a wife of the era could against a move to faraway Florida, so distant from her family. With the memory of the beauty of Pensacola Bay fading, Boone eventually relented as his thoughts once again turned to beyond the mountains of the west.

If Boone's Florida enterprise offered a fitting prelude to the next stage of his life, it was a variation on the leitmotif that had dominated the very theme of his peripatetic existence. For not long after returning from the southern colonies, he sold off his Bear Creek property in the Yadkin to satisfy a tax lien and moved his clan some sixty-five miles farther into the upper stretches of the valley. Even at this remove he found homesteaders sprouting like burdock, and after one hunting season the family again relocated, with Rebecca carrying baby daughter Levina papoose-style to a tract on the margins of a small upper valley that "gradually swelled into mountains." The Boones were, in Draper's words, "at last embosomed in the region that had been well called *The Switzerland of North America.*"

The highlands were in fact the Brushy Mountains, an isolated spur of the Blue Ridge chain on the westernmost edge of North Carolina. Not incidentally, they ran virtually astride the boundary line decreed by the Royal Proclamation of 1763. Within months the Boones were joined in this American Helvetia by a bevy of clan members, which included Daniel's brothers Neddie and George, who were married to Rebecca's sister and cousin respectively; Squire Boone, Jr., and his wife; and John Stewart and Hannah Boone Stewart. Rebecca appreciated the company, for here she gave birth to the family's fourth daughter—also named Rebecca, born in May of 1768. The Boone biographer Lyman Draper, writing with the racial sensibility of the mid-nineteenth century, rapturously described the wilderness site where the family settled as "lands that seemed without an owner."

The Boones and their blood relations may have well agreed. Multiple Indian tribes begged to differ.

It is one of the ironies of Daniel Boone's illustrious life that the first time he set foot in Kentucky he was likely unaware that he had even reached his western lodestar.

Despite the disparate aftershocks of Pontiac's Rebellion that rumbled southward—five North Carolina fur traders killed by Shawnee along the Tennessee River in the spring of 1767; a small party of Virginia emigrants journeying to the Mississippi River similarly wiped out by Cherokee later that summer—in the fall of that year Boone and another Yadkin Valley frontiersman named William Hill set off together on Boone's most wide-ranging hunt yet.

Crossing the Blue Ridge, they forded both the Holston and Clinch Rivers near their sources in the mountainous western fringes of Virginia before reaching the headwaters of the Big Sandy River along what is now the West Virginia–Kentucky border. Assuming that the northerly flowing watercourse emptied into the Ohio, they followed its banks for nearly one hundred miles, hunting rugged and precipitous hills nearly devoid of game. In early December, having skirted the rim of the spectacularly deep five-mile gorge known as Breaks Canyon, they had no way of knowing that they were still a good seventy miles from the Ohio River. It was then and there that they were harrowed to the bone by a blizzard in what is now the eastern periphery of Kentucky. As the storm clouds rolled over them like great black boulders, Boone decided they had no choice but to dig in for the winter.

Kentucky in the eighteenth century was riven by an array of rich salt deposits beneath the land's limestone crust. As underground springs bubbled upward through fissures in the earth, the waters absorbed the mineral, which resulted in a plentiful occurrence of salt licks—broad swaths of muddy, salt-laden soil. Had Boone and Hill not stumbled upon one of the largest of these licks not far from where they had been trapped by the snowstorm, they would likely have never been heard from again.* But such was the appeal of the lick's brackish water and clay to game that the two not only survived the winter but feasted on the carousel of antler-and-hoof circling the site. Other beasts in small herds were also drawn to the lick, whose minerals kept their bowels from binding after feasting on the fibrous stalks in the canebrakes. These were the first buffalo that Boone had ever laid eyes on.†

Though buffalo had swum the Mississippi and tramped the eastern mountains and coastal flats as far south as Florida and as far east as Maryland into the late seventeenth century, decades of hunting by European

---

* The site of Boone's and Hill's winter layover later became one of the largest salt-mining works in the state. As the Kentucky historian Ted Franklin Belue observes, Kentucky's major cities of Frankfurt, Lexington, and Louisville owe much of their origin to the ready availability of the precious preservative, and by the mid-nineteenth century Kentucky was producing more than one hundred tons of salt per year.

† In English, the bastardized word "buffalo" was applied to the herds of *boeufs* encountered by the earliest French trappers in North America sometime around 1635. In 1774 the animals were officially classified as "American bison" in order to taxonomically distinguish them from African and Asian buffalo species. Yet, as these bison were universally referred to as buffalo throughout the seventeenth, eighteenth, and nineteenth centuries, that is the term we have chosen for this book.

settlers had pushed their eastern ranges back into the wild upper country beyond the Piedmont. There they roamed singly and in small droves.
Though nowhere near the size of the mighty herds that blanketed the
Great Plains, it was not unusual to sight forty to fifty buffalo congregating
at one of the salt licks that dotted the riverine system of North America's
backcountry, and throngs numbering in the high hundreds had been recorded by early explorers. Indeed, Boone's father, Squire Boone, had settled his family in North Carolina on land informally named Buffalo Lick.

To North American woodsmen of the 1700s, the buffalo was a lumbering commissary. Its meat was rich in sustaining protein, with the triple del-
icacies of the animal's tongue, hump, and marrow being the most prized
culinary rewards. The hump of the beast consisted of layered streaks of fat
and lean meat that, when roasted properly, would satisfy an urban epicure.
And the nutrients in the fatty tongue, boiled in salt water with wild onions
until the skin slid off, would carry a hunter for weeks. But it was the bone
marrow that sent buffalo hunters into slavering paroxysms.

The choicest marrow was found in the animal's shanks, which frontiersmen would roast one end at a time over aromatic red-hot hickory
logs kindled with fat pine and red cedar. When the bones were deemed
ready, they were split open with a hand ax or tomahawk and the steaming
marrow devoured. Although deer and elk tongues and marrow were also
consumed in the wilderness, it was the buffalo's gifts that often drove the
hunters to gorge on the steamed fat marrow to the point of gluttony.

Other than for meat and marrow, the consensus among chroniclers of
the early wilderness hunts assigns little to no value to the larger elk, bear-,
and buffalo skins that proved too bulky to dress and transport to market towns. The hide of a typical full-grown buffalo, for instance, weighed
around 125 pounds. And unlike the conveyances available to the execu-
tioners who were to wipe clean the herds from America's western plains,
draft wagons were useless in the Eastern Woodlands. That said, though
buffalo hides may have been worthless in terms of the labor-to-market
financial equation, they were more than propitious to the frontiersmen,

"who used them in place of blankets, stretched them over a sapling frame for a lean-to or a hide boat, cut them into tugs, or sewed them into shoe-pacs or other heavy-duty winter garments."

Boone and his hunting companion William Hill did just that, and by the spring of 1768 the two had accumulated such a haul of peltry that it was too large to pack out. They resorted to caching their excess hides underground in hopes of retrieving them at a later date.* Upon their return to the Yadkin with all the treasure that their horses could carry, Hill promptly dropped dead from unknown causes. Boone, ever a fair man, assigned half of the profits from their foray to Hill's widow and family, and used his share to pay off the household debts Rebecca had accrued in his absence.

Throughout the next summer's planting season Boone debated with himself about whether the now-eleven-year-old James was strong enough to accompany him back to the salt springs to retrieve the cached hides. In the end, he again judged the journey too arduous for his son, and the two spent the autumn with a small company of Yadkin men hunting the Watauga River region of the far northeast corner of Tennessee. There was never a doubt in Boone's mind that he would soon be returning to Kentucky. In what form or fashion, he was not certain. He was well aware of the Crown decree prohibiting white men from setting foot on the far side of the mountains; he and his neighbors were breaking the law just by hunting along the Watauga. But if he lent much thought to the proscription, it was surely along the lines of his old Virginia militia commander from the Braddock expedition.

In 1770 George Washington would descend the Ohio as far west as the Kanawha Valley in what is today West Virginia to inspect the tracts he had

---

* Long hunters dug their caches on rises where the soil was most dry, lined the pits with branches and dry leaves, and lowered their furs, often bundled in waterproof bearskin, into the pit. They would then refill the hole with dirt and camouflage the site as best they could against pilfering Indians or even other hunters. This often presented a problem, as the efforts to obscure the cache from intruders sometimes worked so well that the original hunters could not find the location later.

purchased through his land agent and business associate William Craw-ford. Washington killed several buffalo on his journey and even attempted to drive a few young calves back to Virginia in hopes of domesticating the "wild cow." His breeding plans came to naught, although he was so impressed with the country—and with tales friendly Indians related of the beautiful Kanta-ke to the southwest—that upon his return he contracted an agent to recruit settlers in England and Ireland. He also urged Craw-ford "to secure some of the most valuable Lands in the Kings part which I think might be accomplished . . . notwithstanding the Proclamation that restrains it at present."

Washington concluded his letter to Crawford with a sage, if cynical, insight: "I can never look upon the Proclamation in any other light than as a temporary expedient to quiet the Minds of the Indians," he wrote. "Any Person who therefore neglects the present oppertunity [*sic*] of hunting out good lands & in some measure Marking & distinguishing them for their own (in order to keep others from settling them) will never regain it."

In other words, only a fool would put stock in the British king's prom-ise to the primitives. This, Daniel Boone could understand.

14

THE GAP

Not long after Boone and his son returned to the Yadkin around Christmas of 1768, he was surprised to hear the tinkling of a peddler's packhorse moving at a slow clop up the icy trail that led from the river to his cabin. Visitors were rare that high in the Brushy Mountains, especially in midwinter. But as the rider leading his draft animal came into view Boone recognized him immediately. Thirteen years had done little to dull the Irishman John Findlay's beaming countenance. He wore the grin of a man who killed weasels with his teeth.

Findlay had not journeyed up into the mountains to vend the pots and pans, needles and hand mirrors, or, to Boone's surprise, the bolts of Irish linen that weighed down his jument. When the flatlanders below had informed him of Boone's whereabouts, he had been struck by an idea. And now he had arrived to discuss Kentucky, specifically to propose a long hunt. That night the two were joined by Daniel's younger brother Squire, who was soon enough enthralled by Findlay's tales of the veritable paradise that lay to the northwest.

Playing devil's advocate, Boone evinced skepticism, and over a flaming hearth related his adventures with William Hill. If that was indeed Kentucky in which he had wintered over, it was nothing like the lush country

Findlay described. Boone even acknowledged that had he and Hill not stumbled upon the salt lick, they likely would have perished. How could Findlay propose mounting an expedition across mountains where no wagons could travel and where their packhorses might well starve to death before they could find sustainable hunting grounds?

It was then that Findlay reminded the two brothers of the Indian tales of the Warrior's Path that cut through Cumberland Mountain. Based on his memory of what the Shawnee had told him as well as the opaque rumors and tales from white long hunters, Findlay believed the location of the break in the towering mountain was much farther south than the northwest line Boone and Hill had taken following the Big Sandy. Findlay admitted that he was no great woodsman, but surely Boone would have little trouble picking up a trail that had been trod for centuries by animals and humans alike. Once Boone led them into Kentucky, Findlay said, he would recognize key landmarks from his long-ago sojourn with the Indians.

Boone, who in truth probably needed little prodding given the debts he'd again accrued, was convinced. Within days of John Findlay's appearance on his doorstep he laid out a proposition to four trusted Upper Yadkin neighbors, including his twenty-four-year-old brother-in-law John Stewart. The company, with Boone as their pilot, would strike west come the conclusion of the spring planting season. Upon entering Kentucky and deciding on a site to make a permanent station camp, Boone, Findlay, and Stewart would fan out to hunt while the others—William Cooley, James Mooney, and Joseph Holden—would be paid a percentage of the profits to dress and bale the hides and furs as well as maintain subcamps as need be. Boone's brother Squire and Daniel's son James—square-jawed and sandy-haired, James at twelve was by now nearly as tall as his father— would remain behind in North Carolina to assist the other families with the fall harvests. After the crops were in, Squire would follow their trail with resupplies of powder, shot, and fresh packhorses. When each man in turn voiced his enthusiasm, the pact was sealed "per curiam."

Four months later, not long after sunup on the first day of May 1769, the six men saddled their best horses, bade their families farewell, and set out for the Cumberland Gap leading a dozen or so packhorses laden with flint, tinder, spare blankets, camp kettles, extra powder and lead, and molds for making rifle balls. Each toted a long rifle as well as tomahawks and sheathed hunting knives suspended through leather belts that constrained their billowing linen hunting shirts. Powder horns and ample bullet pouches hung from their saddles, and small stocks of salt had been wrapped in the blankets or bearskins draped over their animals' shanks. Their deerskin moccasins, tucked up into their leggings of the same material, had been buttressed by bearskin shoepacs for warmth as well as better purchase on the several mountain ridges they were destined to traverse. None wore a coonskin cap.

Though Boone's name had reached near legendary status up and down the Blue Ridge, outside of that small pocket of the world he remained a relatively unknown frontiersman. This would change, despite the British government's best efforts.

Two months prior to John Findlay's auspicious arrival in the Yadkin, representatives of the Crown had negotiated a set of treaties that would alter the rhythms of tramontane North America.

The first, known as the Treaty of Hard Labor after the name of the South Carolina creek where the talks took place, was signed with the Cherokees in October 1768. It relocated the five-year-old royal proclamation's line of demarcation farther west to encompass settlers like those in Virginia's Holston Valley who had already broken the edict. In exchange for £2,500, factions from all three divisions of the Cherokee Nation ceded to the colonists the vast territory west of the Alleghenies and southeast of the Ohio River along a line that flowed south to the border of East Florida. This included major portions of what are now the states of Kentucky and West Virginia. That the Indians who were party to the deal in no way represented the wishes of a large swath of the Cherokee Nation—not to mention neighboring Creeks, Choctaws, and Chickasaws—carried little weight with the white negotiators.

The British were in effect asking for a course correction—admitting that the king's previous boundary line could not hold back American pioneers set on westering. This time, they promised, it would be different. The Crown would enforce the new borders and finally stem the violent clashes between white and red along the old frontier. Conversely, for what today would be worth a little over a half million dollars, the Cherokee put false faith in the idea that a new line of demarcation might finally check the white invasion.

One month later, in November 1768, the Indian agent William Johnson and representatives of the Six Nations of the Iroquois Confederacy convened at an old battlement named Fort Stanwix near the present city of Rome, New York. In exchange for guarantees that the Iroquois's northern territories would remain off limits to whites, illiterate tribal leaders "touched the pen" to a treaty that resulted in an even more westerly borderline in exchange for just over £13,000.* Lost to the Ohio Country Indians were the hunting grounds of western Pennsylvania, parts of present-day West Virginia, and most of what was left of Kentucky.

Although Gen. Gage was skeptical of the Iroquois's right to hand over land on which they did not even reside, Johnson assured him that the tract "belonged" to the confederacy by dint of their victories over the Shawnee a century earlier. Autocrats and auditors in London grumbled over both the terms and the cost of the treaty. And when it was revealed that among the lands handed over were extensive parcels that Johnson had purchased for personal friends, the clamor to recall him from America echoed through

---

* As all but an infinitesimal number of Native Americans living in what is now southern Mexico had no history of writing as Europeans knew it, an elaborate ceremonial system was instituted when treaties were agreed upon. After the terms of the pact were translated aloud, tribal representatives would come before a scribe one at a time. They would touch the scribe's quill with their index fingers before the scribe "signed" their Anglicized names. In the early nineteenth century a Cherokee blacksmith named Sequoyah invented a protoalphabet called a syllabary, wherein a set of written characters, sixty-five in Sequoyah's case, represented syllables in the Cherokee language.

Whitehall. Wills Hill, the Earl of Hillsborough, Great Britain's secretary of state for the colonies, was particularly incensed that Johnson had usurped his authority. But such was Johnson's standing with King George III that Hillsborough was reduced to sputtering over Johnson's insubordination to anyone who would listen.

Had it been possible to view the lands ceded in the Treaty of Fort Stanwix from on high, the territory now open to white settlement formed the rough outline of a huge arrowhead with its pointed tip resting at the Ohio River's confluence with the Tennessee River in present-day Paducah, Kentucky. Needless to say, both treaties had the opposite effect of their intents. In the South there were not a few factions of the Cherokee Nation who refused to recognize the Hard Labor agreement. While in the North the Shawnee were incensed. Alexander McKee, the Crown's eyes and ears in Shawnee country, reported to Gage that the northern and western tribes who had only so recently allied with Pontiac were responding positively to war belts sent out by the Shawnee. Many bands, he added, had already sent emissaries to the great council house at Chillicothe on the Scioto to hear Shawnee and Mingo war chiefs state their cases.

More worrisome to the British, the Shawnee had also reached out to their ancient enemies the Cherokee. Gage, upon learning from spies that Cherokee, Creek, Chickasaw, and others might be open to an alliance with

MAP ON RIGHT: *In the wake of the British victory in the French and Indian War, King George III desperately attempted to prevent the American colonists from spilling over the mountains into Indian lands. His first effort—the creation of a boundary line by Royal Proclamation in 1763 making it illegal to move west of the line—proved as efficacious as King Canute's admonitions to the tides. Five years later, with settlers continuing to ignore the royal proclamation, British Indian agents renegotiated two new treaties with the tribes—the Treaty of Hard Labor and the Fort Stanwix Treaty—moving the boundary farther west to encompass pioneers who had already settled the lands. In the case of the Fort Stanwix Treaty, American territory bulged all the way to the confluence of the Ohio and Tennessee Rivers. Once again American hunters, pioneers, and land speculators ignored the barely enforced boundaries, and lost to the Indians were western Pennsylvania, parts of Tennessee, and most of Kentucky and present-day West Virginia. The resulting "American invasion" led to a rash of white-red skirmishes, battles, and wars that culminated in the American Revolution.*

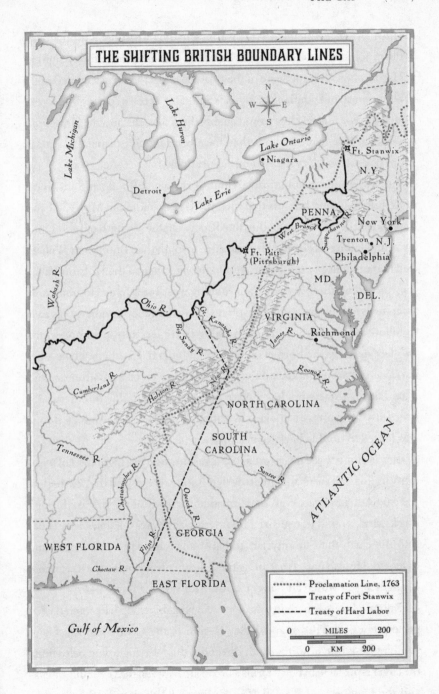

THE SHIFTING BRITISH BOUNDARY LINES

Lake Michigan

Lake Huron

Lake Ontario

• Niagara

Detroit •

Lake Erie

Ft. Stanwix

N.Y.

PENNA.

West Branch

Susquehanna R.

New York •

Trenton • N.J.

Ft. Pitt
(Pittsburgh)

Philadelphia •

Wabash R.

Ohio R.

Gr. Kanawha R.

Big Sandy R.

MD.

DEL.

VIRGINIA

James R.

Richmond •

Cumberland R.

Holston R.

New R.

Roanoke R.

NORTH CAROLINA

Tennessee R.

SOUTH
CAROLINA

Santee R.

ATLANTIC OCEAN

Chattahoochee R.

Ogeechee R.

GEORGIA

Flint R.

WEST FLORIDA

Choctaw R.

EAST FLORIDA

Gulf of Mexico

Legend	
··········	Proclamation Line, 1763
————	Treaty of Fort Stanwix
– – – –	Treaty of Hard Labor

0   MILES   200

0   KM   200

the northern tribes, penned a dire warning to the Indian agent John Stuart, William Johnson's assistant, who had been present for the treaty signing at Hard Labor. "The scheme of the Shawnese [*sic*] to form a confederacy of all the west and southern nations is a notable piece of policy," he wrote Johnson. "For nothing less would enable them to withstand the [Iroquois] and their allies against whom they have been much exasperated on account of the boundary treaty held at Fort Stanwix."

Such were the geopolitical circumstances when Boone and his troop of Kentucky-bound hunters departed the Upper Yadkin in May 1769 and descended the west slope of the Blue Ridge. On the strength of John Findlay's hunch they forded the Holston farther south than Boone and William Hill had on their previous journey. On the far fringe of the Holston Valley they picked up the Warrior's Path running westward. In use for millennia by animals and humans, in some places along the valley floor it was as easy to follow as a modern turnpike, running thirty feet across and pounded two feet deep by the hooves of millions of buffalo. In others, however, it narrowed to accommodate only single-file movement by both beast and man. During these stretches it often became so braided with other trails, overrun with laurel, or choked by canebrakes, that several times Boone was forced to double back to pick up the true trace.

It was along these nose-to-tail passages through the highlands of western Virginia and eastern Tennessee that Boone recognized that the path of the true Athiamiowee, even as it threaded narrowly along ridges, through creeks, and around house-sized boulders, was always cut just a bit deeper into the earth than the myriad Indian trails with which it merged and diverged. He also noted that along these segments it would take a regiment of engineers to widen and level the route for wagons.

Boone, of course, had no way of knowing that his troop had entered what geologists call the Ridge and Valley Region of the Central Appalachians. Running in a rough north–south direction, this physiographic belt within the larger Appalachian range forms a broad arc between the Blue Ridge peaks and the Cumberland Plateau. The Ridge and Valley, gouged by ancient watercourses, is characterized by serrated uplands creased by fertile river troughs. After negotiating a series of corrugated rises, Boone's company passed through Moccasin Gap in Clinch Mountain and dropped into yet another valley. Across the dark green hollow cut by the Clinch River they could see a hogback to the west dominated by Powell Mountain, whose summit reached thirty-five hundred feet. Still following the Warrior's Path, they skirted the north side of the mountain's peak at Kane Gap. By the time they had picked their way across the heights and ridden into eastern Tennessee's Powell Valley, they had traveled some 250 miles in just shy of three weeks.

Powell Valley—what the historian Lyman Draper described as "this lovely vale"—was dominated by towering spinneys of chestnuts rising from the banks of the Powell River. Although the routes through both Moccasin Gap and Kane Gap were fairly well known to long hunters of the era, Boone was taken aback to find some two dozen Virginians throwing up rough-hewn cabins and clearing land to plant corn along Powell Valley's riverbanks. More surprising was that he knew their leader, Joseph Martin, who had also worked as a teamster during Braddock's march. The hunters passed the night with Martin and his troop, who cited the authority of the Loyal Land Company of Virginia for the legality of their presence in what Boone assumed was Indian country. The land company, mostly dormant since its formation two decades earlier by eastern Virginia speculators, had been revivified by the previous year's treaty at Hard Labor.

Boone and his cohort rode off the next morning after bidding farewell to the last white faces they would see for seven months. Boone may have wondered about the legality of Martin's "settlement," but he kept the thoughts to himself. Not so a band of Cherokee who refused to accept the terms of the Treaty of Hard Labor and who but a few weeks later destroyed Martin's huts and fields and drove the company from the valley.

If Boone harbored any doubts about old John Findlay's stamina, the Irishman dispelled them by riding point as the party left Martin's Virginians behind and turned southwest to hug the eastern flank of towering Cumberland Mountain. A frisson of excitement passed through the company when the imposing mountaintop outcropping of sandstone and conglomerate known as the White Rocks hove into view. Wilderness lore held that the pale cliffs, hanging in the sky like phantom drifts of snow, were only a day's travel from the notch in the mountain.

Incredibly, neither Boone nor anyone in his company thought to record the exact date and time when they made the Cumberland Gap. But extrapolating from Joseph Martin's records and Boone's own timeline of reaching subsequent geographical landmarks, it is safe to say that the horsemen ascended the gently sloping sixteen hundred feet to the southeastern entrance of the saddlelike breach in mid-May. As they rode single file, the gap's famed pinnacle jutted and loomed over one thousand feet above them. It resembled the curved beak of an eagle guarding the gateway.

Boone and the others were far from the first European Americans to have traversed the Cumberland Gap. The journals of the French Canadians who had been shown the "elephant" bones at Big Bone Lick some three decades earlier hint that, while heading east, they had passed through a fissure in the Appalachians somewhere in the vicinity. And tales along the borderlands told of various long hunters who had followed Indian trails that converged at a mysterious breach in the mountains.

But the first person to record and describe the gap was the Virginia scientist and naturalist Dr. Thomas Walker, who led a party of five companions through the cut in 1750. Walker christened it the "Cave Gap" after exploring the large cavern on the north side of the passage. But the gap itself was merely the opening to a natural corridor across the rugged Cumberland uplands that led to a second notch in the 120-mile-long Pine Mountain, which runs parallel to Cumberland Mountain some fifteen miles to the west.

To picture the tangled topography between the two mountains, imagine an ancient and colossal sledge being dragged on a north-by-northeast course over one hundred miles across what is now eastern Tennessee to West Virginia. The slag and chuff thrown up by the sledge's eastern edge is Cumberland Mountain, the wall created by its western edge is Pine Mountain. The highlands between the two upheavals contain a mazelike labyrinth of swirling ridgelines, stone towers, ravines that turn back on themselves, and cul-de-sac coves.

Although Walker's discovery was guarded as a state secret among the British governors and bureaucrats of the New World, prior to his report white explorers were certainly aware of several breaches in the east face of Cumberland Mountain, among them the Pennington Gap and the Big Stone Gap. But those notches led only to the snarled uplands. It will never be known how many passed through those gaps and never returned. Even if the most intrepid trailblazers were skillful or lucky enough to pass through the Pennington or Big Stone cuts and traverse the plateau to its western terminus, they were left facing the dead end of the sheer cliffs of Pine Mountain. Walker's feat, if it can be called such, was to "discover" what the Native Americans had known for centuries: once through the Cumberland Gap, a geologic passageway cut by the Cumberland River funneled pathfinders almost due west through a similar gap in Pine Mountain called the Narrows, a defile eroded by millions of years of coursing river water.

The two gaps lined up perfectly, and after following this couloir, Walker named the watercourse in honor of the Duke of Cumberland, the son of Britain's King George II, who had funded his scientific expedition. Thus did Cumberland Mountain and the gash in it receive their appellations.

Now, nearly two decades later, it is not recorded what words, if any, Boone and his Yadkin compatriots exchanged as they passed through the mythic portal. Perhaps they paused to allow their horses to drink from the rushing spring emanating from the cave Dr. Walker had documented, or to plot their descent down the far steeper northwestern slope of the Gap. Standing on the western rim of Cumberland Mountain, they must surely have contemplated what manner of alien object had created the huge and marshy bowl-like depression below them—the "Pondy Woods," as it came to be called—before Boone and his party dropped down into the indentation and followed the bend of the Cumberland River toward the Narrows.*

Though Boone never mentioned what thoughts entered his mind as he and his party negotiated the Cumberland Gap, he no doubt foresaw that his journey opened a new chapter in the history, if not the mythology, of a country that within the decade would become the United States. As noted, individual European American explorers from New England to French Canada to the Spanish southwest had certainly preceded Boone as pathfinders beyond the Appalachians. But none of these long hunters, missionaries, or treasure seekers possessed Boone's vision, which paralleled so precisely American expectations regarding western settlement. As the frontier historian Dr. Craig Thompson Friend observes, "Boone's actions aligned with the language of providential [manifest] destiny emerging in the new nation."

---

* The crater that Boone and his companions were staring at is the astrobleme gouged about 300 million years ago when a meteor measuring some 1,500 feet across slammed into the earth at 40,000 miles per hour. The impact left an indentation 3.7 miles in diameter. Much like a Dutch polder, its swamp waters were drained in the late nineteenth century to create the Kentucky town of Middlesboro, home to about ten thousand people today and the only United States municipality built in a meteor crater.

15

THE WARRIOR'S PATH

Two days ride past the Narrows through Pine Mountain, at a salt spring known as Flat Lick, the main line of the Warrior's Path veered north toward Shawnee country. The Boone party was now traversing their final hurdle, the Appalachian Plateau, which stretches some seventy miles north by northwest of Pine Mountain before breaking into open country. The topography is as brutal as the Cumberland highlands, characterized by alluvial valley floors dense with canebrakes and a thick understory of laurel and rhododendron growing in the shadow of narrow ridges and rugged outcrops topping sheer rock faces. It was here, two decades earlier, where Dr. Walker and his party had faltered.

Having passed through the gap and the Pine Mountain Narrows, Walker had expected to find the "Eden of the West." Instead, he complained in his journals about the ceaseless rain, hail, and bogs of snow impeding his expedition and limiting its movement to seven or eight miles per day. On those rare occasions when the sun did appear, scores of rattlesnakes and copperheads emerged from their lairs to strike at his animals' legs. Landslides and rockfalls abounded; one of his party was mauled by a bear; and during a windstorm that downed trees in their path another slipped with his horse off a hogback ridgeline. The man survived; the horse did not.

After six months of fighting the elements, a frustrated Walker turned back toward Virginia, never knowing that he had come within a day's ride of the edge of the plateau and the Eden he sought.

Not so Boone and his men. After fording a succession of turbulent creeks they reached the west branch of the Rockcastle River, so named for the rococo sandstone parapets and rain-carved shale towers rising from either bank. It was among these edifices—resembling nothing so much as a succession of medieval European castles dropped into the wilderness from the sky—that they paused to reconnoiter and assess their position. Although the outfit was still traveling along the high crumpled fastness of the Appalachian Plateau, Boone later told his earliest amanuensis, the schoolteacher-turned-biographer John Filson, that he somehow sensed that they could not be far from the rich tracts of bottomland that Findlay had described.

On June 7, 1769, while the others went off to hunt their next meal, Boone shouldered his rifle and, following the Red River, rode in the direction of a knobby escarpment to the north that demarcates the uplands from Kentucky's rolling countryside. Ascending the tallest capstone promontory, since christened Pilot Knob, he gazed down as the Kentucky River watershed below fell gently into a series of undulating meadows— the famed "Kentucky levels." Beyond lay the fertile pastures of a new world, he would later recall to the Kentucky Legislature, "unequaled on our earth . . . the fairest claim to the description to the garden of God."

*From the height*s of Pilot Knob, the plains below appeared smooth enough for an Amish buggy. But before reaching the center of the limestone-rich bluegrass territory, Boone's party had to pass through a region where scores of streams had cut the easily eroded shale stone into a series of steep and narrow gullies and ridges. As such, the riders found it more expedient to avoid this "broken beechy country"—so named after the beech trees that favor the shale's sour soils—and double back onto the Warrior's Path. From there Boone followed the trail to a small tributary of the lower Kentucky River called Red Lick Creek.

It was here, amid waist-high grass in what is now the north-central part of the state, that they established their "skin depot," or station camp. It was also at this point that Findlay's memories appeared to overwhelm him. As stubborn as a horse leech, he would not wait for the rough camp shelters to be erected before insisting on heading off to find Eskippakithiki—"Blue Licks Town." With Boone riding at his side, Findlay crossed the Kentucky River and located the remnants of the abandoned village. It was now a theater of organic decay, and for good measure someone had burned most of what was left of the cabins and storage huts. But the Irishman recognized the flame-scarred remains of the town's gatepost and stockade walls. Before long he showed Boone the very spot where the French had attacked his trading party. There was no sign of the tulip-tree bateaux he and his company had carved, and he assumed that this was how the Canadian raiders had packed out their captives and his stolen peltry.

What Findlay did not recall were the waving fields of bluegrass carpeting the open leys between thick copses of hardwood. Of course, he had no way of knowing that he was likely in part responsible for the spread of the *Poa pratensis* plant, which gives the Bluegrass Region its name. For agronomists suggest that Kentucky's famed bluegrass, which is not native to North America, had been seeded in the territory's rich limestone soils by the discarded packaging of the first white traders to Eskippakithiki, who had wrapped their most fragile trade goods in the "English hay" purchased from merchants in the jumping-off towns like Lancaster, Pennsylvania. Once discarded in the interior, bluegrass seeds were spread throughout the northwest section of the territory via the droppings of grazing deer, elk, and buffalo.

Meanwhile, as Findlay had promised, herds of game were indeed thick in and around the woods and shimmering grasslands that spread from Red Lick Fork. As Filson reported Boone saying, "We passed through a great forest, on which stood myriads of trees, some gay with blossoms, other rich with fruits. Nature here was a series of wonders, and a fund of delight. Here she displayed her ingenuity and industry in a variety of flowers, beautifully colored, elegantly shaped, and charmingly flavored, and we were diverted with innumerable animals presenting themselves perpetually to our view."

Even taking into account Filson's propensity for syrupy exaggeration, Boone and his troop found the distinction between this new country and North Carolina stark.* So populated had the Yadkin become by the late 1760s that it seemed to be closing in upon itself; where the valley had once teemed with wildfowl it was now difficult to flush a single turkey for Sunday supper. Yet in Kentucky one merely had to rattle a canebrake to cause a cloud of gobblers to dim the sun.

Boone and his brother-in-law John Stewart were seasoned huntsmen, used to stalking deer during the day's "two rises"—the sun's at dawn and the moon's at dusk. Much like Boone and Hill two winters earlier, however, the trackers found their skills redundant—they need only lie in wait

---

* Filson personally interviewed his subject before publishing *The Adventures of Col. Daniel Boon* [*sic*] in 1784 with a testimonial from Boone himself, that "every word here written is true." Historians, on the other hand, take with an arched eyebrow Filson's claim that he acted only as Boone's stenographer. Boone was indeed literate, although far from lettered enough, as the Kentucky historian Belue notes, "to wax eloquently about great cities of antiquity like Persepolis and Palmyra," as he does in Filson's book. Belue also observes that in Boone's dotage, he delighted in having passages from his "autobiography" read aloud to him.

MAP ON RIGHT: *During Gen. Braddock's long march into the interior, Daniel Boone was beguiled by the Irish-born teamster John Findlay's tales of an Edenlike land teeming with game west of the Appalachians that the Indians called Kanta-ke, which translated roughly as "place of lush meadows." Findlay had previously dropped down from the Ohio River into the Bluegrass section of the territory to trade with the Indians. Although the Appalachian Mountain Range was thought to preclude exploration of Kanta-ke from the east, Findlay further intrigued Boone with the story of a rumored gap in the impassable Cumberland Mountain that led into this tramontane paradise.*

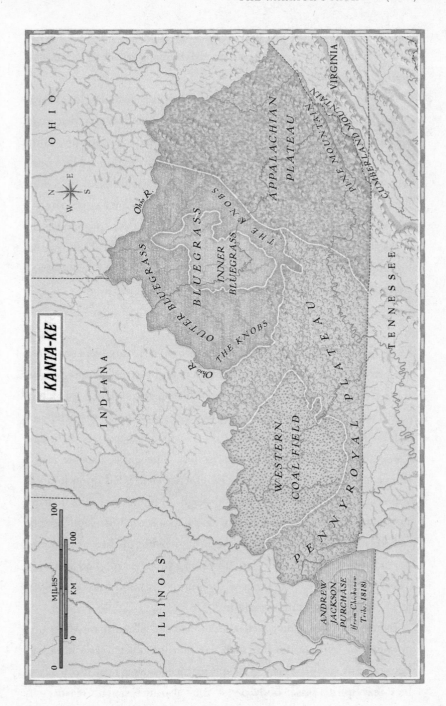

near the area's multiple salt licks for the game to come to them. Such was their haul that within weeks the men were cursing themselves for not having brought more packhorses.

In November of 1769 Boone turned thirty-five. From his June arrival at Red Lick Fork, some five months earlier, until his birthday, neither he nor members of his party had picked up any Indian sign—the tiny cairns of rocks or twigs that warned of evil spirits, the pictographs blazed into trees to mark a trail. They had not even seen a moccasin print embedded into the spongy turf. The frontiersmen had entered Kanta-ke prepared to fight for their take of peltry if need be, but their guard had dropped as the weeks passed and their fortune in hides piled high. This may be the reason, three days before Christmas, Boone and Stewart were caught unawares and captured by a party of Shawnee without a shot being fired.

There was a complicated dynamic at work when it came to encounters between the European American intruders and the indigenous peoples of the frontier. Sometimes a captured white might be killed quickly or slowly, such as the militiaman made to dance while being dismembered alive during the Cherokee wars. At others he or she could be held hostage to trade for Indians held as prisoners. There was also the Native American tradition of adoption. The practice depended upon multiple circumstances. A captive's age carried weight, although there was no hard-and-fast cutoff line. The Indians also took into account how depleted their tribe's clan or band may have become through battle, disease, or starvation due to failed harvests. In the end, however, a prisoner adopted and acclimated into Indian society enjoyed the same rights and freedoms as any man or woman born into the culture.

Indians had been raiding each other's towns and villages in these "mourning wars" for centuries for just such repopulation objectives. And though they generally viewed whites as an inferior race—having been created from the Great Spirit's lesser body parts—they also now saw no reason why captured settlers could not fill the same purpose. The adoption ceremony itself usually required the captive's clothes to be burned in a symbolic fire, after which they were scrubbed with pungent greases or oils, the ablution serving to "wash out their white blood." Certain tribes, the Shawnee among them, also believed in the concept of transmogrification, or "covering the dead," whereby a medicine man's application of mystical rituals allowed a captured prisoner, including white men and women, to assume the identity of deceased kinsmen or kinswomen.

Finally and somewhat counterintuitively, there were occasions when trespassing whites taken in ambush or battle were allowed to walk free with what today would be construed as a mere summons or stern warning. Much depended upon the leader of the Indian party.

Two years earlier, while separated from William Hill along the Big Sandy, Boone had been awakened one snowy night by a Cherokee waving a tomahawk in his face. He did not panic. For all the fantastical attributes and feats attributed to Boone by a succession of hagiographers, he was by all accounts that truly rare breed of human for whom Hemingway seemingly coined his definition of courage—"grace under pressure." On that occasion, with a host of Indian braves eyeing his flowing locks, Boone had flashed his toothsome grin (which thereafter secured him the nickname "Wide Mouth" among the Cherokee) and offered to share what little provisions he carried. After the meal, and possibly the passing of his flask, his captors allowed him to keep his horse and weapons and ordered him to vacate the territory. Boone was undoubtedly fortunate that to this point during their Big Sandy hunt, he and Hill had fared so poorly that he was bereft of any skins, which the Cherokee would have, rightfully, considered their own.

But the Shawnee who now took Boone and his brother-in-law were not as susceptible to the Wide Mouth's charms, if, indeed, what must have appeared to the Indians as the wretched creatures standing before them claimed any. After six months in the wilderness, the two white men— their mended and re-mended clothes smeared from head to toe with the dried viscera of their kills, and no doubt stinking like the carcasses with which they had littered the woods—must have seemed a sorry sight. After Boone's and Stewart's hands were bound, they were marched back to the Indian camp, where Boone again attempted to affect a hail-fellow bonhomie. The head of the hunting party, however, was a wily subchief known as Captain Will, a half-blood Virginia-born William Emery, who now lived in Chillicothe across the Ohio River. He was not about to be taken in by Boone's guile and charisma no matter how wide the white man's smile shone through the dirt encrusting his face.

Although there are no artist's depictions of Captain Will, the many whites with whom he crossed paths, including Boone, were fairly unanimous in their descriptions: although he was taller than the average Indian, he had inherited his Shawnee mother's copper skin tone as well as high cheekbones sharp enough to cut falling silk. He was also said to comport himself with the mien of a natural leader. Aside from his outsize height, it is doubtful that most whites would have been able to physically distinguish Captain Will from his followers. For many native tribes, hair and hairstyles were intimately tied to heritage and identity, and in parlous times the Eastern Woodlands Indians often cut their long, braided hair and plucked their scalps smooth with a mussel shell, leaving only a lock of hair at the crown, which they bear-greased to stand upright. Such did Captain Will's nearly bald head, streaked with vermilion, now appear to his white prisoners. It was said that Captain Will was partial to vermilion. Boone surmised that Captain Will had indeed had the white blood washed out of him.

As one who knew the white man intimately, the former William Emery was also imbued with a deep strain of cynicism toward the Anglo-American pioneers and settlers. He was particularly galled by what he considered their habitual false promises and propensity for playing one tribe off another. The newcomers insisted on borders to protect themselves from the red race, yet they consistently violated those boundaries when their interests demanded it. Had not the Great Father in London promised the Indians all the lands west of the Appalachians a mere six years earlier? If so, by what right did the Cherokee and Iroquois have to barter away Shawnee hunting grounds at Hard Labor and at Fort Stanwix? And if these new treaties overrode the British Proclamation of 1763, what future pacts would override them?

Further, Captain Will continued, it was all too convenient for the white man to look down on the indigenous peoples' nomadic tendencies as nothing more than slothful vagrancy. That the Indians had not put down permanent roots and taken up the plow and loom was merely an excuse to rationalize the seizure of their land. But did Boone not think that the tribes would notice the white man's own peripatetic migrations to slash and burn more trees, to desecrate the earth with more farm furrows, to fence in the open land created by the Great Spirit the Shawnees called the "Master of Life"? These were all existential grievances Captain Will shared with the broader Shawnee Nation.

But perhaps what vexed the Indians most was closer at hand, staring up at Captain Will with his hands bound by buffalo tugs—that is, one of the men representative of the wastefulness of the American hunters in their habit of simply shooting an animal for its pelt and leaving to rot heaps of fine venison or buffalo meat that could feed an entire Indian family.

From Captain Will's and his tribesmen's point of view, this went further than the theft of Indian meat and the white man's habit of littering the meadows and forest floors with rotting carcasses. It was a question of spiritual morality. The great pleasure and the pointed mystery the Native Americans took from studying the animals they hunted lay in the connectivity, even the kinship, they sensed in the winged creatures and four-legged beasts. From this sprang their rituals of the hunt, to give thanks to a beast taken down for providing food, even to ask forgiveness. Watching a white frontiersman kill a buffalo simply to boast that he had done so was incomprehensible to the Indian. Boone and his like had profaned the sacred hunt.

As it was, the Indian leader told Boone and Stewart that he had already decided that the interlopers would not walk free without paying what he considered a fair toll for their trespass along the Warrior's Path—that is, either with their lives or with every hide and pelt they had amassed. He ordered Boone to lead him and his party to their station camp in exchange for their freedom. But Boone, still confident he could outsmart the "untutored Indian," was not about to surrender five months' worth of plunder so readily. Instead he guided the Indians to a temporary dressing post that held a trifling of skins.

Boone knew that the satellite site was manned by one of his Yadkin companions, likely William Cooley. On his approach he made certain to thrash through the underbrush loudly enough to give Cooley time to flee. With luck, Cooley would warn the others at the main camp on the Red Lick Fork to pack up what they could and ride hard for home. But Captain Will was no fool. Surveying the slim pickings at the dressing outpost, he cautioned Boone that his attempt at subterfuge was insulting. For the moment, he said, his braves were content to confiscate his peltry as opposed to his scalp. But Boone had best not again try to take advantage of that forbearance.

Feigning a chastened demeanor, Boone led the Indians on a winding, time-consuming path to what he hoped would be an abandoned station camp. Upon reaching the clearing, however, he was horrified to discover that though his compatriots had indeed taken flight, they had left without packing out any of the peltry. In their haste they had not only left the packhorses behind, but, for some reason, most of the company's spare guns and ammunition as well. The Indians were ecstatic.

Captain Will had the thirteen-horse packtrain loaded with what Boone estimated was several hundred dollars' worth of peltry—nine hundred deerskins and a few large bales of fur. A man of his word, he then furnished Boone and Stewart with a French-made fusil and enough powder and shot to provide for food on their long trudge home. Each was also given two pairs of moccasins and a swath of doeskin for patching the inevitable holes that would tear open along the 360-mile journey. Before releasing the white men, Captain Will issued an admonition couched as words of advice: "Now Brothers, go home and stay there," he told them. "Don't come here anymore, for this is the Indians' hunting ground, and all the animals, skins and furs are ours." Boone would have none of it.

That night, after pretending to head south, he and Stewart doubled back. They stole into the Indian's remuda and unhobbled two horses. After walking the animals out of earshot, they jumped on their bare backs and rode all night. The next morning, thinking themselves secure, they paused to rest the horses. Boone was lying flat on his back on a grassy knoll when he caught the rising sun flashing off the blue steel barrel of a musket pointed at his face. Though Captain Will never dropped his mask of stoicism, his braves appeared greatly amused by the audacity and, in their eyes, stupidity of the white men. This time they again secured their prisoners' wrists with tugs, and also tied a horse collar festooned with small bells around Boone's neck. "Steal horse, ha?" taunted one warrior, and the rest broke into gales of laughter as they set off for the Ohio River.

Seven days later the group made camp on the south bank of the Ohio. Not knowing what plans the Shawnee had for them across the water, that night Boone and Stewart wriggled out of their leather manacles, managed to steal two rifles and a small cache of powder and balls, and crawled backward deep into an enormous canebrake while using their ramrods to flip the cane back up to cover their trails. The Indians utilized the hollow cane sprouts for everything from weaving baskets to fashioning pipes; now Boone and his brother-in-law used it as cover. As the sun broke over the eastern horizon, the two fugitives could hear the Shawnee prowling the edges of their hidey-hole. Then silence. By the time the two white men emerged around midmorning, the Indians were gone.

Boone and Stewart took off southeast at a steady lope, pausing only to roast the occasional raccoon or muskrat and scoop water from streams. Five days later they caught up to their fellow hunters along the banks of the Rockcastle forty miles from the abandoned station camp. Boone was not the sort to reprimand or even openly question the judgment of his companions. He had not been present when the decision was made to abandon their entire kit to the Indians, and, to his way of thinking, squabbling over it now did not change their circumstances. He viewed life with an admirable equanimity—or, as he put it later, "I firmly believe that it takes but a little philosophy to make a man happy in whatever state fortune may place him."

As for Captain Will, that he had kept his original promise to free Boone and Stewart once they led him to the station camp evinced a level of incredulity in contemporaneous and near-contemporaneous retellings of Daniel Boone's capture. Even the typically circumspect biographer Lyman Draper betrays a sniff of condescension when he marvels over the Shawnee leader's "clever shew [*sic*] of mercy."

Some, of course, were eager to credit Captain Will's "mercy" to his father's white blood flowing through his veins. Yet for all of early America's popular descriptions of the "vagabond depredators" of the woodlands, it is an interesting thought experiment to contemplate how a mob of white settlers might have dealt with a pair of "savages" who had been apprehended poaching animals on their property.

Upon reaching the Rockcastle, no small portion of Boone's disappointment and frustration was salved by finding that Findlay, Cooley, Mooney, and Holden had only that morning been joined by his brother, Squire Boone, and another Yadkin man, Alexander Neely. The two, as promised, had followed Boone's trail through the Cumberland Gap and arrived with resupplies, including horses, weapons, ammunition, and beaver traps. The traps, eight inches across the jaws, settled it for Boone. Even in his youth it was noted that his innate patience was equaled only by his stubbornness. Further, with Captain Will riding north with his hard-earned peltry, Boone was again broke.

Most of the provisioning for Boone's long hunts, most particularly those for powder and shot, was done on credit. Because of the sparse hunting conditions when he had stayed closer to home to hunt with James over the past few years, his debts had accumulated faster than he could pay them off. One North Carolina lawyer recalled Boone having had "more suits entered against him for debt than any other man of his day."

In the end, however, Captain Will and his Shawnee band had no idea that Daniel Boone was not a man to be exiled so easily from such rich country. He had not been hunting for half a year to come away with nothing but the clothes on his back. He was also well aware that, at this point in North America's history, the beaver had become the staple of the New World's fur trade.

16

"WITHOUT . . . EVEN A HORSE OR A DOG"

Through much of the eighteenth and early nineteenth centuries, the beaver was to European fashion what the horse was to military might. The soft felt undercoat of the *Castor canadensis* so dominated Europe's markets for men's headwear that between 1700 and 1770 British milliners exported over twenty-one million individual beaver hats across the channel to the Continent. Europe's stock of beaver had long ago given out to overtrapping, which left the North American colonists sitting on a veritable monopoly. In the 1600s it is estimated that as many as four hundred million beavers populated the continent, with a beaver dam built on every half mile on every stream of every watershed in Canada and the contiguous United States. Individual animals of this semiaquatic species, which can weigh up to sixty pounds, prefer to build their watery "lodges" in colder climates afforded either by latitude or elevation. The British and French colonies had an abundance of each.

The Native Americans of the Ohio Country had for decades exchanged beaver pelts with white traders for weapons, tools, blankets, and beads. One French Jesuit priest reported an Indian telling him that "the beaver does everything perfectly well; it makes kettles, hatchets, swords, knives . . . in short, it makes everything." It was (likely apocryphally)

Daniel Boone was born in Exeter, Pennsylvania, in November 1734. The structure shown here replaced the log cabin erected by his parents, Squire and Sarah Boone, although the original basement remains. (*Courtesy of the Historical Society of Pennsylvania.*)

For much of the eighteenth and early nineteenth centuries, beaver pelts were the American frontier's most valuable commodity and often used as backwoods currency. (*Courtesy of the Library of Congress.*)

A depiction of the Delaware chieftain Tishcohan, one of the signatories to the celebrated if underhanded "Walking Purchase" of 1737 that transferred great swaths of the Pennsylvania interior from the Indians to the Quakers. (*Courtesy of the Library of Congress.*)

A portrait of George Washington as he would have appeared as the leader of a Virginia militia company during what North Americans called the French and Indian War—which some believe his rash military actions precipitated. (*Courtesy of the Library of Congress.*)

A sketch of Thomas Walker, the Virginia physician who led an expedition in 1750 through the Cumberland Gap and into southeastern Kentucky. (*Courtesy of the Virginia Historical Society.*)

The disastrous defeat of the British Gen. Edward Braddock during the French and Indian War's Battle of the Monongahela in July 1755 nearly cost the lives of the twenty-year-old Daniel Boone and the twenty-three-year-old George Washington. (*Courtesy of the Library of Congress.*)

The inscription "D. Boon Cilled a Bar 1760" carved into a tree in northeastern Tennessee bears witness to the "literate but not lettered" long hunter's extensive travels. (*Courtesy of the Wisconsin Historical Society.*)

The military strategy of the British Prime Minister William Pitt, 1st Earl of Chatham, was the key to the Crown's ultimate victory in the French and Indian War. (*Courtesy of the Library of Congress.*)

The personal peculiarities of the latter-stage British commander during the French and Indian War, Gen. Jeffery Amherst, included a genocidal desire to wipe clean from the face of the earth the "execrable race" of Native Americans and a penchant for posing for portraits in medieval suits of armor. (*Courtesy of the William L. Clements Library at the University of Michigan.*)

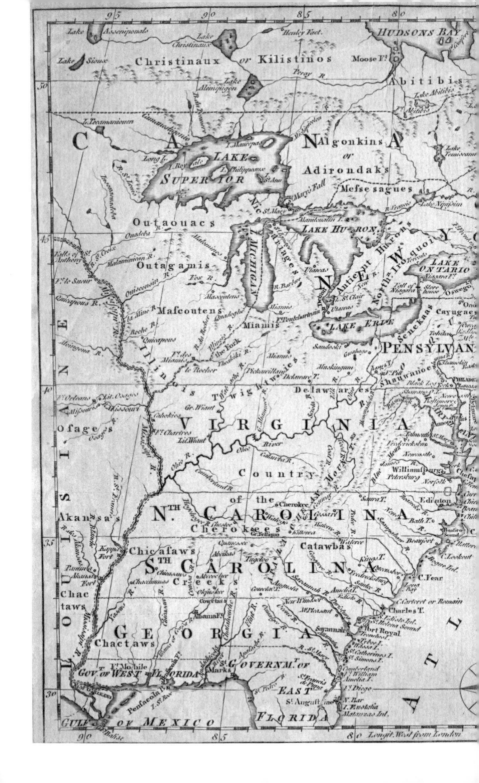

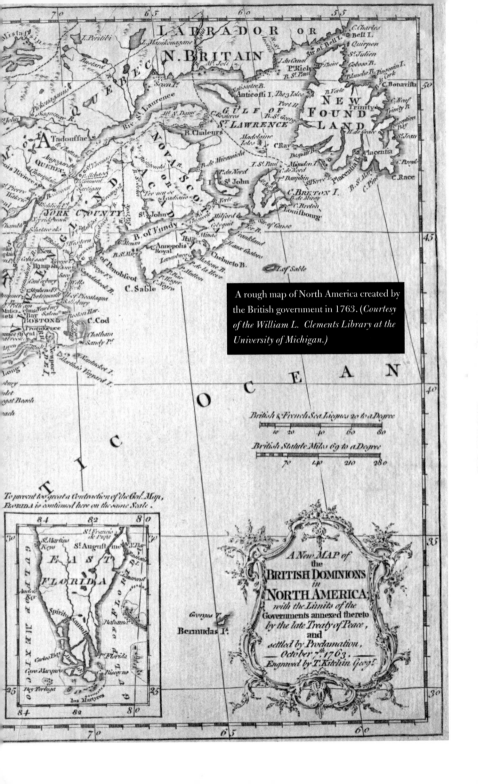

A rough map of North America created by the British government in 1763. (*Courtesy of the William L. Clements Library at the University of Michigan.*)

The Irish-born Sir William Johnson represented the British government as the superintendent of Indian Affairs in North America; unlike most Indian agents, Johnson strived to maintain peace between the tribes and encroaching white settlers. (*Courtesy of the Library of Congress.*)

The "Pontiac Conspiracy," as this illustration depicting the Ottawa war leader's eventual surrender is titled, was one of the names given to a rebellion led by Pontiac against British occupiers of the frontier in 1763. (*Courtesy of the Library of Congress.*)

While in the employ of Gen. Amherst during what came also to be known as "Pontiac's Rebellion," the Swiss mercenary Col. Henry Bouquet devised a plan to gift a contingent of Indian negotiators with blankets purposely infected with the smallpox virus in what is believed to be the first use of biological warfare on the North American continent. (*Courtesy of the National Archives of Canada.*)

The Royal Proclamation of 1763 issued by King George III was a futile attempt to set a boundary line between the coastal British colonies and the more western lands claimed by Native Americans. (*Courtesy of the William L. Clements Library at the University of Michigan.*)

The brutal murder of the family of the Mingo leader known as Logan was a major catalyst for what came to be known as Lord Dunmore's War in 1774. (*Courtesy of the Library of Congress.*)

This eighty-four-foot granite memorial rises at the site of the Battle of Point Pleasant in what is now West Virginia, the largest engagement of Lord Dunmore's War that resulted in a defeat of the Indian army led by the Shawnee chieftain Cornstalk. (*Courtesy of the Library of Congress.*)

reported that the runnels and creeks splashing out of the western slopes of the Cumberland and Allegheny ranges were so rife with beaver that a trapper could walk on the backs of the sleek animals from one bank to the other without getting his moccasins wet—that is, as long as the man was hard enough and restless enough to risk his scalp living beyond the fringes of the eastern settlements. Daniel Boone was such a man. Despite their encounter with Captain Will, he and Stewart were determined to return to Kentucky to recoup at least a portion of the bounty they had lost to the raiders. Squire Boone and Alexander Neely were equally anxious for wilderness adventures. The others preferred to return to their homes.

With that, Boone and his three colleagues bade farewell to Findlay and their Yadkin neighbors, spurred their fresh horses, and rode west. Though Boone would eventually see his North Carolina acquaintances again, not so John Findlay. When the Irishman reached the Holston, he turned his animal north, waved goodbye, and disappeared into the churn of history.

By the time Boone and his replenished company picked their way across the snowbound Appalachian Plateau in mid-January 1770, Kentucky's vast deer herds had lost their reddish-hued summer skins that were so easily dressed. The deeply rooted gray hair of their winter coats had turned their pelts too dense to be properly grained—the leather produced was prone to cracking along the grain line—and the deer were thus virtually worthless except for meat. The unappealing texture of the deep-winter deer hides, conversely, were more than compensated for by the long and luxurious seasonal pelts of beaver and otter.

At first Boone led his brother, brother-in-law, and young Neely back to the station camp on Red Lick Fork. But fearful of another appearance by Captain Will, they salvaged whatever equipment the Indians had left behind and rode some thirty miles northwest before reaching a glade where the Red River empties into the Kentucky. There, in the shadow of the Cumberland and its range, the foursome erected a makeshift lean-to and laid in a stock of jerked venison before heading out with their traps and castor-musk bait to work the banks of the slew of streams cascading out of the mountains. Although a century of trapping by both Indians and whites had dented America's eastern beaver population, the animal was still plentiful. Further, their pelts were easier to bundle and transport, and they brought a better market price: a horse-load of beaver packs might earn a trapper five times as much as the same weight in deerskins, with otter furs even more dear.

As the party settled into camp on the north bank of the Kentucky, their days fell into a rhythm. Squire Boone and Alexander Neely would trap as a team upriver, while Daniel Boone and John Stewart, more familiar with the country, reconnoitered the downstream creeks. The men had constructed a small canoe from broad sheets of green elm bark, and Stewart often used it to paddle across to the south side of the river while Boone trapped the north bank. The four set intermittent dates, usually about every two weeks, to meet back at camp.

If dressing and salting summer deer pelts was messy and fetid work, beaver trapping in the dead of winter was cold and hard. No matter how well crafted his leather moccasins, a trapper's feet and legs were in a near-constant state of numbness from wading into frozen creeks and streams. And his hands, gnarled from prying open the cold steel of the traps and cracked beyond recognition by the hypothermic conditions, were often an indication of the frostbite never far from felling him. One day in late February a freezing and unrelenting rainstorm overflowed the Kentucky's banks. A sodden Boone was the first to arrive at the empty station camp for the appointed rendezvous. He was less fretful about the absence of his brother and Neely—whom, he assumed, were trying to rescue their traps from the swollen upstream currents—than he was apprehensive about Stewart's delay. His brother-in-law knew how to navigate roiling waters; it was not like him to be late.

Boone waited several stormy days for the brown waters to subside, taking advantage of the downtime to prepare his beaver catch for travel. As he weltered in the freezing mire, skinning the animals along a line from the underjaw to the tail, he undoubtedly recognized the finely framed clash between the pageantry of abrading the "king of furs" to the squalor of his own muddy circumstances. When Boone finally deemed the river navigable, he pushed across on a log. On a high and dry piece of ground not far inland he spotted a small cave. Just past its mouth he found the ashes of a recent campfire. Not far away the initials "JS" had been freshly carved into the bark of a tree. There was no blood trail, nor any sign of a struggle.

Every long hunter was aware of the life-altering consequences faced by those who willingly chose to roam the frontier's edges. John Stewart had apparently, somehow, been caught in that backwash. He was never again seen alive. This was a major loss for Boone, who had come to look upon Stewart as a brother. Stewart had been a loving family man, and it went without saying that the Boone brothers and Neely would apportion his share of the hunt to his widow, Daniel's and Squire's youngest sister Hannah. She was left now with a fatherless infant to tend and feed.

But Stewart's unknown fate spooked Alexander Neely. He and Squire Boone had indeed been upstream retrieving their tangled traps from the floodwaters, and after Boone described the murky circumstances of Stewart's vanishing, Neely packed his belongings and set out the next morning for the Yadkin. The Boones did not begrudge his decision. They allotted Neely his share of beaver and otter pelts and asked him to pack out Hannah's portion. Then Daniel and Squire set about constructing a rough cabin in which to ride out the remainder of the winter weeks while they continued to trap. By late April, with the beaver shedding their fur and the hunters' ammunition nearly exhausted, it was decided that Squire would carry the pelts to market on their string of packhorses while Daniel stayed behind to further scout the territory, "without bread or sugar, without company of his fellow creatures, or even a horse or a dog."

Boone would remain alone in the wilds of Kentucky for the next three months, exploring and committing to memory the territory's forest groves, mountain meadows, and rolling hills and bottomlands. He roamed as far north as the state's present-day borders with Ohio and Indiana and as far west as the Falls of the Ohio, "marking the western boundary of Kentucky with inconceivable grandeur."

Already envisioning future settlements, he noted that the farther he tramped from the territory's eastern highlands, the thicker the carpet of buffalo grass, wild rye, and clover. It grew to two to three feet tall and muffled his footfalls as he stalked his meals. The underlying limestone of this geologic zone had been eroded by rivers and streams to yield pasturages more than hearty enough to feed large herds of domestic cattle, while the inky black topsoil, as fertile as Aphrodite, appeared to have attached at least a few grains of itself to his soul. Boone also marked for future reference the ubiquity of the groves of maples, whose sap, rendered in the spring, produced a high-grade form of sugar, as well as the equally voluminous honey locust trees, from whose spiky pea pods an excellent beer could be brewed. Together with the scattered iron deposits and the ubiquitous licks waiting to be boiled for salt, he observed that a good portion of the staples needed for home consumption already existed in Kentucky.

Ever alert for Indian sign, he husbanded his little remaining powder and shot judiciously, taking care to use his balls on only the biggest buck elk and deer that would render the most meat. He was astounded to see buffalo herds numbering in the hundreds lumbering to and from two massive salt-spring deposits along what is appropriately named the Licking River. It would never have dawned on him that within three decades the beasts would be exterminated from the state.

"The buffaloes were more frequent than I have seen cattle in the settlements," Boone told John Filson. And though he noted that a full-grown buffalo when angry or spooked was faster than a mustang, he also found them "Fearless, because ignorant of the violence of man." He took down the occasional bull, and his diet of venison and buffalo meat was supplemented by the plums, pawpaws, asparagus, and lettuce that grew wild almost everywhere.

As a cautious man alone and on foot, Boone preferred to make camp in the countless caves carved by the torrents of ancient rivers now shrunken to the creeks and streams that laced the countryside. He would later relate to his children and grandchildren hair-raising tales of the wolves he faced down over his cookfire, the buffalo stampedes he narrowly avoided, or the Shawnee war party from which he escaped by leaping off a sixty-foot cliff and landing on a dense canopy of large sugar maples. According to Draper, the frontiersman's solitary quest to explore the parameters of the Kentucky territory resulted in Boone considering it "the most extraordinary country that the sun enlightens with his celestial beams."

Whatever the strength of the sunlight that emblazoned the lush lands south of the Ohio River, it is true enough that during the summer of 1770 Boone was the personification of a budding and hungry young nation prepared to not only throw off the constricting chains of the Treaties of Hard Labor and Fort Stanwix, but perhaps of Great Britain herself. He was far from alone in these notions.

As Boone's solitary wanderings took him from one end of Kentucky to the other, he was unaware that sundry hunters and explorers in companies large and small were also beginning to penetrate the wilderness beyond the Appalachians in contravention of the existing treaties. In the spring of 1769 a party of four Virginians—including the father of the future president Zachary Taylor—put in a long boat on the Ohio River near Fort Pitt and, portaging past the Falls of the Ohio, reached the Mississippi. From there they paddled north to the former French outpost of Fort de Chartres in southwest Illinois, only to find it occupied by a small contingent of Redcoats. Aware that in British eyes they were trespassing, they turned back down the Mississippi and spent the winter charting and mapping as far as the Washita River on the future Texas-Oklahoma border. Of all their peregrinations, reports Lyman Draper, "they were decidedly best pleased with Kentucky."

Around the same time, a company of twenty long hunters formed a consortium that departed the New River country in far western Virginia, passed through the Cumberland Gap, and followed the wide buffalo traces adjacent to the Cumberland River along today's Kentucky-Tennessee boundary. Although their numbers were thinned during several skirmishes with the Cherokee, they continued west until stumbling into the midst of a buffalo herd so numerous that the men were afraid to dismount for fear of being trampled. They tarried for several months about midway between the future Tennessee cities of Nashville and Gallatin, slaughtering deer by the hundreds and feasting on buffalo marrow. Then one day they returned to their station camp to find all the equipment and spare ammunition stolen by Indians. The intruders had also destroyed over five hundred dressed deerskins.

Like Boone, these were hard men not prone to easy surrender, and a small group volunteered to return to the eastern settlements to resupply the company. Upon their return the entire troop resumed the hunt until sometime in April 1770, when they split their force. About half the hunters made their way back to Virginia overland, while ten men loaded their haul into two bateaux and descended the Cumberland with trapping gear. At the mouth of the Cumberland they were set upon by two dozen Chickasaw. During the fight the Indians made off with several guns and some iron cookware but not the hunters' peltry. Debarking at the then-Spanish port of Natchez, they sold their cargo and returned home.

Meanwhile, miles to the north, a New Jersey–born Virginia militiaman named Major John McColloch decided to attempt his own trek down the Ohio. McColloch, the son of a Glaswegian immigrant, put out from Fort Pitt in a lone canoe sometime in 1769 accompanied by only his white indentured servant and a black slave. The trio descended the river as far as the mouth of the Wabash River on the current Indiana-Illinois border before they were, predictably, captured by Northern Indians—likely Potawatomi, then in the process of migrating south from their ancestral lands in Michigan and Wisconsin.

Although the fate of Maj. McColloch's companions is lost, the first-generation Scotsman proved as tough as he was daft. He was kept prisoner by the Indians for five months before being granted his freedom with a warning similar to that issued by Captain Will to Boone—leave the country and do not come back. With the assistance of French traders manning a small fleet of pirogues, McColloch wound his way from Indiana to New Orleans via Natchez, where he booked passage for Philadelphia. For unknown reasons the ship's captain and crew abandoned him in Bermuda, where he was stranded for several more months before making it back to his Albemarle County homestead in north-central Virginia. He promptly uprooted his wife and six children and moved over three hundred miles into the wilderness near what is now the city of Wheeling, West Virginia.

McColloch, as hearty as a Scottish thistle, apparently passed the trait to his progeny. His oldest daughter, Elizabeth, would marry the famed explorer Ebenezer Zane (for whom the Ohio city of Zanesville is named) and two of McColloch's sons—John, Jr., and Samuel—would be feted by none other than General George Washington for their scouting and intelligence-gathering feats during the American Revolution. Washington may have first met the McColloch boys some six years before he was appointed commander in chief of the nascent Continental Army. For at the same time that Boone was traipsing Kentucky, the future president was prowling the precincts of the Ohio Country's Kanawha River Basin. He had heard rumors of a proposition to found a new colony abutting western Pennsylvania and western Virginia south of the Ohio River, and he feared that this would somehow affect his landholdings. Better, he felt, to survey and claim ownership now.* But there was a problem, Washington wrote to his brother. He had never seen the Indians in such distemper.

Despite the white onslaught, however, not all Native Americans were anxious to take up the tomahawk against the intruders. That autumn, British Indian agents from across the Ohio Country reported clans and sometimes even entire bands from the woodland tribes harvesting their corn, dismantling their villages, and departing the territory. Some Shawnee journeyed south, to take up residence near the Creek, with whom they had cemented relations a century earlier. Others from a variety of tribes forsook the East altogether and moved their people across the Mississippi to settle in what was then Spanish territory. Those who remained, however, were ever more determined to fight.

---

* The Crown eventually rejected the idea for the proposed colony of "Vandalia"—named in honor of the British queen Charlotte, who was thought to be descended from the ancient Germanic tribe of Vandals. In the wake of the Revolutionary War, the few pioneers who settled "Vandalia"—covering most of what is today West Virginia and northeastern Kentucky—petitioned to be admitted to the union as the state of Westsylvania. Virginia and Pennsylvania politicians, considering the land theirs, successfully blocked the move. The new United States federal government then divided and apportioned the area between the two states along the Mason-Dixon Line. A section of that territory, of course, would become the state of Kentucky in 1792, with West Virginia breaking away and entering the union during the Civil War in 1863.

17

"A SECOND PARADISE"

The pang of the betrayal stung the Shawnee like a copperhead's strike. The tribe had been literally sold out by their neighbors—the Iroquois to the north at Fort Stanwix and the Cherokees to the south at Hard Labor. The promise of the Royal Proclamation of 1763 was now but a black memory. Erased were the eighteen addendums that the Shawnee and their Mingo and Delaware allies had negotiated with the British regarding the finer points of King George's decree. Now, at the dawn of a new decade, tribal leaders had no more faith in the Redcoats to control the Americans swarming over the Appalachians and contaminating their lands than they believed the man sitting on the throne in faraway London had been placed there by the Master of Life.

On the few occasions when the British Army did manage to evict illegal squatters—toppling their cabins, burning their farm fields—more would return like blowflies to a decomposing corpse. The Virginians in particular earned the harshest Indian enmity. Such was that colony's duplicity that at Native American councils across the Ohio Country any promise made by white men came to be known as the "Virginia lie."

Boxed in by enemies to the north, east, and south, a rueful if defiant Shawnee chief told a British agent, "We have always been the frontier." To that end, the Indian added, his people had no choice but to do what they had done for a century. Fight. It was not for nothing that Shawnee warriors boasted that they had killed ten times more whites than any other tribe.

But total war had taken its toll on the Shawnee beyond battlefield losses. A lack of guns and especially ammunition had forced Cornstalk and his warriors to raid farther and farther afield to replenish their arms. This left their towns and villages underdefended for long periods of time against white reprisals. The constant violence had also disrupted Shawnee customs and subsistence to the point that the tribal birthrate had dropped, and no amount of ritual corn-dance performances could preclude winters with barely any food. Cornstalk may have still led men who, like their forebears, were capable of killing ten times more whites than other Indians had. But as the war chief was to learn, it would never be enough.

Not surprisingly, by the summer of 1770, Daniel Boone could see and sense the increasing Indian hostility. His capture and escape from Captain Will had served as a sort of harbinger. During his subsequent solitary journeys through the northern and western districts of the Kentucky territory he was often forced to secret himself amid dense copses of laurel and beech or deep in cane thickets as more and larger bands of Native Americans, their faces painted black or red for war, crossed his paths—the Cherokee journeying north, mounted Chickasaw and Creek riding west, Shawnee and their Mingo and Delaware brethren moving south.

Boone had not had word from the east since his brother had packed out their beaver pelts. What he could not have known was how the frequency with which American intruders following old trails or breaking new ones across the Ohio Country was goading the Indians to heights of retaliation not seen since Pontiac's Rebellion. It was open season on the outlying settlements along the rapidly filling borderlands, with war parties attacking and looting in wild abandon. The Iroquois Confederacy to the north constituted a virtual wall behind which most New England and New York settlers remained safe. But the broad arc from northwestern Pennsylvania to southwestern Virginia remained vulnerable. The Shawnee, following some vestigial connection to William Penn, proclaimed that they might spare the lives of Pennsylvanians after burning them out of their cabins. All Virginians, on the other hand, were marked for death.

In late July 1770, Squire Boone returned to Kentucky with supplies, fresh horses, and the news that Daniel was father to a new baby boy and a namesake at that—Daniel Morgan Boone had been born the previous December 23. To this point the Yadkin remained a relative island of tranquility, so it is doubtful that even the younger Boone was aware of the uptick in white westering activity closer to the Ohio River and the Indian retaliation it was spurring. Over the succeeding weeks, however, the brothers took extra caution as they laid in as many deerskins as their horses could tote. Come September, Squire was once again charged with packing them out. Upon his return three months later, the Boone brothers moved farther down the Kentucky River to trap beaver.

One day in March 1771, with his younger brother out tending their traps, Boone settled into a clearing to sun himself on a bearskin blanket. As had increasingly become his habit, he was singing and whistling aloud when he heard a twig snap. He jumped to his feet and found himself staring at a young white man leveling a large rifle at him. The tall stranger, who despite his size had closed in on Boone with a panther's stealth, introduced himself as Kasper Mansker.

The twenty-year-old Mansker, born during his parents' sea voyage from Bohemia to Pennsylvania, had taken to long hunting in his mid-teens and now called home the Holston country of eastern Tennessee. As he and Boone parleyed over jerked venison, Boone showed a particular interest in Mansker's old-fashioned smoothbore gun. The big German told him he preferred the versatility of a weapon that shot ball, buckshot, or any combination thereof, which a rifled barrel was incapable of. When Squire returned, the three repaired to Mansker's nearby station camp. There, more than a dozen hunters greeted them. As Mansker related their story over firelight, it only solidified Boone's inkling that Indian belligerence might now be coalescing into a concerted, countrywide epidemic.

During the previous autumn, Mansker said, he had joined some fifty frontiersmen from the Holston Valley and Virginia's New River settlements to traverse the Cumberland Gap and hunt and trap the river valleys tumbling out of the Cumberland range. Theirs was perhaps the best-equipped, nonmilitary troop to yet venture into the wilderness, with each rider leading three packhorses laden with additional rifles, spare ammunition for several seasons' worth of hunting, and a plethora of beaver traps. Traveling south by southwest, skirting the Kentucky-Tennessee border, they built various station camps along the Laurel River before turning north toward the Green River. Amid the thickets of ash, elm, walnut, and oak that sprang from the rich soil of the two watersheds they felled deer by the hundreds while taking down the occasional buffalo gathered at the stamped licks. They were not far from the mouth of the Green when a quarrel broke out between two factions of the group.

Mansker explained it as the Virginia men's jealousy over the hunting proficiency of the Tennesseans. Boone nodded and let the comment pass. True? Self-aggrandizing? Tales of nerves failing and tempers flaring among edgy hunters too long in the wilderness were commonplace, a sort of corollary to cabin fever. To avoid any bloodshed, Mansker continued, most of the New River men had opted to return home with their bales of hides, while he and sixteen others remained to spend the winter collecting beaver furs in Kentucky.

But one day he and his trappers had returned to their camp to find it abandoned by the five men left to tend the site. Mansker was certain they had either been run off or killed by Shawnee; he recognized the tribe's markings on a war club found close at hand. It was daubed with vermilion, as was the bark of a nearby tree. At this, Boone thought of Captain Will and his fondness for the flaming crimson paint. The Indians, in habit, took what tools, cookware, and peltry they could carry, and then deliberately destroyed over fifteen hundred deerskins.* Mansker's mounted party, still flush with ammunition and relatively hale horses, refused to be broken. They rode north to trap, and that is how they had run across the Boone brothers.

Given Mansker's departure date from the Holston nearly a year earlier, he and his companions were likely unaware of George Washington's ominous reports of Indian foment along the Ohio River. They could, however, and probably did have knowledge of the fates of the other long-hunting parties that had battled both the Chickasaw and Cherokee along the Tennessee. Despite its vastness, news, particularly bad news, traveled fast on the frontier.

Mansker's tale, while confirming Boone's instincts about the increased tensions roiling the wilderness and its borderlands, did not deter Boone and his brother from spending several weeks riding and trapping with the Holston Valley party. In late March he and Squire said their goodbyes and made course for home, their packhorses laden with beaver pelts and deerskins.

They were camping along the Warrior's Path near Powell Valley when they were approached by a party of six Cherokee. At first the Indians feigned cordiality—Boone noted that they were not painted for war—and the Boones reciprocated, inviting the visitors to share their supper. During the meal, however, the Cherokee managed to surround the brothers, both of whom, at Boone's signal, had kept their rifles close. It was a standoff that Boone knew they could not win. He motioned to Squire to hold fire, and while four of the Indians and the Boone brothers stood aiming their rifles at each other beneath hard stares, two of the intruders stole off with the horseflesh and prized furs. The others, backing away, followed.

---

* Unbeknownst to Mansker as he related the tale to the Boones, one of his camp's keepers had taken ill, and another had volunteered to take him back to the eastern settlements. The three remaining hunters were attacked by Indians. It was later learned that one of the three had escaped into the forest and eventually re-crossed the Appalachians with word of the assault. The two other white men were never heard from again.

The skins and pelts that Squire had twice in the last twenty-four months packed out to the settlements could not make up for the brothers' twin losses, first to Captain Will and now to the Cherokee. After two years of hunting and trapping, of accruing what would have been considered a small fortune for the era, Boone arrived home that May, writes Draper, "poorer than when he departed."

"But he had seen Kentucky," Draper continues, "which he 'esteemed a second paradise,' and that of itself was enough amply to repay him for all his toils, losses, and sufferings."

The sentiment was not likely shared by Boone's creditors.

Also sounding like a story too good to be true is a yarn that still circulates regarding Boone's return to the Yadkin in that spring of 1771. It is told that on the night he and Squire arrived in the valley, a barn dance was taking place on the Bryan property. Boone, covered in the huntsman's normal cuts and scratches in various stages of healing, his clothes torn and filthy, stood at the edge of the crowd awaiting greetings from his friends and neighbors. No one recognized him. Although beards were in fashion along the eastern seaboard, borderlanders were fairly meticulous about shaving, and nearly every long hunter carried a straight razor in his kit.

It suddenly struck Boone that he had neither cut his hair nor shaved during the final few months of his two-year sojourn, and his face had cultivated such a density of facial hair that it qualified as a topiary. With an impish grin, he approached Rebecca and made a motion inviting her to dance. Repelled by the stranger's coarse appearance, she backed away, only to recognize the pitch and tenor of her husband's guffaws as he doubled over in laughter. Soon, it is said, the entire crowd, including the musicians, were gathered about Boone eager to hear his tales of Kentucky.

18

---+---

COLD RAIN MIXED WITH THE TEARS

Perhaps it was the birth of his namesake son. It could have been his inherent optimism. Or maybe some combination of the two. Whatever the rhyme or reason, Daniel Boone remained undeterred by his multiple setbacks and growing debt. He spent the next thirty months cash-cropping in the Upper Yadkin during the spring and summer seasons and returning to the Virginia-Tennessee borderlands with his son James to market-hunt in fall and winter. On these journeys the idea of decamping from North Carolina and relocating to Kentucky was never far from his mind. In early 1772 he put pace to that notion and returned to further scout the bluegrass country with a small party of like-minded long hunters. At one point he led them to a cavelike hollow guarded by a rock overhang that he had called home for a short while nearly three years earlier.

It was during these expeditions that the settlement of the river valleys beyond the Blue Ridge exploded. One by one they filled, the Holston and the New and the Clinch, populated by pioneers squeezed out by the rising price of land in the Piedmont as well as the equally pernicious property taxes. On Boone's way home from his Kentucky sojourn, he stopped to camp along the Clinch River in the western corner of Virginia. There he made the acquaintance of the veteran militia officer Captain William

Russell, a thirty-eight-year-old college-educated descendent of Virginia's
Tidewater elite who had moved west to begin a new life after his wife died.

Capt. Russell, a former member of Virginia's House of Burgesses, now
served as a local justice of the peace while tending his large tobacco plantation, which he named Castle's Wood. Russell was not only a pillar of the
growing community but one of the few slaveholders along the southern
borderlands.* Yet despite his comfortable lifestyle and prosperous status, Russell proved as restless as Boone to establish a community in the
distant wilderness. The captain, his father, and his uncle had all fought
in the French and Indian War, and for their service had been awarded
land grants beyond the mountains called "military warrants," Over open
cookfires of pigs roasting on spits and thick steaks carved from Russell's
cattle herd, the two made arrangements to gather neighbors of similar
bent attracted by the Crown's offer of fifty acres to any settler who cleared
and planted three of the acres, and set off for Kentucky once the following summer's farm fields were sown. Russell would boss the outfit, with
Boone serving as its pilot.

Boone departed the Clinch and returned to the Yadkin in April of
1773 in time to witness the birth of his eighth child and fourth son, Jesse
Bryan Boone, born on May 23. He found enthusiasm for Capt. Russell's
proposed Kentucky expedition not only among his brother Squire and
his family, but also with a fair number of his Bryan in-laws. Boone was not
the only North Carolinian anxious to escape the tax gatherers now ranging through the Lower Yadkin. As the summer progressed, the Boones

* Though greatly outnumbered by pioneers of English heritage, the Scots-Irish settlers who predominantly migrated into Kentucky from the north, particularly from Quaker Pennsylvania, carried with
them a disdain for the concept of the "peculiar institution" of chattel bondage. Slavery thus remained
for them a mostly foreign abstraction. Conversely, given the wealth accrued in the Yadkin Valley by
Daniel Boone's in-laws, the Bryans, several members of the clan most certainly owned black human
beings in the 1750s and 1760s. But in the main slavery and indentured servitude were anomalies
in the uplands labor system. Census results from North Carolina's three most western counties, including Rowan County, indicate that though "Negros" made up 20 percent of the population, they
were concentrated in fewer than 10 percent of households. Later, toward the end of the 1770s, slaves
accounted for perhaps 10 percent of the Kentucky territory's population, including several acquired
by Daniel Boone.

and diverse members of the Bryan clan set about selling their farmsteads, most of their livestock, and any farm equipment too bulky to convey by packhorse. It was not lost on the thirty-eight-year-old Boone that he was following in the footsteps of his father's perambulations over two decades earlier.

On September 25, 1773, Daniel and Squire Boone, accompanied by their wives, Rebecca and Jane, and their eight and three children, respectively, bade the seventy-three-year-old Sarah Morgan Boone tearful good-byes. Both Boone boys understood that it would probably be the last time they saw their mother. The smallest children were then hefted into hickory wicker baskets draped over either side of a pack animal's withers, and the Boones departed the Upper Yadkin Valley, driving small herds of hogs and belled cows before them. Boone's adopted nephews, Jesse and Jonathan, old enough to make their own decisions, opted to remain behind. Boone's son James, now sixteen and a seasoned woodsman, had earned pride of place to ride abreast of his father at the head of the column.

Among the adventurers from the Lower Yadkin wishing to join the migration were two dozen or so solitary horsemen. These were nearly evenly split between unmarried men looking for a fresh start, and those leaving families behind who planned on returning to retrieve them the following summer after establishing Kentucky homesteads. Most of these latter men were not quite ready to depart, and Boone proposed they catch up to the ambling packtrain in Powell Valley. It was there that he also expected to meet a contingent of Virginia emigrants whom Capt. Russell had recruited among the Clinch River settlements. He calculated that their strength in numbers would serve them well enough in deep Indian country.

The packtrain reached Castle's Wood sometime in mid-August. There they tarried for a month making final preparations before the entire group, totaling between forty and fifty souls, set out for the West. Only Capt. Russell stayed behind to facilitate some eleventh-hour business. It took two weeks to cover the hundred or so miles between Russell's homestead and the Kane Gap at Powell Mountain. Boone's scouts had already informed him that the Yadkin men awaited him up ahead. Watching the strung-out, single-file cavalcade slowly advance, he realized that he had grossly undersupplied the party. With this, he dispatched his son James and the two young Mendinall brothers back with a request that the captain acquire additional horses and cattle. It was the last time he saw his eldest boy alive.

After the ambush, torture, and killing of James Boone and Henry Russell, the Shawnee known as Big Jim and his intertribal war party never did circle back to attack Daniel Boone's packtrain. And though the burial party led by Capt. Russell and Squire Boone interred the mangled, arrow-pocked bodies of the two teenage boys in a single grave near the site where they fell, the murder of Henry Russell reverberated much further from the political and social precincts of western Virginia than the killing of James Boone. For all his local celebrity, Daniel Boone was still a relatively unknown entity east of the Blue Ridge. When newspaper reports of the "massacre" circulated, the name Boone was merely a footnote.

Young Russell's father, on the other hand, was a prominent Virginian already honing a public career that would propel him to contribute to the Declaration of Independence as well as serve in the First Continental Congress. Word of the killings was quick to reach the state's colonial capital of Williamsburg, more than four hundred miles to the east. There, Governor John Murray, the 4th Earl of Dunmore and a descendant of the Scottish house of Stuart—and more generally referred to as Lord Dunmore—was quick to scent the political winds calling for vengeance. Young Russell's and Boone's Shawnee and Delaware killers were of course long vanished, if not into the wilds of Kentucky then surely back to the Indian towns and villages on the Scioto in far-off Ohio. But when Dunmore's agents learned the identities of the two Cherokee who had ridden with Big Jim and participated in the attack, he dispatched emissaries to the Cherokee Nation demanding redress.

The governor offered the tribal leaders a choice: serve up the perpetrators in chains or exact your own rough frontier justice. Either way, Dunmore demanded lethal revenge. One of the assailants, a warrior named Not-ta-wa-gua, received his punishment when his brains were bashed in by the equivalent of an Indian firing squad. The second cutthroat managed to temporarily escape into Chickasaw country but was eventually captured, turned over to Virginia authorities, and hanged.

Despite this ruthlessness, Lord Dunmore was not completely unsympathetic to Indian grievances. He made this clear in a letter to William Legge, the 2nd Earl of Dartmouth and the secretary of state for the colonies under the British prime minister, Lord Frederick North. In his communiqué Dunmore complained that no government could hope to restrain the colonists from their western migrations into Indian territory. America's indigenous tribes, he continued, were only doing what any Englishman would do to protect his property.

The Americans, on the other hand, "do and will remove as their avidity and restlessness incite them," Dunmore wrote. "They acquire no attachment to Place but forever imagine the Lands further off are Still better than those upon which they are already Settled." In fact it was not unusual for pioneer families to shift their homes six times or more in their lifetimes. Nonetheless, Dunmore recognized that the Crown had appointed him to govern the provincials no matter their "avidity and restlessness." It would not stand to have hostiles rampaging through his bailiwick torturing and murdering the sons of its prominent citizens. War was brewing, and the governor knew it.

Out in the Powell Valley, Daniel Boone spent the days following the murder of his son attempting to convince the members of the expedition that they should press on for Kentucky. Naturally heavy of heart, he nonetheless argued to Capt. Russell that postponing the expedition would dishonor the sacrifices of their dead boys. Russell, however, better intuited the pall of fear that had fallen over the emigrant train. At an impromptu council he voted with the majority of the travelers to delay the move west for at least several months, perhaps longer if the Indian question had not been resolved. Boone accepted the decision; he had no real option. Pushing on alone with his wife and children into lands swarming with angry Indians, even if his brother Squire and his family joined them, was untenable.

Boone, however, could not stomach the idea of a return to North Carolina, where the memories of James permeated every hunting stand and forest path. While the remainder of his Yadkin party picked their way back east across the Blue Ridge, he accepted an invitation from one of Capt. Russell's neighbors to winter over in an unoccupied cabin on the Clinch. Although the territory was rife with enough game to feed his family, he vowed to make for Kentucky again one day soon. The relocation did not soothe his soul. The loss of his son haunted his dreams.

One night in the spring of 1774 he rode off alone for the Powell Valley. When he arrived at James's gravesite he found sign that wolves had been burrowing among the logs that covered the shallow pit. He pushed aside the lattice of timber and began digging with a hand spike. He breathed a sigh of relief when he found the bodies undisturbed. He slit the woolen sheathing and gazed at the mangled face of his boy. It was so disfigured that he later confessed he would not have been able to tell James from Henry Russell had it not been for his son's fairer hair. His thoughts turned to their cold nights alone on the hunt, when he had wrapped his arms around the little boy to share his own body heat.

Boone removed the tattered sheath, separated the bodies, and covered each with a saddle blanket. He then laid them back down beside each other. He was repositioning the logs atop the tomb when a howling winter storm rolled over the mountains. He put the last piece of wood in place as the skies opened. Cold rain mixed with the tears streaming down his cheeks.

PART III

THE SETTLERS

I think the most important object which can be proposed with such force is the extermination of those hostile tribes of Indians who live between the Ohio and the Illinois.

—Thomas Jefferson

19

A WHITE INVASION

In the aftermath of the killings of young Boone and Russell, reports of the uptick in Indian raids across the Ohio Country began to trickle east. Scores of white hunters, traders, and homesteaders who had taken the Treaties of Hard Labor and Fort Stanwix as settled law found themselves facing Indian intransigence across the territory from roving bands of Shawnee, Delaware, Mingoes, and Cherokee.

In the past, it had not been all that unusual to witness long hunters palavering with Native Americans over pipes of kinnikinnick. Now, wherever white and red men came into contact, writes the historian John Jacobs, "no questions were asked on either side but from the muzzles of their rifles." Among the westering settlers, this "whirlwind of blood and carnage" evinced its greatest fear in the revived idea that the Shawnee and Cherokee, ancestral enemies, would join forces to form a united front against the colonials.

The personification of this nightmare was the rumor that Boone's old Shawnee tormenter Captain Will Emery had successfully recruited some Cherokee to join his raiding parties. Throughout the late winter and spring of 1774, reports of Captain Will sightings took on a spectral nature: one day his band was burning cabins in the vicinity of Fort Pitt, the next they were attacking bargemen on the banks of the Mississippi over six hundred miles away. A feeling set in that if the hostiles had such ghostly presences as Captain Will in their host, what hope for the Anglo-Americans? Cooler minds, however, recognized that renegade "bandits" like Captain Will were merely symptoms of a greater fever.

Not all Native Americans had taken to the warpath, however, as even hardened warriors such as the Shawnee chief Cornstalk appeared to be torn between fighting the whites and somehow accommodating them. To that end, when he heard that a party of explorers including the soon-to-be legendary frontiersman Simon Kenton were traveling through his territory, he invited them to parley. Kenton's assemblage had already lost a man to Indian attack near the Elk River, and he asked Cornstalk why so many of his people had risen. The chief merely pointed to a surveyor's mark on a nearby tree. It was, he said, one of hundreds that had been carved into the Ohio Country's primeval forests. Cornstalk's silent gesture was as eloquent as any words.

Despite the winds of war swirling from the west, Daniel Boone spent the final months of the winter of 1774 more determined than ever to re-enter Kentucky at the head of a settler's train. He had little idea that the territory of his romantic obsession—the lands of rolling meadows and thick forests teeming with deer, of countless waterways bursting with beaver, of myriad salt licks attracting buffalo herds as far as the eye could see—was at the very moment being measured for modernity by a small army of surveyors and mapmakers. Nor could he intuit that their presence would instigate a horrific conflict that would induce even the more moderate Indians to paint their faces.

It was easy enough for the Iroquois who traveled to Fort Stanwix to sign over to the British the fabled lands south of the Ohio River. The members of the confederacy from the far north, after all, did not live there or even hunt there any longer. To a few sympathetic whites, it may have seemed as if the treaty terms were the equivalent of a bank foreclosing on a property its inhabitants were in the midst of paying for with blood and treasure. But for the Shawnee and their indigenous neighbors, the betrayal went deeper.

The Eastern Woodlands Indians did not measure the worth of their lands in the number of council houses or wickiups or cornfields, or even in the depth and breadth of the rivers and mountain meadows. Their heritage and their home were entwined in something more mystical. It was the sun and the moon and the stars above and the earth and forest below. It was the myriad four-legged creatures with whom the Great Spirit had gifted them in order to feed their families. The land was a spiritual entity that transposed mere physical *presence*.

But now whites in the employ of "landjobbers" had crossed the Appalachians and commenced a virtual infestation, measuring and valuing Native American territory merely for the acreage to be plowed under and fenced in. To the whites, soil was for growing, not worshipping. In a letter to his fellow speculator George Washington, the Virginia militia colonel and surveyor William Preston was succinct in his breakdown of what was universally referred to as the "Indian problem."

"It is say'd the [Indians] claim the Land to the Westward . . . between the Cumberland Mountain and the Ohio [River]," Preston wrote. "If so, and our Government gives it up, we lose all the Most Valluable [*sic*] part of the Country. The Northern Indians Sold that Land to the English [and] at that Time neither the Cherrokees [*sic*] nor Others laid no claim to that Land & how they come to do it now I cannot imagine."

Preston went so far as to circulate a petition calling for a volunteer army of Virginians to drive "this useless people" from the backcountry by plundering their towns and burning their farm fields. He was ready to lay waste to Indian presence all the way to the Mississippi if necessary. Preston's may have been one of the more bloodthirsty voices of the movement—many blamed him for the Shawnee predilection of killing Virginians but sparing Pennsylvanians—but his was far from a lonely lust for Indian land. His compeers included not only private explorers and investors like Simon Kenton and the plethora of Tidewater statesmen, but a large company under the command of the French and Indian War veteran Captain Thomas Bullitt. It was Bullitt whom Governor Dunmore had secretly charged with laying out land parcels as far west as the Falls of the Ohio for settlement by Bullitt's fellow veteran officers as payment for their combat service.

Near simultaneous to Bullitt's expedition into the interior, the young Virginia polymath George Rogers Clark was leading a company of settlers to the confluence of the Ohio and Little Kanawha Rivers in what is today northwestern West Virginia. There Clark paused, awaiting another party of Virginians to join him before moving down the Ohio to survey and carve a new community out of western Kentucky.

Clark was the second oldest of nine children born to parents of Anglo-Scots ancestry who had originally established a prosperous plantation on Virginia's Rappahannock River. Three years before Clark's birth in 1752, his father, John, and mother, the former Ann Rogers, had moved west from the Tidewater Region to a 410-acre farm in the shadow of the Blue Ridge, some two miles from present-day Charlottesville. Their neighbors included Peter and Jane Jefferson, whose oldest son Thomas was nine years George Rogers Clark's senior. In 1749 John Clark and Peter Jefferson had joined a group of speculators who formed the Loyal Land Company, a consortium that laid claim to 800,000 acres across parts of Virginia and what are now West Virginia and Kentucky. It was on a swath of this territory where Clark planned to build a new community.

While camped along the confluence of the Ohio and the Little Kanawha, Clark listened to numerous reports of Indian unrest from settlers and Ohio River bargemen abandoning the frontier to seek safety in the East. Some were heading to Fort Pitt, where they hoped to ride out the storm they sensed coming. Others told Clark that the territory could never be tamed, and they intended to recross the Alleghenies for good. Clark was flabbergasted. He was also challenged.

Unlike the scions of most land-hungry immigrants, Clark had been raised on the idea of the frontier as more than just a measurable tract of territory. In a touch of irony that would have been lost on most whites, much like Captain Will Emery he viewed the great American interior as a potent myth, an abstract state of mind, and an aspiration rolled into a single concept that symbolized American freedom: freedom from Great Britain, freedom from the Indians. Unlike Captain Will, however, Clark hated North America's indigenous peoples, and the race-based brutality so crucial to the "conquest" of this land was for him merely a foundational sidebar to national expansion. By the time of the twenty-one-year-old Clark's departure for Kentucky in 1774 he had also been appointed a captain in the Virginia militia. Although his original intent was to settle Loyal Land Company parcels west of the Appalachians, he warned his followers that if the rumors of a coming Indian war proved accurate, he was prepared to rapidly transform the enterprise into a military expedition.

On a more cynical note, as Clark bided time in his Ohio River camp, it undoubtedly occurred to him that any defeatist talk of retreat from the "aborigines" could drive down the value of his Kentucky holdings. The result of his passion for an America unbound was a fit of either boldness or madness, for he now entertained the notion of leading a company of ninety men downriver to attack the main Shawnee town of Chillicothe on the Scioto. Luckily for the combustible Virginian, the more experienced Pennsylvania militia officer Michael Cresap talked him out of the confrontation.

Cresap was a wizened frontiersman who operated a trading post on the Monongahela not far from Fort Pitt. A decade older than Clark, Cresap explained to the young Virginian that even if his raid was successful—an outcome Cresap very much doubted—the all-out war it would undoubtedly spark would leave Clark vulnerable to recriminations from William Johnson's Department of Indian Affairs. Even as Clark was contemplating his raid, Cresap told him that Johnson and a Crown delegation were attempting to reach an accord with the Shawnee similar to their pact with the Iroquois. Should Clark attack Chillicothe unprovoked, the British authorities might even cancel the deed to his Kentucky tracts.

Cresap himself was in the process of putting together an expedition into Kentucky to settle land parcels he had purchased. He suggested to Clark that they combine their operations but, for the time being, retreat some one hundred miles back up the Ohio to the small community of Zanesburg. There, in the town that would eventually grow into present-day Wheeling, West Virginia, they could await word from the Indian agent Johnson before deciding on their next course of action. When they reached the hamlet, they found it overflowing with refugees fleeing war parties.

By late April 1774, with aggrieved settlers still pouring into Zanes-burg, it was clear that negotiations with the Ohio Country tribes were at an impasse. Though the Delaware seemed pliable, the Shawnee had no intention of abiding by the Treaty of Fort Stanwix or forging a separate peace. After ascertaining as much from the authorities at Fort Pitt, Clark and Cresap called a joint council of the leading men in their companies. They shared the news that Fort Pitt's commander had issued a procla-mation giving the local militia commanders wide latitude to protect the region's white settlements. Clark and Cresap took that hazy notion a step further, issuing a declaration of war against the Shawnee—which, it should be noted, carried no official governmental weight.

In the end, it was probably just as well for the majority of Clark's and Cresap's followers that the two eventually abandoned the notion of pro-ceeding into Kentucky, and instead led an out-migration even farther up-river to Cresap's trading post. There were others, however, who had no intention of walking away.

20

LORD DUNMORE'S WAR

Great blood-drenched events often turn on small hinges. In the darker annals of human history there have been no dearth of seemingly insignificant acts that, in retrospect, constituted a flash point igniting an inferno: a Spartan queen abducted by a lovesick Trojan; a clique of Roman senators bringing their conspiracy to a head on the Ides of March; an anonymous Mongol leather craftsman on the Asian steppes inventing a saddle and stirrup that allowed his descendants to gallop from the arid savannah and establish the largest contiguous empire in the history of the world.

By 1774, both the colonists and the indigenous peoples of North America's Eastern Woodlands viewed their coming clash as inevitable if not epochal. It only awaited a spark. That was lit on the final day of April in an obscure backwoods tavern at the mouth of an even more isolated stream, a small tributary known as Yellow Creek, which empties into the Ohio River about forty miles west of Pittsburgh.

Relations between the modest white community of hunters and traders at the mouth of Yellow Creek and the nearby Seneca and Cayuga villages had for months been fraught with ominous undercurrents. The Indians in the vicinity were ethnologically and linguistically a subset of the Iroquois

Confederacy. But since being driven into Ohio from their ancestral lands nearer to New York's Finger Lakes decades earlier, the small tribe of some six hundred had allied themselves both politically and militarily with the larger Algonquian-speaking Shawnee. Known as "Mingoes" to most Anglo-Americans—a corruption of the Eastern Algonquian word *mingwe*, which describes Iroquois language groups in general—they had fought alongside Louis XV's fusiliers during the French and Indian War. Since then, however, they had established a provisional détente with the Anglo-American settlement on Yellow Creek.

The Mingoes' most renowned orator and warrior, Tachnechdorus, was referred to variously by whites as Logan Elrod, James Logan, and Captain John Logan. But it was the single, Anglicized name of Logan by which he was best known throughout the settlements. Logan was not technically a chief. Given the tiny size of the Mingo band, the tribe was probably closer in custom and tradition than even their Indian neighbors to the egalitarian, hunter-gatherer societies that had arisen eleven thousand years earlier in the forests and grasslands of East Africa. In that sense, it is more accurate to describe Logan as the unofficial spokesman for the string of villages that constituted the Mingoes' Yellow Creek community.

By the spring of 1774, most of the European Americans in and around Yellow Creek had fled the area for the walls of Fort Pitt. A tavern owner named Joshua Baker, however, was reluctant to leave, perhaps believing that his rapport with the Mingoes who frequented his establishment would ensure his safety. On April 30, some two dozen vigilantes who had split off from the Clark and Cresap expeditions rode into Yellow Creek. At their head were the Virginian brothers Daniel and Jacob Greathouse. The group hid their horses in a spinney of oaks while Daniel Greathouse induced the tavern keeper Baker to send a runner to Logan's village requesting his presence for a parley. It was a ruse. The Greathouse troop secreted themselves in Baker's storage room. Ironically, Logan was away that very day at an intertribal council making the case for peace with the whites. He even warned his fellow Indians that should they decide to make total war on the settlers, reinforcements numbering "like the trees in the woods" would invade their land.

When word of the tavern keeper's request reached Logan's village, his younger brother decided to answer the invitation. He was accompanied to Baker's tavern by Logan's wife, Logan's nephew, and Logan's sister Koonay, who was married to a white fur trader. Koonay was visibly pregnant. Upon their arrival, Baker attempted to put them at ease by challenging the men to a shooting match. It was a subtle trick to ensure that the Indians had emptied their muskets. Afterward, he invited them inside and poured several rounds of grog.

Logan's brother was soon drunk and playfully reached over and snatched Baker's hat from his head. The Mingo was admiring the jaunty tilt of the headpiece in a hand mirror when Baker reached beneath the rough planking that served as his bar, hoisted his long rifle, and shot him dead. With this, the Greathouse posse burst from their hiding space and massacred the others. Spilling out the tavern's doors, they also killed a small escort of Mingo braves standing guard over the canoes.

After the slayings the Indian bodies were mutilated, with Jacob Greathouse slicing open Koonay's abdomen, removing her unborn son, and scalping the fetus before impaling the tiny body on a stake.

Within days numerous Mingo and Shawnee war parties were attacking white homesteads and communities up and down the Ohio frontier with unremitting fervor. An enraged Logan, whose name throughout the territory was soon to become synonymous with a death rattle, vowed to take ten scalps for each of his family members who had been murdered.

What heretofore had been a series of isolated skirmishes and raids throughout the Ohio Country was now a conflagration that came to be known as Lord Dunmore's War.

Lord Dunmore's initial reaction to the news from Yellow Creek was paradoxical. With the Northern Indians spreading flame and fury across the upper borderlands, the Virginia royal governor's first instincts were to cast a wary eye toward the Cherokee. To this point, the southern tribes, notwithstanding the likes of the renegade followers of the mixed-blood Captain Will, had limited their attacks to any whites who ventured into what the Cherokee considered their hunting grounds beyond the Kentucky River. With the Shawnee and Mingo alliance threatening to pull in Delaware, Wyandot, and perhaps even more westerly tribes, however, Dunmore sensed he could ill afford to count on the Cherokee's continued forbearance.

In the North, the British Department of Indian Affairs superintendent William Johnson had managed to convince the Iroquois to reject the wampum war belts proffered by their Mingo cousins. This was not a difficult argument to make, as there was no love lost between the Confederacy and the Mingoes' Shawnee allies. To the south, Johnson's counterpart, John Stuart, had to this point also held the Cherokee in check. But there were rumors that the enraged Logan was now prowling the Cherokee towns hoping to prod them into an ad hoc confederation. As a precaution, Dunmore sent word to Daniel Boone's old patron Capt. William Russell to begin constructing blockhouses up and down the Clinch River and Powell Valley settlements. The governor then announced and circulated a decree declaring a state of war with the Shawnee and Mingoes. Unlike George Rogers Clark's declaration, this one carried the weight of the Crown. On June 10, 1774, nearly three thousand Virginians found themselves in service to the realm. They were following a long tradition.

In the nearly five hundred years since King Henry II issued his Assize of Arms in 1181, the citizens of England and, later, Great Britain had for the most part assumed a communal responsibility for military defense. This practice had become customary in Crown colonies and holdings around the globe. Within two decades of the landings at Jamestown, for instance, the fledgling Virginia legislature passed laws requiring all able-bodied freemen between the ages of seventeen and sixty to own weapons and be ready to serve in the dominion's militia.

This protective system had inherent deficiencies. Colonial governors of agrarian communities were loath to press farmers into service during the planting and reaping seasons. And, in reality, Henry II's theoretical "defense of King and Country" often stopped at an insular province's borders. But these handicaps were balanced by the relative affordability of a nonprofessional army as well as the combat readiness of citizen-soldiers who had been called to arms on multiple occasions. Many Virginians now primed to fight the Shawnee and Mingoes, for instance, had also borne arms during the Cherokee wars.

Though it was true that the American colonists expected their Crown representatives to conscript able-bodied men to defend their lives and property against Indian threats, Dunmore was not free from ulterior motives in activating the militia. The governor, presiding over the largest and wealthiest colony, had leveraged his position to become one of the major land speculators in the Ohio Country. As such, it was in his financial interest to crush any Native American uprising before influential officials sympathetic to the Indian cause, like William Johnson, convinced the authorities in London that the indigenous peoples were in fact being treated unfairly.

Moreover, Dunmore was not unmindful of the escalating rebel crisis unfolding in Massachusetts. Earlier that spring he had even dissolved the House of Burgesses when its representatives expressed what he considered an untoward solidarity with the firebrand New Englanders. The British blockade of Boston Harbor in retaliation for the Boston Tea Party had gone into effect only ten days before the governor's call to arms.

Dunmore calculated that a popular and winnable war against the Ohio Indians would not only enhance his own personal and political reputation, but also strengthen ties to Mother England among any Virginians inclined to sympathize with America's newly minted and restless Continental Congress. Lastly, for some time Dunmore had been embroiled in a jurisdictional dispute with his Pennsylvania counterpart John Penn, William's grandson, over control of Fort Pitt and the surrounding countryside. If the adage coined in Dunmore's ancestral Scottish Highlands was correct, and possession was indeed nine-tenths of the law, a force of Virginians using Pittsburgh as a base to conduct military operations would effectively stifle any boundary debates.

Meanwhile, out in the western settlements, Capt. Russell was not only throwing up blockhouses and stockades but also positioning scouts along the Warrior's Path as trip wires against Cherokee incursions. Boone volunteered as one of the riders, but Russell needed him elsewhere. Earlier that year the skim ice encrusting the sandy banks of the Ohio River had barely melted before several surveying parties totaling some sixty-odd men in the employ of Lord Dunmore had journeyed downstream to chart and map the Kentucky wilderness. Now, with the governor's declaration of war, they needed to be warned. Russell tapped Boone for the task.

Boone asked a German-born Virginian named Michael Stoner to accompany him. Stoner was known for his forest craft, and Capt. Russell, writing to William Preston, considered them "two of the best hands I could think of." If the surveyors were still alive, Russell added, "it is indisputable but Boone [will] find them." In late June the duo plunged into the wilderness for the dangerous dash from the Clinch River Valley into northwestern Kentucky. Though an experienced woodsman and crack shot himself, Stoner stuck like a limpet to Boone as they moved at a febrile pace. Argus-eyed, the two avoided all Indian trails during the day, and at night if they could not find a cave to hide the light of a cookfire, they made a cold camp and supped on dry jerky and parched corn, often seated back-to-back to guard against ambush.

By the time Boone and Stoner bushwhacked a path to the mouth of the Kentucky River, the first team under the command of the surveyor John Floyd had already fled back over the Appalachians—"well drove in by the Indians," in Boone's report. The two continued on as far as the Falls of the Ohio in search of the others only to discover that all the remaining mappers had also retreated east. Despite its ineffectual denouement, the story of Boone's and Stoner's sixty-one-day journey across nearly eight hundred miles of wild and dangerous country spread like kudzu. Upon their return, word of their feat was reported by newspapers throughout the colonies and also caught the attention of several prominent Virginia militia officers, who recognized in Boone "a very popular Officer where he is known."

When Boone finally arrived back at the Clinch River settlements in late August he was feted as a hero—for what, he could not quite understand. Like others of his trim, he enlisted in the ranks of Virginia's militia, the bulk of which had already set off for the Ohio Country in two columns. The first, eleven hundred men under the command of Colonel Andrew Lewis, planned to traverse the Alleghenies via the New, Greenbrier, and Kanawha River Valleys and penetrate to the mouth of the latter. There, opposite southeastern Ohio in what is today West Virginia, Col. Lewis had been ordered to establish a camp on a triangular spit of land known as Point Pleasant. He was to await orders from Lord Dunmore, who would lead a second prong of about seventeen hundred troops from Fort Pitt.

Boone and a small company of recruits rode out to catch up to Col. Lewis but were overtaken by a rider carrying a message from Capt. Russell instructing them to turn back. Hostiles, taking advantage of the large body of militiamen seemingly abandoning the area to march north, had stepped up their attacks along both the Clinch and Powell Rivers as well as in the Holston Valley. Russell and the settlers needed Boone's unruffled presence, particularly now that it had been confirmed that the Mingo warrior Logan was leading raids across the territory.

Logan erroneously blamed the trader Michael Cresap—and not the Greathouse brothers—for the murders of his wife and family members, and over the next six weeks scores of men, women, and children along the Virginia borderlands were killed and kidnapped. Logan had taken to leaving as a sort of calling card a painted war club on the ground next to his mutilated victims. That some of these talismans were of Cherokee design stoked fears that the Mingo had indeed managed to recruit from the southern tribes. Aside from a few hot-blooded renegades, however, such was not the case.

To modern sensibilities it is difficult to absorb the savageries practiced by both sides of the conflict: the crawling and bawling white toddler found scalped amid the scorched remains of his parents, who had been burned alive; the captured Indians hung from trees with their severed penises jammed into slit throats. North America's contested borders were at the time a place where rough justice from both antagonists sated a barely repressed communal id. In one instance a company of mounted militiamen caught up to a trio of Shawnee who had murdered a septuagenarian homesteader. In the skirmish that ensued the horsemen were certain that they had fatally wounded one of the attackers and suspected that his confederates had concealed his body in a fifty-foot sinkhole. The posse abandoned its chase in order to fashion a rope ladder to descend into the pit for the sole purpose of claiming the corpse's scalp. Scavenging the topknot of one dead Indian was more important than running down two still alive.

Contemporaneous militia documents indicate that Boone—by this time commissioned as a captain and working as both a scout along the backcountry's serrated ridgelines as well as helping to man forts and blockhouses—led several rescue and retaliatory missions during this period. They do not record the outcomes of his pursuits.

Meanwhile, as the butcher's bill escalated along the precincts of western Virginia and northeastern Tennessee, Lord Dunmore pushed his army over five hundred miles to Fort Pitt—which he promptly renamed Fort Dunmore. From there he dispatched a messenger to Col. Lewis instructing him to rendezvous at the mouth of the Scioto. The plan was to march their combined force on Chillicothe and the other Shawnee towns along the river. As Lewis was still preparing to cross the Ohio, however, a mile-long line of seven hundred Shawnee and Mingo braves was silently uncoiling like a snake through the dense forest to his rear. At the column's head was the formerly reluctant warrior Cornstalk.

"I have with great trouble and pains prevailed on the foolish people amongst us to sit still and do no harm until we see whether it is the intention of the white people in general to fall on us," Cornstalk had told a British official not long after he had shown Simon Kenton the surveyor's mark blazed into the tree. But now, with his scouts tracking two armies about to converge on his homeland, he had his answer.

Cornstalk had accepted the black-wampum war belt, and as a sign of the importance of the campaign, had asked several medicine men to accompany his expedition. The night before he sprang his trap, he watched silently as his hunters sliced out the hearts of a dozen deer for examination by the holy men. They found the signs propitious.

21

LOGAN'S LAMENT

What came to be known as the Battle of Point Pleasant raged from dawn to dusk on October 10, 1774. At first the fight followed the contours of a typical woodlands Indian attack. The Shawnee, who had crossed the Ohio the night before, fell on two Virginians who had strayed from the camp for a sunrise hunt. The musket fire was heard by all. Within moments a regimental drum was beating the militiamen to arms. Anticipating a light raiding party, perhaps a few braves hoping to cull a beeve or two from the small herd the militiamen had driven before them during their march from Virginia, Col. Andrew Lewis formed up two columns of 150 men apiece. He dispatched them upriver, in parallel lines, toward the direction of the rifle reports. Cornstalk and his warriors were waiting.

At the head of one column, Col. Lewis's brother Charles Lewis, also a colonel, was one of the first to hear the *thwop* of a musket ball. In fact, he heard it before he felt it. For when he looked down he realized the projectile had pierced his tunic, his hunting shirt, and finally his flesh. The spider's web of blood just below his heart expanded rapidly. With their commander mortally wounded and a virtual hailstorm of bullets blowing sideways from the surrounding forest, the Virginians under Col. Lewis panicked and fled, carrying the dying officer with them. Their fear was infectious; in a moment the militiamen of the second column joined them in the race back to camp. The Shawnee were not far behind.

Col. Andrew Lewis did not have the time to tend to his brother, who was deposited before the company's headquarters tent. Beyond the crumpled body, Col. Lewis beheld a frightening sight. Hundreds of painted warriors were descending from a small ridgeline into his riverside camp. The air was thick with their piercing war cries.

The officer had his drummer beat a retreat. The Virginians fell back about half a mile, where Col. Lewis organized them into an attack line. He ordered a charge. Col. Lewis was an experienced Indian fighter. He expected the outnumbered Shawnee to fall back against the onslaught of over one thousand men. What he did not expect was the slow and orderly fashion in which the Indians withdrew, ducking from tree to tree to reload, take careful aim, and fire. More surprising was what happened when the warriors reached the crest of the ridge. Under Cornstalk's direction, they formed a crescent-shaped defensive line a mile long, and dug in.

By midday the Shawnee had beaten back several frontal attacks. Both sides were exhausted. The fighting paused, and the battle devolved into what was known as a "blackguarding" contest. The combatants from both lines engaging in a foul-mouthed repartee over the bodies of the dead and dying that lay between them—"Sons of bitches!" "Dog fucker!" "White bastards!" "We will eat your hearts!"

Even the Indians whom Cornstalk had left on the north bank of the Ohio to cut off escaping stragglers joined in, urging their fellow Shawnee to "drive the white dogs in [to us]."

Finally, by late afternoon, Cornstalk took a calculated risk. Despite the Virginians' superiority in numbers, he ordered a second advance. He later admitted that he recognized his only hope of fending off Lord Dunmore's combined army was to wipe out the rump force under Col. Lewis at Point Pleasant. Even then, he said, he would need the help of other Indians rushing to join his side once word spread of his victory along the banks of the Ohio. Now, here, was his last chance.

As the sun's fading rays penetrated the sulfur-fused gloaming, polished flintlocks and flashing tomahawks glinted. Men died with their throats cut, their skulls caved in, their hearts pierced by steel and bone. The hand-to-hand fighting ceased only when a flanking maneuver by one of Col. Lewis's company commanders shattered the Indian line. With that, Cornstalk signaled his braves to break off the assault. As the skies darkened the survivors slipped back across the Ohio River, leaving the Virginians to count their dead.

Col. Andrew Lewis recorded 75 militiamen, his brother included, killed during the engagement. Another 140 or so were wounded. The next morning some 33 Native American bodies were collected from the battle-field. Their corpses were promptly scalped. How many of their dead and dying the Indians may have carried away or rolled into the river was never established.* Although colonial losses certainly outnumbered Indian casualties, the battle was a major defeat for the Shawnee and Mingoes, and both sides recognized it.

Back across the Ohio, there were many, including the revered Shawnee warrior Blue Jacket, who argued for another attack on the white camp before they recovered from the surprise and ferocity of the first.† But Cornstalk knew that his people, even with Mingo allies, could not stand against the combined might of the two Virginian forces. Their only chance had been a swift victory at Point Pleasant, which would have drawn

---

* Among the Shawnee casualties was one of Cornstalk's top lieutenants, the Kispoko Shawnee Puckeshinwa. Grievously wounded and ferried back across the Ohio before he died, Puckeshinwa extracted from his sons a promise to never stop battling the white invaders. Puckeshinwa's six-year-old son, Tecumseh, destined to become a fabled warrior-chief, was to hold fast to the vow he made to his father.

† Seventeen years later, at what became known as the Battle of the Wabash, the still-militant Blue Jacket was one of the principal war chiefs who inflicted on the United States the worst defeat the country would suffer at Indian hands when a combined intertribal force of over 1,000 Indians killed 832 American troops and wounded another 264.

the other tribes to their cause. Fearing the annihilation of Chillicothe on the Scioto's women and children, Cornstalk ended the discussion by burying his tomahawk into the center post of the council house. "I will make peace," he said, and immediately sent runners to Dunmore's camp requesting a parley.

It was not long before a theory began to circulate that the Battle of Point Pleasant was in fact the first official engagement of the American Revolution. The thesis put forward placed Lord Dunmore, anticipating the American rebellion, secretly in league with the Indians. The conspirators charged that he never intended to rendezvous with Col. Lewis's force, which he supposed would be annihilated, leaving Virginia's militia too enervated to join the other twelve colonies in revolution. Cornstalk would have been manifestly insulted by such a hypothesis.

The engagement at Point Pleasant may indeed have been a battle for American independence—American Indian independence. Cornstalk was a remarkable figure, but rather than playing the role of Benedict Arnold conspiring with the British against the Americans, he is more easily compared to George Washington. Given the mores of the era, Washington never would have understood the correlation. But the fight Cornstalk waged at Point Pleasant was, from an Indian viewpoint, not all that much different from the skirmish that would occur a year later at North Bridge in Concord, Massachusetts. Only the outcomes differed. It was with a heavy heart that, nine days later, Cornstalk led a contingent of Indian warriors into Lord Dunmore's camp to sign what came to be known as the Treaty of Camp Charlotte.

According to the terms, the Shawnee and their allies agreed to cede to the Anglo-Americans all lands south and east of the Ohio River—present-day Kentucky and West Virginia. They would also cease their raids on river traffic. In exchange they were promised the retention of all territory north of the watercourse. Although several Mingoes were signatories to the pact, Logan—still mistakenly holding Michael Cresap accountable for the Yellow Creek murders—refused to attend the peace council. His legendary oratorical skills were nonetheless on display when one of his emissaries read aloud a message that has come down through history as "Logan's Lament":

I appeal to any white man to say, if ever he entered Logan's cabin hungry, and he gave him not meat; if ever he came cold and naked, and he clothed him not.

During the course of the last long and bloody war, Logan remained idle in his cabin, an advocate for peace. Such was my love for the whites, that my countrymen pointed as they passed, and said, Logan is the friend of white men. I had even thought to have lived with you, but for the injuries of one man. Col. Cresap, the last spring, in cold blood, and unprovoked, murdered all the relations of Logan, not sparing even my women and children. There runs not a drop of my blood in the veins of any living creature. This called on me for revenge. I have sought it: I have killed many: I have fully glutted my vengeance.

For my country, I rejoice at the beams of peace. But do not harbor a thought that mine is the joy of fear. Logan never felt fear. He will not turn on his heel to save his life.

Who is there to mourn for Logan? Not one.

22

BOONE'S TRACE

It was unusually warm for a March morning when Daniel Boone arrived on the south bank of the Watauga River in Tennessee's Holston Valley in 1775. He was there to witness the latest in a series of schemes designed to carve a bit more land away from North America's indigenous peoples. This time the vessel for the transfer of territory was a corporation named the Transylvania Company, and its victims were, again, the Cherokee.

The major figure behind what came to be known as the Transylvania Purchase was the North Carolina lawyer and superior-court justice Richard Henderson. Over the previous year, with Lord Dunmore's War still raging, Henderson and a consortium of prominent associates had hatched yet another plan to establish a separate colony to the west of Virginia. Henderson viewed the Appalachians as a dam holding back a sea of land-hungry farmers, and he wanted the sluice gates opened. That the Royal Proclamation of 1763 barring white settlement on the far side of the mountain chain was nominally still in effect did not faze him or his fellow land speculators. Nor did the subsequent treaties signed at Hard Labor and Fort Stanwix or even the most recent Camp Charlotte accord— all in effect ceding to the Americans what was essentially the same territory south of the Ohio River.

Henderson had argued cases before Boone's father when old Squire sat on the Rowan County Municipal Court, and was familiar with his son Daniel's far-flung peregrinations. Thus, when Boone had been released from militia service four months earlier, Henderson had a job waiting. As the "Wide Mouth" was a known entity among the southern tribes, the Transylvania consortium hired him to circulate among the Cherokee towns to convince their most influential elders to attend a conference at Sycamore Shoals on the Watauga. There, at the foot of Holston Mountain among the eponymous trees that lent the river's white water its name, Henderson had arranged for the delivery of six wagonloads of smoothbore rifles, powder and shot, corn, flour, salt, calico shirts, ribbons, blankets, bearskins, silver trinkets, and, most telling, barrels of rum.

By the time the twelve hundred or so Cherokee began trickling into the site, the train of trade goods was propitiously displayed in tents where all could inspect it. Although historians differ as to the worth of Henderson's haul, the general consensus is that it was equal to anywhere from £2,000 to £10,000—roughly between $420,000 and $1.6 million in today's dollars.

The sight of such a bounty was too tempting for many of the younger Cherokee braves, who comprised about half of all the Indian men, women, and children in attendance. They successfully pressured their three senior chiefs—known by their Anglicized names Stalking Turkey, the Raven, and Little Carpenter—to capitulate to what came to be known as the "Great Grant." In exchange for the seeming treasure on display, the trio of Cherokee leaders—dressed formally for the occasion in bright red and blue matchcoats over ruffle-sleeved shirts—signed over to the Transylvania Company a tract of 18 million acres—28,000 square miles—bounded by the Cumberland River in the south, Cumberland Mountain to the east, and the Kentucky River on the north. In other words, a goodly portion of what is the modern-day state of Kentucky.

As the whites celebrated by passing jugs of corn whiskey, Little Carpenter's son, known to the whites as Dragging Canoe, stepped forward

THE TRANSYLVANIA PURCHASE

OHIO

ILLINOIS

INDIANA

Planned Settlement
by the Colony of Virginia
for Retired Soldiers
and Militiamen

TRANSYLVANIA PURCHASE OF 1775

VIRGINIA

TENNESSEE   0   MILES   60

0   KM   60

Obliterating the boundary lines set by both the Treaty of Hard Labor and the Fort Stanwix Treaty, in 1775 the North Carolina Superior Court Justice Richard Henderson and a consortium of prominent fellow land speculators formed the Transylvania Company to negotiate their own purchase of western lands from the Cherokee Nation. Their plan was to establish a separate colony to the west of Virginia in defiance of the colonial authorities who denounced the "Transylvania Purchase" as illegal. Similarly, a coalition of Eastern Woodland tribes, led by the Shawnee, vowed to make war on any whites attempting to settle what they considered their hunting grounds.

to object. Unlike his elders, Dragging Canoe was still keen to fight. He argued, quite sensibly, that the land the Cherokee had just deeded to the whites was not even theirs to sell. Even if it had been, he told his father, the newcomers would not stop there. Citing the disintegration of the once-proud Delaware in Pennsylvania, he also warned that the Americans would soon force their way into Tennessee, reducing the Cherokee Nation to begging for scraps like the fawning Catawba.

Little Carpenter, a small and wizened elder, was not moved by his son's protests. He had acquired his sobriquet for his purported ability to find diplomatic common ground between tribal factions and the whites, much like a carpenter notching wooden joints using a tongue-and-groove

technique. He judged his actions as best for his people. Dragging Canoe
was livid at his father's intransigence, and before he rode off he sneeringly
told Henderson and Boone that they would come to rue their purchase of
"the bloody ground," and warned them that it would be "dark and difficult to settle." Dragging Canoe's premonition is undoubtedly the source
of the too-common mistranslation of Kanta-ke as "the dark and bloody
ground."

Before the Treaty of Sycamore Shoals was even signed by all parties
on March 17, Henderson had promised Boone two thousand acres of
choice Kentucky bottomland in exchange for blazing an artery from the
Holston Valley, through the Cumberland Gap, and into the protocolony's
Bluegrass Region. Thus did the obscure former farmer and long hunter
from the outskirts of what was then considered civilization further etch
his name into the annals of American history. The "Boone Trace," as the
trail was first labeled, was destined to be trod over the coming decades
by some three hundred thousand immigrants who came to know it as the
"Wilderness Road."

Alas for Henderson and his cohort, their land grab was snakebit from
the start. One month earlier, North Carolina's colonial governor, Josiah
Martin, had caught wind of the scheme and issued a decree condemning
the purchase as contravening the terms of the Royal Proclamation of 1763.
Calling the sale the work of "land Pyrates," Martin declared the Transylvania transaction "null and void" and threatened the company's partners
with jail. Henderson ignored him.

Virginia's governor, Dunmore, added his own protest, labeling Henderson's "pretended purchase" unethical along the same grounds as
North Carolina's Martin.* Dunmore also demanded that Henderson and

---

* Six days after Gov. Dunmore's proclamation—and twenty-three days before Redcoats under the
command of the Massachusetts royal governor Thomas Gage marched on the colonial armory at Concord, Massachusetts—a committee of Virginia legislators, including Thomas Jefferson and Patrick
Henry, convened to investigate the parameters of King George III's authority in granting land. Its first
recommendation was to forbear the sale of any lands west of the mountains by and to anyone. Neither
Jefferson nor Henry admitted to being secret land speculators.

all Anglo-Americans associated with the Sycamore Shoals transaction desist from entering the "Cantucky" territory under penalty of fines and im-
prisonment. With no apparent irony, Dunmore added that the Henderson
deal had illegally appropriated territory that by royal land grant belonged
to Virginia. He was referring of course to previous surveys by the likes of
John Floyd and Capt. Thomas Bullitt, and appeared to be arguing to the
Transylvania Company that you cannot steal what the Crown has already
stolen.

In the face of these threats, Henderson and his partners saw but one
recourse—to settle the Kentucky wilderness as rapidly as possible in
order to make their projected colony a fait accompli. The Cherokee had
barely packed up their payment when Henderson took out newspaper
ads declaring that parcels of land in his new Transylvania would be sold
in five-hundred-acre tracts at twenty shillings per hundred acres—about
$175 today—to any American willing to submit to his corporation's
authority and raise a crop of corn in Kentucky within the next twelve
months.

The initial reaction appeared encouraging. A Virginia militia colonel
monitoring Henderson's machinations reported to Lord Dunmore that
hundreds if not thousands of Virginians and North Carolinians were
preparing to cross the mountains. Short of mustering troops, the officer
advised the governor, there was little that he could do to stop them—not
least because he believed that many of the western sojourners were militia
members themselves.

But Dunmore's agent was far too optimistic about the number of
pioneers heading west, which in fact totaled a few hundred at best.
Yet despite the low turnout, between the westward expansion and the
scent of revolution in the air, it was an electrifying epoch along the
southern borderlands. The Boone biographer Draper encapsulated the
sense of potential and promise the Transylvania Company was offering in the romantic prose of the era: "The fearless frontier men," he
wrote, "heeded not the royal fulminations of Martin and Dunmore, and

probably regarded them only as the expiring throes of tyranny in the New World."

Perhaps.

In the vanguard of Draper's "fearless frontier men" was Daniel Boone and his party of some thirty woodcutters. In return for their services the men had been promised two-acre garden plots in Transylvania's capital city (wherever that might be) as well as wages enough—ten pounds sterling—to purchase one of the larger tracts outside of the projected town. Among the work gang were Squire Boone and a few Yadkin men; a score of hardies from the Clinch River Valley, including Boone's old expedition partner Michael Stoner; and a contingent of North Carolinians from the state's southwestern Rutherford County. There were also two women traveling with the outfit as cooks and camp keepers—Boone's eldest daughter, Susannah, and a slave owned by an officious Virginian named Richard Callaway.

Henderson had hired Callaway, the youngest son in a family of wealthy Shenandoah Valley landowners, to wrangle the teamsters transporting the Indian trade goods to Sycamore Shoals. Callaway, sensing opportunity in the West, signed on with the woodcutters, planning on sending for his wife and fourteen children once he was settled in Kentucky. A large, imposing figure, Callaway's long face—at least judging from a surviving portrait from the era—resembled nothing so much as a melancholy hound's and was hooded, as if by a stage curtain, by a thick mane of silver-streaked black hair, of which he was extraordinarily fond.

Close to twenty years Boone's senior, Callaway had risen to the rank of militia colonel during the French and Indian War and simmered at having to serve under what he considered an unlettered backwoodsman. A fussy and abstemious man, Callaway affected "a quakerish elegance," to borrow Robert Louis Stevenson's phrase, although his stock was pure Southern Baptist. That said, he was the closest thing Boone's outfit had to a gentleman farmer, at least in Callaway's mind, and he fell into that category of easterners who considered men like Boone, with their anarchic wanderings and clan loyalty, little better than the red barbarians from whom they were wresting the country. If you gave the man a grievance, he would hoard it like diamonds. For the moment Callaway banked his fire, though it was evident to most that the budding discord between Callaway and Boone was destined to escalate.

As for the fourteen-year-old Suzy Boone, as she was called, she had only weeks earlier married one of the company's axmen, a twenty-year-old Irish emigrant named Will Hays. Depending on the contemporaneous source, Suzy Boone was either one of the first harlots to make for the Bluegrass Region, or a free-willed protofeminist whose strength of body and mind mirrored that of the men breaking ground into uncharted and dangerous territory. Perhaps both.

A slim woman of medium height and "pretty good looking," according to one of her father's associates, Suzy had met her future husband when the Boone family had forted up with Hays during Lord Dunmore's War. Before emigrating to the colonies, Hays had taken a modicum of schooling in his home country, and Suzy had initially fallen for the Irishman's suave and aristocratic mien. She was further impressed by the way her father had come to rely upon Hays to assist him in penning what passed for his military after-action reports during his defense of the Clinch Valley in Lord Dunmore's War.

Hays in fact did help improve Boone's writing and, in particular, his skill at calculating expenses. But when he asked for Suzy's hand in marriage, the father gently attempted to dissuade the suitor. His daughter, Boone suggested with a diplomat's grace, might have difficulty harnessing her affections to one man. Sure enough, one story the meticulous researcher Lyman Draper managed to uncover had a disconsolate Hays approaching Boone not long after the nuptials to complain about Suzy's "frolicking" ways. Boone, no doubt recalling his own intemperate youth as well as his wife's dalliance with his brother, responded with a shrug. "Didn't I tell you?" he said. "Trot father, trot mother, how could you expect a pacing colt?"

Along their journey west, Boone and company spent cool days and freezing nights fashioning "Boone's Trace." They took their belt axes to saplings, canebrakes, and overhead branches; they hefted dead trees blocking the trail and hewed live ones to bridge streams and the occasional sinkhole. In their wake they left a rough road only just capable of supporting a Conestoga as far as the Cumberland Gap. Upon reaching the notch in the mountain, Boone, riding point, decided that they had neither the manpower nor the tools to make the gap wagon-friendly, much less the rough Kentucky country that lay ahead. It would be another two decades before a wagon's wheels left their first imprint in the gap's soil.

Pausing at the entrance to Kentucky much as he had done six years earlier, Boone announced that their final destination lay 120 miles to the northwest, where a spring-fed stream known as Otter Creek emptied into the Kentucky River. He had scouted the land, just southeast of the current city of Lexington, on his previous rambles through the territory. He knew it to be well stocked with hardwoods for building as well as near the site of two springs. One of the fountainheads, nearly hidden in a holler of sycamore trees, spewed forth clear, sweet water abundant enough to sustain a large community. The other, farther north, contained the brackish salt water so beloved by big game. But hunting was not the priority. Wild animals were too adept to remain in the area where men put up towns. It was the acres of "stamps" that made the salt spring appealing.

Buffalo stamps, or stamping grounds, were coveted by both the land-jobbers and farmers of the era. Located around salt licks that had for centuries attracted untold numbers of the vegetation-destroying herbivores, buffalo stamps at first glance resembled nothing so much as denuded brown moonscapes. But as settlers quickly learned, once the herds were driven off, the tons of manure deposited deep into the earth over the decades converted them into prodigal fields for either farming or grazing. The corollary, of course, was that the stamps also lay at the heart of Indian hunting grounds.

The unrest among the Cherokee followers of Dragging Canoe was

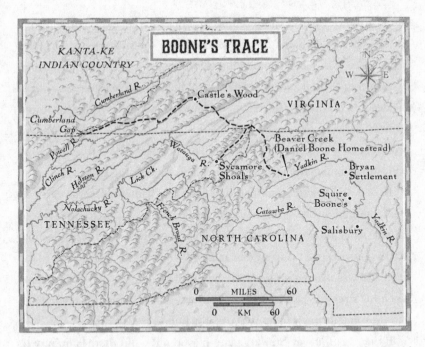

The Transylvania Company's chairman, Richard Henderson, was well aware that Daniel Boone had first traversed the Cumberland Gap in 1769 and had subsequently spent the better part of a year hunting and exploring Kentucky both with fellow long hunters and by himself. In 1775, Henderson hired Boone to lead a company of woodcutters to hack a trail, or "trace," from Sycamore Shoals in northeastern Tennessee—site of where Henderson and his partners had signed the treaty with the Cherokees—and through the rugged Valley and Ridge section of the Appalachians to the Gap and beyond into Kentucky.

no secret to Boone's woodcutting outfit, nor were the sentiments of the Northern Indians still seething over the Camp Charlotte agreement. As such, Boone piloted his axmen on a cautious pace, with he and his brother often acting as flanking scouts through countryside he considered particularly well suited to ambush. Even at this, however, nerves were on edge. The disquiet spiked when a scouting party discovered the bones of a skeleton crammed into the hollow of a great sycamore tree on a ledge overhanging the Rockcastle River.

Boone recognized the moldering hunting shirt shrouding the corpse's bones as that of his brother-in-law John Stewart, vanished half a decade earlier from the beaver camp on the Kentucky River. Although Stewart's rifle was nowhere to be found—Boone's eye for weapons would have pegged the gun's owner immediately—his suspicions were confirmed upon seeing the initials "JS" etched into the decorative brass *bandeau* of the dead man's powder horn. The skeleton's right humerus was fractured midway between the elbow and shoulder, and the telltale discoloration produced by a lead musket ball was still pronounced. Stewart's skull, however, showed no markings from a tomahawk or scalping knife.

Boone deduced that on that long-ago rainy winter's day, Stewart was likely camped on the south bank of the Kentucky waiting for the river to subside when he was set upon by Indians. Though Stewart had somehow lost his gun, despite his wound he managed to elude his attackers, ford the river, and was making for the settlements on the far side of the mountains when his strength gave out. Having no weapon to bring down game, he had presumably nuzzled himself into the hollow tree to die.

If that was the way Stewart's end played out—and there is no way to ever know—it would mark Daniel Boone's brother-in-law as one of the first white men to be killed by Native Americans on the bloody ground over which hung Dragging Canoe's portentous cloud.

23

A NEW WORLD

There were not a few in Daniel Boone's woodcutting party who counted the discovery of John Stewart's desiccated corpse a dark portent. The omen was fulfilled on their seventh day out from the Cumberland Gap, when, thirteen miles from their destination, the company was attacked by Indians just before daybreak. Two men were killed—a Clinch Valley veteran of Lord Dunmore's War named William Twitty, and his slave. The slave, whose name is of course unreported, died instantly. Twitty, shot through both knees, was saved from a scalping by his English bulldog, who seized his assailant by the throat and was tomahawked to death for its loyalty. Twitty was destined to linger for three days. A North Carolinian from Rutherford County, named Felix Walker, was also badly wounded before return fire drove off the Indians.

When the company reorganized, Michael Stoner claimed to recognize the quillwork body tattoos and painted moccasins of their assailants. He told Boone that they were distinct to the Miami tribe, the powerful, Algonquian-speaking people who resided along the Wabash in present-day Indiana. The Miami were certainly aware of the consternation the Camp Charlotte accord had caused among their Shawnee cousins, and

Boone suspected that given the stealth of the raid, the odds of a hunting party merely happening upon his camp in the pitch black of predawn were unlikely. They had been stalked.

With Twitty slowly bleeding out and Walker too badly hurt to yet travel, Boone ordered three lean-tos erected on the spot. They christened the little station Twitty's Fort in honor of their dying comrade, and divided the company into sentries and hunting parties. Two days later, while Boone and his brother were prowling the snow-crusted forest for game, they came upon the teenage woodcutter Will Tate stumbling through the trees. Tate and his father, Samuel, both Upper Yadkin men, had been among a quartet also out hunting. The boy said that they had been attacked the previous evening while drying their moccasins over a campfire, and he and his father had become separated after fleeing barefoot into the forest.

Young Tate led the Boone brothers back to their makeshift camp. There they found the scalped remains of the other two woodsmen but no sign of Tate's father. As they buried the bodies, Will Tate tried to remember everything he could about their assailants. From his descriptions, Boone was fairly certain that the mixed-blood Captain Will Emery and his band were also roaming the area. Miami *and* Shawnee. That night Boone doubled the camp's guard and sent out runners to alert any hunters, surveyors, and settlers also bushwhacking through the Kentucky wilderness that war parties were in the vicinity. Those alerted included pioneers who had entered the territory in groups of twos and threes as well as a party of over one hundred settlers under command of the noted frontiersman James Harrod, who did not recognize the Transylvania Company's imprimatur. Then, dictating to his son-in-law Will Hays, Boone composed a message to Richard Henderson.

"Your company is desired greatly," he wrote, "for the people are very uneasy, but are willing to stay and venture their lives with you. Now is the time to flusterate [*sic*] [the Indians'] intentions, and to keep the country whilst we are in it. If we give way to them now, it will ever be the case. Come or send [reinforcements] as soon as possible."

Boone had just completed his communiqué when an exhausted Samuel Tate stumbled into camp. He warned that there were still Indians about.

Richard Henderson was alarmed and confused. It was April 7, and a weary rider had just delivered Boone's message to him in the Holston Valley, where he and his party of thirty mounted riflemen had been stalled by a fierce spring blizzard. Henderson knew he could not keep secret from his fellow travelers the news that hostiles had taken to the warpath up ahead. And, indeed, when word of the lethal Indian attacks spread among his teamsters, several of the men quit on the spot and rode for home.

Sensing yet again that haste was his surest ally, Henderson and his remaining riders set out for the Cumberland Gap the next morning despite the deep snowdrifts. Their forty or so packhorses—weighed down by sacks of seed corn, powder, and ball, and what Henderson hoped was enough inventory to stock a trader's store—moved slower than ever.

In the meanwhile, once the wounded Felix Walker was well enough to travel, Boone's woodcutters had set off for the mouth of Otter Creek. The twenty-two-year-old Walker, jouncing along in a hammock slung between two horses, credited Boone's knowledge of herbal medicines with his survival, and he later published a journal chronicling the trek. Apparently possessed by the soul of a philosopher, in his diary he admitted, "My wounds, pronounced by some to be mortal, produced very serious reflections."* Now, lifting his head from the litter, he caught his first glimpse

---

* Or perhaps his was the soul of a natural-born politician, for in his later incarnation as a United States congressman, Walker is credited with making a vital contribution to the American lexicon. Elected to represent North Carolina's Buncombe County in 1817, Walker gained a reputation as a stem-winding if not particularly enlightening speaker. On one occasion, much to his colleague's chagrin, he insisted on delivering a long and tedious "speech for Buncombe" on the floor of the house. Today we derive the bastardized term "bunkum" from his efforts.

of Kentucky's rolling meadows, the waist-high bluegrass and white rye studded with scores of buffalo.

The trail-cutting party reached the site of the future Boonesborough in early April, less than a month after the treaty signing at Sycamore Shoals. Boone's immediate priority was to begin construction on a stockade. He chose for its site a broad floodplain that gradually sloped to the south bank of the Kentucky River, an ideal conduit upon which to convey future crop shipments to New Orleans via the Ohio and Mississippi Rivers. Across the watercourse, moving swift with winter runoff, the forested ground rose precipitously to some one hundred feet. This lent the location, in the words of the Boone biographer John Mack Faragher, "a secluded and protected feeling."

Boone envisioned his fort enclosing perhaps an acre, protected by two-story bastions on each corner, with several cabins built into its log walls. There was, however, an impediment: the axmen, having only signed on to clear a road, were less interested in construction work than in claiming their promised two-acre plots and, Indians be damned, roaming farther afield to stake out their larger plantations near the buffalo stamps. Boone was lucky to get a small powder magazine built.

Boone begged and wheedled to little avail; these were headstrong men who had journeyed into the hinterlands precisely to escape monocrats telling them what to do. In truth, Boone probably sympathized. By the time Henderson and his depleted company arrived two weeks later, the stunted walls of a blockhouse that had barely risen were encircled by a mottle of half-built cabins and filthy osnaburg tents made from coarse brown linen scattered among the tree stumps. Taking charge, Henderson deemed Boone's chosen site for the fort too close to the river, and work was begun on a new structure farther away.

With Henderson's arrival, the Boonesborough population had swelled to eighty or so men and boys—including a few slaves—and the two women. They faced not only the Indian threat, but a dwindling cache of supplies that the packtrain could not come near to addressing. There was no flour for bread baking, and the corn crop and vegetable patches planted on the "stamps" were only just past germination. Worst of all, the inexperienced hunters among the group were slaughtering game for target practice, driving the buffalo and deer herds farther and farther away. In addition, competing land claims between the Boonesborough residents and the settlers putting down roots under James Harrod's command—now two hundred or so occupying two separate sites—were edging toward violence.

Astonishingly, in the face of this disorder Henderson felt it an opportune moment to hold what he termed a constitutional convention to elect delegates to deal with the governance of the territory. In early May 1775, he invited Harrod and his followers to attend the meeting at Boonesborough. Boone was surprised when Harrod agreed.

Harrod, tall and lean, was remembered by all who met him as the possessor of a coal-black diagonal of a beard that began at his cheekbones and fell to mid-chest. He was also a man of fierce independence, and Henderson was well aware that Harrod did not accept the Transylvania Company's authority over the territory. He had good reason.

James Harrod was born seven or eight years before Boone, sometime around 1742, the son of an English immigrant who became an early settler in Virginia's Shenandoah Valley. His father was killed by Indians when he was twelve, and by the age of sixteen he was serving as a teamster on the British expedition under Gen. Forbes, which occupied the abandoned Fort Duquesne during the French and Indian War. Five years later he returned to the site, renamed Fort Pitt, as a member of a relief party during Pontiac's Rebellion. When Pontiac made peace, Harrod wandered west as far as what is now Illinois. There he lived among both French traders and Indian tribes and learned to communicate in several Native American languages. He then crossed the Ohio to join Capt. Bullitt's surveying team.

Like Boone, Harrod's youthful journey into the Ohio Country had instilled in him a hunger for more exploration. The hamlet he and Bullitt were

laying out when Lord Dunmore's War erupted, known today as Harrodsburg, is acknowledged as the oldest permanent American settlement west
of the Appalachians. By the time Richard Henderson rode into Boonesborough, Harrodsburg consisted of eight to ten cabins arrayed in an arc
around a communal seventy-acre cornfield. A smaller sister settlement
called Boiling Springs—so named for the brackish water boiled to make
salt—rose several miles away.

Henderson recognized that to convince a man like Harrod of the Transylvania Company's jurisdiction was a tall task, and he employed the full
power of his oratorical skills in hopes of smoothing over the dispute. With
a wink and nod toward Harrod and his followers he opened the ceremo-
nies by emphasizing that "All power is originally in the people."

Though Harrod remained skeptical, by the end of the session nine
bills had been passed pertaining to the executive, legislative, and judicial branches of the nascent colony of Transylvania. These included the
formation of a militia, the establishment of tribunal criminal courts, and
legislation proscribing "profane swearing and Sabbath breaking." As a
compromise to soothe the contentious arguments over land, an initiative
to award individual parcels through a lottery system was also established.

The convocation was concluded with the performance of the feudal
custom of "Livery of Seizin."* In the ceremony, the Indian agent who
had been appointed (by Henderson) to represent the Cherokee at Sycamore Springs gouged a thick piece of sod from the earth and handed it to
Henderson. This signaled the formal transfer of land ownership from the
Cherokee to the Transylvania Company. In terms of political practicality,
however, the conclave may as well have voted to order the sun to shine
eternally on its cornfields while abolishing death and disease west of the
Appalachians.

The following day a rider arrived at Boonesborough with news of the
battles at Lexington and Concord. For the Kentucky colonists, however, a

---

* From the French *saisie,* or "seizure."

more immediate threat took precedence over the announcement of armed conflict nearly one thousand miles away.

In March 1775, two months before Richard Henderson accepted his symbolic slice of Kentucky soil, Virginia's governor, Lord Dunmore, dispatched an emissary to the Cherokee towns to inform them of his decision to declare the Transylvania Purchase illegal. His reasons were a mix of the political and the personal. On the one hand, the English Crown, through its representative in the royal governor's office, had prohibited private companies from buying Indian territories, in no small part for fear that the frontier, once viewed as a safety valve to siphon excess laborers from eastern lands, would now begin to denude its colonies of their most productive citizens. The governor had few qualms about emptying his colony of men of little consequence and less taxable property. But now, Dunmore worried that the acreage claimed by squatters would impinge upon his own land speculations.

When news of Lord Dunmore's intrigues reached Kentucky, the pioneers delivered a message of their own: any attempts by royal surveyors to "stretch the chain" near their western settlements would be met with powder and shot. In the meanwhile, the governor's representatives in Cherokee country found the tribe already experiencing second thoughts about the "deception" that had cost them their hunting grounds.

An American trader living among the tribes reported that Little Carpenter and his fellow negotiators had been under the impression that it was not the Kentucky River that marked the purchase's northern boundary, but a different watercourse altogether—the smaller Louisa, a tributary of the Big Sandy some 125 miles to the east. And in what can be interpreted as a tribal-wide grievance, an influential warrior who had received but a single linen hunting shirt and several gills of rum for his "share" of the "Great Grant" complained that he could kill more deer in a day in the forest and fields of Kanta-ke than the garment was worth. He soon departed with his family to join Dragging Canoe's growing throng of dis-affected tribesmen.

News from the north was no more encouraging. In the late spring of 1775, Boone's old friend Capt. William Russell—now posted on the Ohio River at the fort erected in the wake of the Battle of Point Pleasant—sent a warning to Boonesborough: factions of the Shawnee and Mingo bands who had never recognized the legitimacy of the Treaty of Camp Charlotte were preparing to rise against the white "cabiners" along the Kentucky River. The Indians throughout the Ohio Country, Russell wrote to Boone, were aware of the violent rupture between the Redcoats and the American colonials near Boston. They hoped to use what they viewed as the white man's civil war to reclaim their "stolen" land.

In the early stages of the conflict between colonies and mother country, Great Britain's official Indian policy had been to restrain the northwest tribes from entering the fray. But now, Russell confided to Boone he feared that in the wake of the recent engagements at Concord and Lexington, rogue British agents from Detroit were already circulating among the Native Americans in an effort to turn them toward a warpath that led to Boonesborough's front door.

Boone was conflicted. He was certainly ready to defend the inter-ests of his eponymous community against Indian attacks. But, at least in his words to his contemporaneous biographer John Filson, he felt no animosity toward the British. He was still, in fact, a rather tepid rev-olutionary. It was true that many Kentucky settlers, particularly those drawn to Harrodsburg, leaned toward secession. But James Harrod and his followers, despite their presence at Henderson's assembly, had at best only tentatively accepted the notion of the Transylvania Company's jurisdiction over the territory. Their main priority, in tandem with a real revolutionary zeal, was to convince any new United States federal gov-ernment to reaffirm the long-standing policy of pioneers free to establish homesteads on unclaimed western lands—unclaimed by whites, that is—without paying eastern consortiums like Richard Henderson's for the privilege.

Boonesborough, on the other hand, remained the capital seat of Transylvania, and Boone's fond recollections of Henderson's generosity still meant something to him.

24

REVOLUTION

D aniel Boone was not alone in his ambivalence about breaking ties with England. These were strange times on either side of the Appalachians. Even as General George Washington's Continental Army was besieging British-held Boston, the Second Continental Congress convened in Philadelphia was adopting the "Olive Branch Petition." The document appealed directly to King George III for help in achieving reconciliation between the warring forces.* The wily Richard Henderson, unsure of how to read the swirling political winds, opted to play both ends against the middle.

First, Henderson declared to Lord Dunmore that the Kentucky colonists "by no means forget their allegiance to their sovereign [king]." At the same time, he arranged for a former North Carolina attorney named James Hogg to ride for Philadelphia to volunteer his services to the Continental Congress as a delegate from Transylvania. At Henderson's instruction, Hogg urged "the united Colonies [to] take the infant Colony of Transylvania into their protection; and they, in return, will do everything in their power, and give such assistance in the general cause of America."

---

* George III refused to even open the petition and, instead, issued a proclamation declaring the thirteen colonies to be in open rebellion.

A committee of New Englanders, including John and Samuel Adams, advised Hogg that Transylvania's overture to become the fourteenth colony might fall on more sympathetic ears if Henderson and his fellow Transylvanians forbade the importation of owned "Negroes" into the territory as a precursor to outlawing slavery altogether. Their advice was not heeded. In the end, Virginia and North Carolina delegates, loath to cede any land to a new colony, vetoed Hogg's appointment to the political body.

Henderson received the news of Congress's rejection of Transylvania's application for statehood with outward equanimity. He even took out what he called "booster" advertisements in North Carolina newspapers, once again offering inexpensive five-hundred-acre lots whose "fertility of the soil and the goodness of the range surpass belief." He was of course aware that the Kentucky settlers were slaughtering the buffalo into oblivion. This did not deter him from claiming that the herds were so thick that a man could easily keep his family alive on buffalo meat and indigenous fruits and vegetables until the sale of his planted crops allowed him to purchase beef cattle, milk cows, and hogs. But the fact that he had omitted from his newspaper notices the original settlement stipulation to plant a corn crop hinted at Henderson's desperation.

At Sycamore Shoals the Transylvania Company had laid out what was for the era a small fortune to buy off the Cherokees. Further, the consortium was still supplying the Kentucky pioneers with expensive rifles and ammunition on credit, as well as hiring more axmen to widen Boone's Trace. In addition, several men, including the Boone brothers, remained on the payroll as hunters to provide the colonists with fresh meat.

By this point, the entire "colony" of Transylvania consisted of no more than a few hundred people, with more departing than arriving every day. In private letters to his North Carolina investors, Henderson virtually begged them to "spirit up the people, and convince them of the goodness of our country, and that the Indians in general are friendly." But his public relations efforts were no match for the hard news that defecting Kentuckians were carrying back from the western wilderness. A pilgrim passing through the territory at the time described the settlements as "a bustling hive of squalor" whose occupants lived in constant fear of Indian attack. What few buffalo that remained, he added, were already breaking through rail fences and trampling the weed-filled cornfields of abandoned farmsteads.

And though it was true that no tribe had yet formally declared war on the "Caintucks," sporadic incidents of grisly red-white skirmishes continued apace. On one occasion two boys playing on a hill across the river not far from Boonesborough vanished; the only clue to their disappearance were moccasin tracks heading north. A search party following the trail found the scalped body of one of the teens. The other was never heard from again. These were not the kind of tales to convince, as Henderson told his associates, "the people on the other side of the mountains to take courage and venture out."

Boone, on the other hand, would not be dismayed. Determined to make a home on the two-thousand-acre land grant he had been given "with the thanks of the [Transylvania Company's] proprietors for the signal service he has rendered to the company," in mid-June of 1775, he set off for the Clinch River to fetch his wife and children. He arrived at their cabin in time to witness Rebecca give birth to their ninth child, William, who died several days later. By the time of his return to Kentucky in early September he was not only accompanied by the grieving Rebecca and their children, but by an additional fifty or so emigrants answering Henderson's newspaper notices. These included twenty-one mounted riflemen.

At forty, Boone was now not only the respected leader of the Kentucky pioneers but a wealthy man as well. At least on paper.

The settlers who rode with the Boone family into Kentucky in the fall of 1775 were part of a small wave of emigrants from Virginia, North Carolina, and Pennsylvania who temporarily buoyed Henderson's spirits. Among these were Squire Boone's wife, Jane, and her infant daughter Sarah, as well as the family of Richard Callaway, whose wife and two daughters—joining Rebecca Boone and her four daughters—surged the female population at Boonesborough. Some of the newcomers drove before them herds of cattle, passels of hogs, and carried caged chickens and clipped-wing ducks, believed to be the first domesticated fowl to enter Kentucky. Further, at least a part of the Transylvania Company's hyped promotions proved prescient—the territory's soil was indeed as fecund as promised, and the first crop of corn came in beyond all expectations.

Also arriving at the Kentucky settlements that fall were George Rogers Clark and the frontiersman Simon Kenton. Clark's reputation preceded him, primarily because of his fearless if absurd plan of a year earlier to attack the Shawnee stronghold on the Scioto River with a mere ninety men. And the twenty-year-old Kenton's physical presence—at six feet four he was a giant for the era—matched his reputation as a seasoned hunter, scout, and Indian fighter. Despite their youth—Clark had yet to turn twenty-three—both men had already grown a lot of hard bark, and both would go on to achieve mythic martial renown, although in somewhat different fashions. The rawboned Kenton was destined to save Daniel Boone's life during an Indian fight before being nearly tortured to death as a Shawnee captive. And Clark's military expertise would in the near future be tapped by Patrick Henry. Henry, on the verge of becoming the governor of the newly declared *state* of Virginia, wanted Clark to lead an expedition against the western tribes. For now, however, both remained lone pioneers attempting to scratch out a living in an untamed territory of forest and meadow.

By the close of 1775 the Transylvania Company's land office at Boonesborough had registered more than nine hundred applicants for plots totaling some 560,000 acres. In truth, however, the Christmas celebrations up and down the Kentucky River that season were muted. Most of the new claimants, citing the uncertain Indian question, had yet to make their payments, much less physically move west. The few who did venture over the mountains were for the most part speculators who would rush into the territory, throw up a few "pigsty cabins"—roofless and doorless lean-tos surrounded by a few rows of planted corn—and scuttle back east to sell the properties at a profit.

If on its books the colony appeared to be thriving, it is doubtful that the combined settlements along the Kentucky River contained much more than the few hundred people who had trickled into the territory since the Transylvania Purchase. With the War for Independence threatening to spill over the Appalachians, the future of the colony was decidedly opaque. As Henderson's chief surveyor noted in a letter to a colleague, "I think there will be but small improvements made this year, as many [potential settlers] seem confused, and great numbers are leaving the country."

What Daniel Boone made of the Transylvania Company's attempts to bullyrag a brand-new colony into the national fabric of the nascent United States is murky. Historians have primarily been left to rely on Richard Henderson's self-serving journals and correspondence as the most comprehensive written accounts from the period. Though he slowly grew more sympathetic to the cause of American independence, Boone, like Henderson, was far from a rabid secessionist. There is even sketchy evidence that he received a few British visitors with gracious aplomb when they arrived to feel out his Kentucky hamlet's political leanings. There is also no doubt that he never forgot Henderson's generous land grant. In the end, however, Boone's thoughts about the company's efforts were moot.

Within a year the Transylvania Company would be bankrupt, with Virginia royalists annexing the consortium's holdings in the name of the Crown. Gov. Dunmore, perhaps fearful of a surge in seditious activity among Henderson's backers should he be prosecuted, compensated the judge and his associates by awarding him two hundred thousand acres in the far west of the territory beyond the Falls of the Ohio. Years later the state of North Carolina would similarly nullify the company's claims to the sliver of northern Tennessee along the Cumberland River that had been wrested from the Cherokee at Sycamore Shoals. With that, Henderson returned to North Carolina to run for his old superior-court seat. He won.

In the end, the Transylvania Company's foray into the western frontier occurred at the wrong place and particularly the wrong time for the land speculators. Not the least of their miscalculations was that the carbonated forces driving the American Revolution would allow business barons with even a taint of Tory ties to purchase large swaths of the country they were fighting to free from British rule. As Thomas Jefferson observed, the rents that the company charged were in and of themselves "a mark of vassalage."

As for Boone, the demise of the Transylvania Company also marked the end of his short stint as a gentleman farmer. Within a year his two-thousand-acre grant was invalidated by Virginia's appropriation of the territory. Without complaint, he moved his family into a cabin that in time would become part of Boonesborough's fort complex.

Despite heartening reports from beyond the Appalachians—Washington driving the British from Boston, American troops repelling an assault on Charleston Harbor by the Royal Navy—the Cherokee renegade Dragging Canoe had proven a prophet. Along with the tidings of revolutionary triumphs came news that Dragging Canoe had convinced his followers to take to the warpath. Raiding parties incited by British agents were ravishing homesteads from north Georgia to western Virginia, including up and down the Watauga and Holston River Valleys. Over three hundred warriors had boldly attacked three American stockades simultaneously, including Joseph Martin's rebuilt fort in Virginia's Powell Valley as well as a blockhouse situated on an island in Tennessee's Holston River. The attacks only ebbed when Dragging Canoe was wounded in both legs during the latter fight.

In neighboring Kentucky, the scent of war was also in the air as news spread of Shawnee and Mingo probes into the territory. As such, the presence of settlers and landjobbers noticeably thinned, and even the boldest long hunters kept nearer to the stockaded stations and slept with their rifles loaded. Like the Cherokee, the tribes north of the Ohio River strongly suspected that America's War for Independence was being fought over Indian land despite high-minded slogans about taxation without representation. It was the Shawnee who recognized the earliest that this internecine conflict among the whites could only end badly for the tribe should the rapacious colonists prevail. Native American support of the Crown, in essence, was the lesser of two evils. It was not the British, after all, who had begun desecrating Kanta-ke with cabins and cornfields.

Given the patterns of history repeating itself—in this case, of white empires arming Indians to do their forest fighting—Boone surely suspected that his lonely outpost in the far-off Bluegrass Country was destined to become the western focal point of the war being waged on the other side of the mountains. For as the spring of 1776 bloomed and Indian activity proliferated along the Kentucky River, a pall hung like an illness over Kentucky's pioneer settlements.

Within this tense atmosphere, whenever an incident occurred—a stray surveyor's mangled body discovered, a family burned out of their isolated cabin, a hunter unaccounted for—it was always to Boone, equally adept at stalking hoofs or paws, feet or feathers, whom even the most experienced backwoods hands looked for guidance. "Old Daniel's on the track" became a familiar refrain around campfires along the river. Boone's innate ability to wisp through the forest in order to separate viable threats from mere rumor lent him an unmatched mystique. That skill would soon be put to the test.

25

KIDNAPPED

This time Daniel Boone heard the piercing shrieks and recognized them as only a parent could. He grabbed his rifle, burst from his cabin, and sprinted toward the Kentucky River without pausing to put on his moccasins. When he reached the south bank, the only clues were the two broken oars and the strip of torn calico belonging to his daughter's Sabbath-day dress. He was too late to see the Indians carry off the thirteen-year-old Jemima and the two Callaway girls. But he knew what he had to do to get them back.

Boone, like every man, woman, and child living along the frontier in eighteenth-century America, was accustomed to the quotidian barbarity of life on the borderlands. Scalpings, mutilations, murdered infants—these were no less the trade-offs for whites and Indians alike than a random wolf attack or bear mauling. At least a kidnapping offered the possibility of retrieving the abducted. Only weeks earlier the twin sons of Pennsylvania immigrants had been taken by Mingoes just a few hundred yards from their cabin near Harrodsburg. The Shawnee chief Cornstalk had intervened, and the boys were turned over to an Indian agent at Fort Pitt relatively unharmed. This time, Boone did not intend to let it get that far.

. . .

Sunday, July 14, 1776, had dawned hot and dry as chalk, but the morning's heavy dew rendered the early hours bearable. Jemima Boone had spent most of the previous afternoon tending the family garden before cutting her instep on a broken cane stalk. Now, returning from religious services and still wearing her Sunday dress and bonnet, she invited her friends Betsy Callaway, fifteen, and Fanny Callaway, thirteen, to accompany her to the river, where she could dip her wound into the cool waters.

On the south bank of the watercourse they untethered one of the settlement's dugout canoes and clambered aboard. Neither Callaway girl voiced any concern; Jemima Boone was so at home on the water that her nickname was "Duck." There was a tiny islet less than a half mile downstream, where wild onions grew, and Jemima hoped to grub some up to make a poultice for her injury while the sisters gathered wild fruits. They pushed off with Betsy and Fanny manning the oars and Jemima handling the tiller while dragging her foot through the water.

At the time ten small American communities, or "stations," had risen on or near the banks of the Kentucky River. These consisted of anywhere from a dozen to forty or so cabins, a pointillist belt bookended by the two largest stockade communities—Boonesborough to the east and Harrodsburg to the west. Every child living along the river had been taught that the land to the north was hostile territory and to keep away. But the three girls had drifted less than one hundred yards when the current began to draw their canoe toward the north bank.

The Callaway sisters struggled furiously with their paddles to break from the water flow's pull, but they were not strong enough. The slender canoe was a few feet from shore when five Indians—three Shawnee and two Cherokee—rose from a canebrake. One of them waded into the shallows, grabbed the buffalo-tug rope attached to the bow, and began reeling in the little craft. As Jemima's screams echoed through Boonesborough, Betsy and

Fanny Callaway beat the Indian about the head and shoulders with their oars until the paddles broke.

Once ashore, the Indians marched the girls north as the three did all they could to slow their progress. Their screaming had stopped: one of the Cherokees who spoke passing English threatened to scalp Betsy Callaway on the spot if it continued. But Jemima found so many opportunities to collapse and complain about the wound to her bare foot that one Indian tossed her a pair of moccasins and brandished his tomahawk until she pulled them on, stood, and shuffled on.

When the captives pretended to struggle through the thick, thorny underbrush catching on their clothes, the Indians sliced off their dresses and petticoats at the knees. One noticed Betsy Callaway digging the heavy heels of her Sunday shoes into the soft forest undergrowth of clover and peavine. He lopped off the heels, and thereafter the group kept to the harder ground along ridgelines. While climbing the ridges the girls feigned using the branches of saplings and tall bushes for purchase while making sure to break off as many as they could. And when no one was looking, Betsy Callaway managed to tear bits from her white linen handkerchief and surreptitiously toss them to the side of their path.

It was coming on twilight, and Jemima guessed that they had traveled six miles when they stopped to rest. Fingering the pocketknife hidden in the folds of her dress, she told the English-speaking Cherokee, a minor war leader known to the Americans as Hanging Maw, that she recalled once seeing him outside her family's cabin back on the Clinch. He had been talking to her father, Daniel Boone. At the name, Hanging Maw's lips curled into a speculative half smile. He asked if the others were her sisters. Sensing things would fare better for Betsy and Fanny if she lied, Jemima nodded yes.

The Cherokee snorted a laugh. "Then we have done pretty well for old Boone this time," he said.

. . .

By now more than a dozen armed men had joined Boone racing down the south bank of the river in pursuit of the empty canoe. These included a mounted troop led by Betsy and Fanny's father, Richard Callaway. Callaway was naturally anxious to ride after his daughters, and after a twelve-year-old boy plunged into the fast-flowing water and retrieved the craft, Callaway paused only long enough to inspect it for bloodstains. Finding none, he led his troop to a ford a mile or so downstream while Boone and five others swam the deep watercourse. These latter included the surveyor John Floyd whom Boone and Michael Stoner had set out to warn against Indian attack two years earlier and Betsy Callaway's fiancé, Samuel Henderson, the thirty-year-old nephew of the Transylvania Company's Richard Henderson.

By the time Boone and his companions picked up the Indians' trail running up the steep bluff on the north side of the river, Callaway's party was galloping hard toward them. There were perhaps ninety minutes of daylight remaining. Boone, still barefoot, his Sunday pantaloons dripping, cautioned Callaway that at the first hint of hoofbeats the Indians would surely kill the girls. Given the raiders' route, he suspected that they would keep to a northerly course and cross the Licking River near the spreading salt spring known as the Blue Licks. He ordered Callaway to lead his horsemen on a wide berth to the Licking and form a loose circle out ahead of the kidnappers. Boone and his party would pursue on foot and drive the Indians into Callaway's net.

Callaway bristled, visibly riled. He was used to giving orders, not receiving them. His resentment of Boone's growing notoriety had only increased in the months since they'd reached Kentucky. He was also aware, as common gossip had it, that Boone was not even the father of the girl with his name who had gone missing. But he held his spleen, recognizing that this was neither the place nor time for prolonged argument. He nodded his assent. His revenge on Boone would wait.

Boone and his party silently disappeared into the forest afoot, at first following the deep imprints left by the heels of Betsy Callaway's shoes and, later, the clumps of broken branches and snippets of handkerchief dropped as trail markers. They had made some five miles when it became too dark to continue. They camped that night with a company of nine Virginians they stumbled across erecting a cabin on staked land. Boone sent his best swimmer back to Boonesborough to retrieve extra powder and ball, his breechclout, and his moccasins. It is not recorded how well he slept that night.

The Indians slumbered in a loose circle around their captives. Each girl, kept out of reach from the others, was pinioned at the elbows with rawhide tugs, with the loose end of the makeshift ropes fastened to an Indian's breechclout. Seated with their backs to a large hemlock, Jemima, Betsy, and Fanny spent the night straining to hear rescuers' footfalls above the chirping of insects and the occasional hoot of an owl.

They broke camp at dawn on Monday, with the Indians proffering small hunks of unsalted, smoked buffalo tongue that made the girls retch. The captives continued their ruse of breaking off small branches, twigs, and vines to guide any pursuers, but by this time the Indians had grown wise and positioned one of their party as a trailer to clean up any sign. Sometime around noon one of the Shawnees ran down an aging white nag that had likely strayed too far from a hunting camp. Thinking it would quicken their pace, they placed first Jemima and then Fanny and sometimes all three on the horse's back. Though the girls were expert horsewomen, they feigned fright, and by surreptitiously pinching and jabbing their heels into the poor beast's underbelly they managed to turn it into a bucking bronco from which they were repeatedly thrown. Vexed, the Indians abandoned the horse and doubled their wariness.

The girls were quick to notice that any time they came across a stream running north, the Indians would plunge into the middle and follow it for some distance. If it was too deep for their captives, they would throw them over their shoulders. Similarly, the abductors went out of their way to split up and snake through the thickest canebrakes in their path, often doubling back to break separate courses through the same obstruction. It may have slowed their escape, but if Daniel Boone was indeed dogging them, they would not make it easy for him.

The Indians prodded the girls along at a hard pace, and after traveling close to thirty miles with only intermittent breaks, the party stopped at dusk to camp on a fork of two tributaries flowing into the Licking. Here the suddenly talkative Hanging Maw told Jemima that they were heading for the Shawnee towns on the Scioto, still one hundred miles away. He boasted that he had been among a war party of Cherokees scouting an ambush around Boonesborough for a week or so when he and his companion fell in with the three Shawnee just as they spotted the girls in the canoe. That night they again tied their captives with tugs in a sitting position, but this time allowed them to huddle together. Jemima and Fanny took turns laying down their heads and dozing on Betsy's lap.

Three of the cabin builders had joined Boone's pursuit, bringing his party to eight. By early on Monday morning they had tracked the Indians to their previous night's encampment, but from there the trail went cold. More specifically, the several trails went cold. No longer were Betsy's heel marks acting as a beacon, and the bent and broken shrubbery seemed to be more scattered, with no sign of the shredded handkerchief bits.

Boone deduced that the Indians were not only sporadically splitting up, but also deliberately laying false sign. All the paths, in any case, led in one general direction—almost due north toward the Licking and then into Shawnee country. Boone drew his little troop together and told them that instead of running in circles they would be better off plowing ahead toward the Ohio. On several occasions they recrossed the Indian trail almost by accident. Stifling the few mild protests to follow it, Boone kept his company together at a steady jog.

. . .

By Tuesday midmorning the Indians felt confident enough in their distance from any pursuers to discharge a rifle, shooting and killing a buffalo calf. They sliced out the animal's tongue, cut off a portion of its hump, and continued moving north to find a stream to gather water with which to boil the former. While they were butchering the beast, two of the Shawnee had made grunting noises toward the girls. Hanging Maw translated their words as "pretty squaws." He'd then asked Jemima, described by a contemporary as "real handsome," to remove the combs from her hair. The thirteen-year-old complied, and her long black tresses dangled about her knees as they trod on.

At close to ten o'clock Tuesday morning Boone's troop again picked up the Indians' trail on an old buffalo trace running parallel to the Warrior's Path. This time they followed it, with Boone supposing that by now the raiders had let down their guard. He set a faster pace, and the group had made eight or nine miles when they came across the slaughtered buffalo, the blood still trickling from its severed hump. Boone guessed that the Indians would halt at the nearest water to cook their meal. About midday they reached the next stream, where the sign seemed to end. Boone, sensing that their quarry was near, used hand signals to divide his troop, half the men cautiously slipping downstream while he led the others up the far bank.

The pursuers were separated by no more than a few hundred yards when the northernmost point man was drawn to the smell of smoke and roasting buffalo. Peering down from a small knoll, he signaled to the others that the Indians were but some thirty yards below him. They had made camp in a secluded glen surrounded by a canebrake. One brave was lounging supine near the captives huddled together on a fallen tree, another was gathering wood. A third was kindling the cookfire, while a fourth squatted beside him lighting his pipe. All were barefoot, their wet moccasins ringing the fire to dry. There was no sign of the fifth kidnapper—Hanging Maw, as it turned out—who had returned to the stream with his kettle to scoop more water.

As the remaining seven rescuers belly-crawled toward the rise, Boone ostentatiously removed his finger from the trigger of his rifle as a silent warning that no one should shoot without his go-ahead. But before he and the others could reach the small ridge, the point man lifted his gun to his shoulder and fired. He missed.

The Indian camp was pandemonium in an instant. One of the Shawnees lunged at the girls with his war club. It narrowly missed Jemima's head. As he drew it back a second time he fell, shot through the chest by either Boone or the surveyor Floyd, who had fired simultaneously. Another Shawnee was hit and toppled backward into the flames but somehow recovered and lurched into the thick brush. By now Boone's entire party was descending on the camp shouting their terrible war cries. The two remaining Indians scattered into the cane.

At the crack of the first rifle shot, Jemima had leapt to her feet and cried, "That's daddy." The more composed Betsy Callaway, ducking the swinging war club, jerked her back close. Betsy wrapped her arms around both younger girls and pulled them backward off the log. When Boone reached the camp, all three leapt to their feet, but he barked at them to get back down behind the dead tree. He needed to make certain that the three escaped foes, or even the kidnapper who had been fetching water, were not lurking in the wood with a primed rifle. He needn't have worried. The Indians had left behind all their weapons and ammunition, including their knives, tomahawks, and war clubs. Their moccasins were still drying by the fire.

Years later Jemima Boone told her granddaughter that when the finality of their rescue set in, all three girls collapsed in a weeping cluster. They were joined by Betsy's fiancé, Samuel Henderson, and Boone himself, who sunk to his knees and bawled like an infant. Jemima had never before seen her father cry.

By some good fortune, on their trek home the party happened upon the aged white horse the Indians had captured and released. This time, with no pinching or pounding on its shanks, the animal proved gentler and provided much-needed respite for the exhausted Jemima and Fanny Callaway. Betsy Callaway, who had slept least during the ordeal, was carried home on Samuel Henderson's back.

When they reached the rise on the north bank of the Kentucky overlooking Boonesborough they were met by Colonel Callaway and his mounted patrol. Callaway's troop had made the Licking and, finding no Indian sign, doubled back along a buffalo trace. They had come upon the Indian camp in the glade only to find it empty except for the dead Shawnee. Callaway realized from the tracks leading south that the girls were safe, and he and his men followed Indian sign north for a short while—including a blood trail left by the wounded Shawnee who, as it turned out, was later reported to have died from the gunshot. But they had not been able to run down any of the abductors, and Callaway called off the pursuit. His paternal reward came a month later, when Betsy Callaway and Samuel Henderson became the first couple to be officially married in the Kentucky territory.

Boone himself, who was commissioned as the area's magistrate by none other than Judge Henderson, officiated over the "brush arbor" ceremony. The bride wore a white linen dress, the groom a borrowed and embroidered hunting shirt, his Sunday-best bib and tucker having been shredded during the rescue. Though Col. Callaway resented the fact that Boone had presided over his daughter's nuptials, he readily consented to the union. He did hedge his bet against the legality of the Transylvania Company's civil authority, however, by extracting a promise from his new son-in-law to repeat the rite before a preacher at the first opportunity.

. . .

There is no little irony that the tale of the dramatic rescue of Jemima Boone and the Callaway sisters only hastened the Transylvania Company's disintegration. For the frightening story of pioneer girls taken by "savages" reached the eastern settlements just as Indian attacks in Kentucky temporarily ebbed. Although the Cherokee war party that the kidnapper Hanging Maw had gloated over did manage to burn down a cabin some quarter of a mile from Boonesborough, the raiders and other Cherokee roaming the area were soon recalled by Dragging Canoe, who was still recovering from his wounds and in need of reinforcements.

In the end, Dragging Canoe's endeavor to halt or even push back the trickle of white settlers seeping across trans-Appalachia was smashed when the Continental Army's General Charles Lee—whom Washington had placed in command of his southern forces—initiated what became known as the Cherokee Campaign of 1776. Lee's punitive expedition was a three-pronged affair involving troops from South Carolina, North Carolina, and Virginia invading and crushing the tribe on its home territory. Over fifty Cherokee towns and their adjacent farm fields and vegetable cribs were burned out by Lee's soldiers, leaving the survivors without food or shelter as winter loomed.

Surveying the devastation, many Cherokee abandoned Dragging Canoe and beseeched their older chiefs, including Little Carpenter, to sue for peace. The terms were harsh. The treaties Lee imposed on the Indians marked the first time the tribe ceded ancestral lands to the Americans, including centuries-old settlements, as opposed to wilderness hunting grounds like Kanta-ke. The capitulation caused such a schism that an unrepentant Dragging Canoe and what remained of his followers withdrew deep into the wilds of northern Alabama and the southern Tennessee interior. From there they would continue their resistance against the United States for decades. The remote area to which they repaired to establish new towns along Chickamauga Creek (near modern-day Chattanooga) lent the hostile bands their new name—the Chickamauga Cherokee.

At the same time, fearing further "mischief" from the Shawnee and Mingoes in the wake of the botched kidnapping, a host of Kentucky settlers, including most of the women and children, began a second wave of mass evacuations. An exception to the diaspora was a lone pioneer who arrived to take up residence at Boonesborough in August of 1776. He came bearing a copy of *The Virginia Gazette,* which contained a transcript of America's Declaration of Independence. The community's residents reacted to Thomas Jefferson's sublime document with a celebratory bonfire. Most had, after all, borne the dangers of their new wilderness homes precisely to "dissolve the Political Bands which have connected them" to tyrannical colonial authorities. Boone was more circumspect.

Two months earlier, a Continental Army force of 650 North Carolina volunteers had decimated a loyalist contingent of 750 Tories, primarily Scotsmen, during an engagement along the state's southeastern coast. In what became known as the Battle of Moore's Creek Bridge, the Scots had foolishly charged across the bridge spanning the creek with broadswords raised. They were met by a barrage of rifle fire, which drove them back and effectively ended the engagement, with almost all the king's men who were not killed being captured. The results had not only engorged Continental military rolls, but driven many loyalists to seek succor across the western mountains.

This influx of Tories into Kentucky prompted the settlers in Harrodsburg to elect what they termed a Committee of Safety led by the patriot firebrand George Rogers Clark. Clark was as vociferous in his antipathy for British sympathizers as he was toward Indians, and the committee's first order of business was to petition the new Virginia state government for rifles and ammunition to prevent "the effusion of innocent blood."

Boone, when pressed by some at Boonesborough to form a similar committee, demurred. To fervent revolutionaries this was a certain sign that his wife's family's political tendencies had also infected him. But to

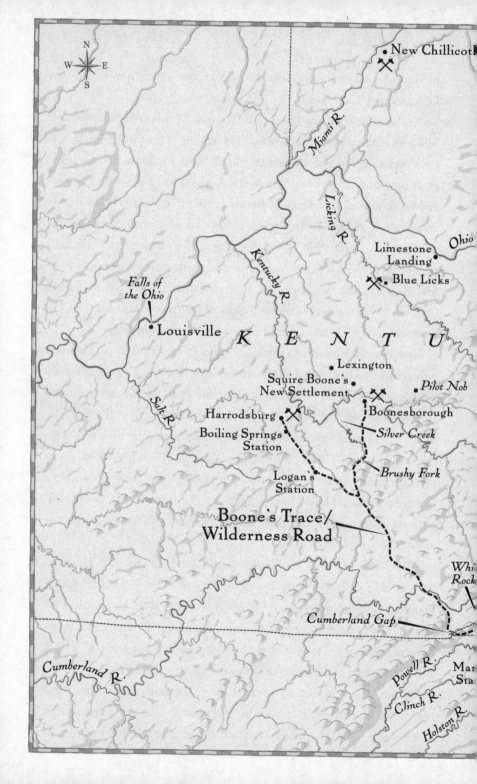

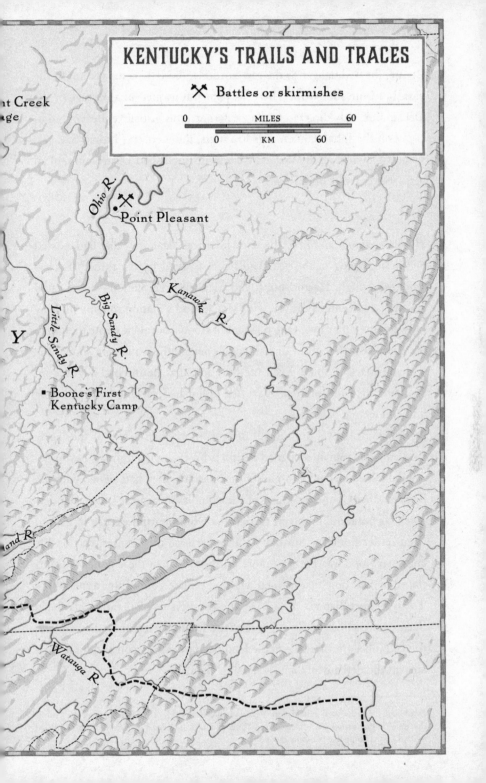

KENTUCKY'S TRAILS AND TRACES

⚔ Battles or skirmishes

| | MILES | |
|0| |60|
| | KM | |
|0| |60|

t Creek
ge

Ohio R.

⚔
•Point Pleasant

Kanawha R.

Big Sandy R.

Little Sandy R.

Y

■ Boone's First
Kentucky Camp

and R.

Watauga R.

Boone, the real danger to the raw borderlands settlements lay not to the east, but from the north. There, as Jefferson warned in a passage of the Declaration slyly directed to the westerners, the British "endeavoured to bring on the Inhabitants of our Frontiers, the merciless Indian Savages, whose known Rule of Warfare, is an undistinguished Destruction, of all Ages, Sexes and Conditions."

By mid-autumn of 1776, the ten wilderness "stations" that had existed at the beginning of the year had been whittled to just three.* Each— Boonesborough, Harrodsburg, and McClelland's Station—was located south of the Kentucky River, with McClelland's Station roughly midway between the other two. One resident of Boonesborough wrote that there were now less than three dozen men to defend the settlement should the Indians attack in force. Even the little fort that Boone had begun constructing the previous year remained unfinished, lacking both picketing and connecting palisades.

Sensing betrayal and abandonment, more than a few of the hardy cabiners who remained signed petitions beseeching Virginia's new independent state assembly to nullify the contracts they had signed with the Transylvania Company. Many of the complaints against Judge Henderson's corporation, however, carried the whiff of artful excuse to get out from under fiduciary burdens to an enterprise they sensed was on life support. None was perhaps more outrageous than the colonists' claims that they had only just learned, eight years later, about the terms of the Treaty of Fort Stanwix. If in 1768 the Iroquois Confederation had been deemed the sole legal proprietors of the Kentucky territory, they argued, the Cherokee transference of the land deed to Henderson and his associates invalidated any of their ownership claims.

---

* Although the terms "station" and "fort" were used interchangeably on the frontier, there was a subtle difference in that a stockade fort was usually larger and more populated than the few cabins arrayed around a blockhouse that constituted a station.

Their grievances were nonetheless heard by the incipient Virginia General Assembly presided over by Governor Patrick Henry. At Henry's urging the political body incorporated into its constitution a law proscribing the purchase of previous Indian lands within the original chartered boundaries of the state. Naturally the patriot politicians still contended, revolution or not, that this line stretched all the way to the Mississippi per the colony's original charter. Not long after, the delegates also enacted legislation organizing the entirety of "Kentucki" into a separate Virginia county. What Lord Dunmore had begun, Patrick Henry had finished, thus effectively sounding the death knell for the Transylvania Company.

Boone, as was his wont, remained aloof from the political ramifications swirling about him. With his daughter's narrow escape fresh in his mind, he spent the rump of 1776 hunting to lay in winter meat and surveying a site for a new fort about three hundred yards downstream from his half-finished stockade. In the meanwhile, for the second straight season, an overwhelming corn crop had come in, although its bounty was offset by Boonesborough's dwindling supply of gunpowder and shot. For all his forest craft, Boone could not outrun a deer or take down a buffalo with a war club or a hunting knife. He husbanded his limited ammunition as best he could, but as the new year drew near, he became more and more anxious over the dearth of powder and shot.

It was more than a matter of putting meat on the table. Boone only needed to glance at one of Ben Franklin's old maps of Kentucky to recognize that if the British and their Indian allies planned to open a western front against the American rebels along the coast, the lonely outposts along the Kentucky River were the only barriers that stood in their way.

—✦—

26

AN INDIAN ARMY

As 1776 drew to a close the fortunes of war had turned against the Americans. The British rout of Gen. Washington's army in a string of battles in and around New York City resulted in his Continental Army fleeing across New Jersey with the British Army's General Charles Cornwallis in close pursuit. This prompted not a few congressmen to consider replacing Washington with Gen. Charles Lee, conqueror of the Cherokee. Farther north, the Royal Navy's near annihilation of a cobbled-together United States fleet on Lake Champlain sparked fears of New England being cut off from the rest of the colonies in a classic divide-and-conquer strategy.

General William Howe, who had replaced Gen. Gage as commander of all Crown forces in North America, had poured the majority of his troop strength—Redcoats and mercenary Hessians alike—into the New York campaign. Given Howe's manpower limitations, this was in part why the key southern port cities of Charleston and Savannah remained in American hands. As such, the delegates in Philadelphia finally recognized what the borderlands settlers had known for some time: if the British were to attempt a pincer movement against the southern colonies from land and sea, they would need the support of Native American tribes ranging from the Ohio Country to the Great Lakes.

In an attempt to preclude just this, the American Indian agent George Morgan invited representatives of the nearest Ohio bands to parley at Fort Pitt, which had been abandoned by the British four years earlier. Not surprisingly, the ever-more-militant Mingoes refused to attend. But several Wyandot and Shawnee elders, including Cornstalk, joined the Delaware chief White Eyes in leading over six hundred of their people to the conclave.

Morgan held no delusions that he could prevail upon the tribes to fight under the American banner. At best he hoped to cajole the Indians into a precarious neutrality. He was well aware of the lies that his British counterpart, Guy Johnson, was spreading.

Two years earlier the British Indian superintendent William Johnson had abruptly dropped dead of a stroke after giving a rousing oration to a throng of Iroquois warriors. After performing a traditional Indian condolence ceremony, the leaders of the Six Nations recognized Johnson's nephew Guy Johnson as his successor. The younger Johnson had subsequently traveled to the Ohio Country and convened an assemblage of Wyandot, Delaware, Mingoes, and Shawnee headmen to warn them of American duplicity. The colonists, the Britisher told the Indians, would invite them to a conference under the ruse of peace talks, and while the warriors were away the rebels would burn their towns, villages, and farm fields. Given this misinformation, Morgan considered the fact that any Indians at all had shown up at Fort Pitt a victory of sorts.

Once the conclave was underway, Morgan explained to the Indians that the new United States government was in the process of drawing up a Constitution. This document would stress that the federal Congress— and not the individual states—would become the sole authority of issues pertaining to the national interest, which included Indian affairs and settlements. Come war's end and the defeat of the British, he promised, the congressional delegates would treat fairly with the indigenous peoples as long as they had not taken to the warpath as Redcoat allies.

In reaction, the chiefs told Morgan that the Ohio Country tribes were

divided. Their council houses continuously erupted in arguments between those who wanted to take up the hatchet against the Americans
and others, including Cornstalk and White Eyes, who had seen too much
hallowed ground soaked by the blood of their tribesmen. Cornstalk told
Morgan that some of his people had simply given up and intended to
cross the Mississippi to reunite with old Corn Cob's Shawnee band in
Spanish territory. Others had joined the unrepentant warrior Blackfish of
the tribe's Chillicothe division. Blackfish had removed his followers from
the Scioto farther west to the Miami River country, a safer location, he felt,
from which to plan for battle.

In the end, Cornstalk agreed to take no side in the conflict between
Great Britain and her rebelling colonials. He stressed, however, that he
only spoke for his Mekoche branch of the Shawnee. The Delaware chief
White Eyes went even further, proposing that the Indian agent Morgan
petition the Continental Congress to declare Ohio a Lenape state of the
nascent union, with voting representation at Philadelphia. In exchange,
he proposed that the Delaware act as guides and auxiliary troops when
the Americans marched through Ohio to attack British holdings at Detroit
and farther north. As a show of good faith, White Eyes promised to en-
courage his people to accommodate the Americans by allowing Moravian
missionaries onto his lands to preach and convert.

Their apparent pacifism notwithstanding, it was certainly not lost on
the war-weary tribal leaders that if the white men stealing their lands were
intent on killing each other in what the Indians considered a civil war, why
should red men interfere?

Morgan reported the success of the negotiations in a euphoric communiqué to the Continental Congress, adding that Cornstalk even planned
to relocate his Mekoche people from Chillicothe on the Scioto to nearer
the Delaware capital town of Coshocton on the Muskingum River. Yet
what the Americans accustomed to hierarchal lines of authority did not
understand—what they could not understand and would not understand
across the Indian Wars of the ensuing century—was that no individual

brave took "orders" from what the whites perceived to be their "kings." With the vast majority of Indians belonging to kin- and clan-based societies, their extreme loyalty to extended family worked naturally against any individual attaining regal eminence.

In reality, a tribal leader's influence was commensurate to his ability to provide for his people and most particularly to his accrued wisdom. The idea that any one man, however well regarded, could be granted absolute authority over his band or tribe, and most especially over its warrior class, was more than anathema to Native American culture. It was incomprehensible. Why not just tell the wind to stop blowing or the rivers to cease flowing?

Nor were the tribes the utopian societies imagined by Enlightenment-era European philosophers composing teleological paeans to aboriginal nature. Eighteen hundred years earlier Plutarch had described the Greek concept of democratic government as the individual being responsible to the group, and the group responsible to its core principles. This was about as close as an eighteenth-century Shawnee or Cherokee or Iroquois could or would come to what the Americans deemed representative government. Anything hinting at formal political titles or fixed terms of office other than the occasional elevation of a war chief was as culturally foreign to the Indian as the fine art of scalp-taking would have been in the corridors of London's Whitehall.

Notwithstanding tribal affiliations, the woodlands Indians of the eastern United States were accustomed to going where they wanted when they wanted and taking what they wanted on the strength of their courage and cunning. Unlike the "civilized" Europeans, they venerated in their leaders the good judgment and common sense acquired with age as opposed to a coat of arms or how well an ancestor had fought in the Crusades. In short, public opinion and ancient custom substituted for both regal lineage and the ballot box.

Despite the Spanish, French, British, and eventually American determination to elevate notable leaders like Cornstalk into "all-commanding

monarchs, with whom to negotiate and sign treaties," the point was beyond moot. The Cherokee Dragging Canoe's break with his own father
was evidence enough of this. To also expect white newcomers to North
America's interior to be able to delineate the subtle power shifts of any
tribe's political, religious, and military societies was folly. Nor did they
much try. Absent war paint, only the most experienced frontiersmen were
capable of physically distinguishing a hostile Mingo from, say, a friendly
Delaware. The fallback reflex for too many whites was too often to shoot
the Indian, any Indian, on sight.

Thus at the very moment when Cornstalk and White Eyes were pledging
their neutrality, British representatives were being dispatched throughout
Indian country to convince the tribes to make war on the Americans. Some
were more successful than others. In the South the British Indian agent John
Stuart, suddenly no longer a peacemaker, accompanied fifteen Shawnee
warriors on a seventy-day trek to the Cherokee seat of Chota in southeastern Tennessee. The Northern Indians entered the town painted black from
head to toe and presented the southern chiefs with a nine-foot war belt. A
few Cherokee warriors were eager to accept the invitation. But the older
leaders, already twice defeated by the whites, sat silent.

North of the Ohio River, however, emissaries circulating among the
Shawnee towns on the Scioto and Little Miami Rivers found greater em-
pathy with warrior clans already bristling over the loss of their Kentucky
hunting grounds and who wanted them back.

The British were vexed. With close to seven thousand British and Hessian
troops soon to assemble in Montreal and march south under General John
"Gentleman Johnny" Burgoyne, the Crown's military strategists were
also seriously pondering an assault from the west on the American-held
Fort Pitt. But Gen. Howe and, more important, Lord George Germain—
London's new secretary of state for the colonies—recognized that the
five hundred or so Redcoats already overextended among Fort Niagara,

Fort Detroit, and Fort Michilimackinac in northern Michigan's Mackinac Straits were too few to constitute the western prong of any military campaign. Into the equation stepped the British Indian agent John Connolly, who offered to scour Canada and the Northwest Territories to raise an auxiliary Canadian-Indian army of what he dubbed "Loyal Foresters."

Gen. Howe gave Connolly his blessing. Howe envisioned Burgoyne's army severing New England from the other rebel colonies while Connolly's patchwork force captured Fort Pitt and then moved south into Kentucky and western Virginia. Simultaneously, an immense British landing party would march inland from the southern seacoast, trapping the southern revolutionaries in a vise. But the plan was banjaxed when Connolly was captured by patriots while traveling to Fort Detroit.

Soon enough the notion of raising Canadian loyalists was discarded in favor of an all-Indian force consisting of multiple tribes. It fell to the civilian commander at Fort Detroit, the former British Army officer Henry Hamilton, to devise a strategy.

The forty-two-year-old Hamilton, the third son of an Irish viscount, possessed a keen martial mind gleaned from his twenty-one years of military service. He had been in North America since 1758, when his unit was dispatched to fight in the French and Indian War, and had eventually risen to the rank of brigade major. Hamilton had familiarized himself with Native American customs by working closely with the Iroquois Confederacy. For this he was groomed for administrative duties by Guy Carleton, the Crown's Quebec-based governor-general of British North America.

At Carleton's urging Hamilton had resigned his military commission in 1775 and been promptly appointed by Carleton to one of the four newly created positions of lieutenant governor. While stationed at Fort Detroit—whose tiny garrison was nominally under the command of Captain Richard Lernoult—Hamilton studied the strategy proposed by the since-captured John Connolly for his "Loyal Foresters." He liked Connolly's ideas, with a twist. He would eschew recruiting Canadian militiamen and rely solely on Indian irregulars.

This plan led to a break with his mentor, Governor Carleton, who considered repugnant the idea of arming red warriors. But officials in London sided with Hamilton and gave him free rein to recruit a Native American force by any means possible. Hamilton immediately convened a grand assemblage of Ottawas, Chippewa, Potawatomi, Miami, Shawnee, Mingoes, and Delaware at Fort Detroit. Breaking with the shibboleths of the Amherst era and taking a page from his French precursors, he supplied them with food, war paint, guns, ammunition, and scalping knives as a good-faith gesture from their "Great Father King" in London.

Hamilton was a student of human nature and recognized that the northern tribes were already skeptical of the United States' cause. He played up the fact that America's weak, young government made promises it could not keep. As evidence, he pointed to its failure to curtail the market hunters, rumrunners, and landjobbers who roamed their lands with impunity. Finally, toward the end of the gathering, he donned Indian garb, painted his face, and sang the tribal war songs. The Indians were won over. That Hamilton was also offering one hundred dollars for a captured Continental soldier or militiaman and fifty dollars for the scalp of a rebel American—prompting George Rogers Clark to damn Hamilton with the sobriquet "Hair Buyer"—was but added incentive.

Hamilton's understanding of North America's indigenous peoples served him so well that over time he displaced Guy Johnson as the Crown's head Indian interlocutor in reality, if not in title. This, in turn, would eventually lead him back onto the battlefield.

On December 6, 1776, with Lord Dunmore having fled Williamsburg for refuge aboard a British man-of-war anchored in Chesapeake Bay, the new Virginia governor, Patrick Henry, officially incorporated Kentucky County as the state's westernmost district. Anticipating this move, six months earlier the territory's voters had selected the bellicose George Rogers Clark to represent their interests in the state assembly. Though not yet technically a member of the legislative body, the twenty-four-year-old Clark had journeyed to Williamsburg, where he spent the late summer and early fall lobbying the delegates to supply the Kentucky stations with gunpowder and lead.

Citing the continued restiveness of the Cherokees and the palpable threat from the Northern Indians, Clark implored Gov. Henry and his Executive Council to spare him some of the much-needed ammunition, nearly all of which had already been earmarked for the war effort along the seaboard. Clark was a persuasive man, and by November he and six volunteers were not only freighting five hundred pounds of powder and galena, the natural mineral form of lead, by way of Fort Pitt, but Gov. Henry had appointed Clark as Kentucky County's justice of the peace and commissioned him a major in the Virginia state militia.

Toting his deadly load to Fort Pitt, Clark was met there by the experienced Kentucky long hunter John Gabriel Jones, who had also been elected to represent the new Kentucky County's interests. Jones had secured a barge, and the group loaded the flatboat with the cargo and floated it nearly three hundred miles down the Ohio. Despite the professions of peace by Cornstalk and White Eyes, Clark feared an Indian raid farther downriver, and ordered the craft docked at a natural harbor where Limestone Creek flows into the Ohio River in what is now Maysville, Kentucky. Clark calculated that he did not have enough hands to withstand an Indian attack while transporting the gunpowder and lead overland, so he ordered the payload buried in a hidden cache. He then left the others to watch over it while he set off to gather reinforcements at Harrodsburg, one hundred miles away.

Not long after Clark departed, Jones was joined by four more frontiersmen. Perhaps foolishly and certainly lethally, he judged his party of nearly a dozen riflemen strong enough to fend off any assault. The little company retrieved the cached ammunition and by Christmas morning had made about thirty miles when they were ambushed by a conglomeration of some forty to fifty Mingoes, Shawnee, Wyandot, Ottawas, and

Chippewa—the warriors from the latter three tribes providing proof that British efforts to turn the Great Lakes tribes was effective. The war party was led by a noted Mingo warrior whose somewhat farcical Anglicized name—"Captain Pluggy"—belied the ferociousness he had displayed as Logan's chief lieutenant during Lord Dunmore's War.

Jones and one of his companions were killed in the fight, and another two whites were captured, including Clark's cousin Joseph Rogers. The remaining seven managed to elude the Indians and reach McClelland's Station with the stores of powder and lead. There they met Clark returning with a party of thirty Harrodsburg men. Four days later the same Indians—likely having tortured their prisoners into revealing the nature of the consignment they carried—executed a bold frontal assault on the station. After failing to set fire to the blockhouse's log walls, they attempted to batter down the gate. It was during this attack that Captain Pluggy fell mortally wounded, picked off by a sharpshooter from the parapets. With their leader bleeding out, the Indians retrieved Captain Pluggy's body, rounded up the settlement's horses, slaughtered its cattle, and blended back into the forest.

27

ABANDONED SETTLEMENTS

In the aftermath of the fight at McClelland's Station, the checkerboard of Kentucky settlements once again rearranged itself. The station's founder and namesake, the former Virginia militia captain John McClelland, had been one of two men killed by Captain Pluggy's raiders. McClelland's slow demise—it took him two days to die from his wounds—was a psychological blow to his followers. With their leader McClelland dead, their horses stolen, and their cattle butchered, the station's remaining inhabitants saw no choice but to abandon the blockhouse and accompany George Rogers Clark back to Harrodsburg.

Among Clark's command was another former Virginian named Benjamin Logan. The thirty-five-year-old Logan was a battle-scarred veteran of both the Cherokee campaigns and Lord Dunmore's War, where he achieved the rank of lieutenant. Logan had emigrated to Kentucky in 1776 and briefly established an eponymous settlement some twenty-two miles southeast of Harrodsburg, one that eventually would grow into the town of Saint Asaph, named in honor of Logan's maternal forebears who had immigrated from Wales. That same year he was appointed Kentucky County's sheriff, the second-ranking officer in the county behind Clark. Though a seasoned and dedicated Indian fighter, Logan was described by a fellow soldier as "a dull narrow body from whom nothing clever need be expected." Which is probably why Clark was astonished when, as his party neared Harrodsburg, Logan and fourteen followers split off to reoccupy his old site.

Once again Kentucky was left with three manned outposts on the western frontier, each over two hundred miles from the nearest Virginia communities. The desperate mood in the settlements was highlighted by the plaintive communiqué dispatched to Patrick Henry by the Harrodsburg resident Hugh McGary. McGary, a volatile man even by frontier standards, was one of the ranking officers in Kentucky County's militia, such as it was. In truth, every man and boy able to heft a long rifle constituted the entirety of Kentucky's official fighting force. Writing to the governor, McGary warned him that the territory the Virginia legislature had only just absorbed as part of the state could very likely be shorn of its entire population when the winter weather broke, and he predicted a resumption of Indian attacks in the spring, "that fills our minds with a thousand fears." He envisioned a massive attack of Cherokee from the south, Shawnee from the north, and even Miami from the west. "We are surrounded with enemies on every side [and] every day increases their number," McGary wrote. "Our fort is already filled with widows and orphans; their necessities call upon us daily for supplies."

McGary proved no less prophetic than Dragging Canoe. Precisely eight days after a courier rode east with his letter, sixty to seventy Shawnee under the war chief Blackfish appeared outside Harrodsburg's gates singing their war song: *"The water will wash them away, / The wind will blow them down, / Darkness will come upon them, / And the earth will cover them."*

The militant Blackfish was a mystery to most of the whites though the Indians knew him well as for some years he had been vying with Cornstalk for tribal leadership. A short, wiry man who, at fifty, was some ten years younger than Cornstalk, Blackfish had been close with Tecumseh's slain father, Puckeshinwa. He had even become a mentor to the fatherless boy. Like his late friend, he, too, refused any accommodation with the Americans. Years later the Native American portraitist Charles Bird King portrayed Blackfish as a man whose still face was dominated by a pair of hooded eyes sparkling ominously, as if both amused and threatening. Moreover, like Logan of the Mingoes, Blackfish considered his excursion south of the Ohio as both a martial and personal journey. Though he and his followers had been encouraged by the British to harass, if not eliminate, the Kentucky "rebels," it had been Blackfish's son whom Boone's party had shot and killed during their rescue of Jemima. This attack was his revenge.

After establishing a central camp for his two hundred or so warriors on the Licking River, Blackfish personally led the rump contingent that fell on Harrodsburg. Initially he instructed his braves to burn a dilapidated cabin adjacent to the stockade in the hope that the sparks would spread to the log walls, which his scouts had splashed with buffalo tallow. When that failed, a long-distance gunfight ensued, with one man from each side struck by a lethal ball. Two more of the stockade's defenders, including Hugh McGary, sustained minor wounds.

Meanwhile, on the same day as the Harrodsburg attack, a separate force of Blackfish's Shawnee raided Boonesborough to much the same result. The Indians were driven away after killing a Negro slave working the communal vegetable garden. Boone immediately posted round-the-clock sentries and assigned armed guards to any farmer venturing out into the surrounding cornfields to continue the essential spring planting. He also led several scouting missions into the deep woods to search for Shawnee sign in an attempt to adjudge just how many hostiles were roaming the territory.

"The Indians seemed determined to persecute us for erecting this fortification," Boone told the biographer Filson. He had no idea that it may have been his musket ball that killed the son of the war leader now attacking the stations.

Boone had recently been commissioned a captain in the Kentucky militia, serving under George Rogers Clark, and had spent the previous months attempting to complete the stockade on the south bank of the Kentucky River. That it had held fast against the Shawnee assault was testament to his engineering skills. Given Blackfish's tactics, however, one is left to marvel over the sagacity of Humphrey Marshall, the great chronicler of Kentucky's frontier era.

In his contemporaneous *The History of Kentucky,* Marshall questioned the curious logic of the Indian sieges, noting that had the Shawnee "possessed the skill which combines individual effort with a concerted attack; and had they directed their whole force against each of the feeble forts in succession, instead of dissipating their strength . . . they could have easily rid Kentucky of its new inhabitants."

Over the next two months the Shawnee at first appeared to heed Marshall's words, first surrounding and besieging Harrodsburg for most of March to the point where the fort faced a serious food shortage. Yet with victory nearly in hand they inexplicably broke off their blockade to turn their attention to Boonesborough.

On the morning of April 24, two of Boonesborough's occupants left the stockade to round up a small remuda of horses grazing just past a cornfield seventy yards away. They had nearly reached the animals when a half dozen Shawnee leapt from a sycamore hollow and fired. As the balls whistled past their ears and kicked up gravel at their feet, the Kentuckians raced back for the fort while two of Boone's scouts, including Simon Kenton, stood near the open gate urging them on. Only one man was fast enough; two of the Indians overtook the other. A warrior split the latter's skull with a tomahawk and took his scalp. As he stood over the dead man waving the bloody trophy, Kenton shot him dead.

Kenton reloaded on the run as he and his fellow scout pursued the remaining Indians down the dirt lane that bisected the cornfields. They were nearly to the edge of the woods when the big frontiersman sensed something amiss. Turning back toward the fort, he saw Boone and a dozen men, including Michael Stoner, racing up the path. Before Kenton could warn them to turn back, half a hundred Shawnee poured from the cornfields and blocked their path of retreat. According to the historian Draper, who interviewed Boone's youngest son, Nathan, for the account, Boone yelled to his company, "Boys, we are gone—let us sell our lives as dearly as we can." With that the Kentuckians fired off a volley and, wielding their rifles as war clubs, charged into the scrum of Indians.

The fight must have seemed a murky whirlwind of gunsmoke, dust, and war cries to those watching from Boonesborough's parapets. In what many attributed to divine providence, no more Kentuckians were killed that day, although several received wounds that required them to be assisted on the dash back to safety. Michael Stoner was one such, his hand shredded by a musket ball that eventually lodged in his hip. Boone was one of the last in the field when, pausing to reload, a ball penetrated the heel of his foot and shattered his ankle as if it were made of spun glass. He had barely hit the ground when he looked up to see his assailant looming over him, tomahawk raised.

Dazed and losing consciousness, Boone was still fumbling for his hunting knife when the Indian's heart appeared to burst from his chest, propelled by a ball from Simon Kenton's long rifle. Another Indian lunged toward Boone with a knife, but Kenton, quick as a big cat, bashed in his skull with the butt of his gun. With that, Kenton threw Boone over his shoulders and lumbered for the log walls. As they neared the gate, Jemima Boone raced out to help carry her father.

Back in his cabin, the musket ball—"mashed as thin as a knife blade"— was drawn from Boone's ankle from the opposite side from which it had entered. While Rebecca and Jemima fashioned strips of linen into a sling for his leg, Boone asked his daughter to find the young Kenton and bring him to his bedside. The two pioneers with the outsize reputations had circled each other warily since Kenton's arrival in Kentucky, two particles of positive charge destined to repel each other. But this incident had apparently bent the immutable laws of physics and sealed what was to become a lifelong friendship.

When Kenton appeared in his doorframe, Boone nodded his thanks. "Simon," he said to the man who had saved his life, "you have behaved like a man today. Indeed, you are a fine fellow."

No one ever accused the laconic Daniel Boone of overstating his case.

28

"THE BEST LITTLE INDIAN FIGHT"

S uch was the perilous nature of existence along the American border-lands through the summer of 1777 that an informal census taken in early May concluded that of the roughly 280 settlers occupying the trio of besieged Kentucky station-forts, less than half were able-bodied fighters. Harrodsburg's 84 men defending forty families was the largest contingent, the 15 at Logan's Station the smallest. Boonesborough counted 22 riflemen among its dozen or so families.* This was the bulwark who stood between the eastern settlements and the over three thousand warriors the combined Shawnee, Delaware, Mingo, and Miami tribes could muster.

As nearly every American horse had been stolen, Daniel Boone, George Rogers Clark at Harrodsburg, and Benjamin Logan at his station relied on Kenton and another long hunter named Thomas Brooks to flit through the forest on foot as couriers relaying news among the three outposts. The two were also charged with acting as early-warning signalmen on the constant lookout for recent Indian sign. The dangerous and cumbersome relay system meant it took days for Boone or Logan, for instance, to learn

---

* Put in perspective, this was roughly 0.02 percent of the twelve thousand Continental troops who would limp into Valley Forge later in the year.

that a man had been killed and another badly wounded gathering water outside of Harrodsburg, or that a war party of close to two hundred Indians had wounded three men during a subsequent forty-eight-hour siege of Boonesborough. Given the distances to be covered, if distress messages did manage to arrive, it is not certain how much good they did.

One day Kenton slipped into Boonesborough with news that Logan's Station was under attack by over fifty Shawnee—with one man already dead and three others wounded. The plea from Logan contained the ominous information that his tiny group of defenders were running out of lead balls, and the settlement's women were at the hearth melting down pewter plates for ammunition. Boone, by now on crutches, asked his brother Squire to lead a company of reinforcements. Although several members of the Boonesborough relief party made it through to help break the siege, the younger Boone had barely stepped into the forest when a rifle shot cracked two of his ribs. He was forced to turn back, his assailants never seen.

Notwithstanding the insight of the historian Humphrey Marshall, it was evident that the hostiles were trying to keep up a steady fire on all three outposts for a twofold purpose—to starve out the pioneers as well as to prevent them from coming to each other's assistance. The Indians continued to slaughter any domestic cattle and hogs they discovered at pasturage, and unlike Boonesborough, Harrodsburg was under such constant surveillance that the settlers dared not venture out to plant spring corn. Volunteers would sneak from the stockade under cover of darkness to tote back as many bushels as possible from the previous season's corncribs cached deep in the woods, while others made water runs to nearby streams. This barely kept the community alive, particularly the growing ranks of orphans and widows. The women were reduced to weaving buffalo hair into the bark-like fibers of prickly nettles that grew wild within the stockade. The result was a facsimile of cloth to patch the riflemen's tattered linsey-woolsey shirts.

As the pressure built, the beleaguered communities took on the miens of prizefighters buckling at the knees after a series of body blows, looking to their corners for answers. Those answers, as everyone knew, lay to the east. By midsummer Boone had dispatched a messenger to the Yadkin to plead for assistance from his old friends, neighbors, and relatives, while a volunteer from Logan's Station had snuck off in the night to the Holston Valley for the same purpose. Clark, meanwhile, had sent Hugh McGary to Fort Pitt to obtain ammunition and, if possible, horses. In response, Gov. Patrick Henry finally acted, and on August 1, a company of one hundred mounted Virginia Rangers rode into Boonesborough to the huzzahs of the ragged survivors.

The Indians were not cowed. Within the week a squad of the Virginians riding to Logan's Station was ambushed; their commander reported two men wounded and another killed. What made this incident stand out from the welter of violence was the proclamation affixed with a makeshift spear to the body of the dead militiaman. It was a letter from Lieutenant Governor Hamilton offering a general pardon, a retention of rank, and two hundred acres of land to any Kentuckian who deserted the rebel cause to fight for the Redcoats. Given the black days of the preceding months, Benjamin Logan wisely kept the overture of the "Hair Buyer" to himself.

As if to emphasize the shift in the military ecosystem, several weeks later a war party of Kickapoo fell on a company of thirty or so volunteers delivering corn to Harrodsburg. The Kickapoo were a nomadic, Algonquian-speaking tribe whom Indian lore (and present-day archaeologists) describe as having calved from the Shawnee at some point in the distant past. They now roamed the lands of what is today western Indiana, Illinois, and Wisconsin—French Jesuits recorded them exploring as far southwest as Texas and Mexico—and allied themselves with the even more western Sauk and Fox. The Kickapoo were rarely spotted south of the Ohio, and their presence in Kentucky only reinforced the British contrails wafting over the new front.

Despite his cracked ribs, Squire Boone had been among those

provisioning Harrodsburg when the Kickapoo broke from the woods. The tale of his actions in the minor engagement that ensued—infinitesimal in proportion to the grand revolutionary battles being waged to the east—is nonetheless indicative of what the newly minted Americans on the western frontier were willing to endure more than half a century before the phrase "Manifest Destiny" was coined.

At the sound of the first Kickapoo war whoops, the younger Boone shouldered his rifle and fired. Before the smoke had cleared his gun's touchhole he dived behind a tree to reload. Another militiaman had chosen the same tree as cover, but an Indian flanked him and shot him dead. His body toppled onto the kneeling Squire Boone, pinning Boone's rifle beneath them both. When the warrior raced in to collect his scalp, he was surprised to discover the quick beneath the dead.

Squire Boone was carrying a saber—a favorite of American militiamen, the three-faceted weapon was the origin of the Indian term "Long Knives"—and the two combatants drew first blood simultaneously. For precisely as the Kickapoo's tomahawk lifted a cleat of flesh from the squirming Squire Boone's forehead—denting but not fracturing his skull—Boone plunged his sword into the Indian's abdomen with his right hand. With his left he seized the warrior's breechclout. He pulled the man toward him until several inches of the blade protruded from the small of his back. The gasping Kickapoo lunged for the sheathed knife hanging from Squire Boone's belt. But the blood pouring from Boone's forehead rendered it too slippery to grasp. The Indian backed away, but Boone would not let go of his breechclout. After several steps back, dragging Boone with him, the Kickapoo fell dead. Not to be outdone by his understated brother, Squire Boone later declared the contest as "the best little Indian fight" he had ever taken part in.

As the Kentucky hardwoods sprouted rainbows of shimmering orange, red, and yellow leaves, so too turned the momentum in the epic settler-Indian struggle. The pioneering outlanders, emboldened by the arrival of the Virginia militia as well as a company of forty-eight North Carolinians from the Yadkin Valley, were no longer content to huddle behind the log walls of their stockades. Equipped now with horses and gunpowder, mounted riflemen became the hunters and the "dusky forces" their prey. The offensive posture only increased when another eighty-eight or so Virginians rode into Harrodsburg during the first week of October. Two weeks later, fifty dragoons under the command of the Scots-born Virginian Charles Watkins arrived in Boonesborough.

With the influx of so many militiamen, the frontal sieges on the Kentucky forts ceased and the fighting deteriorated into a series of deep-forest ambushes. As a relieved Boone recalled, "Now we begin to strengthen [and] our affairs began to wear a new aspect. The enemy, not daring to venture on open war, [could only] practice secret mischief. Hence, for the space of six weeks, we had skirmishes with Indians, in one quarter or another, almost every day. The savages now learned the superiority of the Long Knives."

Such was the reversal that Benjamin Logan felt confident enough to leave his brother in command of his station in order to accompany James Harrod to the Holston for supplementary ammunition. They returned not only with four kegs of powder and a string of packhorses hauling lead, but with the stunning news that Gen. Burgoyne, marching south from Canada, had surrendered his entire army to General Horatio Gates near the Upstate New York hamlet of Saratoga. As Logan and Harrod distributed the powder, shot, and the tale of Gates's victory to their hunters, it is not recorded what buoyed the settlers more—the idea of close to six thousand Redcoats and Hessians as prisoners of the Continental Army or, for the first time in months, the prospect of fresh-killed meat for their cookfires.

Farther south, George Washington's emissaries attempted to leverage word of the northern triumph at Saratoga to America's advantage by reaching out to overtly recruit Indians to the rebel cause. The first target were members of the Overhill Cherokee faction, led by the chief known as Corn

Tassel. For years Corn Tassel had trodden a fine line between keeping his distance from the skirmishes and battles waged between the encroaching white settlers and Dragging Canoe's more militant Chickamauga branch of the tribe. Washington, employing Christopher Gist's brother Nathaniel as his conduit, attempted to exploit this rift.

The Continental Army's commander in chief—whom Gist described as the "great Warrior of all America" to Corn Tassel and his people— had received permission from a wary Continental Congress to recruit no more than four hundred Cherokee to be used primarily as army scouts. It was a sound idea, not least because the prospect of any Native Americans fighting alongside the rebelling colonists was certain to give the British pause. But Washington also had an ulterior motive for the gambit: should he manage to gather enough Overhill Cherokee warriors under his imme- diate command, they would make excellent hostages if Dragging Canoe stepped up his own recruiting efforts from among the neutral factions of the tribe.

Although the Indian reaction to Washington's overtures was tepid— there were few warriors willing to travel to Pennsylvania—the talks did result in a treaty between Corn Tassel and the Americans, which ceded most of western North Carolina and some of eastern Tennessee to the fledgling United States. What Washington had not taken into consider- ation, however, is what military analysts would today call blowback, as scores of disgusted Overhill Cherokee deserted Corn Tassel to join Drag- ging Canoe's militants.

In the meanwhile, in order to keep the northern tribes at bay, Wash- ington personally appointed the Irish-born polymath General Edward Hand as commander at Fort Pitt. Gen. Hand had convinced Washington that the most efficient way to prevent Indian attacks on America's frontier settlements was to bring the war to the enemy's towns and villages. It was an overly optimistic notion, as Hand soon discovered that the troops he envisioned taking the fight to the Indians were sparse in western parts, and Washington could spare no eastern regulars.

Unable to mount an expedition in strength, Hand was forced to dole out portions of his eight-hundred-man garrison piecemeal, sending companies hither and yon to aid whichever Pennsylvania or Virginia militia commander whose situation appeared most dire. As these rapid-response teams usually contained no more than a few hundred men, they were largely futile, in no small part because the Indian raiders often had disappeared by the time they arrived on the scene.

Gen. Hand's ineffectualness notwithstanding, a renewed sense of enthusiasm and resolve had infused the Kentucky pioneers since beating back Blackfish and his hostiles. The corollary to this soaring esprit de corps was to explode with the Native Americans' near rabid thirst for reprisal following one of the more dishonorable episodes of an ignominious epoch on America's frontier.

In early October 1777, Cornstalk and two other Shawnee elders arrived at Fort Randolph, the stockade that had risen at Point Pleasant on the site where three years earlier the old chief had suffered the defeat that ended Lord Dunmore's War. The fort's former commander, the militia officer Capt. Russell, had returned to his home on the Clinch River, and Cornstalk had come to deliver a warning to the garrison's new officer in charge, Captain Matthew Arbuckle. He and his older Mekoche followers, the Shawnee told Arbuckle, were personally willing to continue to "uphold the chain of friendship" with the Americans. But such was the influence of British agents on so many of the tribe's young warriors that their fealty to him had slipped away.

Despite Arbuckle's frontier bona fides—he had only recently been the first white man to chart the Great Kanawha River from its headwaters to the Ohio—Arbuckle was confused. Was not the great Cornstalk the "king" of all Shawnee? Nearly 250 years later one can almost envision the sigh Cornstalk emitted when, as he had explained to the Indian agent George Morgan a year earlier at Fort Pitt, the chief attempted to elucidate the differences between the independence of his peoples' loose tribal fighting coalitions and the top-down military organization of the white man. No warrior was subservient to any civil authority, he told Arbuckle. He could no more command his warriors to stand down than the American revolutionists could order the British to return to England.

His final words betrayed a hint of a fugue state as he reflected on his war weariness. It was as if he longed to escape the endless loop of violence.

"When I was young and went to war," Cornstalk told the white soldier, "I thought that each expedition would prove the last, and I would return no more. Now I am here amongst you. You may kill me if you please. I can die but once."

Arbuckle's response was to take all three Indians hostage as bargaining chips. This was merely a negotiating ploy, he promised Cornstalk and his companions. He would ensure that no harm came to them.

Weeks later Cornstalk's son Elinipsico arrived at Fort Randolph in search of his father. Arbuckle allowed them to visit. As the Indians conferred, the body of a scalped militia courier was carried into the little outpost. Casks of rum were tapped in the dead man's honor, never a good sign among ill-disciplined irregulars. At length the mail carrier's friends gathered outside the cabin where Cornstalk and the others were being held. Sensing the raven come to call, one of the Indians climbed the hut's chimney and began to dismantle the roof shingles. Cornstalk bade him come down. It was, as he had predicted, their time to die. The mob stormed into the makeshift prison. A hail of bullets left all four Shawnee piled in a bloody heap.

Capt. Arbuckle later claimed that the event occurred so fast that there was nothing he could do to stop it. But his explanation was undercut by another officer's journal. In it, Captain John Stuart recorded that the canoe bearing the dead courier's body had barely made shore outside the fort when a cry went up to murder the Indian prisoners. "Every man with his gun in his hand came up the bank pale as death with rage," Capt. Stuart wrote. "Captain Arbuckle and myself met them endeavoring to dissuade them from so unjustifiable an action. But they cocked their guns and threatened us with instant death if we did not desist, and rushed into the fort."

What loomed certain, however, was that there would be repercussions for the murders. In an attempt to forestall the inevitable, Gov. Henry of Virginia and his Pennsylvania counterpart, Thomas Wharton, dispatched emissaries to Cornstalk's Mekoche village expressing their remorse over the "accident." And from Pittsburgh the beleaguered Indian agent George Martin conveyed the Continental Congress's deepest regrets. The American authorities, however, recognized that the Shawnee would see through the crocodile tears. Gen. Hand succinctly summed up the mood: "If we had anything to expect from the [Shawnee] Nation," he wrote, "it is now vanished."

Considering Capt. Arbuckle's broken pledge to Cornstalk that he would not be harmed, it was not lost on some observers that only nine months earlier it had been George Rogers Clark who had evinced so little faith in Cornstalk's solemn word.

PART IV

THE CONQUEST

Never did the Indians pursue so disastrous a policy, as when they
captured me and my salt-boilers, and learned us, what we did not know
before, the way to their towns, and the geography of their country.

—Daniel Boone

29

TAKEN

It was snowing hard by the time Daniel Boone finished packing his horse with over two hundred pounds of fresh buffalo meat. Leading the animal on foot, he had made less than a mile when a shiver in the brittle tree branches, a sixth sense, a numinous whisper running through the forest, caused him to wheel. Four Indians were behind him, perhaps thirty feet distant. In his gut he knew it was already too late. The rushing Licking River to his right was in spate, blocking flight to the north. On his left a near-vertical wall of granite and gneiss rose to over fifty feet. They had chosen well their spot for an ambush.

The hostiles were afoot, and Boone's first instinct was to slice the tugs securing his bales and try for a mounted escape. But his knife, bloody from dressing the buffalo carcass, was frozen in its sheath. His second reaction was to run. Although not fully recovered from his shattered ankle, Boone at forty-three was in better physical shape than most men half his age. Unfortunately, these did not include the three warriors who took off after him as the fourth grabbed his horse's reins.

He could hear their cackles intermixed with mocking war trills as they followed his trail through the fresh powder. When the path broke into forest, the Indians loped up nearly parallel to his either side, one or the other pausing to fire at his feet as if daring him to run faster. Finally, when a musket ball severed the strap of his powder horn, Boone knew the ghost was near given. He ducked behind a tree, tossed his rifle as a sign of surrender, and awaited his fate.

As the biographer Lyman Draper picks up the story, "The Indians now came up, whooping and laughing in great good humor in view of their success, shook him heartily by the hand, and took possession of his gun, knife, and ammunition."

For all the wanton brutality of the eighteenth-century Indian Wars, to a modern observer it sometimes appears as if the white pioneers of America's first frontier and the indigenous peoples whose lands they coveted were playing some great cosmic game, albeit one whose table stakes were torture and death. There is no better example of the Grand Guignol nature of this lethal contest than the events subsequent to Daniel Boone's capture, yet again, by the Shawnee on the Sunday morning of February 8, 1778.

One month earlier, the whites populating the wilderness settlements along the Kentucky River—now in their third year of hand-to-mouth existence—had found themselves precariously bereft of salt. Boonesborough was particularly desperate, as Blackfish's Shawnee had poisoned the brackish spring near the stockade with dead animals, turning it into a mephitic brew. Though the fear of further Indian raids made the tedious method of acquiring salt stores from farther sources a dangerous prospect, the fact was that the settlers could not survive without the salt necessary to cure winter meats.

Depending on a lick's viscosity, between five hundred and six hundred gallons from a salt spring's waters were needed to produce one fifty-pound bushel of the precious preservative. Moreover, with the Shawnee having killed most of their cattle and burned their cornfields, the communities were ever more dependent on storing jerked game to survive until spring.

In consequence, Boone had set out from Boonesborough in early January at the head of a troop of thirty men for the southern bank of the Licking and the multiple springs of briny water that fed the river.

The party, packing several large iron kettles, planned to spend a month boiling and drying before being relieved by a similar-sized company led by Capt. Watkins. With most of the previous autumn's militia reinforcements having returned to their homes in Virginia and North Carolina, Boone and his party counted on the early-winter months remaining the traditional quiet time for warfare on the borderlands.

What Boone, Watkins, and the others in the compounds had failed to take into consideration, however, was the fury the Indians still felt over the murder of Cornstalk, his son, and his confederates. In the wake of the killings, the warrior Blackfish had assumed Shawnee tribal leadership and called a war council to debate how and when to best exact vengeance. His former rivalry with Cornstalk did not mean that the old chief's killing could be left unavenged. Spurred by the promise of British bounties, Indians from myriad tribes answered Blackfish's call to arms, including renegade Creeks from the south and Chippewa from the Canadian border.

Yet even Blackfish recognized that the 120 or so braves gathered under his command on the Little Miami River were too few to assail the well-garrisoned fort at Point Pleasant where Cornstalk had been slain. Instead, he convinced the council to look south to Kentucky, specifically to Boonesborough, where the white trespassers would least expect a midwinter assault.

So confident were the Indians who had run down Boone that they did not bother to bind his hands as they led him to their camp. As he was ushered before Blackfish, Boone was shocked to find over one hundred hostiles on the south side of the Ohio in February. The Shawnee war leader was surrounded by half a dozen of his most elite fighters as well as two Quebecois fur traders in the employ of the British. Blackfish could have summoned one of the two "turncoat" Girty brothers present, either James or George, to translate. Twenty-two years earlier, during the French and Indian War, a combined Shawnee-Delaware raiding party had killed a Pennsylvania Indian trader named John Turner and kidnapped his four stepsons, who still carried their late biological father's surname of Girty, likely a bastardized version of the Irish Geraghty. After British negotiators secured the release of one of the boys, the other three were dispersed among separate tribes, with thirteen-year-old James adopted by the Shawnee, ten-year-old George kept by the Delaware, and their older brother, Simon, fifteen, taken in by the Mingoes.*

But Blackfish, undoubtedly cognizant of the Girtys' reputations along the frontier as "white savages," instead chose a former black slave named Pompey. Pompey, like the Girtys, had been captured as a child and had lived and fought with the Indians since. The Shawnee chief opened the proceedings with the pidgin greeting universally employed by the indigenous Eastern Woodlands peoples: "How d'do, brodder?"†

Though they had never met, Blackfish hailed Boone as if he were indeed a long-lost "brodder," shaking his hand and clapping him on the back. Then the Shawnee warrior stepped aside to allow his Praetorians to do the same. As was the spiritual Indian custom, Blackfish had satisfied his blood debt to his late son by personally killing several Kentucky pioneers during the previous autumn's fighting season. Though that slate was now clean, the deaths of Cornstalk and his son had begun a new one. As Blackfish's inner circle approached one by one to take the measure of

---

* Despised by borderlands pioneers as race traitors, the Girty brothers in fact matured into intelligent and circumspect men who often served as bridges between the white and red worlds. Although never definitively proven, it was rumored that Simon Girty—blood brother to Simon Kenton, it should be noted—was the interlocutor who delivered "Logan's Lament" at the Treaty of Camp Charlotte negotiations. The Girty brothers burned their last American bridge when they offered their services to the British Army in early 1778.

† This is the origin of countless if baffling Hollywood scenes of stoic Indians greeting white men with an upraised and open right hand accompanied by the single word "How." In reality, by the time the original "How d'do" salutation crossed the Mississippi it had been shortened by Plains Indians, first to "How-dee," and finally to "How." The open hand signified that the Indian did not intend to fight.

their prisoner, Boone knew that propriety demanded that captives remain silent unless directly spoken to. But when the last Shawnee in line neared, he could not keep his tongue.

"How d'do, Captain Will?" he said. The half-blood Will Emery took a step back and eyed the white captive suspiciously.

"Eight years ago," Boone prompted. "Two white prisoners on the Kentucky River." With this, a broad smile creased Captain Will's face and he clasped Boone's hand in both of his and shook it so vigorously that he nearly wrenched the frontiersman's arm from its socket. Despite the bonhomie, Boone well understood that a more serious approach to removing his limbs might soon be his fate.

The introductions over, Blackfish casually admitted that he and his war party were on their way to raze Boone's settlement to avenge Cornstalk's murder. But first, he wanted to know, precisely how many white men were on the Licking River making salt? Boone riposted by asking the Indian what made him think that *any* men were on the river? Blackfish swept his arm, and several warriors stepped from the circle about him. Because his scouts had found them, he said. Then, gesticulating ominously, he emitted a series of growls that needed no translation from Pompey: Boone had best not lie to him. Boone nodded and admitted that twenty-eight "salt-boilers" and three hunters, including himself, made up the company. Blackfish said he planned to kill them all.

Boone knew that the men camped on the Licking, outnumbered four to one, stood no chance, and that Boonesborough was equally vulnerable. As if the globules of hoarfrost spangling the surrounding tree branches were thousands of crystal balls, Boone foresaw what tactics the Indians would use to take the settlement.

The hostiles would lay siege to Boonesborough, and at first the settlers would hold out. But at the death of the first Indian, or simply out of frustration, Blackfish would bring forth whomever had been taken alive at the salt-boiling camp—there were always captives—lash them to stakes just out of rifle range, and set them afire one by one. How many would have to burn before the fort surrendered, Boone did not know. But surrender it would. The strategy would then be repeated at Logan's Station and at Harrodsburg, until Kanta-ke was again in Indian hands. He weighed Blackfish's admonition about telling the truth, and lied to him anyway.

Boone painted a scene of a hopeless Indian assault against Boonesborough's fortified walls and exaggerated the number of the stockade's defenders. The pioneers forted up would not hesitate to watch fellow pioneers be tortured in order to protect their own kith and kin, Boone said. He added that the settlement's magazines were bursting with powder and lead and its larders were near to overstocked for the winter. He painted a bleak portrait: the settlers would eat well each morning, noon, and night while Blackfish's braves slowly starved for a lack of seasonal game. And even if by some ill chance the fort should fall, Boone concluded, many if not most of the captured women and children would surely die on the long and frozen trek back to the Ohio River, making them worthless as squaws, adoptees, or hostages. None of this, save the last, was remotely true.

Before the Indian could answer, Boone proffered an alternative—why not take prisoner the whites at the camp along the Licking, and then return to Boonesborough later in the spring or summer? He told Blackfish that he was certain he could convince his salt-boilers to surrender once he described the numbers arrayed against them. Then, when the weather turned, he would accompany Blackfish back to Boonesborough and talk the settlers into doing the same. Would not the captives' living worth increase in fairer weather? Boone then played his last card. He volunteered to live among the Shawnee as one of their own. He had but one condition: if Blackfish agreed to his proposals, none of the men taken captive on the Licking would be made to pass through the gauntlet.

This stymied the Shawnee. On the one hand it was traditional for male white prisoners to display their mettle by completing the run. The ritual was not only a torture, but a precursor to adoption into a tribe. On the other, the idea of taking nearly three dozen whites without a fight and transporting them back across the Ohio as either new tribal members or merchandise to sell to the British was intriguing. If any got out of hand, he would lift their scalps for the "Hair Buyer" Hamilton's fifty dollars. And if Boone was true to his word about convincing the men camped on the Licking to surrender, he might indeed be useful come spring in dismantling Boonesborough, not to mention the other Kentucky forts. After a short deliberation, Blackfish nodded his assent.

The snowfall was tapering when Boone appeared, ghostlike, on a ledge above the salt-boiling camp on the Licking. At first the men below thought that Capt. Watkins and his relief party had arrived. But when a line of Indians fanned to either side of Boone they scrambled for their guns. Boone hollered that if anyone fired, all would be massacred. No one did. He then walked into the camp, where twenty-six of the thirty men gathered about him. Of the missing four, two had been sent back to Boonesborough with the first bushel-sacks of salt, and another pair, including Betsy and Fanny Callaway's cousin Flanders Callaway, were out hunting.

Boone described the bargain he had struck. There were, naturally, grumbles. But Boone emphasized to those who insisted on fighting that he had cut his deal to spare their wives and children back at the settlement as much as to save their own scalps. As if to drive home the point, he swept his hand. By now the whites could make out the scores of painted Indians on the ridgelines overlooking their position.

Finally, with stiff, sullen movements, the frontiersmen lined up to stack their rifles in the center of camp. Within moments the Indians had snatched up their arms and anything else deemed worth taking, including the iron kettles and several bushels of salt. After scattering the rest of the hard-earned crystals to the wind, they marched their prisoners north toward the Ohio River over one hundred miles away.

Later that night, after making camp, Boone noticed several braves snapping frozen cane shoots, bundling them into primitive brooms, and sweeping a path in the snow perhaps six feet across and one hundred yards in length. He demanded that the translator Pompey take him to Blackfish's cookfire. Boone reminded the Shawnee that he had promised not to run his men through a gauntlet. The Indian nodded, and agreed that he had pledged to forgo the ceremony for any captured at the salt-boiling camp. But, he added, he had said nothing about exempting Boone.

Hours after the Indians and their prisoners had set out for the Ohio, Flanders Callaway and his hunting partner rode into the salt-boiling camp. Only months earlier Callaway had wed Jemima Boone. He did not hold his new father-in-law in the same disdain as his uncle, Col. Richard Callaway. The young hunters' initial reaction to finding the camp empty was to assume that Boone had tired of waiting for Capt. Watkins and had decided to return to Boonesborough with their haul. But as they gathered kindling for a cookfire, they came across a Shawnee arrow and not long after noticed that the snow was infused with salt. Searching by torchlight, they picked up the tracks of scores of moccasins leading north. Finding no bodies or blood trails, they surmised that the party had been taken. They mounted immediately.

That night, galloping toward Boonesborough, the two rode headlong into Capt. Watkins's company en route to the Licking. After hearing their report, Watkins turned his troop around and reached the Boonesborough settlement by dawn. In Boone's absence, Col. Richard Callaway had assumed command of the fort. Against Col. Callaway's orders, Simon Kenton and several other long hunters, including his nephew Flanders, insisted on trying to track the raiding party's movements. They made it as far as the Licking by the next morning, but snow had fallen all night, obscuring any Indian sign.

Boone stripped to his breechclout, leggings, and moccasins. He noted that the Shawnee had not painted his face black, too often an augur that the runner was already marked for death. Then, seeing that the greater number of Indians lining the gauntlet wielded only cane switches—and not tomahawks or war clubs—he also gathered that Blackfish was merely toying with him. In that case, he decided, two could play the game. At the starter's signal—a war club smashed into his ass—Boone darted as hard as he could straight at an Indian on the right side of the line and flicked out his fist to within inches of the man's face. While most frontier brawlers relied on raw "wrasslin'" brute strength and wild haymakers to take down a foe, Boone in his youth had taught himself rudimentary boxing skills. He now used them.

When the startled warrior gave ground, Boone pivoted. Snarling and whooping, he barreled toward another would-be tormenter a bit farther ahead on the left, again flicking out his fist. He continued on this zigzag course and, as he had suspected, he felt several switches cutting into the flesh of his bare back and arms. But only one Shawnee had landed a solid blow to the crown of his head with a war club. He could taste the blood flowing into his mouth.

Toward the end of the line a large Indian brandishing a tomahawk broke the rules of the gauntlet and stepped into the center of the path. Perhaps he felt that Boone had gotten off too easily. Boone lowered his shoulders, willed up his body's last ounces of speed and strength, and rammed his head into the big man's chest, sending him flying backward. Boone leapt over him and crossed the end line.

Despite their precarious position, Boone's white comrades let out a string of huzzahs. They may have been drowned out by the gales of laughter and trills emitted by the Indians mocking and trampling the prostrate warrior as they rushed past him to shake Boone's hand.

Over the next few days the translator Pompey proved an amiable enough companion, and during the march north he provided Boone with snippets of gossip as to the mood of the war party. In a sonorous voice he told Boone that the Indians were edgy. Game was sparse, as Boone well knew, having watched the Indians eat the salt party's horses as well as their own dogs.

Moreover, Pompey said, there were those who wanted to slaughter the whites immediately and turn back toward Boonesborough and the full larders of which Boone had bragged. The translator also told Boone that should the captives be allowed to live, one of the Quebecois—he was not certain which—had slyly suggested that inasmuch as they had pledged to join the tribes, their ears should be slit, trimmed, and stretched with weights here and now. Again Boone sought out Blackfish. With Pompey translating, he challenged the Shawnee chief to remain true to his word. He then requested to be allowed to address the entire war party. Blackfish assented.

"These young men will make you fine warriors and excellent hunters to kill game for your squaws and children," Boone told the assembled Indians. "They have done you no harm. I consented to their capitulation on the express condition that they should be made prisoners of war and treated well. Spare them, and the Great Spirit will smile upon you."

With that, Blackfish called for a vote. Fifty-nine of the Shawnee voted to kill the white prisoners, sixty-one to allow them to live. But Boone was not finished. There was this business of the ear-slitting to attend to. Aware that he had pushed his luck to the brink, he took Blackfish aside and couched his argument in practical terms. He told the chief that such a ceremony would not only waste more time during their arduous journey, but also subject the open wounds to frostbite before they could close. Besides, he argued, was not trimming one's ears a tribal warrior's prerogative, and not a requisite? The men should be allowed to decide for themselves once they reached their destination of New Chillicothe on the Little Miami. Blackfish agreed.

They made the Ohio River in just over a week on the move. There the Indians retrieved a large coracle hidden deep in a canebrake. The craft was made from four or five bull buffalo hides sewn together with rawhide cord and fitted over a rude wooden wattle. The craft reminded Boone of the "round boats" he had learned to construct from the Delaware as a child. The vessel's seams were caulked with animal tallow mixed with ashes. It held some twenty men, and after multiple crossings the entire party regrouped on the north bank of the river.

To this point in just over four decades on earth, Boone had explored, hunted, and fought across what today constitutes ten of the current United States. This was the first time he had set foot in Shawnee country.

30

SHEL-TOW-EE

Daniel Boone had always despised, and would for the rest of his life, his outsize reputation as an Indian fighter. He maintained that dealing with belligerent Native Americans, whether via combat or negotiation, was for the most part a matter of luck and instinct. His rescue by Simon Kenton was evidence of the former, his quick thinking on the Licking River, the latter. He was vastly more proud of his ability to endure the burdens of a huntsman's life with a seemingly preternatural stoicism. Now, it was as if the patience he had honed over a lifetime of stalking game through the deep woods was in anticipation of this moment. He would need that gift in the coming months.

On February 18, exactly ten days after their capture, Boone and his fellow prisoners were marched into the Shawnee town of New Chillicothe on the eastern bank of the Little Miami River, not far from where Springfield, Ohio, now rises. Despite a raging blizzard, the appearance of the victorious Indian column was nonetheless cause enough for the community's diminished winter population to pour from their homes and rejoice. Not since Gen. Braddock's defeat at Fort Duquesne over two decades earlier had the tribe enjoyed such a bounty of white captives.

Those among the salt-boilers who had never seen an Indian town were startled. Instead of the simple wattle-and-daub wigwams of their imaginations, the one-room wooden cabins arranged symmetrically around a large council house of notched hickory logs situated on a ridge overlooking the river clearly showed the influence of white frontier architecture. The huts appeared immaculately kept. Moreover, New Chillicothe itself was a model of town planning, with the former expanse of prairie extending from the Little Miami now transformed into fertile fields for planting and grazing horses and, beyond, rolling wooded hills filled with game and wild fruits.

Though most of the town's warriors and their families were spread about the countryside in winter hunting camps, the few-score women, children, and elders on hand insisted on subjecting the whites to the traditional gauntlet. Boone protested, to no avail. In the end, all the salt-boilers made it through largely unscathed, except for one Kentuckian who insisted on fighting his way down the line. He was left with a broken arm for his belligerence. That night a raucous war dance was performed in honor of Blackfish's accomplishment. As the near-naked braves pranced and gyrated around a roaring bonfire, the prisoners strained against their bindings. The reality of their circumstances had begun to set in.

Some now blamed Boone for talking them into surrendering, insisting they could have held their own in any skirmish back on the Licking. A young man named Andrew Johnson accused Boone of being a British spy. Even others who acknowledged the inevitable bloody outcome had they stood and fought now expressed a desire to have been allowed to die like men rather than be enslaved by Indians. Few took seriously Blackfish's stated intention of seeing that they were adopted into Shawnee families. Likely none had any idea what that meant, nor would they have understood had the concept of transmogrification been spelled out for them.

As it happened, over the next several weeks, seventeen of the twenty-seven whites taken from Kentucky were in fact placed into Shawnee families, with all but three of the adoptees being led away to satellite villages and camps.* The trio who remained at New Chillicothe were Boone, the recalcitrant Andy Johnson, and an ornery backwoodsman named Will Hancock, who was, ironically, adopted by Captain Will Emery. Boone was chosen by Blackfish himself to take the place of his slain son. He was rechristened Shel-tow-ee, or "Big Turtle." This was not only a nod to the physical strength packed into the frontiersman's stout frame, but to the spiritual connection Blackfish saw between Boone and the land. In the Shawnee creation myth, the bedrock and soil of North America was an island in a vast ocean literally supported by a giant sea turtle conjured by the Master of Life. At forty-three years old, Boone now had a new "father" and "mother" not much older than himself, as well as two new stepsisters both under the age of ten.

In early March, Blackfish recruited an escort of forty warriors, gathered the remaining ten captives who had proven too bellicose to live with the tribe, and with Boone at his side set off for Detroit 250 miles to the north. By this time, at the direction of a Shawnee medicine man, Boone had been immersed in the river and "cleansed" of his white blood by a team of Indian matrons who plucked clean his scalp, leaving only the traditional Indian topknot. Upon his arrival at the British stronghold he was summoned to the residence of Lt. Gov. Hamilton. Although his ten Kentucky companions were destined for Canadian prison barges, Hamilton offered to ransom the famous frontiersman for one hundred pounds sterling—five times the bounty that each of the other prisoners brought. When Blackfish demurred, Hamilton requested that he at least allow Boone to stay the night so he might interrogate him.

That evening Boone lived up to his woodsman's reputation. He demonstrated his gunsmithing expertise by restocking an Indian trader's broken long rifle, and astonished the lieutenant governor by mixing a batch of

* As evidence that the Indian custom of adopting prisoners was not as successful with older captives, over the ensuing years fifteen of the seventeen adopted salt-boilers either escaped or were killed attempting to escape. Of the remaining two, one moved beyond the Mississippi with his adoptive clan and the other was taken by American soldiers and tortured to death as a race traitor.

homemade gunpowder. Boone had learned the art from a Boonesborough
slave known as Old Monk, who was as adept with a hunting rifle as he was
with a fiddle or a blacksmith's tongs. Boone asked Hamilton to have one
of his adjutants collect bird dung to mix with his own urine in order to
create saltpeter, which he then combined with charcoal and sulfur to create a small cache of black powder. Just as he had back in New Chillicothe,
he played his turncoat role well, proudly brandishing for Hamilton his
captain's commission into Lord Dunmore's colonial militia. He had kept
the mottled slip of paper tucked into the small leather purse, or "budget,"
which most frontiersmen carried in the folds of their hunting shirts. When
Hamilton offered him an officer's commission in a British militia company,
Boone politely declined.

One of Hamilton's final queries to Boone was whether word of Gen.
Burgoyne's surrender had reached Kentucky. Boone told him that it was
common knowledge among the stations. Hamilton appeared taken aback.
For Hamilton and all British officials stationed in the west, Gen. Howe's
dual defeats of Washington's Continental Army at Brandywine Creek and
Germantown outside of Philadelphia were more than offset by the capture
of Burgoyne's army at Saratoga. Hamilton could little afford for the Great
Lakes and Ohio Country tribes to begin to doubt British invincibility. Already there were rumblings among the Iroquois about making a separate
peace with the Americans. If he could not hold on to the Confederacy of
the Six Nations, Britain's oldest and most staunch Native American allies,
what chance did he have to retain the loyalty of the Shawnee and the other
Algonquian tribes?

Hamilton then requested that Boone keep from the Indians the events
of Saratoga. Again Boone replied that it was too late—Gen. Horatio
Gates's victory was also common knowledge throughout the Ohio Country. Boone knew this because he himself had informed the Indians.

When Blackfish arrived the next morning, Hamilton doubled his
offer to buy Boone's freedom. The Shawnee again declined, explaining
that he needed Boone in order to fulfill his plan to take Boonesborough.

As Blackfish and his entourage set off for New Chillicothe, Boone was mounted on a calico pony presented to him as a gift from Hamilton. Blackfish took a circuitous route home via the Scioto River in order to inform any willing warriors of his coming foray into Kentucky. Boone marked the locations of each Shawnee and Mingo village through which they passed. Upon reaching the Little Miami, the Shawnee chief's sunny mood blackened with the news that Andy Johnson had escaped.

Since his capture, Johnson had ostentatiously displayed every indication that he was touched in the head. He acted the part so well that the Indians had mockingly bestowed upon him the pejorative Shawnee name Pe-cu-la, the Little Duck. After his disappearance, a search party had failed to turn up any sign of Johnson, and given his alleged infirmity, his pursuers assumed that Pe-cu-la now lay dead somewhere in the forest. But Johnson had been faking his imbecility the entire time, and neither Boone nor any of the other "adoptees" had betrayed the secret. They all knew that Johnson was in fact more than capable of navigating his way back to Kentucky. Boone was envious.

To this point in his own captivity Boone had been treading a line between languish and flourish, attempting to lull Blackfish into an overconfidence in his loyalty to his new "family" while remaining robust enough to effect his escape. The tipping point in this masquerade came when he entered a series of shooting competitions against the tribe's best marksmen. Remembering the consequences of his youthful humiliation of the Catawba Saucy Jack, Boone was careful to lose several contests on purpose so as not to arouse any unwanted jealousies. He nevertheless shot well enough to be included in subsequent hunting parties. The Shawnee's admiration of his marksmanship, however, was offset by their lingering suspicions, and two warriors always slept close on either side of him during the excursions. But over time, with game taken down by Boone's rifle suffusing the Indian community, Blackfish gradually let down his guard.

Finally there came the day when Boone asked permission to make solitary hunts on his little calico. Blackfish agreed, with a caveat—Boone would only be entrusted with a single charge and ball for his rifle. The chief also ordered braves to surreptitiously track his movements. Boone pretended not to see them. As he continued to gain the Shawnee's trust—and bring in an exorbitant amount of food—the Big Turtle was rationed two, then three, then four charges and balls to carry on his treks.

Though still shadowed by Blackfish's spies, Boone was able to covertly lighten his charging loads of small bits of gunpowder and recover his lead balls from downed prey. In this manner he succeeded in secreting a stash of ammunition in a secured fold of his hunting shirt. Moreover, such was his growing reputation as a gunsmith, particularly at repairing and refitting broken stocks onto gun barrels and the firing mechanisms known as the rifle's "lock," that there were frequently loose locks, stocks, and barrels lying about Blackfish's cabin.

Boone and Blackfish had by now picked up enough of each other's language to forgo Pompey's translations. During evening conversations over flickering firelight, the Kentuckian attempted to enlighten the Shawnee on the gratifications of "civilization." He urged the Shawnee to begin husbanding cattle and volunteered to construct a loom to spin wool fibers into cloth. He also expounded on the superiority of the minimalist, Scandinavian-style log cabins built and occupied by white settlers, although in truth there was very little difference between the Kentucky homesteads and the New Chillicothe abodes, except that the Indians generally constructed their huts without windows or chimneys.

To further ingratiate himself to his new "father," Boone went so far as to suggest the locations for the Indian town's expansion when he convinced the inhabitants of Boonesborough to relocate north of the Ohio River. In turn, Blackfish would smooth over the soil of his cabin's dirt floor to draw precise maps of the topography of Shawnee country as well as the location of farther-flung allied and enemy tribes. He did not suspect that he was imparting a chart of Indian territory that Boone was committing to memory.

Boone later admitted that his interactions with Blackfish and his "simple-hearted people" during his captivity were genuinely pleasant. His thirst for knowledge about Shawnee culture was in part a tentative attempt to bridge the cultural gulf between their two races. Boone had never been influenced by Enlightenment-era thought that divided the world's peoples into "savage" hunter-gatherers, "barbarian" herdsmen, "semi-enlightened" farmers, and "fully civilized" societies reliant on manufacturing and commerce. He considered Blackfish a "noble" adversary, and as he ruefully told his biographer Filson, the Indians "evidently saw the approaching hour when the Long Knife would dispossess them of their desirable habitations."

Boone perhaps naively hoped that it would not come to that, that there would not be a need to exterminate the indigenous peoples so much as teach them to be "white." In the end, however, he certainly recognized that he and his antagonists were, in the Kentucky historian Belue's words, "locked in a duel for land and home." That said, there was never any doubt that he was all the time plotting his desertion from the tender mercies of Blackfish's hearth.

Prior to his brother's capture, Squire Boone had moved his family to a larger cabin near Harrodsburg. In the wake of the disappearance of the salt-boiling party, he returned to Boonesborough and attempted to step into a leadership position. His efforts were stymied not only by the dogmatic Col. Richard Callaway and his Virginia cohort, but by the stigma that had attached itself to the Boone surname.

The backcountry's grapevine was awash with stories limning the circumstances surrounding the bloodless surrender of Boone's company. The tales had rapidly spread east: word had reached Virginia's governor, Patrick Henry, in March. Near simultaneously, the news of Hamilton's overture to any "rebels" willing to come over to the British cause had also become public. Rumors circulated that Boone had taken advantage of the

Lord Dunmore, who had used his influence as colonial governor of Virginia to acquire large swaths of frontier land, sought the safety of a British frigate anchored in Chesapeake Bay after being driven from office by the American revolutionaries. (*Courtesy of the Library of Congress.*)

This oil painting done in 1851 by George Caleb Bingham and titled "Daniel Boone Escorting Settlers through the Cumberland Gap" offers a romantic view of what was a more arduous and less dramatic—yet significant—undertaking. (*Courtesy of the John M. Olin Library, Washington University.*)

A sketch of Boonesborough hard by the Kentucky River done in 1775 by James Reeves Stuart as it was still being constructed. The fort would play a pivotal role on the western front of the American Revolution. (*Courtesy of the Wisconsin Historical Society.*)

An 1852 lithograph by Karl Bodmer titled "The Abduction of the Daughters of Boone and Callaway" depicts the event that would result in one of the defining moments in the life and legend of Daniel Boone. (*Courtesy of the Kemper Art Museum at Washington University.*)

The legendary frontiersman Simon Kenton rescued the wounded Daniel Boone from certain death during a skirmish with the Shawnee outside the gates of Boonesborough in April 1777. (*Courtesy of the Library of Congress.*)

After his famous proclamation of "Give me liberty or give me death," the patriot Patrick Henry served two terms as post-colonial governor of Virginia. (*Courtesy of the Library of Congress.*)

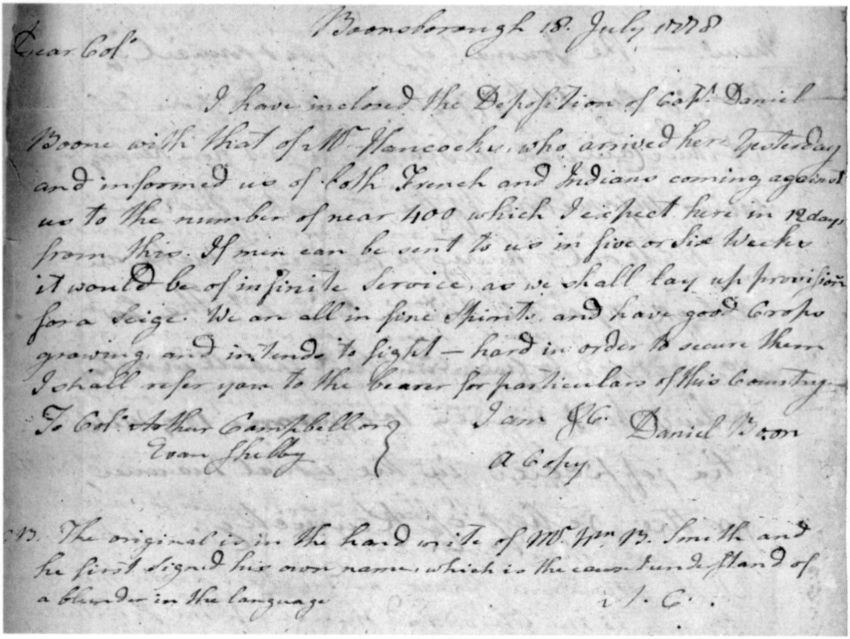

Boonsborough 18. July 1778

Dear Col.

I have inclosed the Deposition of Col. Daniel Boone with that of Mr. Hancocke, who arrived here yesterday and informed us of both French and Indians coming against us to the number of near 400 which I expect here in 12 days from this. If men can be sent to us in five or Six Weeks it would be of infinite Service, as we shall lay up provision for a Seige. We are all in fine Spirits and have good Crops growing and intend to fight — hard in order to secure them. I shall refer you to the bearer for particulars of this Country.

To Col. Arthur Campbell or Evan Shelby } I am &c. Daniel Boon

A Copy

N.B. The original is in the hand write of Mr. Wm. B. Smith and he first signed his own name which is the cause I understand of a blunder in the language

J. C.

This letter, written to a fellow militiaman in 1778, is one of the few surviving documents penned by Daniel Boone. (*Courtesy of the Wisconsin Historical Society.*)

From his base in Detroit, the British colonial administrator Sir Henry Hamilton led the Crown's military efforts on the American Revolution's western frontier that included the long and deadly siege of Boonesborough. (*Courtesy of the Library of Congress.*)

Thomas Jefferson succeeded Patrick Henry as Virginia governor in 1779 as the war in the west reached its peak. (*Courtesy of the Library of Congress.*)

The "race traitor" Simon Girty was one of three brothers who fought alongside the Indians against white militiamen and settlers on the western front during the Revolutionary War. (*Courtesy of the Library of Congress.*)

The dynamic George Rogers Clark (shown here as an older man) led the American forces that defeated Sir Henry Hamilton and the British-backed Indian coalition in the west. (*Courtesy of the Library of Congress.*)

This weathered memorial at the Kentucky site of the 1782 Battle of Blue Licks commemorates one of the last engagements of the American Revolution that also cost Daniel Boone the life of yet another son. (*Courtesy of the Kentucky Historical Society.*)

A fanciful portrait of George Rogers Clark accepting a wampum belt of peace in 1782 which Clark believed—erroneously—would end hostilities on America's first frontier. (*Courtesy of the Library of Congress.*)

John Filson chronicled the early explorations of Daniel Boone into Kentucky and wrote glowingly of the physical beauty of the territory. (*Courtesy of the Filson Historical Society.*)

This portrait of Daniel Boone was painted by Chester Harding at the home of Jemima Boone Callaway in 1820, when the venerable frontiersman was in his eighty-sixth year. (*Courtesy of the Library of Congress.*)

The initial Boone-Bryan burial plots near Marthasville, Missouri, from where the bodies of Daniel and his wife, Rebecca, were allegedly disinterred and moved to the Frankfort Cemetery in Kentucky. (*Courtesy of the Missouri Historical Society.*)

The already widespread legend of Daniel Boone as a frontier hero grew to mythical proportions after his death in 1820; this invented scene shows Boone (and a supportive dog) rescuing his wife, Rebecca, and their child during an Indian attack. (*Courtesy of the Library of Congress.*)

Lyman Copeland Draper, who devoted decades to researching a scrupulous and near-contemporaneous biography of Daniel Boone, died before he could complete his masterwork. (*Courtesy of the Library of Congress.*)

offer, with Col. Callaway's the loudest voice suggesting that he had tricked his men into Indian bondage, including two of Col. Callaway's nephews. When Andy Johnson reappeared at Harrodsburg and described Boone's seemingly complete rejection of the white way of life, suspicions about Boone's motives only ratcheted up.

It was likely these accusations of Tory treachery played a major part in spurring Rebecca Boone's decision to pack up whatever she and her children could carry and return to her people in the Yadkin Valley. Joining them were Will Hays and Suzy Boone Hays, while Flanders Callaway and Jemima Boone Callaway remained. Rebecca may have very well believed, as she told Squire, that her husband was lost to her forever. But the opprobrium she suffered as the wife of a "traitor" had to have affected her decision. Moreover, even absent the sneers and snide remarks from her former friends and neighbors, Boonesborough had turned into the last place a woman of Rebecca Boone's breeding and age would want to raise a family as a single mother.

Col. Callaway had proven such an inept public servant that Boonesborough's day-to-day administration, such as it was, had more or less devolved to a soldier named William Bailey Smith. Smith was a major in the Virginia militia who had arrived with the reinforcements the previous fall and decided to remain. He did what he could to carry on Boone's legacy, but there were few men on the borderlands capable of shouldering that burden. Under Smith's supervision, what had always been a rough and undeveloped community had fallen even further into disrepair, with mire accumulating in and around the cabins and typhoid and dysentery spreading unabated.

Visitors to Boonesborough reported piles of excrement from horses, cattle, and hogs littering the grounds of the stockade. The filth, intermingled with the rotting carcasses of dead dogs, added to the charnel-house miasma that hung over the fort. Cabin roofs sagged under rotting shingles never replaced, and doors hung awarp on fraying, careworn hinges made from the pelage grown by buffaloes in winter. Stores of salt, bread, fruits, and vegetables had become scarce to the point of being rationed. Corn-husking bees were but a memory, and meat from game was now limited by the timidity of hunters fearful of Indian attack. With only intermittent shipments of supplies from the east, the lice-ridden Boonesborough in-habitants had taken on the sallow sheen of the walking dead, their clothes ripped and ragged as they slowly perished from disease. The entire com-plex reeked of the keen smell of misery—a combination of illness, despair, piss, and shit.

There was, however, one flicker of optimism that ran like an electric current between Boonesborough, Logan's Station, and Harrodsburg. It had been sparked by Andy Johnson's escape. For the first time the Ken-tuckians knew the location of the Shawnee towns and villages to the north.

Johnson had been home but a week when he insisted on leading a raid back into Indian country and, in early May, he and five men, all afoot, set off for the Ohio River. They crossed the wide watercourse on makeshift rafts and traveled fourteen miles before creeping upon a Shawnee en-campment. The Indians numbered over two dozen, and the frontiersmen backed away to confer. The sun had nearly set, and the enemy's cookfires reflecting off the low cloud cover bathed the scene in a Rembrandt gloom. Johnson and his band had only just made the decision to circumvent the camp when several Indian dogs caught their scent. With the barking and growling stirring the hostiles, the outnumbered whites had no choice.

Beneath the starless sky they charged the Indians with guns blazing. The Shawnee assumed that such a bold move could only be taken in strength and fled into the night. Johnson and his small troop of riflemen wounded two of the warriors, who later died, and made off with seven fine Indian horses, which they rode back to Kentucky. They were unaware that their actions would precipitate a panic in New Chillicothe.

Blackfish was alarmed and angry when he learned that Kentuckians were prowling his precincts. He was well aware that his villages along the Great

Miami and Little Miami Rivers effectively constituted the British front lines. The Great Lakes Indians who passed through Shawnee territory during their raids on Kentucky and western Virginia may have used the area as forward bases. But when it came time for the Americans to strike back, it would be the Shawnee who took the brunt of their attacks.

Blackfish confronted Boone about the identity of the white assailants, and his adopted son nonchalantly replied that the attackers had more than likely been piloted into Shawnee territory by the escaped Andy Johnson. When the war chief demanded to know why Boone had not informed him of the allegedly addled Little Duck's forest skills, Boone shrugged. "You never asked me," he said, "and you were contented to use him for a laughing stock."

For the first time since striking his bargain with Boone on the Licking, Blackfish experienced a shiver of self-doubt. Simon Girty later recalled that it struck the Shawnee war leader that perhaps he should indeed have just killed the salt-boilers back in February and continued with his original plan to raze the Kentucky forts. What if taking the white prisoners had resulted in a new front being opened on his southern flank?

Though the confrontation between the Shawnee and Andy Johnson's raiding party was but an insignificant engagement, Blackfish could not allow another incursion. He saw only one way to remedy what may have been his strategic error. He immediately dispatched runners to gather as many warriors as possible for the march on Boonesborough.

31

A MISTRUSTED HERO

The opening weeks of June 1778 saw an assortment of painted Shawnee and Mingo warriors drifting into New Chillicothe. When their number topped three hundred, Boone knew it was time.

On the sixteenth day of the month, while he and a cohort of women, including his Indian "mother," were minding the horses of a hunting party not far from the Scioto, he casually unsheathed his knife, cut his calico pony from the remuda, and mounted. Blackfish's wife warned him that her husband would catch him and kill him. And even if he escaped the war chief's wrath, she said, an unarmed man stood little chance of covering the 160 miles to Boonesborough on a lone horse and with no way to bring down game for sustenance. At this, Boone opened the flap of his deerskin rucksack and showed her the flint, gunpowder, and musket balls he had secreted away, as well as a hatchet, short gun barrel, and lock he had spirited from their cabin. All that was missing was a stock for the rifle. As he spurred his horse and laid on the quirt, he could hear the women yelling for their men.

Boone rode hard all night without pause. His pony gave out at midmorning the next day and collapsed beneath him. After removing the saddle, bridle, and horse blanket to lighten the panting animal's load, he took off on foot. Plunging into every stream in his path to hide his trail, he reached the Ohio near sunset. On the north bank he found a dry poplar sapling rotting at the roots. Leaning into it with his back, he managed to bring it down. The moldering wood shattered into three pieces upon hitting the ground. These he lashed together with grapevines. Stripping naked, he positioned his clothes and gear on the makeshift pontoon, which he pushed before him as he swam the river.

He pressed on into the night until he could no longer walk. His sodden moccasins had mottled his feet to the point where great chunks of skin were sloughing from his soles. He hung the footwear from a blackened branch of scrog torched long ago by lightning and slept. A curious fox nipping at the dead skin on his toes awakened him. He scared it off, retrieved his moccasins, lined them with oak and beech leaves, and continued on. But he needed to eat.

Wild summer fruits and vegetables had yet to ripen, so he found a sourwood sapling of about the right size, and broke it off. Shaping it with his hatchet and knife, he fitted it as a stock to his barrel and lock using the buffalo tugs from his rucksack. That an exhausted and hungry man on the run, even an experienced backwoodsman, could restock a rifle with a piece of raw timber beggars the imagination. That Boone's first shot with the gun would take down a small buffalo is even more staggering.

It was still daylight, so he dared to strike fire, and ate well. After replacing the leaves in his moccasins with buffalo wool, he sliced away the animal's tongue and smoked it while he rested. He placed the tongue in his sack to present to his eight-year-old son Daniel Morgan as a homecoming gift.

He made Boonesborough on the twentieth of June, having covered the 160 miles in four days. Limping and spent, he found all of his family excepting Jemima departed. His daughter helped him to his cabin. Jemima, never giving up hope of her father's return, had kept the place much as it was when Boone last saw it. When he entered the empty hut and sank into a cane chair, the family cat jumped into his lap. It was said that the cat had not been seen near the compound in the over four months that he had been gone.

Boone's was far from a hero's welcome. A few of his oldest friends and, of course, his daughter were delighted to see him alive. But the greater part of Boonesborough's residents remained suspicious of his motives. It was as if in his months-long absence the Kodachrome picture of the leader they recalled had begun to turn sepia at the edges, and they now distrusted their own memories.

Boone patiently stated his case to Major William Bailey Smith and the other townsmen. His initial surrender to the Indians, he said, was the only way he saw to save the Kentucky communities from annihilation. And he had played his role as Blackfish's compliant son for so long in an effort to effect a mass-escape with as many of the Kentuckians as possible. But the gathering storm of Indians preparing to march on Boonesborough had forced his hand. He had come to warn them.

There were certainly those who remained leery of Boone's captivity story, if not outright hostile to the man himself. On the other hand, personal doubts about Boone's rationales could not negate his forewarning. And, in fact, his return to Kentucky instilled a sense of quiet determination among the pioneers. Maj. Smith, recognizing his own inadequacies as an administrator, tacitly ceded command of the fort to Boone, and within ten days Boone had overseen the reinforcement of the stockade's rotting southern palisades, the strengthening of its gates and sally ports, and the addition of a new brace of second-story bastions to complement the existing two. All four of these corner strongholds protruded several feet from the fort's facing, and at Boone's direction gun loopholes were drilled through the projecting floors to allow the defenders to repel anyone attempting to torch the log walls.

In the meanwhile, rifle balls were molded and trimmed, early corn was harvested and stored in cabin lofts and rafters, sheets of linen were cut into bandages and stockpiled, cattle were herded into the stockade grounds, and digging began on a new well within the walls of the square-acre compound. All this while the few able-bodied men who could be spared were summoned from Harrodsburg and Logan's Station, perhaps a dozen fighters in all, including Squire Boone.

By early July all was at the ready, though the question hung fire—where were the Indians?

When scouts returned to the Boonesborough fort each night reporting no Indian sign, there was speculation that Blackfish had abandoned his Kentucky plans and was harnessing his forces for action in the Illinois Territory. It was there, during Boone's captivity, that George Rogers Clark had led a long-distance foray with the ultimate aim of besieging Fort Detroit. The British presence at Detroit had long been a burr under George Washington's saddle, particularly as the Continental Congress was unable to supply Washington with additional regular-army troops for a western offensive. In quiet desperation, Washington had Patrick Henry charge Clark and his militia with eliminating the threat by any means possible.

In late 1777—as Washington was desperately attempting to keep the Continental Army from disintegrating at their new winter camp at Valley Forge—Clark and his senior officers had arrived at Fort Pitt to begin planning a secret campaign to infiltrate the British holdings in the Illinois Country. In May 1778, the plan became operational when Clark sailed a force of two hundred or so Kentucky, Pennsylvania, and North Carolina irregulars down the Ohio River to the Falls of the Ohio. There—joined by two dozen more Kentucky marksmen and buoyed by a full solar eclipse, which his men took as a favorable omen—Clark gathered his officers and laid out his strategy. Their first target would be the town of Kaskaskia, a former French fur-trading center on the Mississippi ceded to Great Britain after the French and Indian War.

The usual and easiest route to Kaskaskia would have been to sail up the Mississippi. But Clark was intent on relying on stealth and surprise as even then the river was a major thoroughfare for both white and Indian hunters as well as the occasional British patrol. Instead, he informed his lieutenants, the regiment would traverse 275 miles overland. Before setting off, his scouts spotted a lone man in a dugout paddling down the Ohio. A platoon of militiamen scrambled to their own canoes to intercept him, but this was not necessary. The man aimed his prow directly for Clark's encampment. He was, in fact, looking for Clark to deliver electrifying news: three months earlier, on February 6, 1778, the United States and France had signed treaties of alliance and trade. The French had joined the revolution on the side of the United States. Clark was so overjoyed that he commissioned the courier a captain on the spot.

Two months later, on July 4, Clark and his troops completed their long march and stepped from the forest and into the fields surrounding the small riverfront trading post of Kaskaskia. Not far behind it rose the British fort, not much more than an earthen redoubt. The Americans had indeed surprised the inhabitants. But to Clark's dismay, there were no British troops stationed at the fort, only a few of their Indian allies. Clark immediately made his intentions clear.

Drawing his sword and summoning a translator, he announced, "I glory in war and want enemies to fight us. As the English can't fight us any longer and are become like young children, this is the last speech you can ever expect from the Big Knives; the next will be the tomahawk. And you may expect . . . to see your women and children given to the dogs to eat, while those nations that have kept their words with me will flourish under the care and nourishment under their [new] father."

Any Native Americans who considered honoring their commitment to the British faded into the forest, and the earthen redoubt of Kaskaskia fell without a shot being fired. The following day one of Clark's company commanders captured the nearby village of Cahokia in similar fashion. Clark next set his sights on the key stepping-stone to Detroit—Fort Sackville on the Wabash in present-day Vincennes, Indiana. He dispatched two French Jesuits into the countryside around Vincennes to brandish the Franco-American alliance as a trump card against any French Canadians foolish enough to still stand with the British. The priests returned with news that almost all of their countrymen were eager to sign an oath of allegiance to the United States, and even the British-allied Indians were open to parleying with the American Long Knives.

Thus, two weeks later, on July 20, yet another British outpost fell without a shot being fired when the token Redcoat force garrisoning Fort Sackville fled the scene. Clark renamed the fort in honor of Patrick Henry. But his plans to continue on to Detroit were dashed when most of his Virginia irregulars disbanded, citing the expiring terms of their enlistment contracts. Those men whom Clark managed to persuade to remain with either promises of promotions or outright bribes were predominantly raw French Canadians. Even Clark, usually brimming with overconfidence, recognized that his raiding party was no longer large enough or well-provisioned enough to move on Detroit. In desperation, he left his own token force at the fort under the command of Captain Leonard Helm and set off for Kaskaskia in an attempt to convince the tribal leaders along the Mississippi to fight for the American cause.

Meanwhile, an alarmed Lt. Gov. Hamilton immediately began marshaling forces in and around Detroit to recapture the Indiana outpost. By leaving Capt. Helm and the mostly untrained troops at the newly minted Fort Patrick Henry, Clark had underestimated Hamilton's pluck and, more important, his enterprise. In October of 1778 Hamilton departed Detroit with a small army consisting of eighty English regulars, an equal number of Canadian militiamen, and close to sixty Ottawa warriors. Along the four-hundred-mile march he assembled a constellation of forces by holding councils at various Ojibwa, Wyandot, Potawatomi, Miami, Shawnee, Wea, Kickapoo, and Mascouten villages. At each conclave he enthusiastically took part in tribal war dances; as a result his ranks swelled to over six hundred Indians.

Clark, still at Kaskaskia, was aware that Hamilton was on the march.

But he believed that his British counterpart was moving on a force of Continentals who had been dispatched from Fort Pitt to stand up a small outpost near Lake Erie. Ten weeks later, in mid-December, Hamilton's force arrived at Vincennes.

Capt. Helm's French Canadians, apprised of the numbers in Hamilton's army by their own Indian scouts, had long since abandoned the outpost. When the British and Indian column reached the fort's front gate, they were greeted by Capt. Helm and three Americans manning a single cannon. Hamilton was so impressed by Helm's courage that he offered the officer generous surrender terms for him and his men. Capt. Helm accepted on the spot.

Clark learned of this alarming turn of events while attending a New Year's Day ball some forty miles away in the Illinois Territory town of Prairie du Rocher. He immediately saddled his horse to make for Kaskaskia, no doubt wondering if this pivotal part of the frontier he had worked so hard to conquer was on the verge of slipping away.

32

PRELUDE TO A SIEGE

Though vague rumors had reached Boonesborough that Blackfish's Shawnees might join the British counteroffensive forming at Detroit to retake Fort Patrick Henry at Vincennes, the hearsay was undercut dramatically when another escapee from New Chillicothe arrived at the settlement with dire news.

Will Hancock staggered into Boonesborough on July 17, 1778, after a journey even more grueling than Boone's. Unlike Boone, Hancock had chafed at every moment of captivity under what he considered the "dirty Indians." His adoptive "father," Captain Will Emery, was in turn naturally suspicious of his cantankerous "son" and rarely let Hancock out of his sight. Each evening Captain Will confiscated and hid Hancock's moccasins, leggings, breechclout, and hunting shirt so if he did run, he would run naked.

Late one night, however, a wobbly Captain Will had returned from a council meeting reeking of rum. Several hours later, as the Shawnee snuffled and snored, Hancock crawled naked from their cabin, retrieved a few pints of parched corn he had secreted in a tree hollow, and headed south. It was only dumb luck that as he neared the edge of town he tripped in the dark over the tug of a hobbled horse.

Hancock untied and mounted the animal and, like Boone, rode all day and night until it gave out. When he reached the Ohio it was in high spate due to a week of heavy rain. Like Boone, he used wild grapevines to lash two logs together into a raft, but a floating island of driftwood crashed into his craft and pushed him twenty miles downstream before he made the south bank. As the rainstorms continued, the bruised sky hid the sun and the stars by which he had hoped to navigate. Drenched after three days of wandering, exhausted by the stitch and purl of his journey, Hancock gave up. He ate his last few kernels of corn and lay down to sleep—likely, he thought, for the last time. He was wrong.

Hancock was awakened by the sun finally burning off the brume. A mark in the trunk of a nearby tree caught his eye. When he examined it more closely he recognized that not only had his brother Stephen carved his initials into the bark, but the nearby circle of stones were the remains of a campfire that he, his brother, and their father had made on a hunting trip several years earlier. He realized he was only four miles from Boonesborough. Bruised and bleeding from innumerable cuts and scratches, he forced himself to move on. After a total of nine days on the run, he successfully hailed the settlement's inhabitants from the heights across the Kentucky River. Then he collapsed into unconsciousness.

When Hancock was well enough to speak, he told a harrowing story. As June had turned to July it became as apparent to him as it had to Boone that Blackfish was near to initiating his Kentucky campaign. Moreover, a company of well-armed Canadian militiamen as well as several British officers from Fort Detroit had joined Blackfish and his army of warriors at New Chillicothe. The only reason the host was not yet at Boonesborough's gate, he said, was because Boone's escape had thrown Blackfish into a pique of rage. The Shawnee chief had dispatched runners to Lt. Gov. Hamilton seeking his advice on where best to vent his anger. Were his warriors needed in the Illinois Country to help stem George Rogers Clark's advance? But even before the messengers returned, the answer was clear. The Canadians were speaking openly of besieging Boonesborough.

The numbers were stark. There were some eighty men, women, and children at Boonesborough. Even with the reinforcements from Harrodsburg and Logan's Station, no more than sixty riflemen were capable of mounting a defense. This was counting slaves and boys as young as twelve. As night fell, Boone and Col. Richard Callaway, momentarily putting aside their differences, dispatched a rider to the militia commander in the Holston Valley with a letter asking for relief. Neither really expected help to arrive in time.

And so they waited. And still the Indians did not come. As the tense days and nights passed, Boone found himself under heavier scrutiny.

Will Hancock's tales of Boone's cozy fraternization with the Shawnee at New Chillicothe had revived feelings of hostility among a fair contingent of the settlers. Hancock also reported that Boone had visited Henry Hamilton in Detroit. What the two had discussed, Hancock could not say. But the meeting itself was enough to raise eyebrows. At first, the efficient manner with which Boone had prepared the fort for a long siege had sanded some of the rough edges from the animus. But there remained enough settlers who suspected that this was in fact an elaborate deception intended to lure the Kentuckians into complacency before Boone held up his end of whatever devil's bargain he had struck with either the Indians or the British. In short, Boone had been a loyalist spy on the Licking River, and he was still a spy.*

Boone was aware of the rancor toward him permeating isolated Boonesborough. This was a conundrum. A frontiersman's frontiersman, it was his nature never to act the braggart. Yet his innate modesty was coupled with the conviction that he indeed knew more than most. To square that circle, he decided that the time was right for a show of bravado. As

---

* Luckily for Boone, his townsmen had no way of knowing that by this point in 1778, the "Hair-Buyer" had put in expenses for the 210 American scalps he had collected from his Indian allies.

the Boone biographer John Mack Faragher allows, "Back country settlers, much like the Indians, followed 'big men,' warriors whose prestige and authority rested on their ability to provide honor, adventure, and plunder for their followers." Thus, to counter the innuendo as well as arrest his own frustrations that there was still no sign of an enemy host, in mid-August Boone called a town meeting. In it he put out a call for volunteers to take the fight to the Indians. The proposal struck some as insane. But Boone of course had an ulterior motive.

Before making his announcement, he had consulted with Simon Kenton, telling him he knew of an outlying Shawnee village rich in "speck," or plunder, in this case horses and beaver pelts. During his late-night talks with Blackfish, he told Kenton, the Shawnee had detailed the village's exact location on Paint Creek, not far from the north bank of the Ohio. If he proposed a raid, would Kenton second the motion? Kenton said yes.

Thus did Boone make his case to attack the Paint Creek village. He emphasized the intelligence the Kentuckians might gather on Blackfish's intentions from any captured Indians. More important, he said, an offensive into Shawnee territory might divert whatever ghost force was aligning against Boonesborough. Those were his shared motivations, at any rate. If Boone wanted to change the narrative of his supposed treachery, if he wanted to reclaim his loyal and valorous standing among his fellow overmountain folk, here was his chance.

Col. Callaway opposed the idea of weakening the settlement's defenses. But Simon Kenton's eagerness swung the mood for over a dozen others. On the second-to-last night of August 1778, Boone's party crossed the Ohio on rafts. With Kenton on point, they crept north. The troop was still four or five miles from Paint Creek when Kenton nearly collided head-on with a war party of thirty to forty Shawnee. A brief if violent skirmish ensued. None of the Kentuckians were injured, but Kenton took the scalp of an Indian he had shot dead and found the blood trails of two more, one apparently wounded by Boone.

But something was wrong. That the Shawnee had broken off the fight and vanished into the thick woods was not unusual. That their trail indicated they were continuing south instead of falling back to defend their families and holdings on Paint Creek certainly was. At this Boone changed his plan and decided to follow the Indians. Kenton and another man stayed behind to steal horses from what they gathered would be the now lightly guarded Shawnee village. In fact, it was empty.

Indian sign led Boone and the others back across the Ohio River. They followed the Warrior's Path toward the Blue Licks springs of the Licking River, not far from where Blackfish had captured the salt-boilers six months earlier. The Kentuckians did not have to actually see the hundreds of warriors congregating on the Licking. Their tracks—coming from north, south, east, and west—more than indicated their numbers. The men abandoned the well-trod trail and raced through the woods as fast as they could to warn Boonesborough.

The sun had barely yellowed the morning sky on Monday, September 7, 1778 when the residents of Boonesborough stopped what they were doing to stare at the sight of the jouncing Union Jack. The large flag was moving at the pace of a horse's canter across the elevated ridge rising from the north bank of the Kentucky River. When the woods thinned and the column came into view, Boone counted between three hundred and four hundred Shawnee, Mingoes, Wyandot, and even a few Cherokee. They were trailed by forty to fifty white men—the Canadians and Britishers whom Hancock had described congregating in New Chillicothe. It was the largest Native American army to ever descend on a white settlement on the western frontier.

The procession traversed the heights in single file before crossing the river and emerging from a thicket of sycamores onto the plain some three hundred yards south of the fort. Out of rifle range. The woolen red tunics of the Detroit soldiers flared against the Indians' deerskin attire. A team of axmen split off from the main host, felled a small grove of peach trees the settlers had planted, and arranged the tangled mass of wood into a crude abatis. Blackfish's army made camp behind the timber barrier.

Within the hour the black translator Pompey rode forward waving a white piece of cloth. He appeared to be unarmed. Pompey stopped within hailing distance of the fort and shouted for Boone. Boone stepped through the stockade gate and hesitated until he heard a voice call out his Shawnee name. "Shel-Tow-Ee!" He spotted Blackfish, mounted and hanging back at some distance.

Now Pompey bade Boone to come forward without weapons and to parley. Against his brother Squire's advice, Boone leaned his rifle against the gatepost, unsheathed his knife, and exited the fort. He pointed to a fallen log some sixty yards from the stockade, well within rifle range, and began walking. What followed over the next forty-eight hours was less professional prizefighters circling each other searching for an opening than a debating contest to discern who could dissemble more convincingly.

Blackfish cantered up to the duo and dismounted. Despite the usual courteous greeting—"How d'do, my son"; "How d'do, my father"—the war chief wore a pained look. He fixed Boone with a gimlet-eyed stare and asked why had the Big Turtle so disrespected his hospitality by breaking his word and running away? Boone replied that the ache of missing his wife and children had finally pulled him back home. Blackfish protested that he would have allowed Boone to leave at any time had he been aware of the heaviness in his heart. Boone said nothing.

Blackfish then handed Boone a letter from Lt. Gov. Hamilton. In it, Hamilton promised the Kentuckians that upon their surrender they would be escorted to Detroit rather than New Chillicothe. There, if they pledged fealty to King George, they would be welcomed as British subjects and any loss of property or livestock incurred would be reimbursed by the Crown. Hamilton, as in his earlier proclamation, reiterated that any frontier militiamen willing to fight the rebels would retain their military rank. He had also added a coda: should Boone and his people decline these generous terms, the British could not be responsible for the massacre of men, women, and children that might ensue.

When Boone was done reading, Blackfish pressed home the point. He handed Boone a wampum belt strung with three parallel rows of colored beads. One end of the belt was Boonesborough, he explained, and the other was Detroit. The red line of beads was the warpath the Indians had traveled; the white line the path they could take together to Detroit. The black beads, he said, represented the death and destruction to follow should the Kentuckians refuse to lay down their arms. The Shawnee chief then called on Boone to make good on his word from those months ago. Surrender your stockade.

Boone, anticipating this, answered that circumstances at the settlement had changed during his absence. As he was no longer in charge, he said, his promise to turn over the fort would be more difficult to keep. Now, he added, he would have to confer with the fort's new military commander. Blackfish took the lie in stride and agreed to talk again after the noon hour.

33

A HAZE OF STINKING SULFUROUS SMOKE

The initial consensus was far from unanimous. Some of the settlers gathered in the Boonesborough stockade's square, now faced with an existential threat that had to this point been but a whisper on the wind, wondered if the British offer of safe passage to Detroit could be trusted. Others suggested bargaining for better terms; perhaps the besiegers would allow them to return east. And still others, Richard Callaway among them, were vehement in their preference to die on the ramparts rather than submit to Crown rule or, worse, Indian perfidy. Boone merely listened as the voices shouted over each other.

Finally, someone suggested a show of hands to settle the debate. Callaway shut down the notion by threatening to shoot any man who voted to surrender. So it came to be that the pioneers decided to fight. Boone shrugged. "Well, well," he said, "I'll die with the rest."

At the appointed hour Boone returned to the meeting place, this time accompanied by Maj. William Bailey Smith. A panther skin had been placed over the log, and Blackfish was joined by the commander of the Canadian contingent as well as some twenty warriors, a few of whom carried rifles, tomahawks, war clubs, and knives. Boone presented Maj. Smith to Blackfish and his entourage as the fort's new commandant. The lean, sandy-haired Smith played his role as if born to the boards. Resplendent in a service coat dyed a rich royal scarlet, he ostentatiously greeted the Indians by bending his six-foot frame in a princely bow while doffing and flourishing his short-brimmed macaroni hat. It was decorated with an ostrich plume.

Blackfish spoke first, reiterating Lt. Gov. Hamilton's demands. He told Boone and Smith that as a show of good faith he had brought along forty horses to lessen the hardships of the women and children during the long journey to Detroit. He waved his hand, and several warriors appeared from behind the timber screen leading a remuda stepping in sync, as if dancing a ponderous waltz. Someone, likely Canadian wranglers, had broken and trained them well. The Shawnee chief then reminded the two white men that should their garrison resist, no mercy for anyone could be expected.

On cue, Smith nodded to Boone. Boone told the Indians that he was sorry for the further delay, but they needed another twenty-four hours to convince several recalcitrant but influential Boonesborough inhabitants that capitulation was their only recourse. The Indian entourage fell back to confer. Then Blackfish acceded.

In the interim, Boone suggested that the warriors help themselves to the settlers' corn and any stray cattle; he knew they would do so anyway. In exchange, he asked that the women of the fort to be allowed to fetch water from the spring. Again Blackfish nodded. Before departing, the Shawnee chief presented Boone and Maj. Smith with seven smoked buffalo tongues as a gift for the fort's women and children. Back inside the stockade, they were urged to throw them away as they might be poisoned. Boone ate one anyway. He pronounced it delicious.

The residents of Boonesborough stood worrisome watch atop the fort's battlements all night. Come sunup Boone posted every rifleman in plain sight on the parapets and swung open the fort's gate. Milling about the opening, in view of the enemy host, he placed women in tattered linsey-woolsey shirts and rawhide breeches, their hair pushed up beneath broad-brimmed hunter's hats. They carried guns slung over their shoulders. He doubted the ruse would work, but it was worth a try.

Near to twelve hours passed, and finally, with the sun low on the western horizon, Blackfish and his attendants again approached the meeting log. This time Boone, Smith, Col. Callaway, and Squire Boone walked out to greet them. Boone was in no mood to palaver.

"We are determined to defend our fort while there is a man living," he told the Indians. Turning directly to Blackfish, he said, "We laugh at all your formidable preparations, but thank you for giving us notice and time to provide for our defense. Our gates shall forever deny your admittance." Doubling down on the deception, Squire Boone remarked that even as they spoke, an army under the command of George Rogers Clark was marching toward Boonesborough.

Witnesses reported Blackfish momentarily taken aback. Clark's reputation was chilling along the frontier. But the Shawnee war chief recovered quickly. Pulling Boone aside, Blackfish suggested that the Indians and the Kentuckians make a separate peace outside of British purview, as neither side really wanted bloodshed. He then asked the white delegation to select its nine best fighters to negotiate a treaty with him and eight of his war leaders, and set the meeting for the following morning. It was a transparent stratagem. Boone and the rest knew well that Blackfish's warriors had not traveled all this way to sign a peace pact and forego any plunder. But if it bought more time, it was worth playing along. There was always the chance, however scant, of reinforcements arriving from the Holston.

That night, as the Indians performed a war dance behind the felled peach-tree screen, Boone prepared the fort for an attack.

The ploy was obvious from the moment the unarmed Kentuckians counted the number of Indians trailing Blackfish toward the meeting log—seventeen in all, including the translator Pompey. A few older men accompanied the Shawnee chief, but a good portion of the men were in fighting trim. Two for every white man. They appeared to carry no weapons.

Blackfish waved away the numbers by explaining that ambassadors from the disparate bands of Shawnee as well as the Wyandot and Cherokee insisted on being represented at the "peace" deliberations. There was even a Shawnee war leader from the village on Paint Creek who had accused Boone's raiding party of killing his son several days earlier. Boone remembered the scalp Simon Kenton had taken and lied. Neither he nor his compatriots, he said, had ever been near the area.

In the tense atmosphere, he also noticed that no Canadian or British officer deigned to attend the parley. Perhaps they had guessed that two dozen rifleman were manning every loophole in the Boonesborough stockade facing the assemblage, their long guns loaded and primed. Or maybe they were fearful of staining their "honor" by taking part in what the frontiersmen had already guessed was an elaborate pantomime. It did not matter.

The women of the fort, carrying tables and chairs to the meeting spot, provided the Indians with an elaborate supper of roasted venison and buffalo tongue, corn and garden vegetables, and bread, milk, and cheese. The sumptuous feast was Boone's idea, an attempt to convince the Indians that the stockade was supplied well enough to survive a long siege. In truth, it was about all the food the pioneers could muster. After an awkward meal, Blackfish again spoke first.

Since time immemorial, he said, Indians of many tribes had regarded Kanta-ke as their hunting grounds. By what right had the whites to trespass and establish towns? Boone replied that the Cherokee Nation had sold the land to Richard Henderson's Transylvania Company for a fair and dear price. Blackfish feigned surprise and turned to one of the Cherokee present and asked if this was so. The Cherokee said yes. Blackfish then indicated that this changed everything. The Shawnee and their allies would return home, he said, and the Ohio River would henceforth be the boundary between red man and white man. After a cooling-off period of some months, he suggested, perhaps the Indians and whites could again meet to set expanded hunting parameters on either side of the river. His Shawnee, he added, wanted nothing to do with the war between the Americans and the British. At this the white contingent exchanged wry glances.

Blackfish then produced a pouch of kinnikinnick and filled the bowl of a calumet, or ceremonial feathered peace pipe, that had been shaped from a tomahawk. Once all had smoked, the Shawnee chief maintained that Indian custom decreed that the white men embrace their red counterparts to seal the pact. The nine Kentuckians stood, with a pair of Native Americans facing each. The Indians extended their arms, the whites did the same, and the Indians jumped them.

Blackfish, who along with another warrior had Boone's arms pinned against his body, shouted a single word in Shawnee—"Go!"—and a fusillade of rifle fire opened on the fort. In the same instant the sharpshooters in the stockade let loose their volley.

Several of the Shawnee braves near Boone fell either wounded or dead precisely as he managed to fling Blackfish to the ground. The hard fall stunned the war chief. Thinking their leader shot, for the briefest moment time stood still for the Indians near the meeting log as they gaped at the prostrate Blackfish. When he finally moaned and stirred, it was too late. Col. Callaway had already broken loose, followed by Maj. Smith, Squire Boone, and the rest. Blackfish had asked for Boonesborough's nine best fighters; he had gotten them.

The Indian who had borne the tomahawk pipe swung it at Boone. He ducked, and the blade glanced off the space between his shoulder blades, opening a shallow, two-inch gash on the back of his neck. When the assailant regrouped and lunged again, he caught William Bailey Smith with a similar superficial blow.

The field before the fort was now a haze of stinking sulfurous smoke, and in that moment of chaos each Kentuckian raced toward the stockade's open front gate. Squire Boone trailed the pack. Running a crooked course much as his brother had used to pass through Blackfish's gauntlet, he nonetheless took a ball to his right shoulder, which ricocheted along his back before lodging in his left shoulder. By the time he reached the gate it was closed, but he dived through a sally port left unlocked for just such a contingency.

The heights along the far side of the river overlooking the little fort burst with a cacophony of trilling war shrieks interspersed with rifle fire. In the flats surrounding the stockade, wisps of gun smoke rose from behind every tree stump, bush, and fallen log. The cornfields rippled with movement as hostiles carved paths through the tall stalks. Inside the stockade the cacophony of screams, gunfire, and baying dogs spooked the horses and cattle, which stampeded about the yard. The dust they raised made it nearly impossible to see. Boone had also prepared for this, preassigning defensive positions to each of his riflemen.

He and his fellow "negotiators" grabbed the guns stacked in the center of the courtyard and bolted to their posts. Some joined compatriots at the loopholes; others climbed to the parapets and bastions. Boone ran among them shouting encouragement. When he reached his brother in the southwest corner of the fort, he found Squire struggling to reload his rifle: he could barely lift his ramrod. Boone examined the wound to his shoulder—one of nine Squire Boone would receive over years of Indian fighting—and located the lead ball embedded in his scapula. He dug it out, but the pain remained nearly unbearable. Boone helped his brother back to his cabin, where Squire insisted that Boone leave a hand ax at his bedside in case the Indians scaled the walls.

For the next thirty-six hours the assailants, well supplied by the British, kept up a steady fire. As the livestock fell victim to musket balls and dropped, men and women rushed from the cabins with butcher knives to salvage what meat they could. Many of the women and children huddled in Richard Callaway's cabin in the center of the yard. There Betsy Callaway discovered a German settler hiding under a bed. When she prodded him with a broom, he protested, "I was not made for a fighter; I was made for a potter." She summoned Boone, who leveled his rifle and set the potter to work deepening the stockade's new well. Instead, the man crawled into the hole in the ground and curled into a ball.

At one point during the fight's opening act several dozen hostiles attempted to rush the stockade to pound down its gate. They were beaten back easily. Later, under cover of darkness, the Indians seized a supply of combustible flax the settlers had stockpiled outside the walls and festooned it across the length of a plank fence that ran the sixty yards from the Kentucky River to the northwest corner of the fort. They lit the dry fiber, but as the flames snaked toward the compound, a sole defender burst from a sally port and, facing scores of muzzle flashes that turned the sky livid with blinding neurons of white-orange fire, yanked down the end of the fencing. The flames fizzled like a fuse connected to nothing.

Throughout the fray, Pompey's booming baritone could be heard either exhorting the pioneers to surrender before they were all wiped out or mocking them with obscenities for their terrible aim. The defenders hollered back, daring the black man to step into the open to see precisely how off the mark they might be. A booming laugh was the only response. Other Indians were also joyously blackguarding the defenders, but Pompey's brash affronts particularly rankled. Given the racial attitudes of the era, how dare a black man who should by all rights be a slave so casually toss filthy curses at white men?

By Friday, September 11, the gunfight had settled into a desultory siege. None of the Boonesborough occupants had been killed as yet, and fewer than a half dozen had been wounded. These included Boone's daughter Jemima, whose backside was grazed by a nearly spent ball as she ran ammunition to her father. The Kentucky River was at low current, and that afternoon a rifleman stationed on a parapet reported that its waters appeared unusually muddy. There was also an odd series of cracking sounds emanating from below the steep southern bank, and one end of a hewn cedar tree could be viewed working itself back and forth above the embankment, as if walking sentry.

Boone guessed that the Indians were attempting to tunnel beneath the stockade from the riverbank, likely at the direction of either the British officers or Canadian sappers. Whether their goal was to insert a large petard, or gunpowder bomb, to blow the stockade's walls or to use the underground passageway to burst into the fort, he did not know. But he recognized the swaying cedar tree as a digging lever operated by several men, and the cracking noises as the snapping of large tree roots.

That night, with the heaviest fire of the siege commencing at dusk, he assigned a half dozen men to begin shoveling a trench, two to three feet wide by ten feet deep, from the northwest corner of the stockade parallel to the walls. Should the enemy tunnel reach that far, there would be a surprise awaiting them. In the meanwhile, each boulder the diggers uncovered was promptly rolled down the slope to the riverbank.*

On Saturday morning, concentrated Indian rifle fire finally snapped the wooden, fifty-foot flagstaff that rose from the center of the Boonesborough compound. When the American colors fell, the Indians trilled in ecstasy, with Pompey's bellows perhaps the most audible. Not long after, the unmistakable visage of the black warrior was spotted on several occasions popping up over the riverbank not far from the mouth of the tunnel, apparently to survey what further damage the fort had suffered and, of course, to challenge the frontiersmen's manhood. Several balls fired toward the peeping and dodging translator failed to find their mark. Finally, an imperturbable long hunter named William Collins nestled in behind a gun loop, shouldered his rifle, and waited. The next time Pompey showed his face, Collins blew it into the Kentucky River.

---

* According to the Boone biographer Lyman Draper, to whom Boone's youngest son, Nathan, related the story, the Indians taunted the settlers to stand up and gunfight like men instead of throwing rocks like children.

34

"WIDDER MAKER"

After six days of fighting the tide began to turn incrementally in favor of the Boonesborough defenders. The previous night a brief but raging rain squall had so soaked the earth that the Indian tunnel collapsed. And though the Kentuckians were unaware of that development, they sensed that the enemy was beginning to flag under the lethal sting of the fort's marksmen. Examples were myriad.

Some one hundred yards above the stockade near the riverbank, for instance, two Indians had found cover behind a large fallen sycamore tree. Employing a patience unusual in the heat of a firefight, they had taken fine and special aim at the loopholes cut into the compound's walls, some of which not in use had been stopped up with rocks. They had done damage, killing the defender David Bundrin with a direct shot into a blocked loophole that exploded the rock into Bundrin's forehead, and injuring a second when a near-miss sent shards of wood shrapnel into the rifleman's face.* Moreover, their ingenuity was equal to their skills with a weapon. One had

---

* The German-born Bundrin, Booneborough's first fatality, took eerie hours to die. Carried into a cabin and, at his insistence, placed on a rocking chair, Bundrin rocked back and forth until his face had taken on the waxy color and texture of artificial fruit and most of his brains had oozed from the bullet wound in his forehead onto the dirt floor.

carried with him a lifelike wooden mask, and when he thrust it above the log to draw fire, the other would shoot from the far end of the downed tree. This continued for some while—the attackers, decoy and shooter, shifting positions on each pull of the trigger—until someone behind the palisades caught on to the ruse. The next time the "false face" was thrust aloft, one settler dutifully fired at it while another waited the split second for the second Indian to appear. When he did, he shot him dead.

Not long after, a warrior firing from behind a tree stump in the flats inadvertently exposed his knee. A rifleman promptly exploded it with a ball. When the wounded brave attempted to crawl off, a gutshot stopped him where he lay. And when an Indian, thinking he was out of rifle range, was observed seated carelessly on a fence beside the staff that held the waving Union Jack, three long hunters overloaded their large-bore muskets with heavy charges, calculated a rough azimuth, and fired simultaneously. The unlucky fighter was blasted backward off the fence and moved no more.

Similarly, a Shawnee—recognizable from his bear-greased topknot—climbed to the fork of a tree atop the ridgeline on the opposite side of the Kentucky River 260 yards from the fort. He proceeded to repeatedly arc musket balls over the walls. Given the distance and the dwindling gunpowder stores forcing the Indians to undercharge their muskets, his shots were more nuisance than mortal threat. What most riled the defenders, however, was the warrior's habit of firing off a round and then turning and lifting his breechclout to waggle and pat his bare ass at the pioneers. Boone was summoned.

After surveying the situation from the fort's rear parapet, Boone sent for a rifle of a slightly larger caliber than his own "widder maker." He packed it with an extra charge of black powder, and loaded it with a one-ounce, .66-caliber ball, a bit heavier than usual. His shot was sublime and sent the Indian tumbling from his perch.

A moment later, as Boone scampered across the stockade's open grounds, he was hit by a ball. Jemima helped him to his cabin, where, as she tended his wound, he could hear the chants from beyond the walls.

"We killed Boone. We killed Boone." As soon as his daughter had finished her bandaging he climbed back to the parapets. "I'm here ready for you yellow rascals," he shouted.

Squire Boone, dragging himself from his sickbed, also taught the besiegers that it was unwise to gather in packs. When a large party of warriors were spotted conferring near the felled peach trees, the younger Boone unveiled the homemade wooden cannon he had earlier constructed from the hollow trunk of a black gum tree. He angled the contraption's steel-banded wooden barrel for an arcing shot and loaded it with scores of spent balls retrieved from the compound's grounds. The cannon's barrel cracked into pieces when fired, but its only shot blew several Indians into the timber screen.

Having experienced the futility of their bold charges against the fort's sturdy walls, the attackers at length resorted to long-range attempts to burn out the Kentuckians. Flaming arrows, some with small pouches of gunpowder attached to the shafts, fell on Boonesborough like orange rain. The brittle shingles that roofed the compound's cabins were particularly vulnerable to spreading sparks, but Squire Boone had also anticipated this. Before the Indians had even arrived, he had unbreeched several old muskets from their locks and fitted them with hand-pumped pistons that, when attached to a water bucket, could splash out close to a quart of liquid with each "shot." Moreover, the cabin roofs had purposely been constructed to slope inward from the stockade walls on an oblique angle, with the rows of shingles held in place by a single large pin at their apex. A rawhide tug was tied to the pin, and if the water guns could not douse a shingle fire, a woman inside a cabin would yank the tug, the pin would disengage, and the burning mass would fall harmlessly onto the dirt.

The settlers also faced a more insidious type of incendiary device when the Indians wrapped tufts of flax around thick strips of flammable hickory bark several feet in length and coated the contrivance with moistened gunpowder. These makeshift hand grenades were then affixed to a stick, which served as a throwing handle. They would light the flax fiber and, darting from behind the cover of trees or up from below the riverbank, lob the firebombs over the walls in hopes of sparking a flame. Most fell harmlessly onto the fort's grounds; the rest were easily extinguished.

Finally, on the night of September 17, scores of warriors made a final rush toward the stockade wielding these fiery faggots. The deafening series of discharges that cut them down made the Kentuckians' gun barrels so hot that their dampened wiping patches sizzled in the rifle bores. Though most of the attackers lay dead or dying before they could reach the walls, enough made it through that several cabins burst into flames. Water-bucket brigades were finally able to douse the fires, but not before a long hunter returning to Boonesborough and watching the conflagration from a distant knoll hied off to Logan's Station to report the fort fallen. He was mistaken.

The next morning, after eight days of fighting, birdsong was the only sound emanating from the heights and fields surrounding Boonesborough. The Indians were gone.

During the siege, the Boonesborough garrison suffered two men dead with another half dozen wounded, including Boone, his brother, and his daughter. When Boone led a squad of riflemen through the front gate to inspect the battleground, the only corpse they found was Pompey's. Superstition forbade an Indian from touching a dead black man, or "bearskin," and the big-voiced translator's remains had been left where he had fallen, splayed near the collapsed tunnel shaft. When Boone examined its mouth he found a plethora of ten-foot poles wrapped with scaly hickory bark held in place by tugs of dry flax. The Indian objective, he then understood, was to tunnel up to the walls of the stockade, pop up from the underground passageway, and jam the mega-torches between the logs of the fort's walls. He thought it might have worked, particularly if some sort of gunpowder mines had been employed in tandem.

Following blood trails large and small—and discovering the bullet-riddled wooden mask behind the fallen sycamore—Boone estimated that between thirty-five and forty of the enemy had been killed, with untold wounded. Most of the dead had likely been collected, weighted with rocks, and slipped into the Kentucky River. A fat flock of vultures circling the stony outcroppings on the far side of the river indicated that the rest may have been buried in the deep crevasses that laced the jagged ridges. The British and Canadians, he knew, would have carried off their slain, either back to Detroit or to be buried on the trail north.

Trudging back to the fort, the Kentuckians were astonished by the sheer firepower the enemy had let loose. At least 125 pounds of lead balls were retrieved, most from the ground beneath the gun loopholes. Boone also estimated that another 100 pounds of lead were embedded in the facade of the stockade facing the river.

Two days later Simon Kenton and his partner returned to Boonesborough atop stolen Shawnee ponies; not far behind them was a detachment of one hundred or so mounted Virginia militia volunteers finally answering Boone's and Callaway's pleas for help. At Boone's suggestion the Virginians rode for Logan's Station to ensure that no war parties circled back to attack the smaller blockhouse.

Across the ensuing days, scattered reports from Harrodsburg and Logan's Station brought news of small Indian raiding parties, likely Cherokee traveling to their homelands in the South, stealing cattle and sniping at lone settlers and hunters along the way. But for now, the pivotal moment for both Kentucky and, in a sense, the American Revolution, had passed.

Had Blackfish's host managed to destroy Boonesborough, there was little doubt they would have similarly overrun Harrodsburg and Logan's Station. Emboldened by the fall of the rebellion's western outposts, Henry Hamilton would have faced little opposition to raising a combined Redcoat–Native American army to flank the coastal revolutionaries from the rear, forcing Washington's Continental Army to defend two fronts. Gen. Cornwallis was already planning to open a southern theater, and it is easy to imagine

Cornwallis and Hamilton crushing the southern rebels between them. More-over, how far the psychological blow would have reverberated had the fabled Daniel Boone been killed or captured at Boonesborough is unknowable.

As it was, the threat was now over for the settlers of Kentucky and, perhaps, for the United States. Not so for Boone.

Despite Boone's cool leadership during the siege of Boonesborough, Col. Richard Callaway still had a grudging score to settle. Not only had Cal-laway continue to seethe at what he considered Boone's impertinence during the rescue of his kidnapped daughters, he blamed Boone for the captivity of two of his nephews, Micajah and James, who had been taken at the salt camp and were still held by the Shawnee. From Callaway's point of view, who knew what fiendish treatment the sullen and defeated Blackfish had in store for them upon his return to the Ohio Country?

With the tacit complicity of Benjamin Logan—who was also put off by the glory accruing to Boone—Callaway used his elected councilman's po-sition to bring court-martial charges against the frontiersman. He accused Boone of four treasonous acts—voluntarily surrendering the salt-boilers to the Indians; plotting with Blackfish in New Chillicothe and with Ham-ilton in Detroit to effect the surrender of Boonesborough; abandoning the fort in the face of an imminent enemy assault to lead the raid on the Paint Creek village; and endangering the lives of the men who accompanied him to the ersatz peace parley outside the stockade.

The trial was convened within days at Logan's Station, with a panel of Kentucky militia officers serving as judges and jury. The court called four witnesses—Richard Callaway, the escaped captives William Hancock and Andy Johnson, and finally Boone. In his testimony Callaway mostly fumed and sputtered, while Johnson and Hancock admitted that the members of the salt-boiling party had indeed been given the opportunity to debate their fate on the Licking River and had freely surrendered under advice but not pressure from Boone. Though Johnson's antipathy toward Boone's friendliness with the Indians remained strong, Hancock conceded that Boone was probably correct in that Boonesborough would likely have fallen to Blackfish back in February if Boone and the war chief had not struck their deal.

When it came Boone's turn to testify, he defended his conduct with grace and aplomb. The first two actions listed as crimes, he argued yet again, were in reality mere ruses to stall the Shawnee from attacking the unprepared settlements. The latter two were undertaken to discover more information as to the enemy's intentions. Though transcripts of the proceedings have not survived, lore has it that the militia officers debated the verdict for about the time it took to pass the jug. When they returned to the makeshift courtroom they not only acquitted Boone of all charges but—much to Col. Callaway's ire—promoted him to major in the Virginia militia. Although Boone never betrayed his emotions during the trial, he later told confidants that the ordeal was one of his life's darkest moments.

With his conduct fully vindicated and his reputation soaring along the frontier and beyond, Boone set off for the Yadkin with Jemima and her husband to retrieve his wife and family. Weeks later, in early November 1778, he walked through the doorway of the small cabin on his in-law's property in the North Carolina piedmont. Rebecca and his children, in the words of Lyman Draper, "could not have been much more surprised had he risen from the dead." Boone proceeded to explain to them how they weren't far wrong.

35

WAR IN THE WEST

Given the multiple hardships Rebecca Boone had endured on the far side of the mountains—squalid housing, food shortages, churlish neighbors, the kidnapping of her daughter, the murder of her eldest son—it was hardly a surprise that she was not anxious to return. There was also the matter of her family, many of whom did not bother to hide their loyalist feelings. According to the Boones' youngest son, Nathan, his maternal grandfather, Joseph Bryan, in particular exerted an inordinate influence on Rebecca to dissuade her from rejoining the patriots of the West.

Considering the circumstances, Boone walked a fine line. He had been mulling the notion of founding a new Kentucky station and was anxious to put his plan in motion. But he understood and sympathized with his wife's bad memories. Nor was he ignorant of the pull his father-in-law had on her. He spoke of their rift over the matter just once, cryptically referring to the "series of difficulties" befalling his relationship with Rebecca over the winter of 1778–1779.

Inherently sensing Rebecca's need for emotional space, Boone moved his family into a two-room cabin on the Bryan property in the Upper Yadkin. Yet even this remained a crowded proposition, with their five children still living at home joined by Jemima and Flanders Callaway and Will Hays and Suzy Boone Hays. Hunting his old pathways along the Blue Ridge and the Holston to feed the large brood—sometimes with his sons-in-law, but more often alone—Boone found Rebecca's intransigence more and more frustrating as the months passed. Then fate intervened, in the form of a dual British offensive.

It was George Washington's startling defeat of General Henry Clinton's British Army at the New Jersey hamlet of Monmouth Court House in late June of 1778 that had shifted the War for Independence's theaters of operations. Formerly concentrated in the colonial Northeast, most of the fighting now moved south and west. The siege of Boonesborough that September had only been a harbinger of the British strategy to come.

Four and a half months after Washington's victory at Monmouth Court House, and six weeks after Blackfish's retreat from Kentucky, for instance, the British major John Butler's combined Tory-Mohawk force swept through western Pennsylvania and Upstate New York wreaking havoc. His raids culminated in the infamous massacre of four hundred unarmed men, women, and children near the New York village of Cherry Creek. Farther west, Henry Hamilton at Fort Sackville in Vincennes had amassed a regiment of ninety British regulars and several hundred Indian allies. Once he drove George Rogers Clark from Kaskaskia and Cahokia, the Crown would again control the Upper Mississippi. With that, Hamilton would turn east to rendezvous with Gen. Cornwallis, who by early 1779 was already in the process of transporting a Redcoat army to implement his "southern strategy."

Clark suspected that Hamilton would wait until the spring "fighting season" to march on the Mississippi posts. He also concluded that Hamilton would never expect a surprise midwinter attack on Fort Sackville. To that end he urged Virginia's governor, Patrick Henry, to supply him the manpower and provisions for just such an assault. "Brave Officers and Soldiers are Determined to share my Fate," he wrote to Gov. Henry.

"I know the Case is Desperate but Great things have been affected by a few Men well Conducted. Our cause is just, our country will be grateful."

If his surprise attack failed, he concluded his communiqué, "This country as well as Kentucky I believe is lost."

His eloquence was unrequited. Gov. Henry told Clark that with Virginia pouring most of its material and manpower into the defense of Charleston, South Carolina, Gen. Cornwallis's initial target, he would have to be left to his own devices in the far west. Clark was not an unenterprising soldier. Investing his own funds and borrowing from friends and family, Clark managed to raise enough money to entice 170 irregulars, roughly half of them French Canadians from the Illinois Country, to enlist in his campaign.

Clark first sent forty troopers up the Ohio in an armed row galley to block any British escape by water. Then, on February 5, 1779, he and the remainder of his regiment undertook the nearly two-hundred-mile trek from Kaskaskia. They marched through incessant rain, which saw them wade through freezing swamps and creeks, sometimes chest deep, across what is today the state of Illinois. At various points they were forced to pause to construct watercraft to shuttle the force across the territory's flooded rivers.

Eighteen days later, at dusk, an American army, albeit much reduced, appeared from the forests surrounding Vincennes for the second time in less than a year. This time Clark was familiar with the lay of the land, although he admitted his surprise to the improvements Hamilton had made to the fort. The Englishman had added blockhouses to each corner of the outpost, built barracks for his troops, and mounted cannons he had transported from Detroit on the parapets. For all that, Clark was lucky in one sense: most of the warriors with whom Hamilton had arrived at Vincennes had grown bored sitting around the fort and were either off hunting or raiding Kentucky settlements. Moreover, several of his Detroit-area volunteers had also departed, leaving him with a force of thirty Redcoats and fifty Canadian militiamen.

Clark led his troops on a winding route that kept a small rise between the town and his marchers. The settlers could only see his regimental banners wafting above the raised meadows. Clark had deliberately carried enough of the pennants to give the impression that he was at the head of nearly one thousand men. This was his precaution against the town's predominantly Franco-American residents forgetting their oaths of allegiance to the United States solicited over seven months earlier by the Jesuit priests. He needn't have worried. No one in Vincennes sounded the alarm, and the British and Canadian soldiers garrisoning the fort remained blissfully unaware of the American presence. Several inhabitants even volunteered to supply Clark's men with dry gunpowder.

When darkness fell, Clark lit tallow torches and moved his troops through the muddy streets of Vincennes toward the fort beyond. British sentries, had they noticed, would have been put in mind of a procession of monks carrying guttering votive candles to Canterbury. Until, that is, the solemn mood was broken by the crack of rifle fire. Henry Hamilton was in his headquarters cabin with several aides sharing hot apple toddies and playing cards with his captive Capt. Leonard Helm when the first gunshots echoed through the compound's courtyard.

Hamilton's first instincts were that his Indians had broken into the rum supply. It was only when an officer standing beside him fell to the floor, wounded by a ball that had shattered a window, that the British commander leapt to his feet and demanded that someone find out the meaning of the rifle reports. According to the Clark biographer William Nester, Helm laconically replied, "It means that you and all your men are prisoners of George Rogers Clark." Hamilton ignored him and ordered his remaining seventy-nine troopers to their posts.

The ensuing firefight raged for some fourteen hours. Clark had hastily thrown up an earthen rampart, which proved effective against the British artillery. Conversely, the Americans took heavy casualties each time they charged the outpost's fortified walls. Just past sunrise, with the fort surrounded, Clark issued a surrender order to Hamilton. In response, the

British commander, assessing his position, dispatched the prisoner Capt. Helm to Clark with a message requesting a meeting to discuss terms. Capt. Helm returned to the fort with Clark's terse reply: he would accept nothing less than unconditional surrender. Again using Capt. Helm as a courier, Hamilton countered by proposing a truce while the two met in the town's only church, but Clark's patience had been stretched taut.

The previous day American sentries had captured an Indian raiding party returning from Kentucky herding four white prisoners and carrying a string of scalps. Now, to demonstrate for Hamilton his lethal intent—"a fair opportunity of making an impression," he called it—he paraded six of his captives before his front lines, out of rifle range. Four of the prisoners were British-allied Ottawas while two were renegade whites who had been raised by the tribe since childhood. Clark ordered them lined up in full view of the fort's eastern wall and forced to their knees. An executioner then passed behind each, splitting the first five skulls one by one with a single blow from a tomahawk. But what was intended as the sixth and final lethal chop failed to even drop its victim, much less kill him. The Ottawa, a war chief named Macutte Mong, lowered his brow, reached up, and yanked the embedded tomahawk from his skull. He then calmly offered it back to his stunned executioner. It took two more swings before Macutte Mong, still gasping for air, was hog-tied and tossed into the Wabash's roiling currents.

With this, Clark stepped forward and dipped both hands into the blood pooling in the mud. He smeared it on his cheeks and performed his version of a shrieking Shawnee war dance. He then strode toward the British fort and demanded that Hamilton cede the stronghold. The lieutenant governor surrendered without any further fighting.

The next day, Hamilton and his officers, resigned to the "disagreeable terms of [our] capitulation," began the long march to Williamsburg, Virginia, as prisoners of war. When news of Clark's triumph reached Gov. Henry, he and his Executive Council rapidly incorporated the far-western territory as Virginia's Illinois County. Further, word of Clark's victory sparked an influx of westward immigration, which was to include a large contingent from North Carolina's Yadkin Valley.

During the early stages of the Revolutionary War's southern engagements, the Yadkin and its environs had remained relatively untouched by the fighting. Yet by mid-1779, as the conflict intensified in South Carolina and Georgia, partisan emotions inevitably spilled over to western North Carolina. The valley's loyalists—not least a good portion of the Bryan clan—found themselves vastly outnumbered by increasingly vociferous patriots influenced not only by Clark's triumphs in the Illinois Country but also by the previous year's victories at Monmouth Court House and Boonesborough. There is no hate like the hate of a civil war, and when several of Rebecca Bryan Boone's family members saw no choice but to flee to the west to start new lives, she finally agreed to return to Kentucky.* The decision was a timely one for her husband.

Beginning in June 1779, the Virginia General Assembly under the new governor, Thomas Jefferson, passed a series of laws intending to regulate the sale of land in Kentucky County. The legislature set the price at $40 per hundred acres—about $840 today—with a purchase limit of one thousand acres for anyone who had built a cabin on the far side of the Appalachians prior to January 1, 1778. For those like Boone who had actually settled on a plot and raised a crop of corn before that date,

---

* Two of Rebecca Bryan Boone's uncles who settled their families in Kentucky returned to North Carolina to fight in Tory militias. One was killed in action and the other was captured near the war's end and sentenced to be hanged. His sentence was commuted at the cessation of hostilities.

MAP TO RIGHT: *In February 1779, the American general George Rogers Clark sprung a winter surprise attack on the stunned Redcoats forted up adjacent to the town of Vincennes in present-day Indiana. Following an eighteen-day, two-hundred-mile march through Illinois Territory swamps and across shoulder-deep rivers and streams while being drenched by unceasing freezing rains, Clark captured Fort Sackville in what would prove to be the largest victory on the western front of the American Revolution.*

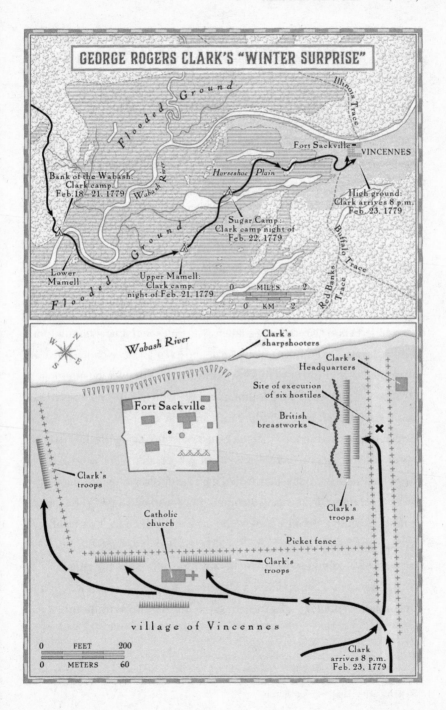

GEORGE ROGERS CLARK'S "WINTER SURPRISE"

Flooded Ground

Illinois Trace

Fort Sackville

VINCENNES

Bank of the Wabash:
Clark camp,
Feb. 18–21. 1779

Horseshoe Plain

High ground:
Clark arrives 8 p.m.
Feb. 23, 1779

Wabash River

Sugar Camp:
Clark camp night of
Feb. 22, 1779

Lower
Mamell

Upper Mamell:
Clark camp,
night of Feb. 21, 1779

Flooded Ground

Buffalo Trace

Red Banks Trace

0   MILES   2
0   KM   2

N W E S

Wabash River

Clark's
sharpshooters

Clark's
Headquarters

Fort Sackville

Site of execution
of six hostiles

British
breastworks

✗

Clark's
troops

Clark's
troops

Catholic
church

Picket fence

Clark's
troops

village of Vincennes

Clark
arrives 8 p.m.
Feb. 23, 1779

0   FEET   200
0   METERS   60

a one-hundred-acre tract could be had for the extraordinary bargain of $2.25. Governor Jefferson also announced that a land commission would meet in Kentucky at some point over the winter of 1779–1780 to adjudicate all claims. The one condition was that claimants must appear in person to state their cases.

In mid-September Boone again found himself at the head of a train of westering immigrants numbering one hundred men, women, and children. The caravan, a half mile long, was made up of a fair number of his Bryan in-laws, including Rebecca's sister Martha, who was accompanied by her reluctant, homebody husband, Neddie Boone, and their five children. It was a motley procession, with members ranging from Rebecca's Uncle Billy Bryan, whose string of twenty-eight packhorses was tended to by his slaves, to barefoot sharecroppers who had barely scraped together enough money to secure a single animal to transport their entire household. Boone himself led six or seven horses laden with rifles and spare ammunition, kettles, farming equipment, seed corn, and even a butter churn. He also attempted to transport two ninety-pound swivel guns over the mountains.

A swivel gun was a small cannon, usually with a barrel no longer than two feet, mounted on a swiveling fork for swift and easy rotation. A year earlier, rumors had swirled that the British accompanying Blackfish's army to Boonesborough carried several swivel guns. Had the besiegers actually possessed such weapons, they would have easily blasted the stockade's log walls to kindling. As it was, not counting his brother Squire's homemade gum-tree cannon, Boone's haul would have constituted the first "artillery" to enter the Kentucky territory. But after the horse carrying the guns collapsed and died under the strain, he was forced to cache the guns.

At Moccasin Gap on Clinch Mountain, Boone's caravan was joined by a smaller company of Virginians.* With this addition, Boone's was

---

* These Virginians included a militia captain named Abraham Lincoln. Though Lincoln, a tanner by trade, was destined to be killed by Indians six years later, before his death he fathered a son named Thomas. In 1809, Thomas Lincoln's wife, Nancy, gave birth to the sixteenth president of the United States, named in honor of his grandfather.

now the largest party to ever set off for Kentucky. After an uneventful six-week journey, the expedition arrived at Boonesborough in late October. Boone was taken aback to see that much of the damage inflicted during Blackfish's siege had yet to be repaired and that the community had slid back into a fetor of decay that, to be fair, characterized most borderlands settlements under constant sniping. For in Boone's absence the climate of red-white conflict may have slowed, but it never completely halted.

Five months earlier, for instance, Benjamin Logan and a Virginia militia colonel named John Bowman had taken revenge for the Boonesborough siege by leading three hundred Kentuckians across the Ohio. They planned to attack New Chillicothe at dawn, but a lone brave stumbled upon their presence around midnight, forcing their hand. By this time so many Shawnee had quit the Ohio Country—nearly the entire Kispoko, Pekowi, and Thawekila divisions had traversed the Mississippi to settle in Spanish Missouri—that the town on the Little Miami was defended by no more than forty warriors, including Blackfish.

As the chief directed a spirited defense, a rifle ball smashed his kneecap, ricocheted upward, and exited his thigh. The Indians, carrying Blackfish, barricaded themselves in the town's council house. Rather than charge headlong into the gunfire pouring from the building's loopholes, the Americans were content to plunder and burn the outlying structures and fields. Though the militiamen made off with a large remuda of Indian horses, the fight concluded with the whites suffering nine men killed, while only one Shawnee fell on the field. Several days later, however, Blackfish's infected wound resulted in his agonizing death.

The Shawnee retaliated in early October, nearly wiping out some forty Kentucky irregulars who were returning from an expedition to New Orleans. Near simultaneously, in what would prove to be their last foray before winter set in, a war party intercepted a pair of poled keelboats transporting gunpowder and other supplies from New Orleans to Fort Pitt. The attackers were led by Simon Girty, who had assumed a greater mantle of leadership after Blackfish's death. The Indians captured one of the river craft while killing or taking prisoner over fifty Americans.

These were but preludes. For the British, recovering from Hamilton's surrender of Fort Sackville, were preparing anew to lead the Indians across the Ohio River come spring. Their plan was to implement a comprehensive offensive that would sweep clear the West of both Americans and Spanish, from the Great Lakes to the Gulf of Mexico.

36

BOONE'S STATION

O n Christmas Day, 1779, on-site commissioners from Virginia's land
office approved the claim on a tract of some fourteen hundred acres
six miles northwest of Boonesborough in the names of Daniel Boone, his
brother George Boone, and Daniel's oldest surviving son, Israel. Within
the week Boone and his clan had abandoned their old cabin and set off
for their new home. They were accompanied by fifteen to twenty pioneer
families, including many of both his and Rebecca's kin. In the first week
of 1780 the troop declared Boone's Station, on Stoner Creek just north of
the Kentucky River, as Kentucky County's newest community. It would
prove an inauspicious debut.

Over the next several months Boone and his followers barely survived
what has passed into Kentucky lore as the "Hard Winter" of 1780. Livestock froze to death, deer and elk starved, and the mighty Ohio River and
its tributaries iced completely over in the extended subzero temperatures,
halting the delivery of any relief supplies. Waist-deep snow blanketed
the territory from the solstice to late spring, and even the buffalo could
not plow their hairy muzzles through the drifts that piled up against the
canebrakes. The animals died where they dropped, their carcasses silent
witness to nature's shuddering menace.

Several of the Boone's Station settlers succumbed to hypothermia, and frostbite was common among the residents who huddled together in three-sided lean-tos made of logs, sticks, and bark. It was only Boone's inimitable forest-foraging skills that kept his little community intact, and even at that he often returned from hunting trips with a frozen haunch, hump, or shoulder from an animal long dead and picked over by wolves. Perhaps the only warmth that winter in Boone's Station was Eros's binding will, for as spring's thaw brought forth a glorious summer, several of the women, including the forty-year-old Rebecca Boone, announced that they were pregnant.

Amid the family celebrations at the news of the Boones' tenth child about to enter the world, one of their own took leave. Squire Boone, who had been a near-constant presence at his brother's side for eleven years, announced that he, thirteen families, and several single riflemen were departing to construct their own station near a sweet-water creek fifty miles to the northwest of Boonesborough. Boone bid his younger brother Godspeed and promised to visit him soon.

Five months before Squire Boone's departure, in January of 1780, Virginia Gov. Thomas Jefferson had ordered George Rogers Clark to establish a fort on the confluence of the Ohio and Mississippi. Fort Jefferson, as Clark named the outpost, was a psychological boost to Boone's little community, who now felt their western flank protected. As the harsh winter receded they celebrated by falling back into the familiar rhythms of the frontier—erecting sturdy log cabins, planting corn, and importing cattle and horses to replace the livestock that had perished in the deep freeze.

While the pregnant Rebecca's and Daniel's daughters tended the family's fields and livestock, Boone continued his hunting forays. By now, however, with the territory brimming with new settlers who sensed that the lands over the mountains were finally safe, the Virginia General

Assembly redistricted Kentucky into three counties—Fayette, Jefferson, and Lincoln. Both Boone's Station and Boonesborough fell within the Fayette County lines. Boone was not ignorant of what this wave of immigration might mean financially, and he soon parlayed his knowledge of the countryside and his skill as a surveyor into a lucrative sideline as a real estate broker.

In addition to the land upon which Boone's Station rose, he put a down payment on another fourteen hundred acres abutting a section of the Licking River fourteen miles to the northeast. In order to pay for the tract, he took to hiring himself out to speculators who knew of his reputation as a man with a keen eye for good bottomland. In most cases these were jobbers from the east who had already purchased warrants for thousands of acres in Kentucky and needed a seasoned hand to tell them where to begin surveying and building. He was compensated for this fieldwork with land grants in the areas he had recommended, which he promptly sold to pay down his own mortgages.

Such was the confidence the easterners had in Boone's integrity that he was often entrusted with down payments in large amounts of American dollars and British pounds. On one such occasion, while traveling east to Williamsburg to secure land warrants with $20,000 in investors' currency, the money was stolen under cloudy circumstances. Boone had stopped at an inn, and when he awoke the next day his rucksack was empty. Though he suspected that he had been somehow drugged and robbed by the tavern keeper, he could not prove it. Most of the major investors took Boone at his word and shrugged off the loss as the price of doing business on the borderlands. But he struggled for years to ensure that all who doubted his story were repaid. Decades later his youngest son, Nathan, recalled that the mortification his father suffered over the incident was second only to the humiliation of his court-martial.

Perhaps Boone was just not cut from a businessman's cloth. In any case, as the year wound down, rumblings from across the Ohio once again signaled that the British were inciting the northern tribes to the warpath. As Boone had just been promoted to the rank of lieutenant colonel in the Virginia militia, he would soon find work more suited to his skills.

By the summer of 1780, George Rogers Clark was spoiling for another fight. After capturing Fort Sackville for the second time, he had returned to his Kentucky station on the Falls of the Ohio and spent most of the spring coordinating defenses with the Spanish. It was well known up and down the Mississippi that the British intended one last-gasp offensive to win back the American interior. Although Clark relished the idea of the coming campaign, he worried incessantly that he did not have enough fighters. He needn't have. The British were trying to plant cut flowers.

Their baleful campaign began far to the south. A flotilla of Royal Navy troop ships planned to embark from Pensacola, capture New Orleans, and sweep through Natchez before sailing up the Mississippi to the former French fur-trading town of Saint Louis. The strategy was dashed, however, when the vessels were attacked and decimated by a Spanish fleet in Pensacola Bay.

Near simultaneously, a British regiment of 150 Redcoat regulars and 800–1,000 Native American auxiliaries were rolling south from Fort Detroit. Their target was George Rogers Clark's headquarters on the Falls of the Ohio. This campaign stalled when the Indians, spooked by Clark's bloodthirsty reputation, instead insisted on plundering several less well defended settlements in northern Kentucky. Captain Henry Byrd, the expedition's commander, allowed the detours on the theory that a few easy victories would set the blood tone for an assault on Clark. It was a mistake. For when the warriors began deserting with their loot and captives, even Capt. Byrd's pleas to Simon Girty and the British Indian agent Alexander McKee to help turn them back were met with inscrutable shrugs. Byrd was forced to call off the operation.

Though most of this fighting had taken place to the west of Boones-borough and Boone's Station, the settlers on both sites continued to face threats. In March, Col. Richard Callaway was killed in a skirmish with Shawnee at the site of his newly established river ferry, a mile and a half from Boonesborough. The Indians stripped Callaway of his clothes, desecrated his body, and lifted the thick salt-and-pepper mane that had been his life's pride. They then rolled his corpse into the mudflats on the north bank of the river. Yet it always seemed to be Boone who found himself facing down the Indians.

One night, for instance, while scouting for a hunting party of some two dozen Kentuckians, he spied a band of hostiles sneaking toward the camp. Racing back, he instructed the hunters to stoke their fire and stuff their bedrolls with hides and fur pelts. He then led them into the surrounding woods. At sunrise, a salvo of musket balls thudded into the blankets followed by a tomahawk charge. As the warriors entered the firelight the forest erupted with rifle reports. Those who survived the fusillade bled back into the dark.

On another occasion Boone was hunting by himself near the Blue Licks when a musket ball cracked a tree branch above his head. He dived into a thicket, worked himself down a small stream, cocked his rifle, and waited. Soon enough he spotted two painted braves making their way down the middle of the creek. For a brief instant, both Indians lined up in his sights, and he fired. His ball passed through the head of the first and ricocheted into the shoulder of the second, who crawled away.

Although these and similar incidents did much to burnish Boone's reputation along the frontier, the gashing assaults were all too much for George Rogers Clark. Intending to halt the cross-river raids once and for all, the soldier whom the Indians had dubbed the "Tall Long Knife" set his gunsights on New Chillicothe. He would finish the job Benjamin Logan and John Bowman had left hanging fire a year earlier.

If Clark had absorbed any hard lessons studying the reports of the previous attack on the Shawnee town on the Little Miami, the paramount red flag was to follow through. Maintaining discipline was where he felt

Logan and Bowman had failed. To ensure there would be no repeat of the fiasco, he spread word that any trooper neglecting his fighting orders to instead plunder for loot would be shot on sight. This time, he made it clear to his subordinates, there would be no survivors. Clark, however, had not reckoned on the pioneers' distaste for Indian fighting absent the prospect of Indian speck.

Clark spent the better part of June and July circulating among the Kentucky River settlements calling for volunteers. Boone and his brother Neddie were two of the first to step forward. Clark appointed the elder Boone a chief scout in Colonel James Harrod's regiment of some two hundred men. Neddie Boone was the surprise. He knew his way around a plow, a pulpit, and even a sister-in-law in mourning. But he was too leaky a vessel to carry much hope as a fighting man. Benjamin Logan also eagerly signed on to help finish the job he had begun a year earlier. But Clark was surprised at the general lack of enthusiasm among the Kentuckians. Leveraging his rank and reputation into what was most certainly an extralegal action, he ordered a squad of veteran troops to occupy the Wilderness Road and turn back anyone attempting to leave the territory. He subsequently swept through the stations pressing men of fighting age into service.

On the first day of August, Clark's grumbling, ill-provisioned, and underequipped force of over one thousand debarked on the Ohio's north bank. The first forward troops were barely ashore before they were ambushed by Shawnee scouts. The Indians killed nine Kentuckians before falling back to alert Blackfish's successor Moluntha, the new Shawnee war leader known to the Americans as Black Hoof. It was Black Hoof's son whom Simon Kenton had killed on Paint Creek. With many of his lieutenants and warriors away in Detroit conferring with the British, Black Hoof saw no choice but to order the town and its crops burned. He then led his people several miles north to the village of Piqua, an old trading post on the Mad River in western Ohio. One week later, Black Hoof and his three hundred or so Shawnee warriors, joined by a smattering of Mingoes, Wyandot, and Delaware, made their stand.

The macabre brutality of the ensuing fight shocked no one. The Kentuckians not only scalped men, women, and children, but skirted Clark's orders by disinterring Indian graves to lift the hair from the corpses. What did surprise Clark was the stalwartness of the Shawnee defense. "The Indians stood at the Pickaway battle 'til they were powder burnt," one participant later recalled, using the town's Anglicized name.

Despite his youth, Clark was by now a hardened field commander, and as both sides traded musket fire, he ordered Benjamin Logan to lead a flanking maneuver that would put him behind the Shawnee. While Logan's force circled through the woods, Clark himself led a frontal assault on the enemy line. As the defenders grudgingly gave ground, there was no lack of heroic scenes. Emblematic of the hard fighting was the experience of a North Carolina militia captain named Joseph McMurtry. While charging toward a makeshift breastwork constructed of two fallen oak trees, a Shawnee ball stopped McMurtry in his tracks, severing his right trigger finger, exploding his powder horn, and ricocheting into his breastbone. As his men gathered about what they assumed was the corpse of their company commander, McMurtry sat up, dug his left thumb into the wound, worked out the disfigured musket ball, tossed it aside, and wrapped his right hand in a handkerchief. He then ran forward to reassume his position at the front.

After hours of such close-in fighting, the invading irregulars found themselves stymied by a rearguard of some fifty braves defending a triangular stockade the Shawnee had erected to make a last stand. Clark finally ordered a brace of six-pound cannons hauled up onto the cliffs overlooking the building's palisades. At this, with the cannoneers well out of his warriors' rifle range and daylight failing, Black Hoof signaled a withdrawal into the surrounding forest. This exposed the flaw in Clark's "no survivors" strategy: the very men needed to drag the artillery to the heights were those he planned to secret in the woods to block an Indian retreat.

It was around this point, as the Shawnee melted into the trees, that an

"Indian" ran forward calling in English for the Kentuckians to hold their fire. In the heat of the firefight, however, someone shot the man down. As a small squad of militiamen gathered about him, he gasped that he wanted to see his cousin George Rogers Clark. The man who lay dying was Joseph Rogers, captured three years earlier by Captain Pluggy's raiding party.

Clark was summoned to the scene, where he exhibited nothing but contempt for his dying relation. As Clark's biographer, William Nester, reports, "The shame of having a turncoat in the family was too much for Clark to bear, let alone admit."

In the end, Clark's "victory" proved as Pyrrhic as Logan's and Bowman's the previous year. The Indian body count may have been slightly higher—the remains of five Shawnee were recovered—but Clark's was appalling. Though he initially reported fourteen of his troops killed and another thirteen wounded, eyewitness accounts later revised that number upward nearer to forty dead and an equal amount wounded. Even as the Americans were burning Piqua's council house and cabins and putting the torch to nearly five hundred acres of Indian cornfields, the Shawnee were moving north and west toward the Great Miami River, where within the year they had reconstructed a new capital town nearer to the Great Lakes tribes. Clark could only take solace in the fact that the Battle of Piqua is forever etched in the history books as the Revolutionary War's largest engagement west of the Alleghenies.

When Clark's joyless army recrossed the Ohio on their return from Piqua, Boone and his brother received permission to split from the main body of troops to hunt the Blue Licks region of the Licking. It took them but several days to load their packhorses with meat, and on the trek home to Boone's Station they stopped near a stream to rest and water their mounts. Neddie settled beneath a walnut tree and was smashing nuts with a small rock when Boone heard a rustling in nearby bushes. A hand signal quieted Neddie until Boone realized that they had flushed a bear. He shouldered his rifle and fired. The animal, struck by a lethal round, lumbered into a thick copse of chestnuts to die.

Boone headed into the trees to retrieve his kill, warning his brother to keep a sharp lookout. He was dressing the bear's carcass when he heard the rifle reports. Racing back toward the creek, he saw four or five Shawnee dancing over the prostrate Neddie. One screamed, "We've killed Daniel Boone." The others yipped and clapped. According to the biographer Faragher, it was in this instant that Boone recalled his wife, thinking him dead, admitting to having slept with his brother because he and Neddie looked so much alike.

Boone's reminiscence was interrupted by a growl and sharp bark from one of the Indians' dogs. With this the Shawnee spotted him and gave chase. He dived headfirst into a canebrake and burrowed like a mole through the loamy soil. Boone estimated that he crawled several miles before he could no longer see the moccasins of his pursuers through the lower stalks of the thick cane. The Indians had seen him carrying a rifle; perhaps, they thought, it was not worth the trouble and risk. More likely they were too anxious to ride north and revel in the celebrity of having dispatched Daniel Boone. In either case, the Shawnee returned to Neddie Boone's corpse and sawed off his head as proof of their kill. They hitched the frontiersmen's horses to their own, and disappeared.

Boone ran the twenty miles to Boone's Station without stopping. He rounded up a mounted posse that included his twenty-one-year-old son, Israel, and raced back to the scene of the killing. A panther was gnawing on Neddie Boone's headless torso when they arrived. They interred the body in a shallow grave before spurring their horses north, but the Shawnee trail ended at the Ohio River. Boone asked his fellow riders to remain in the field to hunt—Neddie's widow, Martha, and her five children would need meat for their table. He and Israel returned to the stream to retrieve his brother's remains for a proper burial.

At one point during the journey home, Boone reined in his horse. He looked about with an expectant air, like a wolf scenting a coming storm. He told his son that they were not far from the very spot where, four years earlier, he had rescued Jemima from Hanging Maw's kidnapping party. It is not recorded if he confessed to Israel that Neddie Boone was Jemima's biological father.

—+—

37

THE MORAVIAN MASSACRE

Daniel and Rebecca Boone celebrated the birth of their ninth surviving child and fifth son, Nathan, on March 3, 1781. Blessed events that season were a family affair, as Suzy Boone Hays and Jemima Boone Callaway also delivered healthy babies. Nathan Boone later told Lyman Draper that when Boone was initially presented with the three infants simultaneously, he hesitated for but a moment before picking out his last son from his grandchildren.

Mere days later, in one of the universe's more impressive stabs at irony, Boone was elected to represent Fayette County in the Virginia General Assembly. The man who rarely held truck with politicians was now one of them. How he felt about this as he set off to join the other delegates was never recorded.

With the Redcoats under the turncoat Benedict Arnold wreaking havoc along North America's southern seaboard, the Virginia legislators had voted to remove their spring session to Charlottesville, some seventy miles inland.* Boone arrived there in May to take his place among

---

* George Washington had dispatched an army to defeat the marauding British forces. Among its commanders was the Marquis de Lafayette, who was under orders from Washington to hang Arnold summarily if he was captured. However, Arnold was able to find safety in New York, and in December 1781 he sailed for England.

the tobacco-planting aristocracy of the lowlands. He had barely taken his
seat in the makeshift chamber when British cavalry, sweeping west, forced
the delegates to again evacuate, this time over the mountains to the town
of Staunton in the Shenandoah Valley. Although luminaries such as Gov.
Thomas Jefferson and his predecessor, Patrick Henry, managed to escape,
such was the speed and stealth with which the enemy fell on Charlottesville
that several of the representatives, including Boone, were captured.

Legend has it that, like Henry Hamilton before him, Gen. Lord Cornwallis, who upon his arrival had relieved Benedict Arnold of command,
was curious to take the measure of the famous Daniel Boone. As the story
goes, when the frontiersman was brought before him, Boone did not dis-
appoint, regaling the haughty Britisher with tales of his backwoods journeys and adventures. Cornwallis was so taken with Boone that he offered
to set him free in exchange for Boone signing a pledge affirming that he
would no longer bear arms against the Crown—fairly standard procedure
for "gentlemen" of the era. There is also a counter-narrative promulgated
by some Boone descendants that has the famous pathfinder, having been
imprisoned in a coal bin, so covered in coal dust that he was deemed a
man of no importance and was thus freed without ever having met the
British general. In either case, Boone was back in Kentucky by June.

How seriously Boone took his "parole" from British custody is debated to this day. To those Kentuckians whose enmity toward him had
simmered since his surrender to Blackfish, the enemy's clemency was yet
one more sign that he was in league with the British. Boone's capture occurred not long after Gen. Cornwallis appointed Major Patrick Ferguson
to recruit loyalists from among the over-mountain settlers to secure the
Crown's western flank from Clark's troops. Ferguson subsequently issued
a ham-handed ultimatum to the westerners: stop opposing British arms or
he would personally march his army across the Appalachians, hang their
leaders, "and lay their country waste with fire and sword."

Ferguson's threat had the opposite effect intended, and his force of
one thousand Tories was ultimately decimated by an army of frontiersmen

at the Battle of King's Mountain in the borderlands between the Carolinas and Tennessee. Ferguson himself died in the fight. Still, that Boone—treated so well by Ferguson's commanding officer—was not dangling at the end of a British noose was, for some, proof enough of his duplicity.

Whether Boone took part in any militia actions that summer against the Redcoats or their Indian allies is not recorded. Although given what he himself recalled as the Kentucky stations being "continually infested with savages," it is hard to fathom that he was not a member of the several detachments of riflemen who rushed hither and yon across the southern and western sections of the territory in the aftermath of Indian raids. These included one skirmish in which his brother Squire yet again took a grievous wound, this time to his arm. What is verifiable is that Boone was seated with the other Virginia delegates in Staunton for the legislative body's fall session when Cornwallis surrendered his sword to George Washington at Yorktown in October 1781.

Although America's War for Independence was to officially drag on for another twenty-three months, the British capitulation at Yorktown signaled the de facto victory for the newly formed United States.

Yet in striking similarity to the circumstances surrounding the conclusion of the French and Indian War, Newton's Third Law again took effect: as hostilities ground down in the East, the viciousness of the conflict increased exponentially in the West. The British still occupied Detroit and Canada, and a consortium of Indians led by the Shawnee still relied on the British for guns and ammunition. Thus it was that 1782 became, in Kentucky, the "Year of Blood."

It began in March, when some 150 American Rangers from western Pennsylvania were mustered to attack British-allied Indian raiders along the Upper Sandusky River. The militiamen instead fell on the Delaware village of Gnadenhutten along the Muskingum in southeastern Ohio. What followed came to be known as the "Moravian Massacre"—the premeditated murders of ninety-six unarmed men, women, and children. The killings were astonishingly savage, even by frontier standards.

The seeds of the animosity had been sown four years earlier when the Delaware leader White Eyes was slain by a drunken Continental militia officer while guiding the Americans on a military expedition near the Great Lakes. To disguise the crime, a story was concocted that White Eyes had succumbed to smallpox. Tribal leaders saw through the lie, and in the wake of their chief's killing, Delaware warriors streamed to the British cause.* This prompted the Continentals to destroy the principal Delaware town of Coshocton despite the fact that most of the Indians who remained in the surrounding villages had converted to the Moravian faith. In accordance with the Protestant sect's well-known nonaggression tenets, their dedication to evangelism prohibited them from taking up arms to support either side in American Revolution.

Because of this pacifism, the Moravian converts were mistrusted by both whites and their fellow Indians, with many on either side suspecting them of being spies. It was for this reason that, after the Coshocton incident, more militant Wyandot descended on the Moravian towns and in late 1781 forced the occupants to relocate farther northwest. The Delaware were either settled or held prisoner, depending on one's point of view, in a bleak village not far from Lake Erie, which came to be known as Captive Town. The area around Captive Town had been virtually stripped of game, and by February of 1782 the residents were facing starvation. In desperation, a contingent returned to their old villages to collect cached food and harvest whatever corn crops remained. It was there, in the fields of Gnadenhutten, where the Pennsylvanians found them.

Once surrounded, the Delaware—twenty-eight men, twenty-nine women, and thirty-nine children—yet again proclaimed their neutrality and denied having participated in any military actions. They were

---

* Years later the Indian trader George Morgan wrote to Congress affirming that White Eyes had indeed been murdered.

nonetheless locked away in their mission building while the American militia officers debated their fates. The Indians spent the night praying and singing hymns.

In the early-morning hours of March 8, the Pennsylvanians voted over-whelmingly to execute them all. A few irregulars who had argued to spare the women and children left the scene in disgust. Most remained. At just past sunrise the Delaware men were led to one "killing house," their women and children to another. They were bound, gagged, and, one by one, their heads were stove in with heavy mallets. And thus were ninety-six souls, in the words of the Moravian minister Reverend John Heckewelder, "trans-lated from earth to heaven."

After each corpse was scalped, the bodies were piled in the mission building. The Pennsylvanians loaded eighty packhorses with Indian plun-der, ranging from beaver skins to tea sets, before torching the village, in-cluding the mission house.* No criminal charges were ever filed for the atrocity. An Indian boy hiding in a corncrib was the only survivor. The child somehow survived the trek north to report the horror to his fellow tribesmen. With the Delaware howling for revenge, George Washington issued a general order cautioning all Continental soldiers and irregulars to avoid being captured by the Delaware. In hindsight, this seems redundant.

One man who did not or could not heed Washington's warning was his close friend and fellow land speculator Colonel William Crawford, a mili-tia commander who had not been present at Gnadenhutten. Two months after the massacre, while leading raids on the Delaware villages along the Upper Sandusky, Crawford was taken alive. A fellow captive who later escaped relayed the details of Crawford's demise. He was first stripped naked, painted black—a certain sign that a prisoner had been marked for death—and forced to run the gauntlet between parallel rows of warriors, who brained him repeatedly with tomahawks, war clubs, and whiplike

---

* After the war, Rev. Heckewelder gathered the remains of the Delaware and buried them in a mass grave at the southern end of the village. The burial mound is visible today.

switches. It might have ended there with a sympathetic Indian shooting the bruised and bloodied Crawford and lifting his scalp.

But specifically citing the Moravian victims, the Delaware next led the barefoot Crawford over a bed of fiery coals and lashed him to a stake. They punctured his head with twigs that had been soaked in buffalo tallow, and lit the tiny torches as they flayed the skin from his torso. In a moment of semiconsciousness, Crawford recognized Simon Girty among his tormenters. As the flames engulfed him, he pleaded with the renegade to shoot him. Girty later claimed that had he acted on the request, the Delaware would have burned him alive instead. Finally the rawhide tugs with which Crawford had been shackled burned away and he collapsed onto the hot coals. As women poured shovelfuls of the burning embers over his body, the brains boiling and bubbling in Crawford's skull caused hissing steam to whistle from his nostrils.

It took American authorities, in the form of Teddy Roosevelt, over a century to officially apologize for the massacre at Gnadenhutten, with the twenty-sixth president pronouncing the murders "a stain on frontier character that the lapse of time cannot wash away." The Indians did not wait that long.

Within a month of the Moravian Massacre, large bands of painted warriors from multiple tribes—Shawnee, Mingo, Delaware, Miami, and Potawatomi—began attacking settlements on both sides of the Ohio River. One Mingo war party managed to evade the network of American scouts and mounted picket posts called videttes stationed around Fort Pitt and burned out several settlements east of the outpost. And in and around Boonesborough and Boone's Station, scattered firefights became the norm. Most vulnerable were the multiple and lightly defended outlying farmsteads that had sprouted since Boone's return.

As spring turned to summer, a skirmish between a party of some forty Wyandot and about an equal number of Kentuckians from a settlement fifteen miles south of Boonesborough introduced a new tribe into the mix. The small battle with the Wyandot left six militiamen dead and another seven wounded. More menacing to experienced frontiersmen like Boone, the appearance of the Wyandot in force foreshadowed another mass offensive. Within months his suspicions would manifest in reality.

In August 1782, over three hundred Indians from six separate tribes convened with fifty British-Canadian Rangers and three British officers on the north bank of the Ohio River across from Kentucky. Before manning their canoes and coracles, it was left to Simon Girty, the pariah now fully integrated into Native American culture, to state their purpose. His face painted, his scalp plucked but for the ubiquitous topknot, Girty stepped onto a fallen log and gathered the small army about him. Among them was his brother George.

"Brothers," he began, "the Long Knives have overrun your country and usurped your hunting grounds. They have destroyed the cane, trodden down the clover, killed the deer and the buffalo, the bear and the raccoon. The beaver has been chased from his dam and forced to leave the country."

Here, according to witnesses, Girty appeared to swoon into a trance. In a loud, hollow voice that raked the forest morning, he decried the so-called civilized ways of the whites. They penned in and fenced, they slaughtered indiscriminately, they burned and hewed the sacred woods. Lifting his hands high, he cried, "Were there a voice in the trees in the forest, it would call on you to chase away these ruthless invaders who are laying it to waste."

With that, howling blood oaths to the gods of war thrummed across the river.

And thus were fired the first metaphorical shots of what came to be known as the Battle of Blue Licks.

38

DEATH AT BLUE LICKS

The initial target was Bryan's Station, the settlement founded by
Boone's in-laws six miles north of another recently established settlement of Lexington. The invading Indian host, heeding the advice of the
British officers, began by destroying the settlers' crops, killing their livestock, and torching the peripheral cabins abandoned by pioneers fleeing
to fort up in the stockade. Multiple attempts to fire the fort's walls failed,
so the Indians settled in for a siege to starve out the Americans. But as the
blazing cornfields sent thick columns of soot into the night sky, several
messengers managed to exit the sally ports and slip through the smoke to
run for help.

By the next afternoon, after another frontal attack on the stockade
failed, scouts informed Simon Girty that a mounted force of over 180 militiamen from several communities below the Kentucky River were galloping north. Of those riders forty-five were from Fayette County under the
nominal command of Colonel John Todd of Lexington, a former Virginia
lawyer whose exploits with Gen. Clark in the Illinois Territory had bur-
nished his martial reputation. Todd's second-in-command was Lieutenant
Colonel Daniel Boone.

As they rode north Boone kept a weather eye on his three nephews, sons of his older brother Samuel, as well as his twenty-three-year-old boy Israel. Israel Boone was only just recovering from a high fever when word circulated that volunteers were needed to relieve Bryan's Station. When his cousins signed up without him, Israel was questioned, albeit lightly, by his father. Within the hour he had left his sickbed and added his name to the roster.

The irregulars arrived at Bryan's Station that night to find the Indians gone. Col. Todd and Lieutenant Colonel Stephen Trigg, in command of the Lincoln County contingent out of Harrodsburg, convened a war council of the fifteen or so officers on hand. Todd told the others that Colonel Benjamin Logan had sent word that he was rounding up an additional several hundred reinforcements and would reach them in no less than two days. Most of the officers at the council, noting that the Indians already had a forty-mile head start, voiced enthusiasm for immediately setting off in pursuit. But Major Hugh McGary, riding under Lt. Col. Trigg's command, suggested that the more expedient strategy might be to await Col. Logan's arrival.

With a doleful look, Todd chided McGary for his craven "timidity." This was a mistake. Even for the extreme personalities populating the frontier, McGary's reputation for a volatile instability bordering on psychosis was well known. He had once taken revenge for the murder of his fifteen-year-old stepson by shooting and killing a Shawnee brave he spotted wearing what he thought might have been the dead boy's shirt. He then tomahawked the corpse to pulp and boasted of feeding the remains to his dogs. He now took Col. Todd's mention of timidity as an affront to his manhood. Worse, it had occurred in front of his peers. The perceived insult set in motion a disaster neither man could have foretold.

As the horsemen followed the hostiles' trail toward the Lower Blue Licks, Boone became more and more unsettled. It was Indian habit to retreat from an engagement like the siege of Bryan's Station by breaking into small groups to confuse any pursuers. Yet the Indian sign—sign they made no effort to conceal—suggested that the entire force was moving together along an old buffalo trace. Moreover, the defenders of Bryan's Station had put Girty's attacking force at somewhere over one hundred—less the half dozen or so they had killed during the brief engagement. But Boone knew that troop estimates from men engaged in a firefight were notoriously inaccurate, and he soon suspected that the retreating warriors were intentionally concealing their greater number by carefully walking in each other's tracks. When the militiamen rushed through the most recent Indian camp, Boone lingered to count the doused fires. He was now convinced that his party was in reality outnumbered two-to-one. For Boone it all added up to one notion—they were riding into a trap.

As dawn broke on August 19, the frontier company reached the south bank of the Licking where the river oxbows around a dark cape of rock that rises over a thousand feet from the opposite bank. As their horses drank, a number of warriors appeared at the crest of the hill. They seemed to take the arrival of the white men without a care, staring wordlessly and casually smoking pipes. Several militiamen suggested that they might be stragglers. Boone suspected otherwise.

When Col. Todd called another war council, he turned first to Boone. Boone informed his superior that the Indians were finished running. He pointed to the heights across the river. "They wish to seduce us into an ambush," he said.

Boone added that he knew this backcountry well—they were only a mile or so from where Blackfish had captured his salt-boilers four years earlier. The crest of the hill across the river was riven with long gullies wide enough to conceal a regiment. The Indians, he told his fellow officers, had chosen a near-unassailable defensive position.

Boone then suggested to Col. Todd that if he was intent on fighting, he at least divide his company. He knew of a ford less than a mile upstream. Their only possible hope for victory, he said, was for half their force to swim the river on horseback at their current position while the remainder crossed at the ford. Even at that, he added, he was not certain a pincer attack would work. "They largely outnumber us," he told Col. Todd, "and it is not prudent to pursue."

Boone was the most experienced woodsman in the party, and the others grunted murmurs of assent. Not so Hugh McGary. Still stung by Col. Todd's accusation, he now performed a perfect about-face. His cheeks red with rage, the spittle flying from his mouth, McGary scoffed at any delay. "By Godly," he said, "what did we come here for?"

Then he turned to Boone. "I never saw any signs of cowardice about you before."

If, as Col. Todd had it, McGary's "timidity" in the face of the enemy was the gravest of insults, the mention of "cowardice" was a mortal blow. One of Boone's nephews later recalled seeing the tendons coil and tighten in the frontiersman's neck as he took a step toward McGary. His next words were clipped, delivered through a clenched jaw and salted with an operatic fury. "I can go as far in an Indian fight as any other man," Boone said.

An icy silence hung over the assemblage. It continued as McGary ran to his horse, mounted, and splashed into the shallows. "Them that ain't cowards follow me," he bellowed. "I'll show where the yellow dogs are."

It was a galvanic moment. As more than a few military historians have observed, a capable commanding officer such as George Rogers Clark would have shot McGary on the spot for insubordination. Instead, Col. Todd, Lt. Col. Trigg, and the others stood slack-jawed as the Harrodsburg company sent up a roar and rushed to their horses to follow their major. The momentum had swung wildly, the word "cowards" having served its purpose. Everyone, including Boone, recognized that there was no turning back.

Todd, Trigg, Boone, and the other officers all mounted. Their men followed. As they rode for the river, Boone turned and waved his rifle over his head. "Come on," he cried, "we are all slaughtered men."

Once across the river, Col. Todd attempted to form some semblance of order out of the chaotic charge. He signaled for all enlisted men to dismount and hobble their horses. He then assembled them into three ragged formations behind the still-mounted officers. Col. Todd took the center command, with McGary and two dozen riflemen already out in front. Lt. Col. Trigg and his company formed a loose right flank. On the left, Boone led the fighters from Boonesborough and Boone's Station. At Col. Todd's signal they charged the hill.

They had nearly reached the crest when the rows of Indians appeared. Boone remembers them in a line stretching from one end of the oxbow to the other. There were more than even he suspected. Selecting McGary's lead squad as their first targets, the hostiles fired a murderous volley. Twenty-two men fell, with McGary among the three left alive.

Boone and his company fought from boulder to fallen tree. The Indians before them fell back. Shouts and war whoops went up as the Fayette men reached the top. But when Boone turned to look for Todd, the pride pumping through his veins dissipated. The colonel was nowhere to be seen through the gun smoke. Instead, a lone rider galloped toward him. It was Hugh McGary.

"Boone, why are you not retreating?" McGary cried. "Todd's and Trigg's lines have given way."

In fact, both officers were dead or dying. Lt. Col. Trigg had been shot from his horse and lay bleeding out among the bodies of his decimated company. Col. Todd had been gutshot and was last seen slumped over his saddle horn while his horse careered madly into the forest. Boone was now in command. He looked back down the hill. Through the swirling smoke and dust he saw Indians closing the circle, collecting the mounts hobbled by the river. He signaled his men to fall back.

Not five minutes had passed, and already the fighting was hand-to-hand. The bodies of forty Kentuckians littered the hill, with the Indians pressing the attack. The militiamen still standing dashed madly into the throng of warriors who had circled about and now lined the north bank of the

Licking. Knives and tomahawks flashed. Screams and war cries echoed off the rock face.

Some men carried clinging Indians into the water as they attempted to swim to safety. Boone sped up and down the riverbank hollering for any men within earshot to form up about him. At one point he overloaded an old fowling piece with several balls and a handful of buckshot and shot an Indian from the saddle of his own horse; the animal reared and streaked away.

When he had gathered what was left of his Fayette company, Boone pointed toward a spinney of trees and instructed his men to use them as cover while they made their way to the ford in the river a half mile upstream. He and a few others would remain in an attempt to cover them. Among those by his side was his son Israel. As the fighting ebbed and flowed, one by one Boone released his rear guard. Soon it was just Daniel and Israel standing alone. Before Boone could say a word, Israel shook his head. "Father, I won't leave you," he said.

Boone looked about frantically for a horse. If he could find a stray, he and his son could mount and plunge into the river. He turned toward the riverbank, and in the same instant he heard the thud. He wheeled to find Israel lying flat on his back. One arm was outstretched and his eyes were glazing over. Boone felt for the wound. The musket ball had nicked his heart.

Boone picked up his son, threw him over his shoulders, and began to sprint. "A very large Indian," as Boone later recalled, was gaining on him. He lowered Israel to the ground, turned, and fired. The warrior fell dead. By now the boy's body was convulsing, gouts of blood spuming from his mouth with each fading heartbeat. Boone waited for his son to die before running off to rejoin his company.

The Licking River was clogged with the dead and wounded at the broad, shallow ford. Most were white men. Some witnesses later claimed that the water ran red. This is unlikely. Other stories ring true. The combination of adrenaline and shock does strange things to men in battle. One dazed Kentuckian, impervious to the musket balls and arrows pocking the ground around him, was spotted seated on the south bank attempting to hang his sopping moccasins and leggings from a tree branch to dry. Another was bent over the water, cupping handfuls into his mouth as bullets sent up small geysers to either side of his face.

When Boone crossed the water he bade his men to stand and cover any stragglers. But already the Indians were moving off. Rallying his company, he counted six missing. These included his brother Samuel's son Thomas, who lay dead on the far side of the river. He found Thomas's younger brother Squire curled up beneath a bramble of blackberry bushes. His thigh bone had been shattered by a lead ball; the wound would leave him crippled for life.

Col. Todd's and Lt. Col. Trigg's companies were already scampering wildly down the buffalo trace, backtracking along the path that had carried them to the Blue Licks. Boone organized the Fayette County men and fell in behind them. He took the rear guard. Every few moments he would stop, kneel, and listen for the sounds of pursuit. There were none.

Boone barely paused at Bryan's Station before securing a horse and making for home to break the news to Rebecca. Another of their sons was dead.

39

"BLOOD AND TREASURE"

Five days after what came to be known as the Battle of Blue Licks, Daniel Boone was among those who returned with Col. Benjamin Logan's regiment to bury the dead. The approaching horses scattered the swarms of vultures picking at the scalped and mutilated bodies, black and bloated in the August heat—"a horror almost unparalleled," Boone later recalled. Within hours a detail had interred either sixty-seven or sixty-eight Kentuckians in a mass grave in the shadow of the hill whose crest so many never reached.* The discrepancy centers on Israel Boone. Although there were no witnesses, and Boone never discussed it publicly, decades later his youngest son, Nathan, told Lyman Draper that his father had recovered Israel's body and buried it separately from the others.

For the remainder of his life, Boone wept openly on the few occasions he deigned to talk about Israel's death. He blamed himself not only for goading the boy from his sickbed, but for allowing Hugh McGary to bait him into a show of bravado that led to a disaster he so clearly foresaw. Few

---

* It was later determined that eleven Kentuckians had been captured and either killed along the march back to the Ohio Territory or kept as prisoners. Indians killed at Blue Licks numbered fewer than ten.

others held Boone responsible, although in the aftermath of the debacle there was no dearth of recriminations.

The survivor upon whom the most opprobrium was heaped was of course Hugh McGary. In his defense, McGary wrote to Col. Logan that the "rumors" of his insubordination were started by glory-hunting rival officers who refused to heed his early warning to wait on reinforcements. Having reached the banks of the Licking, McGary argued, he had no choice but to lead the charge up the hill while the others hesitated in the face of the clear and present danger. Logan took McGary at his word, apparently adhering to the code of the frontier that elevated mad courage, however misplaced, over sound military tactics. Logan's lingering antipathy toward Boone likely played into his decision.

Nor did George Rogers Clark escape criticism. As supreme commander of the Kentucky and Illinois militias, his charge was to patrol and defend the territorial borders. How had he allowed such a large war party to slip unnoticed into Kentucky? Where were his patrol boats, his riverfront scouts, his spies in the Ohio Country? Some critics intimated that Clark was more concerned with protecting his settlement on the Falls of the Ohio with draftees from Kentucky's eastern stations. Boone himself later wrote that the disaster at the Blue Licks could have been averted had not Clark drained the communities along the Kentucky River of fighting men.

Clark attempted to deflect the accusations by shifting the responsibility to the commanders on the ground. Although he ascribed no culpability to Boone, he publicly censured what he called the reprehensible command-and-control leadership of the conveniently dead Col. Todd and Lt. Col. Trigg. In a further attempt to obscure if not remove the stain of Blue Licks from his résumé, he immediately began organizing a retaliatory raid. It was not lost on Clark and others that though the British and their Indian allies may have "won" the Battle of Blue Licks, their retreat back across the Ohio River signaled the beginning of American hegemony over the entire Ohio Country.

Moreover, if, as most Kentuckians feared, the British were again massing the Indians for a second foray south of the Ohio River, Clark's preemptive strike would not only snuff that out but serve as punitive retribution to those who had fallen on the hill near the Licking River.

In late October 1782, less than a month before the United States and Great Britain signed the Preliminary Articles of Peace, George Rogers Clark ferried eleven hundred riflemen across the Ohio in what is often referred to as the "last offensive of the American Revolution."

With both Col. Logan and Lt. Col. Boone at his side and Simon Kenton acting as chief scout, Clark's force found the Shawnee vanished from the Third Chillicothe on the Great Miami River. The Indians had been, in fact, expecting repercussions for Blue Licks, and had fled to a new base fifty miles away on the Mad River. Instead of pursuing them, Clark and his troops were content to raze an abandoned British trading post, destroy five near-empty villages—including the remnants of Piqua as well as Willstown, named for Boone's longtime adversary Captain Will—and burn ten thousand bushels of Indian corn. In mid-November, with scant opposition having materialized, Clark led his troops back across the river. Three men dead and several more wounded were the extent of the destructive campaign's casualties.

Though the climactic battle Clark envisioned never materialized, his scorched-earth policy induced a winter famine among the Shawnee that the scant rations doled out by the British could not stem. This in itself foretold a dramatic conclusion to the battle for America's first frontier.

Boone, ruminating on the lack of an Indian threat, put it succinctly: "Their connexions [*sic*] were dissolved, their armies scattered, and a future invasion put entirely out of their power." Benjamin Harrison, Virginia's new governor, sent word to George Rogers Clark to stand down. The Blue Licks dead had been avenged and the war was over.

The Indians of North America's Eastern Woodlands may not have recognized it, but their last, best chance of stemming the white infestation destined to pour over the Appalachian Mountains had been lost.

Ten months after George Rogers Clark's final Ohio campaign, on September 3, 1783, the signing of the Treaty of Paris ended the War for American Independence. The Crown's betrayal of the tribes was complete. Great Britain, ignoring its multiple promises to protect Indian sovereignty, ceded to the United States the territory from old Spanish Florida to the Mississippi River to the Canadian border. There were no conditions. The treaty itself did not include a single mention of the indigenous nations that had fought alongside the British.

To the east of the Mississippi there would of course follow myriad red-white skirmishes, battles, and even wars—not least the conflict known as the Northwest Indian War led by Blackfish's adopted son Tecumseh. These proved as evanescent as the victory at Blue Licks. Not incidentally, an American military template had been established for defeating and subduing the plains tribes west of what the Native Americans called the "Father of Waters." Goliath's terrible sword had been unsheathed and removed from the temple.

Daniel Boone, approaching his forty-ninth year on earth, recognized the tableau for what it was: the end of an epoch. Prodded by the interviewer John Filson to look back on his life experiences, he shied neither from responsibility nor regret.

"My footsteps have often been mixed with blood," he told Filson. "Two darling sons and a brother have I lost by savage hands. But now I live in peace and safety in this delightful country which I have seen purchased with a vast expence [sic] of blood and treasure."

His words, flecked by dull melancholy, were a recognition of the inevitability of the passing of a bygone world.

Boone would live another thirty-seven years to pursue the bounty reaped by those bloody footsteps. Not so the indigenous peoples of eastern North America, who had conducted a violent symphony of resistance against the white intruders for nearly two centuries. For them, the crescendo was no less fraught than the overture. The land they occupied, if not yet taken, would soon be. Their venerable cultures, if not yet erased, would soon be. Their spirit, if not yet broken, would soon be.

The era of what Frederick Jackson Turner in his famous treatise would label the "fighting frontier" had come to an end. In its place, Turner observed, "A new society had been established" and its "Indian question" all but eradicated. Thus did the "hither edge" of America's first frontier fall not with a whimper, but with the blare of a battalion bugle, the tattoo of a regimental drum, and the deafening discharge of a Kentucky long rifle.

EPILOGUE

As Mark Twain was said to observe decades after the United States won its independence from Great Britain, history may not always repeat itself, but it often rhymes. So it was that despite his advancing age, Daniel Boone had one more Indian fight left in him. On the occasion, several scores were settled—one equitable, one regrettable.

In the wake of the American Revolution, Boone drifted about the territories and counties of what was still western Virginia—the current states of Kentucky and West Virginia—trying his hand at tavern keeping, horse trading, operating an Ohio River shipping company, and even opening a sort of trading post, sending furs and pelts he purchased from hunters to Pittsburgh in exchange for seed corn, beef and pork, and sundry dry goods he sold to westering pioneers.

His first stop was Limestone Landing—the same natural harbor on the Ohio where in 1776 George Rogers Clark had unloaded his cargo of powder and shot and that was incorporated by the Virginia legislature into the town of Maysville in 1786. Discouraged by the lack of river traffic, he moved farther up the Ohio to Point Pleasant at the mouth of the Kanawah, where Simon Kenton had founded a postwar settlement to service the keelboats and barges filled with emigrating easterners. After several years on the Kanawah, Boone and his family returned to their roots, retiring to a one-room cabin in the deep woods of Kentucky County so Boone could resume hunting and trapping. Thereafter he undertook his last great adventure.

Through the Revolutionary War years of 1775 to 1783, the American population west of the Appalachians suffered a far more egregious proportion of death and destruction than the eastern rebels in arms. Close to 7 percent of the westerners met violent ends during the insurrection, as opposed to around 1 percent of the population of the thirteen colonies. It left a bitter taste among the over-mountain settlers, and while the newborn United States federal government attempted to negotiate treaties with the various tribes spread about the Ohio Country, Kentucky residents in particular were of no mind to sit patiently and ignore the uptick of raids from desperate and starving Indians.

In response to these incursions, in October of 1786 eight hundred Kentucky militiamen under the command of Col. Benjamin Logan descended on one of the Shawnee's central village complexes on the Mad River. The nearly fifty-two-year-old Boone still retained his rank of lieutenant colonel in the militia, and with Simon Kenton at his side he rode at the head of one of Col. Logan's companies. That most of the Shawnee, including their chief, Moluntha—old Black Hoof himself—had signed a peace treaty with the federal government was of little consequence to the irregulars.

In the midst of the assault, Boone was attracted to the baying of Indian hounds. Instinctively following the sounds, he and his Rangers spotted several warriors fleeing across a meadow. As the mounted pursuers bore down on them, one of the Indians turned, shouldered his musket, and fired. A Kentuckian not far from Boone fell, mortally wounded. Boone was stunned numb to recognize the gun-wielding Shawnee as Big Jim, the man who had tortured and killed his eldest son James thirteen years earlier, nearly to the day. As Boone sat frozen in his saddle, Kenton charged. Big

Jim was frantically attempting to reload as Kenton plunged his hunting knife deep into the tall Indian's chest. By the time the militiamen had finished mutilating his body, Big Jim was virtually unrecognizable.

Boone's company then returned to the Shawnee village complex to discover that most of the hostiles, including Simon Girty, had escaped into the forest. Those who voluntarily remained included several headmen and their families, Black Hoof among them. Col. Logan ordered that they be taken hostage to trade for white captives.

As day faded to dusk, Boone, Kenton, and a few other veteran Indian hands sat around a campfire with the old chief and his wife, passing a clay pipe and recalling past adventures and battles. Suddenly Hugh McGary stormed into their circle. He approached Black Hoof and demanded to know if he had been at the Battle of Blue Licks. The Shawnee, who had not been present for the fight, was not fluent in "white speak" and likely misunderstood the question. He nodded and, witnesses recalled, smiled. Before anyone could react, McGary drew his tomahawk and sundered the Shawnee's skull. As Black Hoof's brains dampened the soil, Simon Kenton had to be restrained by several men from killing McGary.

Hugh McGary was expelled from the militia for the murder. No charges were ever filed against him. He lived for another twenty years before dying peacefully in bed at his Indiana homestead at the age of sixty-two.

How to apportion and govern the allegedly virgin western wilderness suddenly filling with settlers proved a near-intractable dilemma for postrevolutionary American statesmen. But this was strictly a bureaucratic problem. That the tribes occupying the territory would eventually be removed or eliminated was never in question, previous treaties notwithstanding. What use haggling with a race of men "with the reasoning powers of a child," as the naturalist and historian George Grinnell described the Indians, when you could simply seize their land through duplicity or, if need be, by force.

Thus was Black Hoof's fate the fate of too many Native Americans who dared to stand in the way of American expansion. These included the famed Tecumseh, killed at the Battle of the Thames in 1813. But at least one Indian protagonist, despite an early death, departed this vale of tears presumably with joy in his heart. On the last day of February 1792, a band of Chickamauga Cherokee led by Dragging Canoe gathered to celebrate a successful assault on a white settlement along the Cumberland River. So enthused was Dragging Canoe by the Muskogee and Choctaw warriors drifting into the Chickamauga camp as news of the victory spread that the son of Little Carpenter danced wildly all night around a ceremonial bonfire. As the sun rose, Dragging Canoe dropped dead either from exhaustion or a heart attack. He was fifty-four years old.

Though Tecumseh's and Dragging Canoe's lights blazed to the end, the tribal authors of the mid-eighteenth century's Indian Wars were just as likely to have suffered the ignoble fate of the broken and abandoned Ottawa war chief Pontiac. The Mingo orator Logan, for instance, whose "Lament" Thomas Jefferson considered moving enough to include in his book *Notes on the State of Virginia,* never forgot nor forgave the Americans for murdering his wife and family. After fighting alongside the British auxiliary Mohawk warriors during the revolution, Logan was said to have lost himself to the white man's "firewater" and, in 1780, was killed by unknown Indians, possibly on the orders of Iroquois headmen jealous of his notoriety. It took eleven more years for Logan's tribesmen, to paraphrase Dickens, to tighten the chains of death that had been fitted in life. In March 1791, the killer of Logan's family, Daniel Greathouse, and his wife were captured by a Mingo war party on an Ohio River flatboat bound for western Kentucky. The Indians killed the vessel's crew immediately but, recognizing Greathouse, took revenge by slowly torturing both husband and wife to their deaths.

There is no little irony in the fact that the one tribal war leader whom fate allowed to die peacefully was the "white savage" Simon Girty, who in February of 1818 passed away at the age of seventy-six on his Canadian farm. It is not recorded how much solace Girty took from outliving by twenty-two years Henry Hamilton, the British officer who represented the Crown's ultimate betrayal of the Indian nations of America's northwest woods. Hamilton, who had been released as a prisoner of war at the close of the revolution and transferred to a post in Antigua, died on the island at the age of sixty-two in 1796.

Simon Girty's passing occurred within the same week as the death of his cohort's most zealous antagonist, George Rogers Clark. Clark, whom the Virginia statesman George Mason ostentatiously labeled the "Conqueror of the Northwest," never did achieve his ultimate goal of capturing Fort Detroit. In fact, his anticlimactic razing of the Shawnee villages along the Great Miami River in 1782 was the last expedition he led across the Ohio before the revolution's end.

Amazingly, Clark was still only thirty years old when the Treaty of Paris was signed, but his martial expeditions continued. In the mid-1780s, riding at the head of an army of Virginia militiamen, Clark negotiated several treaties with various Native American tribes along the border of the Illinois-Indiana territories. Each failed to hold, and in 1786 he precipitated what was destined to be called the Northwest Indian War against Tecumseh and his allies by leading a force of twelve hundred Kentucky draftees into Indiana. The campaign was a disaster. A quarter of his impressed troops mutinied over a dearth of food and ammunition. And though Clark managed to broker a fig-leaf ceasefire, it was promptly ignored by Indian raiders. It was during this campaign that Clark's reputation was forever sullied by accusations that he had spent much of the march in a drunken haze.

The Virginia legislature declined to investigate the dereliction-of-duty charges against Clark and instead awarded him a 150,000-acre land grant in southern Indiana in gratitude for his war service. It was to this homestead where he retired as his descent into alcoholism propelled him into deep debt. He attempted to revive his fortunes by offering his military expertise to revolutionary France's efforts to reclaim the Louisiana Territory from Spain. But this only resulted in President Washington threatening to dispatch a federal army to subdue any Americans violating the neutrality between the United States and the European powers.

Thereafter a series of strokes and injuries incapacitated Clark—his left leg was amputated after being severely burned in a gristmill accident—and he was forced to return to Louisville on the Falls of the Ohio, where he was cared for by his sister Lucy and her husband, William Croghan, until his death at sixty-five in 1818.* In what Clark considered a final indignation, his historical legacy was dwarfed by his younger brother William's groundbreaking expedition to the Pacific with Meriwether Lewis.

Mixed fates also awaited the men with whom Daniel Boone had settled and protected what was to become the state of Kentucky. Some, like Benjamin Logan and Boone's fellow long hunter Michael Stoner, died in the arms of their families. Logan, after leading the effort to attain Kentucky's statehood, dropped dead from a stroke in 1802 at the age of sixty in his home at Shelbyville, Kentucky. Stoner passed thirteen years later, at sixty-seven, at his own home not far away. For others, such as James Harrod, mystery continues to cloud their demises.

There are those who contend that Daniel Boone's enduring legacy may have been shared by James Harrod if not for the latter's untimely—and mysterious—death at about the age of forty-five. After the revolution, Harrod married and settled outside of Harrodsburg in the small community of Boiling Springs. There he fathered a daughter, and with holdings of over twenty thousand acres of prime bottomland, he appeared poised to become one of the civic leaders responsible for ushering the territory into the union. But in February 1792—mere months before Kentucky achieved statehood—Harrod abruptly wrote out his last will and testament. He informed his family that he was joining two other treasure seekers in search of a long-lost silver mine rumored to have been discovered in eastern

---

* Another of Clark's brothers-in-law, the Kentuckian William Whitley, was such a rabid revolutionary that when he constructed one of the first horse tracks in the bluegrass country, he deliberately ran his races counterclockwise, opposite of the British style, setting the American precedent that lasts to this day.

Kentucky sometime in the 1760s. He was never seen again. Although it is just as likely that Harrod succumbed to disease, fatal accident, or Indian attack, his wife and daughter went to their graves convinced that he had been murdered by his associates. Fortune hunters to this day continue to comb the Appalachian Plateau near the three forks of the Kentucky River searching for the mythical mine.

For some time before and after the final raid on Black Hoof's village, Daniel Boone's various business ventures were profitable enough that Maysville County tax records show him purchasing seven slaves, including several mothers and their children, whom he put to work in his tavern and store. But Boone's Achilles' heel as an entrepreneur had always been his naivete as a land speculator. It was this flaw that once again crashed his financial world.

Boone's stab at speculation during the early stages of the Kentucky land boom eventually resulted in a plethora of lawsuits and court rulings against him. In many cases he had failed to properly register a number of the tracts that he had received as recompense from eastern conglomerates and landjobbers for his scouting missions. Over time, most of this acreage was seized and resold. But there was a hitch: Boone still owed massive amounts of property tax on land he could no longer call his own. Moreover, evicted settlers who had paid Boone for the plots were naturally inclined to appeal to the courts to recover their investments. Despite his business foibles, Boone was an honest man with a strong sense of decency, and he vowed to repay every debt he owed. To that end, as his son Nathan told Lyman Draper, "Little by little his wealth melted away."

Boone's complete bankruptcy was temporarily averted by the several postwar terms he served in the Virginia State Assembly. But even as a respected and iconic statesman, he could not outrun the writs and summonses piling up against him. In November of 1798, with Boone having departed Richmond, a territorial judge ordered the Mason County sheriff to serve a warrant and arrest Boone, who was in arrears to various entities for the lordly sum of £6,000, over $100,000 today. When the lawman arrived at Boone's one-room cabin in the Kentucky woods, Boone and his family were gone.

The old frontiersman had become so disillusioned with what he felt was the ingratitude of the people of the territory he had "purchased with a vast expence [sic] of blood and treasure," that he made a decision that heretofore he would have deemed unthinkable. He decided to abandon the United States.

As the eighteenth century came to a close, Spanish authorities in New Orleans were ever more fearful of British Canada's designs on their holdings west of the Mississippi. As a buffer, they sought to populate the interior by offering midwestern land to American pioneers at greatly reduced prices. An impoverished Boone accepted an overture from Spain to lead a train of families to settle a large tract in the community of Femme Osage on the north side of the Missouri River, some thirty miles west of Saint Charles. Such was the frontiersman's fame that the Spanish governor in Saint Louis waived Boone's entry fee as well as the stipulation that all émigrés must convert to the Roman Catholic faith.

Throughout his life, the heart of Boone's identity had been marked by his strong and affectionate attachment to family. So it was that as he moved west in the fall of 1799, he and Rebecca were joined in their exodus by four of their progeny—their sons Daniel Morgan and the teenage Nathan and his new bride, the sixteen-year-old Olive Van Bibber; and their daughters Suzy and Jemima and sons-in-law Will Hays and Flanders Callaway. At the last moment Daniel's brother Squire decided to join the entourage of fifteen or so families herding their cattle, horses, and hogs toward yet another American frontier.

Much like his older brother, Squire had led a peripatetic life since the end of the revolution. Hobbled by his multiple wounds, some of which would never fully heal, Squire had attempted to settle in the Mississippi

Territory, in New Orleans, in Spanish Florida, and had even returned to Pennsylvania to live with relatives for several years. Yet, again like his brother, he proved unsophisticated in the world of business, and by the early nineteenth century found himself hounded by creditors and tax collectors to the point where he was once reduced to stealing food from a slave to feed his family. Along his travels Squire had also become immersed in the Baptist faith and fancied himself a lay circuit preacher.

Though Squire's wife, Jane, exhausted from their many relocations, declined to cross the Mississippi with him, he was certain that she would relent once he had established a homestead in Missouri. This was never to be, and five years later Squire returned east to settle with Jane, their four sons, and his brother Samuel's four surviving sons just north of the Ohio River in the Indiana Territory. There his financial fortunes finally turned, and while serving as justice of the peace for what is today Boone Township, Indiana, he acquired a large tract of land upon which he built a stone house, operated a thriving quarry and gunsmith business, and founded one of the territory's first churches.

Squire Boone would die of heart failure at the age of seventy in August 1815. His final request was that he be buried in a cavern on his property, the same cave where he and his brother Daniel had once hidden from hostile Indians decades earlier.

During the Boone party's trek to Spanish Missouri, Suzy Boone contracted what was then known as bilious fever, most likely malaria. Only days after the emigrant train reached its destination, she died after a short vigil. She was two weeks shy of her fortieth birthday. It took the heartbroken Daniel and Rebecca several months to recover from the demise of their eldest daughter, yet within the year Boone seemed rejuvenated by his new surroundings. He spent his time hunting and trapping the wild Missouri River's feeder tributaries with his sons and sons-in-law while, as in the old days, leading attempts to reconcile disputes between the pioneers and the often-hostile Osage Indians naturally suspicious of the intruders settling on what they considered their lands.

Boone was initially angry when the Louisiana Purchase of 1803 allowed the United States to take possession of the territory and invalidate his Spanish land grants. But he eventually took the decision with equanimity and was content to move himself and Rebecca first into a cabin on Daniel Morgan Boone's land and, later, onto the property of Nathan and Olive. There he delighted in regaling his dozens of grandchildren with adventure stories from his youth. These included the eight children his son-in-law Joseph Scholl brought to Missouri from Kentucky after the untimely death of the thirty-six-year-old Levina Boone Scholl. Three years later, in 1805, the Boones received word that their daughter Rebecca Boone Goe, who had also remained in Kentucky, was dead from "consumption" at thirty-seven. This left Jemima as the only Boone daughter to survive past what was then considered childbearing age.

Like almost all men who had spent their lives wandering cold and wet forests, the elderly Boone suffered from bouts of near-disabling rheumatic disorders in all his joints, which often curtailed his hunts. But despite the fact that his thinning hair had turned badger gray, and his patchy white skin highlighted his red-rimmed eyes, those eyes never lost their light, particularly when his old friend Simon Kenton paid a visit to Femme Osage around Boone's seventy-fifth birthday in 1809. Boone, ever the optimist, had spent the occasion carving a new powder horn, polishing his rifle, and hoping that he could negotiate the steps from his rocking chair and disappear into the woods for one more adventure with the frontiersman who had once saved his life. It was not to be, although he and Kenton passed several weeks reliving old times.

Kenton's travails had been equal to Boone's. Over time he had lost all his Kentucky lands and landed in debtor's prison. It was only through the largesse of his son and daughter, with whom he now lived, that he had not died behind bars. As it was, Kenton returned to Kentucky long before Boone summoned the energy for one final long hunt. That occurred in the fall of 1810 when, at the age of seventy-six, he and his sons-in-law Will Hays and Flanders Callaway joined a company of visiting Kentucky riflemen journeying up the Missouri. Hays later reported that their party made it as far as the Yellowstone River—an assertion never verified—although it is known that the company returned after six months in the mountains laden with valuable beaver and otter furs. A mountain man who had crossed paths with Boone on this final wilderness trek described him thusly: "The old man was still erect in form, strong in limb, and unflinching in spirit."

There are some who would attempt to deconstruct the *myth* of Daniel Boone as merely a creation of his early biographers. In their eyes, Boone was just one of many frontiersmen and long hunters who explored and settled the lands west of the Appalachians in the mid-1700s. And while it is true that the likes of John Filson, Lyman Draper, and others certainly created a process of conferring lasting celebrity and fame upon Boone, his lifetime of adventures and achievements were very much real. Boone's traverse of the Cumberland Gap into Kanta-ke did indeed resonate among white settlers hungering for new territory. Boone's rescue of his kidnapped daughter Jemima did lay the basis for James Fenimore Cooper's most famous narrative. Boone's epic escape and wilderness journey to warn Boonesborough of an imminent Indian attack and his subsequent leadership in the defense of that lonely outpost did have an impact on the western front of the American Revolution.

By no means did Filson or Draper invent Daniel Boone as the first American frontier hero. In the end, their roles as interviewers, researchers, and writers was only to broadcast and publicize the outsize life of a genuine pioneer and adventurer.

Some years ago, a visiting lecturer from the history department of China's People's Liberation Army surprised an auditorium at the U.S. Army

Command and General Staff College when he mentioned that the United States had undoubtedly fought the longest war in recorded history. The American officers in attendance were left to wonder what the man could possibly mean. Even today, as America approaches nearly two decades in Afghanistan, the country's armed forces have never slogged through anything like Europe's vicious Thirty Years' War, much less the continent's Hundred Years' War. The answer came in the lecturer's next breath: he said that he was referring to the three-hundred-year conflict against the Western Hemisphere's indigenous peoples.

"From the perspective of military historians this was a dubious assertion," the history professor Peter Maslowski noted in an essay he contributed to the book *Between War and Peace: How America Ends Its Wars.* "Few of them viewed the Euro-Americans' struggle against the indigenous peoples as a single, continuous war of subjugation."

Upon further reflection, however, Maslowski and others came around to the Chinese general's point of view. In fact, Maslowski wrote, "Euro-Americans did wage a protracted war to conquer Indian nations in order to acquire their land and its resources."

The proof, of course, lies in the numbers. Of today's more than 330 million Americans, some 46 million are descendants of pioneers and settlers who passed through the Cumberland Gap. Before Boone's death in 1820 at the age of eighty-five—outliving his wife of fifty-six years Rebecca by seven years—the pathfinder most associated with that famous breach in the Appalachians survived long enough to see the United States grow from its original thirteen states to twenty-three, including Kentucky, accepted into the Union almost three decades earlier. In his lifetime Boone also witnessed six presidential campaigns, while the country's population increased eightfold from the day he first rode through the notch in the mountains.

Men rarely deviate from their life's philosophy, particularly in old age. No less a personage than Alexander Hamilton recognized this in Federalist Paper No. 27, employing the proverbial phrase, "Man is very much a creature of habit," while arguing for a standing American military force. Daniel Boone was no different. He had once been a man of a certain place and time, and as the first frontier he had helped tame expanded, matured, and eventually disappeared under the trappings of "civilization," he, like so many other pathfinders, passed down to his lineage his sense of wonder and adventure.

Others—men like Cornstalk and Blackfish, like Pontiac and Tecumseh and Black Hoof and Dragging Canoe—were not so fortunate. As Cornstalk himself once observed, "It is better for the red men to die like warriors than to diminish away by inches."

Prophecy fulfilled. More's the pity.

ACKNOWLEDGMENTS

We could not possibly have written this book without the assistance and courtesy of archivists, curators, librarians, historians, and park rangers at multiple organizations and institutions devoted to America's eighteenth-century expansion and the men and women who played significant roles in it. We especially want to recognize the help provided by the Library of Congress, particularly its Prints and Photographs Division; Filson Historical Society; The Boone Society; Kentucky Historical Society; Missouri Historical Society; Crown-Indigenous Relations and Northern Affairs Canada; New York Public Library; John Jermain Memorial Library; Katherine Ludwig of the David Library of the American Revolution; and everyone else at institutions and organizations who proved to be invaluable to our research and reporting.

A special thank-you goes to the National and State Park Service rangers, particularly the indefatigable Ranger Pamela Eddy and Ranger Carol Borneman at Cumberland Gap National Historical Park, master fort builder Ranger Billy Heck at Wilderness Road State Park, and Rangers Chad Bogart and Faith Reeves at Sycamore Shoals State Park. We'd also like to extend our appreciation to Dr. Craig Thompson Friend of North Carolina State University and Dr. John P. Bowes of Eastern Kentucky University for their expertise and insights. We benefited greatly from the knowledge and experience of Neal O. Hammon, who was very generous with his time and insights. We do want to point out, however, that the authors take full responsibility for any errors that still found their way into the text.

We are also grateful for the hospitality provided by John and Jill West in Middlesboro, Kentucky. And yet again, we cannot express enough thanks for the insights and suggestions of the underground editors David Hughes, Bobby Kelly, and Denise McDonald.

Like all modern chroniclers of the lives and times of Daniel Boone's frontier world, we owe a deep debt of gratitude to the dogged nineteenth-century researcher, reporter, and writer Lyman Copeland Draper. He devoted his life and career to preserving the tales of pioneer history, and his archives at the Wisconsin Historical Society were a crucial resource. Of Draper's nearly seventy-five years on earth, he spent fifty of them collecting research material and interviewing hundreds of contemporaneous witnesses. These included Daniel Boone's youngest son, Nathan, who entrusted him with the Boone family papers. Draper once estimated that he'd traveled fifty thousand miles by horse in his quest for the truths of the period, which run close to five hundred volumes. We have been humbled to journey along the trail he blazed.

From the onset of this project and through its completion we have benefited from the enthusiastic support of our editor, Marc Resnick. Others in the St. Martin's Press family to whom we owe a Kanta-ke–sized dept of gratitude include Sally Richardson, Lily Cronig, Hannah O'Grady, Rebecca Lang, Tracey Guest, Kate Davis, Rafal Gibek, Rob Grom, David Lindroth, and, of course, Andy Martin. And, as always, we survive to write another day thanks to Nat Sobel and his merry band of elves at Sobel Weber Associates, particularly Adia Wright. Kudos, too, to the efforts on our behalf of Michael Prevett at the Circle of Confusion agency.

As with any long writing project, we depended on the ongoing support and encouragement of family and friends. You know who you are, but let us single out the inestimable Divine Ms. D, Liam-Antoine DeBusschere-Drury, Leslie Reingold, Kathryn Clavin VunKannon, and Brendan Clavin.

ENDNOTES

Epigraph

xv *"Stand at the Cumberland Gap"*: Turner, *The Frontier in American History*, p. 5.

Prologue

4   *For the first European Americans*: Francisco Cantú, "Boundary Conditions," *New Yorker*, March 11, 2019, p. 73.

4   *"the procession of civilization"*: Turner, *The Frontier in American History*, p. 35.

4   *Conversely, to the continent's indigenous tribes*: Ibid., p. 3.

PART I: THE FRONTIER

7   *"Europeans . . . did not conquer wilderness"*: Jennings, *The Founders of America*, p. 16.

1. A Patient Pathfinder

10 *"forest dark"*: Alighieri, *The Divine Comedy: Inferno*, Canto 1.

12 *"a man of rather small stature, fair complexion, red hair and grey eyes"*: Draper, *The Life of Daniel Boone*, p. 108.

12 *speaks to her Welsh forebears*: Ibid.

14 *"though literate"*: Ibid.

16 *"the Far East beyond Persia and Armenia"*: "Prester John," *Encyclopaedia Britannica*. www.britannica.com/topic/Prester-John-legendary-ruler.

2. "The Single Nation to Fear"

19 *"Children of Satan"*: Storl and Gladstar, *The Herbal Lore of Wise Women and Wortcunners,* p. 85.

20 *"common" pace*: Ibid.

20 *and perhaps even a rest*: Faragher, *Daniel Boone,* p. 34.

21 *"the most bloody and terrible"*: Stuart, *Memoirs of Indian Wars and Other Occurrences,* p. 49.

21 *Twigtwee, or Miami tribe*: Warren, *The Shawnees and Their Neighbors,* p. 19.

22 *"invaders had eroded Indian country"*: Calloway, *The Shawnees and the War for America,* p. 2.

23 *"the single nation to fear" in America*: D'Iberville, *Iberville's Gulf Journals,* p. 175.

24 *"dealing with the English colonies"*: Anderson, *Crucible of War,* p. 23.

3. The Long Hunters

29 *"where conscience was free"*: Draper, *The Life of Daniel Boone,* p. 107.

33 *would need more than eight years to earn $1,000*: Wright, *Comparative Wages, Prices, and Cost of Living,* pp. 44–49.

34 *setting off for North Carolina*: Faragher, *Daniel Boone,* p. 29.

34 *exhibit for the rest of his life*: Brown, *Frontiersman,* p. 9.

4. Into the Yadkin

36 *spiked from one hundred in 1746 to some three thousand by 1753*: Turner, *The Frontier in American History,* p. 36.

37 *crosshatched by dozens of small creeks*: Draper, *The Life of Daniel Boone,* p. 125.

38 *as he dressed the carcasses*: Faragher, *Daniel Boone,* p. 31.

5. The Ohio Country

50 *"So complicated are the political interests"*: Preston, "The Trigger," *Smithsonian Magazine,* October 2019, p. 34.

50 *"Linear warfare may have been effective"*: Glatthaar, *The American Military,* p. 4.

51 *"the colonists considered them fools"*: Ibid.

6. Kanta-Ke

52 *"No Savage Should Inherit the Land," he wrote*: Faragher, *Daniel Boone,* p. 37.

54 *"are the common Receptacle and Rendezvous"*: *The Virginia Gazette,* April 11, 1751.

54 *"Drunkenness, Swearing, Cursing"*: Ibid.

57 *"the great country back of the Appalachian Mountains"*: Haselby, *The Origins of American Religious Nationalism,* p. 11.

7. Braddock's Folly

59 *"with colors flying"*: Draper, *The Life of Daniel Boone,* p. 129.
60 *To that end*: Foster, *The Ohio Frontier,* p. 42.
60 *"were sacrificed by the soldiers"*: Draper, *The Life of Daniel Boone,* p. 132.
60 *"broke and ran like sheep"*: Calloway, *The Indian World of George Washington,* p. 111.
62 *"Who is Mr. Washington?"*: Draper, *The Life of Daniel Boone,* p. 133.
62 *"Providence was saving him"*: Drury and Clavin, *Valley Forge,* p. 111.

8. Rebecca Bryan

66 *"my little girl"*: Faragher, *Daniel Boone,* p. 43.
71 *"incited by French propaganda and rum"*: Draper, *The Life of Daniel Boone,* p. 161.

9. The Cherokee Wars

75 *"We fatten our dogs"*: *South-Carolina Gazette,* February 9, 1760.
76 *Lacking immunity*: Calloway, *The Indian World of George Washington,* p. 164.

10. "Boone's Surprise"

83 *"So much the better"*: Faragher, *Daniel Boone,* p. 58.
85 *"Daniel Boone . . . Come on boys"*: Ibid., p. 57.
86 *"take an exact Account"*: Foster, *The Ohio Frontier,* p. 11.
86 *"in short"*: Ibid., p. 14.
86 *"Walnut, Ash, Sugar Trees, Cherry Trees, &c"*: Ibid.
87 *"habit of contemplation"*: Faragher, *Daniel Boone,* p. 55.

PART II: THE EXPLORERS

89 *"The American . . . acquire no attachment"*: Thwaites and Kellogg, *Documentary History of Dunmore's War, 1774,* p. 371.

11. "An Execrable Race"

93 *"Execrable Race"*: Lord Jeffrey Amherst to Col. Henry Bouquet, July 7, 1763. Amherst College.
93 *"Indians . . . are the only Brutes & Cowards"*: Heinl, *Dictionary of Military and Naval Quotations,* p. 155.
94 *"the English want to dispossess"*: Calloway, *The Shawnees and the War for America,* p. 41.
97 *"Johnson certainly took much pleasure"*: Flexner, *Mohawk Baronet,* p. 87.
97 *"Whilst they have any men"*: Calloway, *The Shawnees and the War for America,* p. xxxvi.
100 *"At the onset"*: Calloway, *The Scratch of a Pen,* p. 12.
100 *"By the time of"*: Ibid.

12. Pontiac's Demise

102 *"search for soil"*: Turner, *The Frontier in American History*, p. 7.
106 *"And we now surround you"*: The Papers of Henry Bouquet, November 17, 1761–July 17, 1765. National Archives.
107 *"Chain of Friendship"*: Calloway, *The Shawnees and the War for America*, p. 40.

13. By Royal Proclamation

112 *"gradually swelled into mountains"*: Draper, *The Life of Daniel Boone*, p. 193.
112 *"at last embosomed"*: Ibid.
113 *"lands that seemed without an owner"*: Ibid.
116 *"who used them in place of blankets"*: Ibid., p. 226.
117 *"to secure some"*: Abbot and Twohig, *The Papers of George Washington, vol. 8*, pp. 26–32.
117 *"I can never look upon"*: Ibid.

14. The Gap

122 *"But such was Johnson's standing"*: Flexner, *Mohawk Baronet*, p. 328.
124 *"The scheme of the Shawnese"*: Calloway, *The Shawnees and the War for America*, p. 47.
125 *"this lovely vale"*: Draper, *The Life of Daniel Boone*, p. 208.
128 *"Boone's actions aligned"*: author interview with Craig Thompson Friend.

15. The Warrior's Path

129 *"Eden of the West"*: Kentucky Geological Society map.
130 *"unequaled on our earth"*: Lofaro, *Daniel Boone*, p. 169.
132 *"We passed through a great forest"*: Boone and Hawks, *Daniel Boone's Own Story*, p. 3.
135 *"wash out their white blood"*: Draper, *The Life of Daniel Boone*, p. 470.
135 *"covering the dead"*: Ibid., p. 491.
138 *"untutored Indian"*: Ibid., p. 216.
139 *"Now Brothers"*: Ibid.
139 *"Steal horse, ha"*: Hammon, *My Father, Daniel Boone*, p. 25.
140 *"I firmly believe"*: Draper, *The Life of Daniel Boone*, p. 252.
140 *"clever shew [sic] of mercy"* Ibid., p. 216.
140 *"vagabond depredators"*: Ibid., p. 228.
141 *"more suits entered against him"*: Brown, *Frontiersman*, p. 40.

16. "Without . . . Even a Horse or a Dog"

142 *"the beaver does everything"*: Allen, *His Majesty's Indian Allies*, p. 19.
146 *"without bread or sugar"*: Draper, *The Life of Daniel Boone*, p. 239.
146 *"marking the western boundary"*: Boone and Hawks, *Daniel Boone's Own Story*, p. 5.
146 *"The buffaloes were more frequent"*: Filson, *The Adventures of Daniel Boone*, p. 51.

147 *"the most extraordinary country"*: Draper, *The Life of Daniel Boone*, p. 242.
148 *"they were decidedly best pleased"*: Ibid., p. 254.

17. "A Second Paradise"

151 *"We have always been"*: Calloway, *The Shawnees and the War for America*, p. xxiv.
156 *"poorer than when he departed"*: Draper, *The Life of Daniel Boone*, p. 268.
156 *"But he had seen"*: Ibid.

18. Cold Rain Mixed with the Tears

161 *"do and will remove"*: Thwaites and Kellogg, *Documentary History of Dunmore's War, 1774*, p. 371.
161 *six times or more*: Billington and Ridge, *Westward Expansion*, p. 6.

PART III: THE SETTLERS

163 *"I think the most important"*: Thomas Jefferson to George Rogers Clark, January 1, 1780.

19. A White Invasion

165 *"the muzzles of their rifles"*: Calloway, *The Shawnees and the War for America*, p. 54.
165 *"whirlwind of blood and carnage"*: Ibid.
167 *"It is say'd"*: Abbot and Twohig, *The Papers of George Washington, vol. 12*, pp. 70–71.
167 *"this useless people"*: Calloway, *The Shawnees and the War for America*, p. 53.

20. Lord Dunmore's War

176 *"two of the best hands"*: Draper, *The Life of Daniel Boone*, p. 306.
176 *"well drove in by the Indians"*: Ibid., p. 327.
177 *"a very popular Officer"*: Thwaites and Kellogg, *Documentary History of Dunmore's War, 1774*, p. 171.
179 *"I have with great trouble and pains"*: Cozzens, *Tecumseh and the Prophet*, p. 3.

21. Logan's Lament

181 *"drive the white dogs"*: Sugden, *Blue Jacket*, p. 44.
183 *"I will make peace"*: Ibid., p. 45.

22. Boone's Trace

188 *"dark and difficult"*: Draper, *The Life of Daniel Boone*, p. 362.

188 *"land Pyrates"*: Faragher, *Daniel Boone*, p. 108.
188 *"pretended purchase"*: Draper, *The Life of Daniel Boone*, p. 334.
189 *"Cantucky"*: Ibid., p. 393.
189 *"The fearless frontier men"*: Ibid., p. 335.
190 *"a quakerish elegance"*: Stevenson, *Travels with a Donkey in the Cévennes*, p. 6.
191 *"pretty good looking"*: Faragher, *Daniel Boone*, p. 109.
191 *"Didn't I tell you"*: Ibid., p. 110.

23. A New World

196 *"Your company is desired greatly"*: Draper, *The Life of Daniel Boone*, p. 335.
197 *"My wounds"*: *Debow's Review*, February 1854, p. 153.
198 *"a secluded and protected feeling"*: Faragher, *Daniel Boone*, p. 120.
200 *"All power is originally in the people"*: Draper, *The Life of Daniel Boone*, pg. 366.
200 *"a profane swearing and Sabbath breaking"*: Belue, *The Long Hunt*, p. xvi.

24. Revolution

204 *"by no means forget"*: Draper, *The Life of Daniel Boone*, p. 388.
204 *"the united Colonies [to] take"*: Ibid.
205 *"fertility of the soil"*: Ibid., p. 389.
205 *"spirit up the people"*: Ibid., p. 381.
206 *"a bustling hive of squalor"*: Belue, *The Long Hunt*, p. 111.
206 *"the people on the other side"*: Draper, *The Life of Daniel Boone*, 381.
206 *"with the thanks of the [Transylvania Company's]"*: Ibid., p. 387.
208 *"I think there will be"*: Ibid., p. 393.
209 *"a mark of vassalage"*: Ranck, *Boonesborough: Its Founding, Pioneer Struggles, Indian Experiences, Transylvania Days, and Revolutionary Annals*, p. 43.

25. Kidnapped

213 *"Then we have done pretty well"*: Draper, *The Life of Daniel Boone*, p. 413.
217 *"pretty squaws"*: Ibid., p. 415.
217 *"real handsome"*: Cushow to Draper, March 14, 1885. Wisconsin Historical Society.
218 *"That's daddy"*: Draper, *The Life of Daniel Boone*, p. 419.
221 *"to dissolve the Political Bands"*: Declaration of Independence.
221 *"the effusion of innocent blood"*: Harrodsburg Memorial to the Virginia Convention, June 20, 1776. Virginia State Archives.
224 *"endeavoured to bring on"*: Declaration of Independence.

26. An Indian Army

232 *"Hair Buyer"*: Draper, *The Life of Daniel Boone*, p. 527.

27. Abandoned Settlements

236 *"a dull narrow body"*: Col. Arthur Campbell to Col. William Davies, October 3, 1782.

236 *"that fills our minds"*: Draper, *The Life of Daniel Boone*, p. 435.

236 *"The water will wash them away"*: Faragher, *Daniel Boone*, p. 146.

237 *"The Indians seemed determined"*: Boone and Hawks, *Daniel Boone's Own Story*, p. 9.

238 *"possessed the skill"*: Draper, *The Life of Daniel Boone*, p. 437.

239 *"Boys, we are gone"*: Ibid., p. 440.

239 *"mashed as thin"*: Boone and Hawks, *Daniel Boone's Own Story*, p. 51.

240 *"Simon . . . you are a fine fellow"*: Faragher, *Daniel Boone*, p. 149.

28. "The Best Little Indian Fight"

244 *"the best little Indian fight"*: Draper, *The Life of Daniel Boone*, p. 448.

245 *"dusky forces"*: Ibid.

245 *"Now we begin"*: Boone and Hawks, *Daniel Boone's Own Story*, p. 11.

248 *"When I was young"*: Cozzens, *Tecumseh and the Prophet*.

248 *"Every man with his gun"*: *The Narrative of Capt. John Stuart*, pp. 159–160.

249 *"If we had anything"*: Hand to Jasper Yeates, December 24, 1777.

PART IV: THE CONQUEST

251 *"Never did the Indians"*: Draper, *The Life of Daniel Bone*, p. 481.

29. Taken

254 *"The Indians now came up"*: Draper, *The Life of Daniel Boone*, p. 461.

257 *"How d'do, Captain Will?" he said*: Boone and Hawks, *Daniel Boone's Own Story*, pp. 54–55.

257 *"Eight years ago"*: Ibid.

262 *"These young men"*: Brown, *Frontiersman*, p. 130.

30. Shel-tow-ee

270 *"simple-hearted people"*: Filson, *The Adventures of Daniel Boone*, p. 123.

270 *"savage" hunter-gatherers*: Calloway, *The Shawnees and the War for America*, p. xxxi.

270 *"noble" adversary*: Filson, *The Adventures of Daniel Boone*, p. 14.

270 *"locked in a duel"*: Draper, *The Life of Daniel Boone*, p. 493.

273 *"You never asked me"*: Hammon, *My Father, Daniel Boone*, p. 58.

31. A Mistrusted Hero

278 *"I glory in war"*: The Papers of George Mason, p. 583. University of North Carolina.

32. Prelude to a Siege

281 *"dirty Indians"*: Draper, *The Life of Daniel Boone*, p. 481.
283 *"Hair-Buyer"*: Nester, *George Rogers Clark*, pp. 102–104.
284 *"Back country settlers"*: Faragher, *Daniel Boone*, p. 181.

33. A Haze of Stinking Sulfurous Smoke

288 *"Well, well"*: Draper, *The Life of Daniel Boone*, p. 501.
290 *"We are determined to defend"*: Ibid., p. 503.
292 *"Go!"*: Ibid., p. 506.
294 *"I was not made for a fighter"*: Brown, *Frontiersman*, pp. 155–156.

34. "Widder Maker"

298 *"We killed Boone"*: Faragher, *Daniel Boone*, p. 197.
302 *"could not have been much more"*: Draper, *The Life of Daniel Boone*, p. 521.

35. War in the West

303 *"series of difficulties"*: Boone and Hawks, *Daniel Boone's Own Story*, p. 19.
304 *"Brave Officers and Soldiers"*: George Rogers Clark to Patrick Henry, February 3, 1779. Library of Virginia.
306 *"It means that you"*: Nester, *George Rogers Clark*, p. 141.
307 *"a fair opportunity"*: Ibid., pp. 146–147.
307 *"disagreeable terms"*: Barnhart, *Henry Hamilton and George Rogers Clark in the American Revolution*, p. 185.

36. Boone's Station

319 *"The Indians stood"*: Faragher, *Daniel Boone*, p. 210.
320 *"The shame of having"*: Nester, *George Rogers Clark*, pp. 196–197.
321 *"We've killed Daniel Boone"*: Faragher, *Daniel Boone*, p. 212.

37. The Moravian Massacre

324 *"and lay their country waste"*: U.S. National Park Service map, "Overmountain Victory."
325 *"continually infested with savages"*: Boone and Hawks, *Daniel Boone's Own Story*, p. 20.
325 *"Year of Blood"*: Belue, *The Long Hunt*, p. 124.
327 *"translated from earth to heaven"*: Foster, *The Ohio Frontier*, p. 64.
328 *"a stain on frontier character"*: Roosevelt, *The Winning of the West*, vol. 2, p. 145.
329 *"Brothers"*: Faragher, *Daniel Boone*, p. 216.

38. Death at Blue Licks

331　*"timidity"*: Hammon, *Daniel Boone and the Defeat at Blue Licks*, p. 39.
332　*"They wish to"*: Faragher, *Daniel Boone*, pp. 217–218.
333　*"They largely outnumber us"*: Ibid.
333　*"By Godly"*: Ibid., p. 218.
333　*"I can go as far"*: Ibid.
333　*"Come on"*: Ibid., p. 219.
335　*"Father, I won't leave you,"*: Ibid., p. 221.

39. "Blood and Treasure"

337　*"a horror almost unparalleled,"*: Boone and Hawks, *Daniel Boone's Own Story*, pp. 22–23.
338　*"rumors"*: Hugh McGary to Benjamin Logan, August 28, 1782. Kentucky Historical Society.
339　*"Their connexions"*: Boone and Hawks, *Daniel Boone's Own Story*, pp. 23–24.
340　*"My footsteps"*: Ibid., p. 25.
341　*"A new society"*: Billington and Ridge, *Westward Expansion*, p. 2.

Epilogue

345　*"with the reasoning powers"*: Taliaferro, *Grinnell: America's Environmental Pioneer*, p. 267.
347　*"Conqueror of the Northwest"*: Palmer, *Clark of the Ohio*, p. 79.
349　*"Little by little"*: Hammon, *My Father, Daniel Boone*, p. 110.
350　*"purchased with"*: Boone and Hawks, *Daniel Boone's Own Story*, p. 25.
353　*"The old man"*: Irving, *Astoria*, p. 219.
354　*"From the perspective"*: Moten, *Between War and Peace*, p. 129.
354　*"Euro-Americans did wage"*: Ibid.
355　*"It is better"*: Brown, *Frontiersman*, p. 106.

SELECTED BIBLIOGRAPHY

Abbot, W. W., and Dorothy Twohig, eds. *The Papers of George Washington. Colonial Series, vol. 8.* Charlottesville: University of Virginia Press, 1993.

———. *The Papers of George Washington. Colonial Series, vol. 10.* Charlottesville: University of Virginia Press, 1995.

Alighieri, Dante. *The Divine Comedy.* New York: Everyman's Library, 1995.

Allen, Robert S. *His Majesty's Indian Allies: British Policy in the Defence of Canada, 1774–1815.* Toronto: Dundurn Press, 1992.

Anderson, Fred. *Crucible of War: The Seven Years' War and the Fate of Empire in British North America, 1754–1766.* New York: Knopf, 2000.

Barnhart, John D., ed. *Henry Hamilton and George Rogers Clark in the American Revolution. With the Unpublished Journal of Lieut. Gov. Henry Hamilton.* Crawfordsville, IN: R. E. Banta, 1951.

Belue, Ted Franklin. *The Long Hunt: Death of the Buffalo East of the Mississippi.* Mechanicsburg, PA: Stackpole Books, 1996.

Billington, Ray Allen, and Martin Ridge. *Westward Expansion: A History of the American Frontier.* Washington, DC: Library of Congress, 2001.

Boone, Daniel, and Francis Lister Hawks. *Daniel Boone's Own Story and The Adventures of Daniel Boone.* Mineola, NY: Dover Publications, 2010.

Brown, Meredith Mason. *Frontiersman: Daniel Boone and the Making of America.* Baton Rouge: Louisiana State University Press, 2008.

Calloway, Colin G. *The Indian World of George Washington.* New York: Oxford University Press, 2018.

———. *The Scratch of a Pen: 1763 and the Transformation of North America.* New York: Oxford University Press, 2006.

———. *The Shawnees and the War for America.* New York: Penguin Books, 2007.

Cantú, Francisco. "Boundary Conditions." *The New Yorker,* March 11, 2019, p. 73.

Cozzens, Peter. *Tecumseh and the Prophet: The Shawnee Brothers Who Defied a Nation.* New York: Knopf, 2020.

Diamond, Jared. *Guns, Germs, and Steel: The Fates of Human Societies.* New York: W. W. Norton, 2005.

D'Iberville, Pierre Le Moyne. *Iberville's Gulf Journals.* Tuscaloosa: University of Alabama Press, 1991.

Doddridge, Joseph. *The Settlement and Indian Wars of the Western Parts of Virginia and Pennsylvania, 1763–1783.* Bowie, MD: Heritage Books, 1988.

Dolan, Terrance. *The Shawnee Indians.* New York: Chelsea House, 1996.

Draper, Lyman C. *The Life of Daniel Boone.* Edited by and with introduction by Ted Franklin Belue. Mechanicsville, PA: Stackpole Books, 1998.

Drury, Bob, and Tom Clavin. *Valley Forge.* New York: Simon & Schuster, 2018.

Eckert, Allen W. *The Frontiersmen.* New York: Little, Brown, 1967.

Faragher, John Mack. *Daniel Boone: The Life and Legend of an American Pioneer.* New York: Henry Holt, 1992.

Filson, John. *The Adventures of Daniel Boone & The Discovery, Settlement and Present State of Kentucke.* New York: Cosimo, 2010.

Flexner, James. *Mohawk Baronet: A Biography of Sir William Johnson.* Syracuse, NY: Syracuse University Press, 1990.

Foster, Emily, ed. *The Ohio Frontier: An Anthology of Early Writings.* Lexington: University Press of Kentucky, 1996.

Glatthaar, Joseph T. *The American Military: A Precise History.* New York: Oxford University Press, 2018.

Hammon, Neal O., ed. *Daniel Boone and the Defeat at Blue Licks.* Hendersonville, TN: Boone Society, 2005.

———. *My Father, Daniel Boone: The Draper Interviews with Nathan Boone.* Lexington: University Press of Kentucky, 1999.

Haselby, Sam. *The Origins of American Religious Nationalism.* New York: Oxford University Press, 2015.

Heinl, Robert Debs, Jr. *Dictionary of Military and Naval Quotations.* Annapolis, MD: Naval Institute Press, 1966.

Irving, Washington. *Astoria, or, Anecdotes of an Enterprise Beyond the Rocky Mountains.* Philadelphia: J. P. Lippincott, 1836.

Jennings, Francis. *The Founders of America.* New York: W. W. Norton, 1994.

Kellogg, Louise Phelps, and Reuben Gold Thwaites, eds. *Documentary History of Dunmore's War, 1774.* Los Angeles: HardPress Publishing, 2012.

Klinck, Carl F., ed. *Tecumseh: Fact and Fiction in Early Records.* Englewood Cliffs, NJ: Prentice-Hall, 1961.

Lakomaki, Sami. *Gathering Together: The Shawnee People Through Diaspora and Nationhood, 1600–1870.* New Haven, CT: Yale University Press, 2014.

Lofaro, Michael A. *Daniel Boone: An American Life.* Lexington: University Press of Kentucky, 2003.

Marshall, Humphrey. *The History of Kentucky.* Pasadena, CA: Davies Press, 2010.

Merrell, James H. *Into the American Woods: Negotiators on the Pennsylvania Frontier.* New York: W. W. Norton, 1999.

Moten, Col. Matthew, ed. *Between War and Peace: How America Ends Its Wars.* New York: Free Press, 2011.

Nelson, Larry. *A Man of Distinction Among Them: Alexander McKee and the Ohio Country Frontier, 1754–1799.* Kent, OH: Kent State University Press, 1999.

Nester, William R. *George Rogers Clark: "I Glory In War."* Norman: University of Oklahoma Press, 2012.

O'Donnell, James H., III. *Ohio's First Peoples.* Athens: Ohio University Press, 2004.

Palmer, Frederick. *Clark of the Ohio: A Life of George Rogers Clark.* Whitefish, MT: Kessinger Publishing, 1929.

Preston, David. "The Trigger." *Smithsonian Magazine,* October 2019, p. 34.

Ranck, George Washington. *Boonesborough.* J.R. Morton Printers, 1901.

Reid, Darren R., ed. *Daniel Boone and Others on the Kentucky Frontier.* Jefferson, NC: McFarland, 2009.

Roosevelt, Theodore. *The Winning of the West.* Vol. 2. New York: G. P. Putnam's Sons, 1889.

Spero, Patrick. *Frontier Rebels: The Fight for Independence in the American West, 1765–1776.* New York: W. W. Norton, 2018.

Stevenson, Robert Louis. *Travels with a Donkey in the Cévennes.* Mineola, NY: Dover Publications, 2019.

Storl, Wolf-Dieter, and Rosemary Gladstar. *The Herbal Lore of Wise Women and Wortcunners: The Healing Power of Medicinal Plants.* Berkeley, CA: North Atlantic Books, 2012.

Stuart, John. *Memoirs of Indian Wars and Other Occurrences by the Late Colonel Stuart of Greenbrier.* New York: Arno Press, 1971.

Sugden, John. *Blue Jacket: Warrior of the Shawnees.* Lincoln: University of Nebraska Press, 2000.

———. *Tecumseh: A Life.* New York: Henry Holt, 1997.

Taliaferro, John. *Grinnell: America's Environmental Pioneer and His Restless Drive to Save the West.* New York: Liveright, 2019.

Thwaites, Reuben Gold, and Louise Phelps Kellogg, eds. *Documentary History of Dunmore's War, 1774.* London: Sagwan Press, 2015.

Turner, Frederick Jackson. *The Frontier in American History.* San Francisco: Okitoks Press, 2017.

Waller, George. *The American Revolution in the West.* Chicago: Nelson-Hall, 1976.

Warren. Stephen. *The Shawnees and Their Neighbors, 1795–1870.* Champaign: University of Illinois Press, 2005.

———. *The Worlds the Shawnees Made.* Chapel Hill: University of North Carolina Press, 2014.

Williams, Glenn F. *Dunmore's War: The Last Conflict of America's Colonial Era.* Yardley, PA: Westholme Publishing, 2017.

Wright, Carroll D. *Comparative Wages, Prices, and Cost of Living.* Boston: Wright and
    Potter Printing, 1889.

COLLECTIONS
Amherst College Archives & Special Collections
Daniel Boone Papers, Archibald Henderson Collection, University of North Carolina
Eastern Kentucky University Special Collections & Archives
George Washington Papers, Manuscript Division, Library of Congress
Hand Papers, New York Public Library
Public Record Office, London, Colonial Office Records
The Draper Collection in the Wisconsin State Historical Society
The Papers of George Mason, 1725–1792, University of North Carolina
The Papers of George Rogers Clark in the Illinois State Historical Archives
The Papers of Henry Bouquet, November 17, 1761–July 17, 1765, Historical Society of
    Pennsylvania
The Preston Family Papers, Kegley Library at Wytheville Community College
University of Kentucky Archives

INDEX

Turn the page for a sneak peek at
Bob Drury and Tom Clavin's new biography

THE LAST HILL:

The Epic Story of a Ranger Battalion and the Battle That Defined WWII

Available Fall 2022

PROLOGUE: A VAST GREEN CAVE

Omaha Beach. Pointe du Hoc. Fortress Brest. Crucibles all. None had prepared the men of the United States Army's 2nd Ranger Battalion for the Hürtgen Forest. It was as if they were walking into the imaginations of the Brothers Grimm. With more bloodshed.

The roughly sixty-square-mile patch of densely timbered hills and gorges straddling the Belgian-German frontier screened the southern rim of the ancient fortress of Aachen, the first German city to fall to the Allies in the Second World War. It was at Aachen, more than a millennium earlier, where the Emperor Charlemagne had established his seat of power and where his bones remained interred. Had the ghost of the King of the Franks miraculously arisen to greet the American Rangers on that morning, November 14, 1944, he would not have recognized the cheerless slagscape of bombed-out collieries, blackened smokestacks, and cindered railheads that now surrounded the capital city he had known as Aix-la-Chapelle. He would, however, have been quite at home among the pristine Hürtgen conifers, whose one-hundred-foot canopy cast the forest floor in shimmering blue shadow, a perpetual twilight even at high noon.

The sodden ground beneath the towering trees was nearly devoid of underbrush, and as the Rangers slogged through ankle-deep mud along a man-made firebreak, they stooped to pass beneath low-hanging pine boughs that lent the woodland a claustrophobic ambience. One trooper, noting the pungent tang rising from the loamy forest floor, likened it to walking into a vast green cave. The utter absence of wildlife, even bird-song, compounded the eeriness. "Everywhere the forest scowled," the customarily sober U.S. Army's official history records in a jarring flight of anthropomorphism. "Wet, cold, and seemingly impenetrable."

The first snowstorm of the season had swept through the Hürtgen a day earlier, and the Rangers had only broached the forest's southwestern edge when a relentless mix of sleet and freezing rain again began to fall. According to army meteorologists, there was no end in sight to the grim overcast. The wretched weather blowing in from the west, in fact, por-tended the most dismal winter recorded in the region in almost a century.

The waning sunlight was near to being swallowed by the night when the battalion reached the base of their ridgeline bivouac eleven miles into the wood. The heights loomed not so much to climb but, like Calvary, to suffer. "Frost and cold making life so miserable . . . wet snow dogging our every footstep . . . had us all bitching and cursing," the Able Company Private First Class Morris Prince jotted in his journal. "Slime and filth soaked our shoes, and great mud splotches blended into the wetness of our overcoats."

The raw conditions not only cut to the bone but, as the Rangers knew well, the low cloud cover would continue to prevent Allied aircraft from leaving their tarmacs in liberated Belgium. Over the past thirty days, the number of Army Air Force and RAF sorties providing close air support to American infantry and armor advancing against a dug-in enemy had fallen by a third. In the coming weeks, those prospects appeared even more bleak.

The autumn murk, however, could not obscure the bloody detritus of months of forest fighting—the scattered rucksacks and bullet-riddled helmets; the smashed hulks of burned-out Sherman tanks and Jeeps; the blackened corpses of American boys fused together for eternity by direct artillery hits. Near the rotting remains of a German supply horse—one of hundreds of thousands killed that autumn—a Ranger rifleman absent-

mindedly kicked at a lone American combat boot by the side of the foot-
path. A foot fell out; the putrescent strips of flesh and muscle still clinging
to bone were black with maggots. Farther on, dead GIs, bloated and gray,
were stacked along the trail in haphazard rows, waiting to be tagged and
bagged. To the Rangers they appeared to have been speared by medieval
pikemen, their bodies punctured and shredded when razor-sharp wooden
shards sheared from the treetops by airburst shells rained death on the
forest floor. At first a light patter, then a heavy downpour.

The Ranger battalion, one of only two American Special Forces units
operating in the European Theater, was a collection of some five hundred
recon men and night fighters, of cliff climbers and bunker busters, of ath-
letes and aesthetes as adept with an M3 trench knife as with a Thompson
submachine gun. Led by the rough-hewn former college football star Lieutenant Colonel James Earl Rudder, they thought they had seen the worst of
what war had to offer. But as they spiraled deeper into the Hürtgen, even
the most battle-scarred among them were staggered by the sight of the soldiers from the U.S. Army's 28th Infantry Division they had come to relieve.

After twelve days of continuous combat, the Germans had nicknamed
the 28th the *Blutiger Eimer*—the Bloody Bucket—a reference to the shape
and color of the division's red keystone badge. It is unlikely that the Wehr-
macht soldiers had any idea that the outfit's ancestry dated to units stood
up by Benjamin Franklin during the Revolutionary War, or that its insignia
paid tribute to those origins in Pennsylvania, the Keystone State. Not that
it would have mattered. For here, in the Hürtgen, the Bloody Bucketeers—
as the division's survivors had sardonically taken to calling themselves—
had lived up to the sobriquet.

Less than eight weeks earlier, the proud soldiers of the 28th Division—
their boots polished, sunlight reflecting off the gleaming barrels of their
M1 rifles—had strutted down the Champs-Élysées to the raucous cheers
of Parisians crowding the sidewalk. Now, as the Rangers approached,
these same GIs emerged from rime-crusted foxholes and tumbledown
bunkers like wraiths, their drawn faces tinged gray, as if dipped in soot.

Their eyes were hollow, without expression. Some looked as if daylight would hurt them; others resembled pallbearers in search of a funeral. The foul stench of gas gangrene from infected wounds was omnipresent, permeating the woodland like a crepuscular mist.

There is an ancient battlefield bromide—rarely believe a casualty and never believe a straggler. In this case, the soldiers of the 28th did not have to speak for the Rangers to piece together what had occurred. When the Ranger battalion's chief medical officer, Captain Walter E. "Doc" Block, stumbled into a former German troop shelter that had been converted into an American aid station, he was appalled to find wounded GIs left unattended, their rasping voices pleading for water or, in some cases, to be put out of their misery. Block managed to salvage one of the few working Jeeps from the 28th's ravaged motor pool, and, after jerry-rigging a litter to the vehicle, he and his aid men stuffed their musette bags with bandages, plasma, and temporary splints to begin combing the forest in search of more wounded. Picking their way through random artillery and small-arms fire, avoiding impassable roads, and keenly aware that German sappers had rigged the trailside trees with mines, they managed to gather nineteen more survivors before Lt. Col. Rudder called a halt to their efforts. "You might get hit" was Rudder's terse explanation. The commander could ill afford to lose his battalion surgeon.

Not far from the Rangers' temporary aid station, the executive officer of the battalion's Able Company, Lieutenant Bob Edlin, spotted a bomb-battered chapel, veiled in mist and rising from the floor of a moss-green dell like a ghostly clipper ship impaled on a reef. "What an odd place for a church," he remembered thinking. He moved closer to inspect the wreckage. As he neared the crumbling structure, he blanched at the plethora of American M1 rifles scattered about. He could only conclude that soldiers seeking sanctuary in the little shrine had tossed their weapons in flight. It had not done them any good. Twenty-one days earlier, the 28th Division and its various attachments had entered the forest with approximately twenty-five thousand effectives. Over six thousand of those men were now dead, wounded, or missing.

More than a few Rangers were startled by the ferocity with which the

Germans, on the run for months, fought in the Hürtgen. Lt. Edlin in particular felt the pangs of the carnage more sharply than most. Before volunteering for the Rangers, he had been a member of the 28th Infantry Division's 112th Regiment and had known many of the GIs who would now never return home. Not long after his inspection of the chapel, Edlin crossed paths with one of his best friends from his old outfit, a captain named Preston Jackson. Jackson begged Edlin to turn around and get out while he could. Edlin was shocked. He remembered Jackson as a solid soldier, eager for action. Yet now Jackson stared at Edlin with vacant eyes, as if something had cankered his soul.

"I wish you wouldn't go," Jackson repeated in a numb voice. "I wish you'd just flat tell them you're not going any further." Jackson cocked his chin toward the enemy front. "It's the most miserable thing that you've ever seen in your life."

Edlin was not sure how to react. For a moment, a baleful silence hung between the two. Finally, Edling blurted, "Well, we'll calm things down." The pained look on his old companion's face made Edlin doubt his own words.

Similar misgivings were racing through the mind of the Dog Company 2nd Lieutenant Len "Bud" Lomell. The Ranger battalion's former sergeant major had only recently received a battlefield commission—one of thirty thousand U.S. enlisted men promoted into the officer ranks during the war—and still retained a noncommissioned officer's close connection to his charges. As Lomell watched his appalled troopers absorb the ravages about them, he began to compile a mental list of how to prevent them from meeting a similar fate. He vowed that wherever this mission led, the men of Dog Company would never be without hot coffee and clean socks. Quotidian goals, perhaps, but in the lethal heat of battle more important than any quests for glory or valor. How Lomell would accomplish this, he had yet to figure out.

Just as the Rangers were taken aback by the savagery of the fighting in the Hürtgen, the members of the general staff at Supreme Headquarters

Allied Expeditionary Force, or SHAEF, were equally baffled by the stiff German resistance. General Dwight D. Eisenhower and his war planners, only recently relocated from London to the Trianon Hotel in Versailles, were inexplicably slow to recognize that as precious as the capture of Paris or Brussels or Amsterdam may have once been to the Third Reich, its soldiers were now defending the Fatherland. "Stand or die" was Adolph Hitler's mantra. The Rangers were willing to oblige the Führer on the second count. Although as they tread farther into the forest, more than a few could not fail to recognize an irony as dark as the vast green cave.

In September and October, it had been the 9th American Infantry Division, accompanied by a smattering of tanks from the 3rd Armored Division, that had been tasked with driving the Germans from the Hürt-gen. The combined units had suffered forty-five hundred casualties while moving forward less than two miles beneath sheets of artillery fire—one man down, the War Department's history of the campaign notes, for every three feet gained. Now it was the 28th Division that had failed to clear the forest. All told, upward of fifty thousand American soldiers had been thrown into the three attempts, suffering over fifteen thousand casualties.

Now it was the Rangers' turn, although a few of the outfit's veterans wondered what twenty-seven officers and four hundred and eighty-five enlisted men could accomplish where so many before them had faltered. If there was a sliver of saving grace to their unenviable task, at least the men of the 2nd Ranger Battalion understood what awaited them. It was the key to the woodland assault. The Germans called it Burg-berg, or Castle Mound, an homage to the ruins of the medieval schloss that had once dominated its precipice. American Army historians, perhaps in deference, also referred to it as Castle Hill. On Allied topography maps it was known as Hill 400 for its height in meters. To the Rangers, it would become, simply, the Hill. The Last Hill.

43rd Bomb Group

Gordon M. Grant

BOB DRURY and TOM CLAVIN are the number-one *New York Times* bestselling authors of *The Heart of Everything That Is, Lucky 666, Halsey's Typhoon, Last Men Out,* and *The Last Stand of Fox Company,* which won the Marine Corps Heritage Foundation's General Wallace M. Greene, Jr. Award. Tom Clavin is also the author of several stand-alone bestselling St. Martin's Press titles, including *Dodge City, Wild Bill,* and *Tombstone.* They live in Manasquan, New Jersey, and Sag Harbor, New York, respectively.